The Diary of Philip Hone

1828-1851

Philip Hone

APPLEWOOD BOOKS
Carlisle, Massachusetts

The Diary of Philip Hone
was originally published in
1889

ISBN: 978-1-4290-2116-6

APPLEWOOD'S
AMERICAN CITIES
SERIES

Thank you for purchasing an Applewood book.
Applewood reprints America's lively classics—books from the past
that are still of interest to modern readers.
Our mission is to build a picture of the past through primary sources.
We do not change a word of the editions we reissue, believing that it is
important to present the past without editing it. Sometimes words, thoughts,
images or ideas from the past may seem inappropriate to the
modern reader. We apologize for any discomfort this may bring.
We believe in the value of bringing the past back, just as it was,
for the purposes of informing the present and future.
This facsimile was printed using many new technologies together
to bring our tradition-bound mission to you. Applewood's facsimile
edition of this work may include library stamps, scribbles, and margin notes
as they exist in the original book. These interesting historical artifacts
celebrate the place the book was read or the person who read the book.
In addition to these artifacts, the work may have additional errors
that were either in the original, in the digital scans,
or introduced as we prepared the book for printing. If you believe the work has such
errors, please let us know by writing to us at the address below.

For a free copy of our current print catalog featuring our bestselling books, write to:

APPLEWOOD BOOKS
P.O. Box 27
Carlisle, MA 01741

For more complete listings, visit us on the web at www.awb.com

PREPARED FOR PRINTING BY HP

THE DIARY

of

PHILIP HONE

1828–1851

EDITED, WITH AN INTRODUCTION

BY

BAYARD TUCKERMAN

IN TWO VOLUMES

VOLUME I

NEW YORK
DODD, MEAD AND COMPANY
1889

Copyright, 1889
By DODD, MEAD & COMPANY

All rights reserved

INTRODUCTION.

PHILIP HONE was born on the 25th of October, 1780, in Dutch street, New York. Four years later his father bought a wooden house, on the corner of Dutch and John streets, where Philip passed his boyhood. He received a common-school education, and at seventeen years of age began his mercantile career as clerk to his elder brother John. The business was that of an auctioneer, which, at that time, consisted chiefly in selling the cargoes brought to the port of New York by the fleet of American merchantmen. Philip displayed so much ability and fidelity in his work, that in 1799, when nineteen years of age, his brother took him into partnership. The firm became extremely prosperous, and bore an honoured name throughout the United States. On the 1st of October, 1801, in his twenty-second year, Mr. Hone married Catherine Dunscomb, by whom he had three sons and three daughters.

In 1820, Mr. Hone, although only forty years of age, had accumulated a fortune then considered very large. His mature life still lay before him, and the choice was open as to the manner in which it should be spent. With no love of money for money's sake, with a sincere desire to improve himself and to be useful to others, he retired from business, in the flood-tide of his powers and his prosperity, to enter a higher sphere of effort.

In 1821 he sailed for Europe in the "James Monroe," Captain Rogers, of four hundred tons burden. This journey to foreign lands made a deep impression, and strengthened his determination to devote his energies to self-cultivation and to objects of public interest. Immediately after his return, he purchased the house, No. 235 Broadway, just below the corner of Park place, for $25,000. This house was one of the largest private residences in the city, and was pointed out to strangers as an object of civic pride. Its windows looked out upon the City Hall Park, then the principal park in New York, surrounded by a fence of wooden palings, and considered up town. When installed in his new house, Mr. Hone began his career of social and public-spirited activity. The most able and influential men in New York were his constant guests. Men from other States, such as Daniel Webster, Henry Clay, Harrison Gray Otis, made his house their rendezvous while passing through the city. Foreigners of note, such as Lord Morpeth, Fanny Kemble, Captain Marryat, John Galt, Charles Dickens, met with a hearty welcome. As his children grew up the house became a resort for the young people; and it was an ordinary question for the beaux and belles walking on Broadway: "Shall we meet to-night at Mr. Hone's, or at Dr. Hosack's?"— these being the two houses in town most constantly open.

In 1824 Mr. Hone was elected an assistant alderman, which office he held until 1826, when he became Mayor. His administration of the affairs of the city was characterized by an intelligent public spirit, untrammelled by party; and his mayoralty, praiseworthy as it was for the wise performance of duty, was especially distinguished in the annals of New York municipal government by the fact that Mr. Hone represented the city socially as well as politically. He entertained officially; and visiting strangers during his term enjoyed a hospitality which reflected credit upon the whole community.

In 1816 was established the first bank for savings. This, the best of all philanthropic institutions, had immediately enlisted Mr. Hone's coöperation. On its foundation he was appointed a trustee by the Legislature, and he continued his gratuitous labours on behalf of the bank for more than thirty years, becoming its president in 1841. For twenty-one years he served as a governor of the

New York Hospital and as a trustee of the Bloomingdale Asylum. He ceased to occupy these positions only when rendered ineligible by his appointment by the Governor of the State as an inspector of all public institutions. He was the founder of the Clinton Hall Association and of the Mercantile Library Association, of which he continued to be the president for many years. Other institutions and corporations of which Mr. Hone was an officer for considerable periods are as follows : Trustee of Columbia College, of the New York Life Insurance and Trust Company, of the Merchants' Exchange ; president of the American Exchange Bank, of the Glenham Manufacturing Company; vice-president of the Institution for the Instruction of the Deaf and Dumb, of the American Seamen's Fund Society, of the New York Historical Society, of the Fuel Savings Society; a director in the Matteawan Cotton and Machine Company, the Eagle Fire Insurance Company, the National Insurance Company, the Delaware and Hudson Canal Company ; a member of the Chamber of Commerce, of the Vestry of Trinity Church ; a manager of the Literary and Philosophical Society, of the Mechanics and Scientific Association ; president of the German Society ; a founder and a governor of the Union Club. By his labours on behalf of the insurance and manufacturing companies, and the Delaware & Hudson Canal, which first connected the coal-fields of Pennsylvania with tide-water, Mr. Hone kept abreast of the industrial interests of the country. The positions held by him in philanthropic institutions were never treated as honorary titles. In each case he worked with the same assiduity that a man could apply to his own business. An ordinary day's occupation for him was to ride out on horseback to the Bloomingdale Asylum, to return and pass the afternoon at the Bank for Savings, thence to attend a meeting of the Trinity Vestry, or to preside over the Mercantile Library Association. He was never voluntarily absent from a meeting where the interests of others demanded his presence, and many were the good dinners which he lost in consequence.

In 1837, the encroachments of trade upon the buildings in the vicinity of the City Hall Park made Mr. Hone's house there less desirable as a place of residence. He sold it, and built the house at the south-east corner of Broadway and Great Jones street, then the upper limit of the city, where he lived during the remainder of his life. The front room on the ground floor, now occupied by the East River Bank, was his library, and there the greater part of his Diary was written.

During the prolonged period of commercial depression, which began with the attacks of President Jackson upon the Bank of the United States in 1836, Mr. Hone met with financial losses, in consequence of assistance extended by him to others, which compelled him to return to active business. He became president of the American Mutual Insurance Company, which was ruined by the great fire of July 19, 1845, and the affairs of which he wound up as receiver. In recognition of the courageous and honourable manner in which he had met his reverses, a number of leading merchants placed in the Mercantile Library a marble bust of Mr. Hone, which Clevenger began and Powers finished. In 1849 he was appointed Naval Officer of the port of New York by President Taylor, which office he held during the short remainder of his life.

In politics, Mr. Hone was first a Federalist, and afterwards a Whig, having given its name to the latter party. The Jackson administration, characterized as it was by unwarrantable assumption of power by the Executive and a cringing party subserviency, excited his detestation; and he was an important factor in the great campaign which ended in the election of General Harrison. He was an able speaker, and his services were called into requisition at all times of public commotion. He presided with success at party conventions, where his fine presence, strong voice, and dignified language swayed and moderated great assemblages.

He had personal gifts which extended the influence due to his character. Tall and spare, his bearing was distinguished, his face handsome and refined; his manners were courtly, of what is known as the "old school;" his tact was great, — he had a faculty for saying the right thing. In his own house his hospitality was enhanced by a graceful urbanity and a ready wit. He was fond of riding on horseback, always had a spirited horse, and for many years his figure was a familiar sight as he rode up and down Broadway. His popularity as a diner-out is sufficiently illustrated in the pages of the Diary, and is well remembered through the institution of the Hone Club.

Mr. Hone's taste for literature and the arts was self-cultivated. With few advantages in early life, he owed his education to his own efforts. He was an assiduous reader of serious books, the contents of which he impressed on his mind by copying striking passages in his common-place book, with comments of his own. He took every opportunity of seeing good pictures, and obtained an artistic judgment by the same system of self-instruction which he applied to literature. Authors and painters were frequent guests at his table, and not a few were assisted by him. He was much interested in the drama, owned a box at the Park Theatre; and when actors like Matthews, Kemble, or the elder Wallack were playing in New York, they always enjoyed his hospitality.

As a merchant, distinguished for intelligence and integrity; as an enlightened philanthropist, as a public-spirited citizen and a social leader, Mr. Hone took pleasure in recording the events which took place under his eyes during the first half of the present century. He saw New York grow from a town of twenty thousand inhabitants into a city of five hundred thousand; he saw the residence portion of the city extend up Broadway to Union square, up Fifth avenue as far as Twentieth street. And in this enormous growth and all the changes which it involved, he had borne an influential part. He had been an American who recognized no division of North and South, and a Knickerbocker who gloried in the progress of his native city. In 1847 he made a journey into the far West, the hardships of which brought on an illness from which he never fully recovered. In 1850 he lost his wife, and on the 4th of May, 1851, he died, in his seventy-first year.

On the termination of his mayoralty, in 1827, Mr. Hone began to keep a record of various events, chiefly of a business and personal description, for convenience of reference, rather than as a literary occupation. But his interest in the life of his day, combined with a natural gift for expression which demanded gratification, caused this record gradually to assume a more elaborate character. In May, 1828, he found that he had only to go a step further to convert his common-place book into a diary, and this step he determined to take. During the rest of his life the Diary became his favourite exercise and relaxation. He devoted an hour or more daily to chronicling events of interest, to comments on politics, literature, art, the drama, or industrial subjects. He wrote without any view to publication. His thoughts were put down as they occurred to him, without previous preparation or subsequent correction. Their expression was the pleasurable one of an active mind which is relieved by giving form to ideas. The keeping of the Diary became a rooted habit; so that, when infirmity had curtailed other occupations, he adhered to this one almost to the day of his death. The somewhat fragmentary character of a common-place book is discernible in the beginning of the Diary; but the reader will perceive a steady improvement as regards both style and continuity.

In its original form, the Diary consists of twenty-eight quarto volumes, closely written on both sides of the page. Not more than a quarter of the work is now published. Mr. Hone made extended comments on new books, with extracts from them; he made summaries of the foreign news brought by the packet-ships; he kept records of political statistics and local political meetings; he copied extracts from the speeches of public men and periodical articles of interest at that time; he kept a record of the journeys which he took about the country on business or for pleasure. Such subjects as the above have been omitted or abridged. The portions of the Diary relating to industrial changes, to political and social life, to public men and other individuals of note, to the history of the city of New York, have been retained as far as allowed by the limits of the two volumes here presented.

BAYARD TUCKERMAN.

THE DIARY

OF

PHILIP HONE.

1828.

SUNDAY, MAY 18.— The tariff bill, having been returned from the Senate, passed by that body with various amendments, was finally passed by the House of Representatives on Thursday last. This bill has been warmly discussed, and has caused great excitement. It increases the duties on all those descriptions of manufactured goods imported from foreign countries which are supposed to come into competition with our manufactures. The success of this measure will be considered a triumph of the manufacturing over the mercantile interest. Some of the Southern States view it as hostile to their prosperity, and I much fear it will lead to violent measures among some of the political Hotspurs of that sanguine portion of our fellow-citizens.

BALLSTON SPRINGS, SATURDAY, JULY 26. — Mr. Stevenson told me the following anecdote of Tecumseh, which was related to him by General Harrison, and which is descriptive of the Indian's romantic character and sublime sentiments. When General Harrison, at that time Governor of the Indian Territory, was engaged with the chief in making the treaty of Vincennes, a misunderstanding occurred, and Tecumseh gave the General the lie. The General was very indignant, and was with difficulty restrained from chastising him on the spot; this, however, would have been attended with consequences fatal to the pending negotiation, and he was prevailed upon to signify to him through the interpreter that his offence was forgiven, and that he was allowed the privilege of being seated in the presence of the Governor, his great father. The haughty chief, throwing himself on the ground, replied with scorn and indignation, "I have no father but the glorious Sun; the Earth is my mother, and I will repose upon her bosom."

ALBANY, TUESDAY, SEPT. 2.— After seeing three of my children, with the horses and carriage, under way in the safety barge "Lady Clinton" for New York, we started at ten o'clock in an extra stage for Boston, by the way of Lebanon, Northampton, etc. We gave seventy dollars for the coach to convey the party of seven persons to Boston.

THURSDAY, SEPT. 4.— Left Lebanon after breakfast. To Pittsfield, seven miles; to Hinsdale, nine; to Peru, four, where we dined; to Worthington, a neat, pretty little town, six; to Chesterfield, six, where we lodged.

FRIDAY, SEPT. 5.— Fine westerly wind and clear weather. We left Chesterfield after breakfast and came to Northampton, thirteen miles. Everything looks delightful in this most beautiful town, which has improved much. We visited in the afternoon the Round Hill School, and were politely entertained by Mr. Bancroft. In the evening we went to a pleasant party at Mrs. Henry Cary's, of New York, who has been passing the summer in this place.

SUNDAY, SEPT. 7.— To Spencer, seven miles; to Leicester, five; to Worcester, six, to breakfast. Worcester is one of the finest towns in Massachusetts, and much improved within a few years. It is the residence of Governor Lincoln. The Blackstone canal commences at Worcester. To Needham, eight miles; to Newton, four; to Boston, by Brighton, nine. We entered the city by the

Mill Dam road, about six o'clock, of a most beautiful Sunday afternoon. I shall never forget the delightful impression I received from this *entrée*. We took lodgings at Mrs. Lekain's, Pearl street.

BOSTON, MONDAY, SEPT. 8. — After breakfast I commenced my Boston rambles, and saw most of the lions of this fine city. Mr. Quincy, the Mayor, took us through the new market-house, which is his hobby, and well worth seeing. The length of this splendid receptacle of beef, poultry, and potatoes is five hundred and thirty-six feet, its width fifty feet, and the improvement of the vicinity consequent upon its erection renders it an object of admiration. We visited Faneuil Hall, the armory, the noble art museum, its exhibition room (where at present is exhibited a collection of Stuart's portraits, for the benefit of his family), the new hotel building at the corner of Tremont and School streets, the docks, etc. After dinner, Mr. H. G. Otis called and took me out to Quincy to visit the President, but we found that he had departed suddenly this afternoon for Washington. We had, however, a pleasant ride, saw the Quincy railroad and quarry of granite, and returned to town by the way of Roxbury. In the evening I went for a short time to the theatre in Tremont street; a handsome theatre, but not a first-rate company.

THURSDAY, SEPT. 11. — We rode out after dinner with the Mayor to see Quincy, etc. The railroad and granite quarry are objects of great curiosity, and are now in fine operation. On our return from the quarry we stopped to see a handsome edifice in the village of Quincy, — a new meeting-house, nearly finished. It is a beautiful piece of architecture, and its massy columns of granite are probably the best specimens of that fine material which have yet been brought into use. They are single shafts, formed each of an entire block, very perfect, twenty-five feet in height, and twelve feet eight inches in circumference. We took tea with Mrs. Quincy, and returned to Boston in the evening.

FRIDAY, SEPT. 12. — This morning was employed in a visit with Mr. Otis to the City Hospital, and to the hospital for lunatics at

Lechmore Point. The last-named establishment occupies a large house, formerly the residence of Mr. Barrell, to which spacious wings have been added, and several court-yards for the recreation of the patients. The arrangement of these courts and of the buildings admits of a classification of the patients, which has been much wanted in our asylum at Bloomingdale. I dined with an agreeable party at Mr. Otis's, and in the evening accompanied my daughter to a party at Mrs. Otis's, and another party at Mrs. Derby's.

SUNDAY, SEPT. 14. — Went to St. Paul's Church in the forenoon, and heard a sermon from Mr. Alonzo Potter, the pastor of that church. This gentleman is son-in-law to Dr. Nott, President of Union College. After dinner we rode out to Colonel Perkins's, at Brookline, where we took tea; and in the evening went to Mr. Otis's. Colonel Perkins has one of the finest places in the neighbourhood; his wall fruit and grapery are justly celebrated, and are now in great perfection.

TUESDAY, SEPT. 16. — We went on an excursion to Waltham, accompanied by Mr. and Mrs. Tilden and Mr. Payne; visited the celebrated seat and ground of Mr. Lyman, and the splendid mansion of the late Governor Gore, where we were kindly received and entertained by Mrs. Gore. This great man has been dead eighteen months, and his widow has lived in retirement ever since. I dined at Gen. Theodore Lyman's, who lives in very handsome style, and has the best library I have seen in Boston. Passed the evening with a party at Mrs. Cunningham's. This lady, who is lately married, is the daughter of Rufus Amory.

FRIDAY, SEPT. 19. — We started for Providence at twelve o'clock; came to Dedham, ten miles, to dinner. A fine morning, with fair wind, made the latter part of our voyage very pleasant, and we arrived in New York at twelve o'clock noon, having performed the voyage from Providence in seventeen hours and a half.

WEDNESDAY, OCT. 15. — The following party dined with us: Lord Bishop Inglis, of Nova Scotia, his lady, and two daughters;

Mr. R. Cochran, Mr. Henry Hone, Mr. H. Brevoort, Mr. D. Lynch, Mr. and Mrs. W. B. Astor, Mr. C. and Miss Brugiere, Mr. Eugene Cruger. Declined: Dr. Wainwright and lady, Bishop Hobart, Chancellor and Mrs. Kent, Mr. and Mrs. I. S. Hone, Mr. and Mrs. J. A. Hamilton, Mr. and Mrs. Thomas W. Ludlow, Rev. Mr. Schroeder.

WEDNESDAY, Nov. 5. — Mrs. Montgomery, widow of General Montgomery, died this day at her residence on the North river, aged eighty-six years.

SATURDAY, Nov. 8. — This being the day fixed upon for the delivery of Dr. Hosack's eulogium on the character of the late Governor Clinton, which was prepared at the joint request of the Committee of Citizens and the Literary and Philosophical Society, I formed one of a large collection of gentlemen who assembled at the City Hall and walked in procession to the Middle Dutch Church. The doctor's oration or memoir was extremely interesting, and secured the attention of a highly respectable audience during the whole of its delivery, which occupied two hours and a quarter, although he left out one-half of that which he had prepared. This part will be restored in the publication of the work, and I am of the opinion that Dr. Hosack will add to his literary reputation by this elaborate and able production.

FRIDAY, Nov. 14. — Visited the Asylum this morning, accompanied by Mr. Richards; dined with Mr. D. S. Jones. On my return home, the Bishop, who had made an appointment with me at Mr. Jones's, called at my house and proposed in confidence the plan of a cathedral to be erected on Washington Square. The idea of a magnificent diocesan church is a very imposing one, and strikes my mind favourably, and it is certain that the location suggested by the Bishop is the best in the city, and can be obtained at a moderate price. Independently of the advantages which our church would derive from such an establishment, the erection of such an edifice would improve the property in its vicinity and render the square the most desirable residence in the city. But where is the money, where the public spirit, where the liberality, to carry such a noble plan into execution? Above all, who will take a lead in it? I cannot; I am already engaged in more business of this kind than I can do justice to, and it has been my fate to be so often repulsed by the cold, calculating objections of that portion of my fellow-citizens who have the ability to promote objects of public improvement, that I am discouraged from attempting again to encounter them. I note in this place the conference above mentioned, as it is possible that this glorious project may, one of these days, be carried into effect, and I believe this is the first time it has ever been hinted. Riding home from Mr. Jones's with Mr. Martin Van Buren, the governor-elect, I took occasion to interest him in the subject of the Delaware and Hudson canal, and hope he may be induced to direct, in his inaugural message, the attention of the Legislature to this object.

SATURDAY, DEC. 6. — Chancellor Kent delivered an address this day before the Historical Society, — a most beautiful production, interesting in its details, affecting and impressive in its style, and read in a chaste and elegant manner. By the exertions of a few individuals this society has been resuscitated, its affairs relieved from embarrassment, the valuable library rescued from the neglect and confusion in which it has lain for years, the apartments cleaned and beautified, and the whole rendered entirely worthy of the patronage and support of the public. These important changes have been principally effected by the zeal, industry, and good taste of Mr. John Delafield, who has, for several months past, devoted much of his time and attention to that object.

WEDNESDAY, DEC. 10. — I dined with Mr. Goold Hoyt, and in the evening attended, in the circuit court-room, City Hall, Judge Betts's introductory lecture to a course of commercial-law lectures which he has undertaken to deliver at the request of the Mercantile Library Association. The sloop "Toleration" arrived this day from Kingston with a cargo of coal, the first-fruits of the Delaware and Hudson canal.

THURSDAY, DEC. 11. — Dined with Mr. Robert Lenox, and in the evening Anthon, Van Schaick, Isaac S. Hone, and their wives supped with us.

MONDAY, DEC. 29. — The new Board of Common Council was organized this day, and proceeded to elect a Mayor for the ensuing year. The following was the result of the first ballot: For Walter Bowne, 25 ; Peter A. Jay, 1 ; Philip Hone, 1. Harrison Gray Otis was elected a few days since to the office of Mayor of Boston.

1829.

WEDNESDAY, JAN. 14. — Being engaged from eleven o'clock this morning until nine in the evening as a juror on a difficult cause, I was prevented from dining with Mr. James G. King, as I intended. The officers of the Literary and Philosophical Society assembled at my house and supped, together with Chancellor Kent, Dr. Matthews, Messrs. Morse, Cole, and Sullivan as visitors. My detention in court prevented me from being at home when the company assembled.

TUESDAY, JAN. 20. — The long-talked-of fancy ball at Mrs. Brugiere's took place this evening. We were present, and much pleased. A large proportion of the company went in character; the dresses were generally appropriate, some of them exceedingly splendid, and many of the characters were supported with much spirit. The rooms were crowded, but it went off well.

FRIDAY, FEB. 6. — I dined with Isaac S. Hone. In the evening attended a fancy ball at Mrs. Abraham Schermerhorn's, — a very splendid and delightful affair.

WEDNESDAY, FEB. 11. — I dined with Mr. Robert Maitland, and afterward met the officers of the Literary and Philosophical Society, and supped at the house of the Rev. Dr. Wainwright.

TUESDAY, FEB. 17. — Died this morning, Simon, the celebrated cook. He was a respectable man, who has for many years been the fashionable cook in New York, and his loss will be felt on all occasions of large dinner and evening parties, unless it should be found that some suitable shoulders should be ready to receive the mantle of this distinguished *cuisinier*.

WEDNESDAY, APRIL 1. — A lot of ground on the west side of Broadway, nearly opposite Bowling Green, and next, I believe, to

Mr. Brevoort's, was sold at auction this day for $19,500. Lot about forty-four feet by one hundred and eighteen.

MONDAY, APRIL 6. — This is the commencement of the second volume of my diary, which I began on the first day of last May, and have continued since, with tolerable regularity. I have occasionally introduced matters of trifling importance, and have omitted others which were entitled to a place; but the employment has afforded me some pleasure, and after its use shall have become confirmed by longer practice, I have no doubt it will be more agreeable and exceedingly useful.

SATURDAY, APRIL 11. — Weekly attendance at the Bloomingdale Asylum. Dined with Mr. G. G. Howland, where I met Mr. Jonathan Meredith, of Baltimore, the father of the very agreeable young lady whom we met last summer at the Springs, and subsequently at Boston, and for whom it is a little expected that our host of to-day has conceived a tender *penchant*.

MONDAY, APRIL 13. — Went with my wife to Wallack's benefit at the Park Theatre, — a very great house. The play was "Julius Cæsar:" Brutus, J. Wallack; Cassius, H. Wallack; Marc Antony, Hamblin; Portia, Mrs. Barnes; but notwithstanding this strong cast, it went off heavily, as this tragedy (intrinsically excellent as it is) always does.

MONDAY, APRIL 20. — I saw this day two celebrated personages, — the Indian chief, Red-Jacket, and the original of the Harvey Birch of Cooper's "Spy." The former is a venerable-looking old man, with gray hair, and less of the Indian in his looks and countenance than I would have expected; and the latter is a tall old man, who looks in all respects the character which he has been made to assume.

WEDNESDAY, APRIL 29. — Charles Kneeland, son of Mr. Henry Kneeland, was married this evening to Joanna Hone, only child of my deceased nephew, Philip J. Hone. He is a fine young man of excellent character, and the union promises to be a happy one. The wedding was celebrated at my brother John's. A large party supped, and the evening was passed very pleasantly for a wedding party.

TUESDAY, MAY 19. — The venerable, the patriotic, the virtuous, John Jay died on Tuesday last, at his seat, Bedford, Westchester County, in the eighty-fourth year of his age. The Supreme Court (which is now in session) adjourned at its hour of opening, as did the other courts now sitting. This delicate mark of respect was alike honourable to the feelings of the gentlemen constituting the several courts, as reverential to the memory of the illustrious deceased.

WEDNESDAY, MAY 27. — Immediately after dinner at home, I took Miss Helen Kane to the ship-yards to witness the launch of the ship "Erie," — a fine vessel, intended as one of the Havre line of packets, — whence I went to Abeel & Dunscomb's foundry to meet a large party of gentlemen who were assembled by invitation to see one of the new locomotive engines in operation, which was recently imported from England for the use of the railroad belonging to the Delaware and Hudson Canal Company.

THURSDAY, MAY 28. — The second locomotive steam-engine which was imported for the Delaware and Hudson Canal Company was set in operation this afternoon at the works of the Messrs. Kemble, in presence of a large number of gentlemen, and succeeded as well as the one I saw yesterday at Abeel & Dunscomb's.

SATURDAY, JUNE 6. — I accompanied the young Count Ney and Count Girardin to dine with Mr. Prime at Hurl Gate. The former gentleman brought me, on his arrival in this country, a letter from General Lafayette, and more recently, on his return from a visit to Count Survilliers (Joseph Bonaparte), a letter from my venerable friend, Count Real. He is the third son of the gallant Marshal Ney, Prince of Moskowa, whose brilliant career in arms and unhappy death have rendered him distinguished in the annals of Europe. The count is twenty-two years of age, and is said to resemble his father. The Count Girardin was a distinguished officer in the army of Bonaparte, and has seen much service.

TUESDAY, AUG. 4. — The house and lot No. 49 Wall street, recently occupied by the Pacific Insurance Company, twenty-nine feet on Wall street, and about one hundred and thirty feet deep, was sold this day at auction to Joel Post for $38,100.

FRIDAY, NOV. 27. — The Hon. Bushrod Washington, one of the judges of the Supreme Court of the United States, died yesterday at the Mansion House Hotel, Philadelphia, in the seventy-first year of his age. He had been engaged in holding the Circuit Court in New Jersey, and was taken ill in Philadelphia on his return.

1830.

FRIDAY, FEB. 5. — I dined with Mr. Charles McEvers, after which I attended Professor Renwick's first lecture on the steam-engine. This lecture was confined to the doctrine and principles of heat and its application, and was illustrated by many beautiful experiments, in which the Professor was assisted by Dr. Eller. Professor Renwick's clear, familiar, and colloquial manner of lecturing is peculiarly satisfactory and interesting, and extremely well calculated to impart instruction to his auditors. The lecture was attended by a large and respectable auditory of ladies and gentlemen.

THURSDAY, MARCH 4. — Died yesterday morning, Col. Richard Platt, in his seventy-sixth year. This gentleman was a veteran of the Revolutionary War. He joined the army in 1775 as lieutenant in Colonel McDougal's regiment, was in the army which invaded Canada under General Schuyler, was acting adjutant-general under General Montgomery in the attack upon Quebec on the 31st of December, 1775, and was deputy quartermaster-general at the surrender of the British army under Cornwallis on the 21st of October, 1781.

TUESDAY, MARCH 9. — The following party dined with us: General Lewis, M. Livingston, G. G. Howland, George Griffin, P. A. Jay, R. L. Patterson, A. Schermerhorn, President W. A. Duer, Mr. William B. Astor, P. G. Stuyvesant, Henry Cary, Chancellor Kent, Henry Hone, Richard C. Derby, Rev. Dr. Wainwright.

FRIDAY, MARCH 12. — I left this morning on an excursion to Washington at six o'clock precisely. The steamboat "Thistle," belonging to the Union Line, started from the Battery, arrived at Brunswick before ten, and the passengers started immediately in nine post-coaches. We found the road very fine, and took the steamboat "Swan" seven miles below Trenton, on the Pennsylvania side of the Delaware. The Union Line has been running only nine days. It is exceedingly well conducted, and the accommodations by land and water are very good. I arrived in Philadelphia at six P.M., and put up at Head's Mansion House.

BALTIMORE, SUNDAY, MARCH 14. — The steam-packet was to have left Philadelphia at six o'clock yesterday morning, but did not till noon. I then started, and arrived at Newcastle on the Delaware at half-past four; from thence in stages to French Town, where we again took a steamboat, and arrived here at half-past two this morning. I am very pleasantly lodged at Barnum's Hotel, Monument square. The Washington monument in Howard Park is nearly finished, being surmounted by the figure of the father of his country. It is well proportioned, and the material — a fine gray granite — is beautiful. The situation, on the slope of a hill, is well chosen to display the grandeur and simplicity of this noble specimen of art.

I paid this morning a visit, which I have long been wishing for, to the venerable Charles Carroll, the only surviving signer of the Declaration of Independence. He will be ninety-four years of age next September. His faculties are very little impaired, except his sight, which within the last few months has failed a little, and deprives him of the pleasure of reading at all times, which he has heretofore enjoyed. He is gay, cheerful, polite, and talkative. He described to me his manner of living: he takes a cold bath every morning in the summer, plunging headlong into it; rides on horseback from eight to twelve miles; drinks water at dinner; has never drunk spirituous liquors at any period of his life, but drinks a glass or two of Madeira wine every day, and sometimes champagne and claret; takes as much exercise as possible; goes to bed at nine o'clock, and rises before day.

WEDNESDAY, MARCH 17. — Continual rain during the day confined me to the house until noon. I then walked out to pay a few visits, and dined with a very agreeable party at Mr. Robert

Gilmor's. This gentleman lives in handsome style; nobody in America gives better dinners or more exquisite wines. His collection of pictures is very fine, and his house is filled with specimens of the fine arts and objects of taste and *virtu*.

THURSDAY, MARCH 18. — The morning being fine, Mr. Brown, one of the acting directors of the Baltimore and Ohio Railroad Company, called after breakfast to take me out to see the commencement of this great work, which is the cause of so much pride and such sanguine expectations to the Baltimoreans. Besides Mr. Brown and myself, our party consisted of Professor McVickar and his daughter, of New York; Mr. DeGraffe, of Schenectady; Mr. Derby and two other Bostonians; and Mr. Meredith. The wind being strong from the north-west, we were conveyed with great rapidity a short distance in a car propelled by sails, a very pleasant mode of travelling.

WASHINGTON, SUNDAY, MARCH 21. — I left Baltimore after breakfast, arrived here at two o'clock, and put up at Gadsby's. After dinner, I walked with Mr. C. P. White, member of Congress from New York, nearly to Georgetown. The weather is remarkably fine, and I met many of my acquaintances in my walk.

MONDAY, MARCH 22. — I called upon the Secretary of State this morning; also upon the Secretary of the Navy; Mr. Berrien, Attorney-General; Mr. Huygens, Minister of the Netherlands; Mr. Vaughan, British Minister, etc. The remainder of the day until dinner was occupied at the Capitol. The Speaker gave me the *entrée* to the floor of the House of Representatives, and Mr. Webster to the Senate and to the Supreme Court, which adjourned its session while I was present. I was introduced to the judges, and had the pleasure of a few minutes' conversation with that great and good man, John Marshall.

TUESDAY, MARCH 23. — I dined with Mr. Vaughan, the British Minister. He lives in handsome style, and his dinners are more *recherché* than those of any other person here. Our party consisted of the following gentlemen: Messrs. Webster, Tazewell, Archer,

McTavish, Cambreling; Colonel Drayton; Judge Vanderpoel, of New York; Professor McVickar; Baron Stackelberg, chargé from Sweden; Pedersen, from Denmark; Neiderstetter, from Prussia; Tacon, Minister Resident of Spain; Mr. Bankhead, British Secretary of Legation; and Count de Menon, chargé of France.

WEDNESDAY, MARCH 24. — I dined with Mr. Webster, where I met General Harrison; Governor Tyler, of Virginia; Mr. Edward Everett and Mr. Silsbee, of Massachusetts; Mr. Grundy, of Tennessee; Count de Menon; Mr. Vaughan; Mr. Devereux; Professor McVickar, his daughter, etc.

THURSDAY, MARCH 25. — I called this morning with Mr. Webster to visit Mr. Adams, late President. His health and spirits are good, and we paid an agreeable visit.

FRIDAY, MARCH 26. — I passed two or three hours this morning in returning visits, after which I went to the House. No business of importance is under consideration, but I have had an opportunity of talking with all the leading members. I infer from what I hear that the administration is losing ground. The proscriptive course which has been pursued in relation to removals and appointments has served to cool their friends and to exasperate their enemies, and the difficulties which exist in the Senate in regard to several important nominations is considered an indication of public opinion. If Jackson succeeds for another term, it will be owing to the difficulty of agreeing upon his successor, rather than to the popularity of his administration. If DeWitt Clinton had lived, what a chance New York would now have had for a President! As it is, I am inclined to think that Van Buren is the prominent candidate. The Virginians say that if he had refused to take office with his present associates, or exerted himself to procure a better selection, he would have been their candidate.

Dined with Mr. Stevenson, Speaker of the House of Representatives, where I met The following party: The Vice-President; Mr. Tazewell; Mr. Livingston, of Louisiana; Drayton; Poinsett; Cambreling; General Harrison; Martin White, of Florida; C. P. White;

and General Wood. In the evening I went to a ladies' party at Mrs. Silsbee's.

BALTIMORE, MONDAY, MARCH 29. — I took my leave of the magnificent Wilderness at nine o'clock, and a very pleasant ride of five hours and a half brought me to Baltimore. I passed the first part of the day in walking and visiting, and dined at Mr. Meredith's with a very pleasant little party, consisting of Messrs. Gilmor, Fricke, Glenn, John Hoffman, Judge Randall, and Mr. Wirt. This is the first time during this visit that I have met the latter gentleman. He was, as usual, gay, agreeable, and instructive.

NEW YORK, SATURDAY, APRIL 10. — Married, on Tuesday evening last, Byam Kirby Stevens, to Frances, daughter of Albert Gallatin.

WEDNESDAY, APRIL 28. — The following party dined with us: Mr. and Mrs. Howland, Mr. Meredith, of Baltimore, Commander Chauncey, F. E. Granger, Mr. Charles Hammond, Thomas L. Ogden, Mr. Abr'm Ogden, S. S. Howland, Isaac S. Hone, Nath. Amory, James Stevenson, A. Schermerhorn, Edward R. Jones. Mr. Robert Gilmor joined us after dinner, immediately on his arrival from Baltimore. Mr. Bradish, who was expected from Albany, did not arrive. In the evening we went to a whist party, and supped at Mrs. Edgar's.

FRIDAY, APRIL 30. — I attended, with my wife and daughters, the opening of the Spring exhibition of the National Academy of Design. A large number of ladies and gentlemen were assembled, and a collation was provided. The exhibition is better than usual, but the crowd was too great to admit of the pictures being seen to advantage. There are some fine pictures of Weir's. This artist is improving astonishingly. There are also some good things by Inman.

MONDAY, MAY 10. — I went this morning with my wife and the girls to take leave of our friends who have sailed in the fine ship "De Rham" for Havre. We went down in the steamboat to the ship, which lay in the bay between Governor's and Bedlow's Islands. She has about thirty-six passengers, among whom are Mr.

and Mrs. Depau; Miss Stephanie and Mr. Louis Depau; Miss Mary E. Livingston, daughter of Maturin Livingston; Capt. John B. Nicolson, U.S.N.; Mr. and Mrs. Breese; Robert Cutting; and a young son of James G. King.

A match race was run on the Union course between Arietta, a Southern mare belonging to Colonel Johnson, and Ariel, belonging to Hamilton Wilkes; and a race between Slender, a Virginia mare, and John C. Stevens's mare, Black Maria. Both these races were easily won by the Southern people, at considerable expense to our sportsmen.

A singularly ridiculous article appeared under the signature of Mr. J. W. Webb in the " Courier and Enquirer " of this morning, of which he is editor, relating an account of a fracas between him and Duff Green in Washington on Thursday last. Webb went on to flog Green, and the latter armed himself with a pistol, and was so unreasonable as to refuse his consent to let the other pull his nose and slap his face. The public might say, with Iago, in relation to this quarrel, —

> "Now whether he kill Cassio,
> Or Cassio him, or each do kill the other,
> Every way makes my gain."

FRIDAY, MAY 14. — I attended a meeting this evening, by invitation, at Dr. Wainwright's, of the Literary Club, which meet at stated periods at the houses of each other, consisting of Chancellor Kent, Mr. Gallatin, the professors of the college, and other gentlemen, with several strangers of eminence and learned acquirements.

MONDAY, MAY 31. — I went this evening to see Booth play Iago to Cooper's Othello; Desdemona, Mrs. Barnes. I do not remember to have ever seen Booth, and was rather disappointed in his performance. It was respectable, but wanted spirit, raciness, and point; but I do not wonder at it, for Cooper is a perfect wet-blanket resting upon all around, stale, flat, and unprofitable. Oh, most lame and impotent conclusion! Is this the man whom I remember to have seen in my boyish days at the theatre, then in Greenwich street? We have both grown older, but I am only a looker-on in Verona, and am not compelled to obtrude my infirmities upon the public notice. *Tant mieux pour moi.*

SUNDAY, JULY 4.— I am wearing the black-silk vest which was presented to me on the 4th of July, 1827, and which was imported into New York in the year 1776. The condition of its acceptance was that I should wear it on every 4th of July during my life, and that it should descend to my oldest son.

MONDAY, JULY 5.— I dined with the Corporation pretty much in the usual way, — a mixture of public characters and of persons who should not have been invited. A poor dinner poorly served up and a want of tact and good management characterized this annual *fête* of the municipality. The presence of the new French Minister gave occasion to some speeches and toasts mutually complimentary to his country and its sovereign, and to the little sovereigns of our city. In the evening I walked down to Castle Garden with Lieutenant Cooke of the Fifteenth Regiment, British Infantry, who has just brought me a letter of introduction from Captain Hope at Quebec. We found this charming place filled with respectable, orderly people, and witnessed a good display of fireworks. The evening was fine, and the beauty of the scene made amends for some of the disgusting objects which our streets have exhibited during the day.

FRIDAY, JULY 16. — The following party dined with us: Mr. C. Bankhead, Secretary of the British Legation, and his lady; Baron Krudener, Baron Stackelberg, Count Ney, Mrs. Cornwall, Mr. James Bowdoin, Dom. Lynch, James A. Hamilton, Isaac Hone.

BALLSTON SPRINGS, WEDNESDAY, JULY 21.— We arrived in Albany at six o'clock this morning, breakfasted on board the boat, and started at eight o'clock in my barouche and a post-coach, and got to Sans-Souci at seven in the evening. Loomis's House has never been so full so early in the season as this. Among his boarders we found Mr. and Mrs. and Miss Brown, Chevalier Huygens and his family, Mrs. Joshua Jones and her daughter, Mr. Isaac I. Jones and wife, the Misses Mason, the families of Messrs. Kernochan, Parish, and Suffern, Mrs. Charles Clinton, Miss Joanna Anthon, the Misses Bridgen, Mr. and Mrs. J. C. Hamilton and their family, Major Fowler, Mr. Hall, etc., which, with the addition of my large party, will form a formidable array at the breakfast table to-morrow morning.

NEW YORK, TUESDAY, AUG. 3. — Commencement of Columbia College at St. John's Church this morning. I attended during the whole time and was much interested in the exercises. The young gentlemen generally made a very respectable appearance. The first honours in the senior class were awarded to Franklin Miller, son of Sylvanus Miller, and in the junior class to Robert Emery, who is the head of his class. The degree of Bachelor of Arts was conferred upon James Bowdoin, Hugh T. Dickey, Benjamin F. Ferguson, Lewis C. Gusen, Nicholas C. Heyward, George Kneeland, Jr., Edward Jones, John T. Kneeland, Henry Ledyard, Franklin Miller, Henry C. Murphy, Henry Nicoll, Charles H. Ogden, William Steele, Jr., William D. Waddington, and George Wm. Wright; also upon William B. Boggs, Robert L. Cutting, and John Delafield, Jr., members of the senior class who are absent by permission. The degree of Master of Arts was conferred upon John M. Forbes and Henry J. Morton, the two young gentlemen who were on Sunday ordained deacons in Trinity Church, and also upon Hamilton Fish, J. Trumbull Backus, and Grenville Temple Winthrop. The Latin salutatory was delivered by Franklin Miller, the English salutatory by Henry Nicoll, and the valedictory by Edward Jones.

WEDNESDAY, AUG. 4. — I left home this morning at seven o'clock in the "Albany" with my wife, two sons, Miss Louisa Fairlie, and Miss Harriet Kane, who are to accompany us to the Springs.

BALLSTON, SATURDAY, AUG. 14. — A fancy ball was given last evening at Sans-Souci, which was confined to the boarders in the house. It was gotten up at short notice, but went off remarkably well. The characters were supported by the following ladies: —

Mrs. James Thomson, a Swiss peasant; Mrs. Isaac Jones, la dame blanche; Mrs. Talmadge, a black nun; Miss Fairlie, a Bohemian fortune-teller; Miss Lawrence, brigand's wife; Miss Dennison, a Sultana; Miss French, French peasant; Miss Mason, character from La Rossignol; Miss Sarah Mason, Virginia; Miss Margaret Hone, a white nun; Miss Mary Hone, an Austrian peasant; Miss Sarah Livingston, a Scotch lassie; Miss Matilda Livingston, a Quakeress; Miss Harriet Kane, a French pedler; Miss Morris, a peasant.

Gentlemen: Mr. P. Hone, Lord Ogilby; Mr. James Thomson, Uncle Ben; Mr. Cooper, Mrs. Lobden and a tiger; Dr. Greenhow, Voltaire; Mr. Van Zandt, a Tryolese hunter; Mr. Van Schaick, Peter McGrowler; Mr. John C. Hamilton, an astrologer; General Fleming, a friar; Judge Morris, a fireman; Mr. Vail, a French village bridegroom; Messrs. Allston, Schermerhorn, John P. Hone, and John Kane, four Austrian hussars; Mr. John Mason, an Albanian; Mr. Washington Coster, Scotch lassie; Robert S. Hone, Bob, the sailor boy; Mr. Carter Lee, Paul; Mr. Whetton, an old gentleman.

NEW YORK, TUESDAY, AUG. 24. — Died yesterday, Col. Marinus Willet, aged ninety years and eleven days. His name is advantageously identified with the events of the Revolutionary War, in which he was a gallant soldier and distinguished officer. He was buried with the honours of war, and his funeral was attended by the Mayor and Corporation, the Society of Cincinnati, and by the members of the Court of Errors, now in session.

SATURDAY, AUG. 28. — Our fair countrywoman, the Marchioness of Wellesley, granddaughter of the venerable Charles Carroll, has been appointed first lady of the bed-chamber to Queen Adelaide, consort of King William IV.

WEDNESDAY, SEPT. 1. — I went over to the Park Theatre to witness the first appearance in America of Charles Kean, the son of the celebrated tragedian. He appeared in his father's great part, Richard III., and brought an overflowing house. But making every allowance for the disadvantages of a first appearance, I cannot perceive that he inherits any great proportion of his father's genius, and is, in my opinion, quite deficient in the requisite physical qualities of voice, figure, and deportment. Booth is playing tragedy at the Bowery Theatre, and I have no doubt will be greatly preferred by theatrical amateurs.

HYDE PARK, SATURDAY, SEPT. 11.— The weather is delightful, and we have passed the day in walking and riding over Dr. Hosack's splendid grounds. Isaac and Eliza Hone came here this morning from Poughkeepsie, and Mr. Poinsett, accompanied by Don Lorenzo de Zavalla, Governor of Mexico, came in the steamboat. The doctor and I went to dine with Judge Pendleton, where we met Mr. Allen, Judge Johnson, Mr. James Duane Livingston, and Mr. Guilliard.

MONDAY, SEPT. 13. — After breakfast, I went with my wife and Miss Eliza Hosack to visit at Governor Lewis's, Judge Pendleton's, and Mr. James Thomson's; this latter superb place is in its usual fine order, and the weather enabled us to enjoy the splendid prospect to great advantage. Our visits were all very pleasant, and our friends glad to see us. We returned home to dinner, and the remainder of the day was spent among the fine walks on the doctor's place, and in the literary delights of his splendid library.

WEDNESDAY, SEPT. 15.— I attended this evening at the house of my niece, Mrs. Maria Hone, the wedding of Mr. William Wood, of Glasgow, who was married to my sweet young friend, Harriet Kane. May she be as happy as she is good and beautiful! They intend to start on Friday on a journey to Niagara, and will probably sail for Europe about the 1st of November.

THURSDAY, SEPT. 16. — The funeral of Bishop Hobart took place this afternoon, under the direction of the committee of arrangements appointed by the vestry, of which I was one. The procession, embracing the governor, mayor of the city, Court of Errors, judges, vestry of Trinity Church, and the other vestries of Episcopal churches, the several religious and literary and benevolent societies of which he was a member, and the clergy of different denominations to the number of more than one hundred, moved from his late residence in Varick street to Trinity Church, where the funeral service was performed by Bishop Moon, of Virginia, Mr. Schroeder, and Dr. Lyell, and a sermon was preached by Dr. Onderdonk. The procession is said to have contained five thousand persons, and the streets on its route were crowded with spectators. The church was filled almost to suffocation, but everything was conducted with great decorum and propriety. The corpse is interred in the chancel, immediately under the communion table, and the grave is to be walled up and an arch to be thrown over it.

TUESDAY, SEPT. 28. — The accounts from France, which were written after the excitement of the Revolution had in some degree subsided, are filled with interesting details, but no part of them excites so much admiration as those in which Lafayette is mentioned. It seems to be allowed on all sides that to this veteran soldier of liberty the king owes his crown. If he had come out for a republic, his popularity was so great, and his influence over public opinion so absolute, that the great mass of the principal actors in the events of the 27th, 28th, and 29th of July would have been satisfied with nothing short of it, and, in all probability, the French people would now have been employed in cutting each other's throats instead of being settled quietly down under a liberal form of government and a patriotic king, with as much liberty as the people of this country enjoy, but under another name. This great citizen of France has now seen, in his latter days, the predictions of his former life verified, and the glory and good fortune which accompanied him in the morning and meridian of his eventful day have not deserted him at its close.

What a strange, eventful period in the affairs of this world has been the brief fifty years during which I have been in it, and how interesting a moment in its history is the present!

THURSDAY, OCT. 14. — The fair of the American Institute has been held yesterday and to-day at Masonic Hall. The exhibition has embraced an immense variety of manufactures, — furniture of every description, and every object which the versatility of invention and the ingenuity of our artisans and manufacturers could produce. In the evening Mr. Tristram Burgess, the great champion of the American system, delivered an address before the members of the institution and a large number of spectators, at the new court-room in the apartments formerly of the American Museum. I had the misfortune to be one of the audience, and was tired out by a heavy, inappropriate jumble of far-fetched facts and unimaginable imaginings, and left the place before the oration was concluded. I marvel much that the members of the institute, with their professed aversion to importation, and their encouragement of home manufactures, should import nonsense from Rhode Island when we have so good a stock of the indigenous article.

TUESDAY, OCT. 19. — Francis Child died at Burlington, Vt., a few days since, aged sixty-seven years. He established the New York "Daily Advertiser," the first daily paper in New York, the first number of which was published March 1, 1785.

MONDAY, OCT. 25. — This day completes my fiftieth year, and we had a large family party to celebrate it. The party consisted of Mr. and Mrs. Anthon, Miss Caroline Anthon, Mr. and Mrs. I. S. Hone, Mr. Van Schaick, Mr. and Mrs. William Wood, Miss Charlotte Kane, Miss Joanna Anthon, Dr. and Mrs. Matthews, Mr. and Mrs. Henry Hone, Mrs. Maria Hone, Mr. and Mrs. Charles Kneeland, Mr. and Mrs. S. S. Howland.

THURSDAY, OCT. 28. — I rented the shop and cellar of Clinton Hotel for five years from May next, at $700 for the first two and $800 for the last three years, to Joshua Leavitt, bookseller for Mr. Appleton.

THURSDAY, NOV. 18. — One of the locomotive engines on the Liverpool and Manchester Railroad traversed the distance between the two places, thirty-two miles, in thirty-three minutes, — about *fifty-eight miles an hour!*

MONDAY, Nov. 22. — Master Burke, a precocious Roscius from the Emerald Isle, who arrived on Thursday from Liverpool, made his first appearance this evening at the Park Theatre in "Norval," and Dr. O'Toole, in the "Irish Tutor." I saw him for a short time in the farce, and think him a remarkably clever boy.

SUNDAY, Nov. 27. — Yesterday took place the New York celebration of the late revolution in France. The procession, divided into sixteen divisions, was formed in Canal street, with its right on the North river and extending up Broadway. At ten o'clock the line of march was formed and went down Broadway to the Park, around the Park, up Chatham street and the Bowery to Broome street, down Broome street to Broadway, up Broadway to Fourth street, down Fourth street to the Washington parade-ground. At this place a stage had been erected, on which the following ceremonies were performed: A prayer by the Rev. Mr. Day; an address to the French people, written by Mr. John Duer, was read; the oration, by Mr. Samuel L. Gouverneur; after which the Marseillaise hymn and an ode prepared for the occasion by Samuel Woodworth were sung by the choir.

I rode during the day and superintended the whole as chairman of the committee of arrangements. The procession was so long that when the right entered Broadway from Broome street, the military, who formed an unusually splendid array, had not yet left Canal street, and when we arrived at the parade-ground, the whole were not yet in motion. The whole route must have been two miles and a half. The ex-President, Monroe, drove in his carriage, as did Mr. Gallatin and the orator and reader of the address. An interesting group occupied a barouche, consisting of Anthony Glenn, who raised the flag at the fort on the retreat of the British, 25th of November, 1783; John Van Arsdale, the sailor who mounted the staff to remove the obstructions; and the identical flag itself, which has been preserved in Scudder's Museum. This group of octogenarians was completed by David Williams, the survivor of the three captors of Major André, and Enoch Crosby, the Harvey Birch of the Revolution. The president, faculty, and students of Columbia College were conspicuous in the procession, and the citizens of France, with their splendid banner, made a proud display. Their banner was formally presented on the ground to the first division of artillery. Among the trades and societies the most prominent were the fire department, with their beautiful engines, badges, and other decorations, to the number of fifteen hundred persons; the printers, who were employed at two places in striking off and distributing among the multitude copies of the ode, etc.; the butchers on horseback, to the number of three hundred, in leg-of-mutton sleeves; the cartmen on horseback in white frocks; a steamboat with her steam up and machinery in motion; the famous Whitehall boat, carried by the pilots and watermen; and a great many stages, displaying the emblems of different trades, and on which mechanical operations were carried on during the march. The procession was closed by the military, who formed on the grounds north of the square and fired a *feu-de-joie* after the civic ceremonies were concluded.

SUNDAY, Nov. 28. — I made a pleasant visit this morning to Colonel Monroe, ex-President of the United States, who is residing with his son-in-law, Mr. S. Gouverneur, in Prince street. Mr. Monroe is very feeble and appears in worse health than usual, the effect of a cold; but his mental faculties are unimpaired, and his manner and conversation are exceedingly interesting.

SATURDAY, DEC. 18. — Moore, Giraud, and I went yesterday to dine at Delmonico's, a French *restaurateur*, in William street, which I had heard was upon the Parisian plan, and very good. We satisfied our curiosity, but not our appetites; and I think are prepared, when our opinions are asked, to say with the Irishman who used lamp-oil with his salad instead of olive-oil, that if it were not for the name of the thing he had as lief eat butter.

FRIDAY, DEC. 24. — Mr. Ball Hughes's model for the statue of Hamilton, on which he has been employed for a long time past, being now completed, the committee who were named to decide upon its merits assembled at the *atelier* of the artist, at twelve o'clock. Of that committee were present: Mr. Wilkes, Dr. Hosack, Colonel Trumbull, and myself; and of the Exchange committee, Messrs. Woolsey, Tibbits, Wyckoff, and George Griswold, with Messrs. D. B. Ogden and James R. Murray. The fullest testimony of approbation was unanimously given, and I have no doubt that if the artist finishes the statue agreeably to the promise given by the model, it will be the best piece of statuary in the United States.

1831.

SUNDAY, JAN. 2. — A decidedly pleasant day, the first I believe during the present autumn and winter. I paid a few visits which were left over from yesterday. The old custom of visiting on New Year's Day, and the happy greetings which have so long been given on that occasion, have been well kept up this year. I am glad of it; few of those good old customs remain which mark the overflow of unsophisticated good feeling, and I rejoice whenever I can recognize any part of the wreck which the innovations of fashion have left afloat.

WEDNESDAY, FEB. 2. — The following gentlemen were on Monday last elected officers of the new university in this city: Albert Gallatin, president of the council; Morgan Lewis, vice-president; John Delafield, secretary; Samuel Ward, treasurer; James M. Mathews, D.D., chancellor of the university.

Dinner to Lafayette. On the 8th of December a grand dinner was given by the Americans in Paris to General Lafayette, the account of which is very interesting from the circumstance of so many Americans of my acquaintance having been engaged in it. James Fenimore Cooper, of New York, presided, assisted by Peter Schermerhorn, of New York, and Capt. John Nicolson, U.S.N. Among the guests were Mr. Serrurier, Minister to the United States; Odillon Barrot, Prefect of the Seine; Gen. Matthias Dumas, adjutant-general of the National Guards; M. Du Perron, grandson-in-law of Lafayette; Mons. De Remusat, deputy, and grandson-in-law of the General; General Carbonel; Mons. Joubert; Mr. Rives, American Minister; Charles de Lameth, deputy of Paris, who fought and was wounded at Yorktown; George W. Lafayette; Jules de Lasteyrie, etc.

TUESDAY, FEB. 22. — I went this evening with my wife and

daughters to the Assembly, where I was introduced to Mr. Serrurier, the new French Minister, and conversed with him about the late occurrences in France. He speaks in the highest terms of the conduct of Lafayette in the affair of the ex-ministers of Charles X. His firmness and courage contributed greatly to preserve the peace of Paris in that interesting crisis. Mr. Serrurier regrets his resignation of the command of the National Guard, and considers it somewhat hasty. But the General has desired him to state to his American friends that it did not arise from any motives of a personal nature.

SATURDAY, MARCH 12. — The following gentlemen dined with us: Judge Spencer, Judge Irving, Mr. John Hone, Dr. Hosack, Mr. Granger, Governor Coles, Judge Oakley, General Scott, Chancellor Kent.

And thus endeth the third volume of my diary. It has become a habit with me to write in it, and affords me pleasure. It is not like writing letters, which may be done or let alone, and becomes, therefore, a task, and as such is more or less irksome; but this is part of my daily occupation. If I should live some dozen or twenty years I shall enjoy the retrospection, or my children, if they revere the memory of their father, will, in turning over the pages of this book, have something to remind them of him, — something that will "prate of his whereabouts," and inform them how he thought and what he did "about these times."

MARCH 15. — Went this morning to see the Siamese boys, who returned last week from England. I did not see them when they were exhibited formerly in this city. This astonishing freak of nature is exceedingly interesting, and the sight of it is not disagreeable, as I expected to find it. They are now nearly twenty years old, kind, good-tempered, and playful; their limbs are well proportioned and strong, but their faces are devoid of intelligence, and have that stupid expression which is characteristic of the natives of the East. They are united by a strong ligament of flesh or gristle, without bone, about three inches in breadth and five in length. Their movements are, of course, simultaneous. They walk, sit down, play, eat and drink, and perform all the functions of nature in unison; their dispositions and their very thoughts are alike; when one is sick the other partakes of his illness, and the stroke of death will, no doubt, lay them both in the same grave; and yet their bodies, heads, and limbs are all perfect and distinct. They speak English tolerably well, and appear fond of talking.

Bachelor's Grand Fancy Ball. FRIDAY, MARCH 18. — This splendid affair, so long the theme of conversation and the subject of preparation, took place this evening at the City Hotel, and I believe no expectations had been formed which were disappointed by the result. The rooms were handsomely fitted up with mirrors, curtains, pier tables, and lamps; the supper tables were splendidly and most abundantly furnished. The number of guests was very great, of which about one-third appeared in fancy dress, some of which were well conceived and supported with wit and address; and others failing in those respects were thought by some to make up in magnificence and lustre. It is not necessary for me to go into the particulars of a *catalogue raisonné*, and if it were, "I am not i' the vein," and I think my time will be better spent in reading Moore's "Byron." My daughter Mary went as "Sweet Anne Page," and looked sweetly in the costume of Leslie's inimitable picture. The rest of us went *sans caractère*, — my wife and I, because we were too old to join the "Masquers and Mummies;" John, because a sprained ankle had prevented him for several days past from making his preparations; Robert, because he couldn't; and Margaret, because she wouldn't. Our party was graced by the addition of our fair visitor, Helen Kane, who was said to look well *for an Albanian*. Mrs. Hughes, as a flower girl, was very näive and lively, and distributed to each of her friends an appropriate flower, with a pretty card describing its attributes, and conveying her good wishes to those whom she selected as the recipients of her favours.

MONDAY, MARCH 28. — Left home on a fishing excursion to Long Island with Giraud. The weather was doubtful, but improved in the course of the day. Dined at Timothy Carman's, and went to Jackson's, where we lodged. Mr. Morris and Mr. Constant were here, having overtaken us at dinner-time.

FRIDAY, APRIL 1. — A gale from the north-west. We went on the pond after breakfast, and caught a fine mess of fish to take home. A deer crossed the creek near the boat while we were fishing. Mr. Giraud and I have taken sixty-five trout. After dinner we started for home at three o'clock, intending to go no further than Jackson's; but our horses were fresh, and we came on to Timothy Carman's, where we lodged. Immense quantities of wild-fowl have been killed in the bay this week. A man had at Babylon this evening, on his way to the New York market, six hundred broad-bills.

SATURDAY, APRIL 2. — Went to dine at Isaac's with a party, among whom were Messrs. Sturgis and Cabot, of Boston. I added a handsome mess of fresh trout to the dinner.

WEDNESDAY, APRIL 6. — Mr. John Mason was elected, on Monday last, president of the Chemical Bank, in place of Mr. B. P. Melick.

WEDNESDAY, APRIL 20. — While I was shaving this morning at eight o'clock, I witnessed from the front window an encounter in the street nearly opposite, between William C. Bryant and William L. Stone; the former one of the editors of the "Evening Post," and the latter editor of the "Commercial Advertiser." The former commenced the attack by striking Stone over the head with a cowskin; after a few blows the men closed, and the whip was wrested from Bryant and carried off by Stone. When I saw them first, two younger persons were engaged, but soon discontinued their fight. A crowd soon closed in and separated the combatants.

SATURDAY, APRIL 30. — A public dinner was given on Thursday last to G. C. Verplanck, Esq., member of Congress from this city, by the *literati*, artists, and booksellers, avowedly for his exertions to procure the passage of the copyright law. Judge Irving was president, and Professor Renwick and Mr. Dunlap, vice-presidents. Mr. Verplanck made a long speech, which is much praised by those who were present.

MONDAY, MAY 2. — The following party dined with us: Sir William Campbell, late Chief Justice of Canada; James Maury, late Consul to Liverpool; Luther Bradish; James G. King; Capt. James Rogers; Isaac S. Hone; Charles McEvers; Isaac Carow; Rutsen Maury; G. G. Howland; James Haggerty.

THURSDAY, MAY 5. — It is an interesting and gratifying subject of reflection that our country at large, and particularly this city, is at this time prosperous beyond all former example, and somewhat remarkable that different interests, usually considered opposed to each other, are equally successful. Foreign commerce is in a thriving condition; vessels are worth fifty per cent. more than they were two years since, and freights are nearly double; real estate, up and down town, equally high; houses in great demand, at advanced rents; the dealers in imported goods doing a safe and profitable business; the farmer selling his wool at seventy-five cents per pound, which two years ago was worth only thirty-seven and one-half cents per pound, and availing himself of the increased price of bread-stuffs, occasioned by the brisk foreign demand; the manufacturers, both of woollen and cotton goods, fully employed, and doing better than at any former period; and the lawyers doing nothing. This is cause of great exultation to our citizens, and should inspire them with gratitude to the Dispenser of all good things. We are more apt to complain when things go wrong than to be thankful when they go right.

MONDAY, MAY 9. — The city is now undergoing its usual annual metamorphosis; many stores and houses are being pulled down, and others altered, to make every inch of ground productive to its utmost extent. Pearl street and Broadway in particular are rendered almost impassable by the quantity of rubbish with which they are obstructed, and by the dust which is blown about by a keen north-west wind.

SATURDAY, MAY 21. — I went with the girls to Hoboken this afternoon, and had a delightful walk on the high banks nearly to Weehawken.

I received this day a letter from Samuel F. B. Morse, dated at Rome, February 15. He informs me that he has shipped for me at Leghorn a fine portrait by himself of Thorvaldsen, the celebrated sculptor, and a cast executed by that artist of the "Triumph of Alexander the Great," from the original *bas-relief* made for the Marquis Sommariva.

TUESDAY, MAY 24. — Died on the 17th inst., at Rochester, Col. Nathaniel Rochester, in the eightieth year of his age. He was an officer in the Revolutionary War, and removed from his native State to Steuben County in this State in 1802, soon after which he removed to the village of Rochester, a great part of which he owned. It is now a town of considerable magnitude, the wonder of the western empire of New York.

THURSDAY, JULY 5. — In the midst of the festivities of the celebration of independence yesterday, the death of James Monroe was announced. He died at the house of his son-in-law, Mr. Samuel L. Gouverneur, in this city. This venerable patriot has been ill and his life despaired of for some months past, and he seems to have lingered until this time to add to the number of the Revolutionary patriots whose deaths have occurred on this memorable anniversary. Of four ex-Presidents who have died, three have departed on the 4th of July, and of this number two, who were signers of the august instrument which declared the political birth of our country, died on the fiftieth anniversary, 4th of July, 1826. Mr. Monroe has now made the third, and has closed his mortal career, respected and honoured by his countrymen. Measures will be adopted by the civil and military authorities to render his funeral obsequies worthy of his character and the important services he has performed and the exalted stations he has filled.

MONDAY, JULY 11. — The hard rains have been followed by bright, cool weather and clear skies. I attended by invitation a *fête champêtre* given by the Messrs. Stevens at the Elysian Fields above Hoboken. This beautiful spot has been cleaned, the grounds laid out with great taste, and a handsome pavilion erected, as a place of public resort connected with the ferry. At three o'clock, the company, consisting of about two hundred gentlemen, assembled on board the steamboat "Chief Justice Marshall." Among them were the mayor and corporation, and many other public characters, and a number of the Stevens's personal friends.

When we arrived on the ground, we were conducted to a spot in the woods enclosed by flags, and decorated in a tasteful manner, where tables were spread, and a dinner of turtle soup and every refreshment furnished to the guests which the taste and liberality of our entertainers had taught us to expect. Some time after our arrival, the party was increased by the New York and Jersey City Boat Clubs, who came in their several boats, dressed in white jackets and trousers, round chip hats, and checked shirts, the becoming costume of the clubs. John Stevens presided at the feast, with spirits as abundant and sparkling as his champagne; and the beautiful grove, under the branches of which we were seated, echoed the sounds of merriment and good-humour, inspired by the toasts, the songs, and the laughter, to which each guest seemed disposed to contribute his share.

MONDAY, AUG. 1. — Col. Richard Varick died on Saturday night at his residence, Jersey City, in the seventy-ninth year of his age, of cholera morbus. He complained of lameness in his feet when I last saw him, which was about a fortnight since, but his general health was good. He attended, as president of the Society of Cincinnati, the corporation dinner on the 4th ult., and was a pall-bearer at the funeral of President Monroe on the 7th ult. Measures are taking to pay great respect to his memory. General orders are issued for the Division of Artillery. The Society of Cincinnati have announced his death, and the order of the funeral ceremonies under direction of Gen. Morgan Lewis, vice-president. Both houses of the Common Council and the Court of Sessions, which were sitting, adjourned this morning on the announcement of his death. The pall-bearers at Colonel Varick's funeral are: Lynde Catlin, Peter A. Jay, Col. Aaron Ogden, Col. John Trumbull, John Pintard, William W. Woolsey, Chancellor Kent, Col. Nicholas Fish.

FRIDAY, AUG. 5.—I left Albany this morning at eight o'clock, in company with Messrs. Charles Graham,
<small>Saratoga Springs.</small>
Lispenard Stewart, Fehrman, and my son John, and after an exceedingly pleasant ride came to Congress Hall and got very good colonial quarters, near the bath-house. We were delighted this morning with the view of the Cohoes Falls; the rains this season have been frequent, and the river rushes in an entire sheet, covering the whole face of the rock. I have never before seen the water so high, nor consequently the cataract so fine. The wreck of a canal-boat is on the edge of the great dam, where she was wrecked yesterday. Her towing line was broken by the force of the current while passing below the bridge, and she was carried down to the place where she now lies. The only man on board and her cargo of firewood were saved.

Congress Hall is filled with company, amongst whom are many distinguished men and fine women, and nearly about the usual proportion of people who are neither distinguished nor fine, but rich, and that, in their opinion, entitles them to more consideration than either. Amongst the first description of persons are Mr. Buchanan, of Pennsylvania, who they say is to supply the place of Mr. Randolph, our *extraordinary* Minister to Russia; Meredith; Gilmor; Gibbes; Hoffman; and Martin, of Maryland; Jonathan Mason and George Blake, of Massachusetts; Mr. and Mrs. Howland; the Cuttings; Carys; my brother and sister; Mrs. Abbott; Oliver Kane and his daughters; William Sullivan, of Boston, and his pretty daughter; Miss Fulton; Mrs. Davis; Mr. and Mrs. Dickenson; the Tayloes, etc.

TUESDAY, AUG. 9.— A party of us went out to dine yesterday at Barhuyt's, consisting of General Van Rensselaer, Mr. Meredith,

Charles E. Davis, Morgan Gibbes, G. G. Howland, Mr. J. Hare Powel, R. Gilmor, J. D. Dickenson, T. L. Gibbes, D. Lynch, Crafts, and myself. The old man gave us several dishes of his little trout fried, two chickens, and that was all; but he charged us well. The party, however, was gay and the conversation brilliant, and Lynch sang for us. The fashionables are leaving Saratoga in great numbers, and no new-comers supply their places. Some go to New York, some to Lake George, and others to Lebanon.

HONESDALE, SUNDAY, AUG. 21.— I went to church this morning, and after an early dinner left Carbondale in a wagon with Captain Goodale and Mr. Archbald and came to this place by the way of Canaan. I never witnessed a more reverential observance of the Sabbath than in both these villages; notwithstanding the vast number of workmen, amongst whom are a large proportion of Irish and Welsh people, who are employed as miners and otherwise, all occupation has ceased; the coal valley which resounded yesterday with the noise of machinery, the rattling of cars, the explosion of gunpowder, and the clinking of pickaxes is now as still as the tomb of the Capulets; and the miners who were yesterday begrimed with coal and looked like citizens of the nether world are seen this morning on their way to church, clean and well dressed, with long coats and gilt buttons, high shirt-collars, and brooches in their bosoms. So much for a good example; the company suspends its operations of every sort on Sunday.

NEW YORK, THURSDAY, SEPT. 8.— A meeting was held at five o'clock this afternoon at the Merchants' Exchange, of which Preserved Fish was chairman and Jonathan Goodhue secretary, at which delegates were appointed to attend the Free Trade Convention at Philadelphia, on the 30th inst., and resolutions passed disapproving the tariff laws, and expressing a determination to take measures to procure a modification of them by the next Congress; the following are the names of the delegates: Albert Gallatin, James Kent, Stephen Allen, Morgan Lewis, Peter A. Jay, Jacob Lorillard, David B. Ogden, James Boorman,

Henry J. Wyckoff, Zebedee Ring, Benjamin L. Swan, James G. King, John A. Stevens, James Heard, Frederick Sheldon, Charles H. Russell, Stephen Smith, Silas M. Stilwell, Moses H. Grinnell, Preserved Fish, Isaac Bronson, John Haggerty, Thomas R. Mercein, Isaac Carow, John L. Crary, J. T. Trimble, George Griswold, J. McVicar, H. Kneeland, Jonathan Goodhue.

WEDNESDAY, SEPT. 14. — A fatal duel was fought at St. Louis, Mo., on August 26, between Major Biddle, paymaster of the United States Army, and Spencer Pettis, Esq.; the former was brother to Nicholas Biddle, of Philadelphia, president of the Bank of the United States, and to Commodore Biddle of the navy, and the latter was recently elected a member of Congress. They fought at five feet distance, and were both mortally wounded on the first discharge. Mr. Pettis died on the same day and Major Biddle on the following. The quarrel originated in political differences and in the publication of an article written by Biddle to operate against Pettis's election.

Excursion to Albany and West Point. FRIDAY, SEPT. 23. — Having received an invitation to visit the Mohawk and Hudson Railroad, I proposed to the girls to take them with me, and leave them at West Point until my return from Albany. I started this afternoon, at five o'clock, in the steamboat "DeWitt Clinton." The weather had been bad all day, and was still very doubtful when we left home, but soon became pleasant. The rest of the party landed at West Point, and I continued on my way to Albany. I went to the American Hotel, and after breakfast joined a large party at the Eagle Tavern. We proceeded in carriages under the orders of Mr. Cambreling, the superintendent, to the starting-place on the railroad, about two miles from the city. The road from this point is finished, a distance of twelve and a half miles, nearly level. The inclined planes at each end of the road are finished. The whole length of the railroad when completed will be fifteen miles and a half.

SUNDAY, SEPT. 25. — My intention of going to church this morning was frustrated by a pressing invitation from Cambreling to take another ride on the railroad with Bucknor and Edward Prime, who came up last evening. We started at ten o'clock, under the orders of Cambreling and Mr. DeGruff, who has been master of the ceremonies on this occasion, and we returned with the American locomotive twelve and a half miles in thirty-seven minutes, which is at the rate of twenty miles an hour, — quite fast enough in all conscience, and exceedingly pleasant.

MONDAY, OCT. 3. — The anti-tariff, or free-trade, Anti-tariff Convention. convention assembled in Philadelphia on Thursday last, but the accounts this morning state that they had not organized by the appointment of officers. What can they want? At least, what can the delegates from New York have to complain of, in thus lending their aid to the excited politicians of the South to destroy a state of prosperity unexampled in the history of our country? If the system of protecting duties should be abandoned, our great manufacturing interests will be prostrated; the wholesome competition with foreign countries which now keeps down the prices of imported goods will exist no longer. Foreigners will receive the benefit of the reduction of duties, and consumers will be compelled to pay double for everything of foreign manufacture. The opinion of New York is not expressed in this convention; our meeting was gotten up by two or three persons, not to obtain the sentiments of our citizens on the propriety of uniting with the nullifiers of the South, for in that they would have failed, but the friends of the measure only were called, and delegates were appointed, in the number of whom are many of our most respected citizens; but the names of several were used without their consent, and although some of them declined as soon as they saw their names published, on the ground of their opposition to the proceedings, the managers had not the candour and fairness to publish their declinations, but were willing to avail themselves of the influence which the use of such names would exercise upon public opinion in other States, where their disapprobation could not be known. Chancellor Kent is one of the number of those whose names, so well known and so much respected, are permitted to stand on the list of delegates. He was at my house last evening, and told me that he sent in his resignation immediately, because he disapproved of the proceeding, and was not opposed to the tariff. But this artifice has accomplished its object, and James Kent is quoted as one of the good and great men of New York who sanction a measure opposed to the true interest of our State and city. Verily, we are an unthankful people, and one that waxes fat and kicks.

MONDAY, OCT. 10. — The convention which has been sitting in Philadelphia adjourned on Friday evening, *sine die.* An address was reported by Judge Berrien, late Attorney-General of the United States, in which the tariff laws were declared to be unconstitutional. This occasioned some difficulty. Mr. Gallatin, from this city, moved to strike out that part, which motion was negatived. Of our delegates, sixteen had the grace to vote for striking out, and four, — Fish, Leonard, Bergh, and Kneeland, — against it; and the address was carried, one hundred and fifty-eight to twenty-nine. Thus the Southern nullifiers have accomplished their object, in getting New York to go with them; for although the delegates from this city do not represent this community, and were appointed nobody knows how, yet they will be claimed by the Southern people, who had rallied all their forces and out-voted our men, and were, in fact, representatives of their respective States. This is the way we are always managed. Such men as Gallatin, Griswold, Carow, and King should never have meddled in this concern, or should have protested and seceded from the convention when a proposition so monstrous as the denying to Congress the constitutional right to pass these laws was about to be adopted. Those gentlemen thought, no doubt honestly, that it was inexpedient and oppressive to pass laws which they considered unequal in their operation; but they are too enlightened to believe for a moment that those laws are unconstitutional. It is but a short time since they took the lead in paying a merited compliment to Mr. Webster for his manly and eloquent defence of the Constitution against the nullifying doctrines of the South, and now we see them bound hand and foot, and led forth to grace the triumph of his adroit competitors.

THURSDAY, OCT. 13. — Mr. Anderson, who came out lately from England, was announced this evening at the Park Theatre, for his first appearance in America, in the character of Henry Bertram in the opera of "Guy Mannering." The house was filled by persons who had prepared to assist in or witness the riot which was expected. He is said to have behaved ill on the passage and abused the Yankees, and a quarrel with the mate was settled after his arrival by the latter giving him a flogging, the effects of which has prevented him from appearing until now.

Row at the Theatre.

SATURDAY, OCT. 15. — Mr. Anderson was announced again for this evening in the part of Henry Bertram. The house was filled very early to suffocation. When I went in the whole interior was a solid mass of men. Not a single female present, except two or three in the upper tier. The first part of the opera was listened to, and when Mrs. Sharpe appeared she was received with the most marked approbation, intended, no doubt, as the *amende honorable* for the share which she was compelled to receive of the ill-treatment intended for Mr. Anderson on Thursday. At the commencement of the second act, previously to the time when he should have appeared, Simpson came forward and attempted to read his apology. This was the signal for the commencement of the riot, and from that time the disturbance continued during the whole night. Apples, eggs, and other missiles were showered upon the stage, and although Barry announced that the unhappy wight was withdrawn who had committed the unatonable offence which called down the vengeance of the sovereigns, and that the play would be changed, they would not be pacified. They went to the theatre for a row, and they would not be disappointed. The only interval of order was during the time that little Burke was brought forward and played on his violin in the overture to " Guy

Mannering," at the unanimous call of the house. The street in front of the theatre was filled by the mob, the lamps were broken, and the interior of the theatre sustained considerable injury, notwithstanding a strong force of watchmen and constables in attendance.

MONDAY, OCT. 17.— The disgraceful riots of Thursday and Saturday nights were continued on a more extensive scale last night. During the whole of yesterday the sanctity of the day was violated by the collection of groups of idlers in front of the theatre, and soon after dark the numbers had increased in a manner which caused serious alarm to the neighbourhood. Cries, shouts, and huzzas marked the commencement of the attack, and about nine o'clock I was disturbed by the noise of the crash of broken windows and the battering of the front doors. This continued half an hour without the interference of the municipal authorities. I then went out to find the Mayor. He was not at home, and could not be found. I then went around to the scene of action, when I found that the whole of this outrage was committed by about twenty boys, who were instigated and encouraged by the mob, and every crash of broken glass was followed by their shouts. At this time Hays came up with a pretty strong body of watchmen, and order was for a time restored. Several men and boys were carried to the watch-house, of whom nearly the whole were discharged in a short time, and several at my solicitation. The mob in front of the theatre continued, but no more injury was done to the building. Indeed, there was not much left to be done, unless the mob could have forced an entrance, when the scene would have been dreadful. The American and tricoloured flags were exhibited from the upper windows to appease the populace, which served to allay the tumult; but the noise continued all night, and I doubt if any person in the neighbourhood of the park had what is called a *good night's rest.*

To-day the front of the theatre is covered with transparencies of patriotic subjects, — flags and eagles in abundance, — which appears

to have propitiated the mob. I went into the house. Burke is
playing, and things go on tolerably quietly. The crowd in front is
tremendously great, but orderly, and there is a large body of
watchmen, with the Mayor in person, so that there is reason to
hope that this foolish affair has come to an end.

THURSDAY, OCT. 27. — The corner-stone of a hospital for sailors,
on the foundation of charity created by Robert Richard Randall,
was laid yesterday at Staten Island, by Chancellor Walworth. The
property left by Captain Randall has increased greatly in value
within the last year, and must be ample now for the objects of his
munificent bequest.

FRIDAY, OCT. 28. — I attended the tariff convention this morning,
and am much interested in their proceedings. The salt of the land
is there, and a little pepper, too; but in my opinion the cause must
be triumphant. It is the only true national triumph, and the only
effectual bond of union. I dined with Nathaniel Richards; Robert
G. Shaw and his wife, Mr. and Mrs. Abbot Lawrence, and several
of the Eastern members of the convention formed the party.

President Adams.

MONDAY, OCT. 31. — I was highly gratified by a circumstance which occurred in the convention this
morning, which proves that good feeling and courtesy
have not yet been voted out of fashion by the American people.
On the appearance of the ex-President, John Quincy Adams, in the
lobby, General Talmadge, one of the vice-presidents, left his seat
and handed him through the body of the house to a seat on the
platform; as soon as he was recognized, the whole assembly, including the spectators in the galleries and lobby, rose from their
seats, and received him with plaudits, which were continued until
he became seated.

FRIDAY, Nov. 4. — The following party dined with us: Hon.
John Quincy Adams, Mr. C. H. Hammond, Charles King, Charles
A. Davis, Peter H. Schenck, Isaac S. Hone, Chancellor Kent,
General Talmadge, John Hone, R. L. Colt, Dr. Wainwright, Miss
Helen Davis, Miss A. Church.

WEDNESDAY, Nov. 9. — Died on Saturday evening at his seat, Westchester, Gen. Philip Van Courtlandt, aged eighty-two years.

FRIDAY, Nov. 11. — The packet " New York " arrived yesterday. Among her passengers are Mr. Jonathan Ogden and his three daughters, and young John Haggerty, of this city, and my friend, Mr. J. R. Poinsett.

I do not know when I have been so delighted as I was last evening in seeing young Kean play Hamlet. It is a chaste, classical performance.

MONDAY, DEC. 26. — The East river was closed by ice this morning, and two or three hundred persons walked across from Fulton street to Brooklyn. On the turn of the tide the ice went out, and the steamboats were again plying.

Henry D. Sedgwick, late of this city, died at Stockbridge, Mass., on the 23d inst., in the forty-seventh year of his age. He was a man of talents, of celebrity as a lawyer, but eccentric.

1832.

THE New Year commences propitiously; the fine weather, clear sunshine, and lively appearance of the streets, covered with snow are emblematical of the happy state of our country and the prosperity of the city, and I ought also to add, of my own situation, which calls upon me for a grateful acknowledgment of the kindness and bounty of Divine Providence. Blessed with good health, my wife and children virtuous and in the enjoyment of health and happiness, easy in my circumstances (although not quite so rich as I have been), and enjoying, as I trust I do, the affections of my friends and the good opinions of my fellow-citizens, I have only to pray that I may not by an act of my own forfeit any of the blessings I enjoy, and that succeeding anniversaries of this day may, like this, be to me "a happy New Year."

FRIDAY, JAN. 9.— The following persons have been elected directors of the Bank of the United States: Nicholas Biddle, John Bohlen, Richard Willing, Henry Pratt, Matthew L. Bevan, John R. Neff, Horace Binney, Edward Coleman, Manuel Eyre, William Platt, Ambrose White, J. S. Henry, Thomas Cadwallader, of Philadelphia; John Potter, of South Carolina; Robert Gilmor, of Maryland; Isaac Carow, John Rathbone, Jr., of New York; Thomas N. Perkins, B. W. Crowninshield, of Massachusetts. The following government directors were appointed by the President of the United States: Nicholas Biddle, Joshua Lippincott, and J. T. Sullivan, of Pennsylvania; James Campbell, of New York; and Hugh McEldery, of Maryland. Nicholas Biddle was unanimously reëlected president.

WEDNESDAY, JAN. 11.— Halsted E. Haight's property sold this day. The three-story house and lot, 22 Vesey street, formerly occupied by the late Bishop Hobart, twenty-five feet front and rear by about a hundred and two feet in depth, bought by Mr. Ward for $18,500. The lot of ground next to my residence, corner of Broadway and Park place, with three tenements, one on Broadway and two on Park place, the lot twenty-five feet on Broadway, twenty-four feet eight inches in the rear, in length on Park place a hundred and twenty-one feet ten inches, and along my line a hundred and twenty feet six inches, bought by L. Bronson for $37,000. I bid for this lot $36,750, and regret since the sale that I had not gone further. It is worth more to me than to any other person.

The house, No. 18 Park place, occupied by Charles McEvers, was sold at auction on Saturday to James J. Roosevelt, Jr., for $14,200; lot twenty-five feet by seventy-five.

THURSDAY, JAN. 19.—The following party dined with us: Mr. and Mrs. Hamilton Wilkes, Mr. and Mrs. Pendleton Hosack, George Parish, Washington Coster, Mrs. A. E. Hosack, D. Lynch, P. Church, Mrs. Maria Hone, Captain Nicholson.

Bryant's Poems. A volume of beautiful poetry by William Cullen Bryant has just been published by Bliss. It contains several pieces which have been published in the periodicals before, with some new things. Bryant may be considered the best of American poets, with the exception of Halleck. A vein of sadness pervades all his writings, which is occasionally lighted up by soft and beautiful images. It is sad and melancholy, but never harsh or gloomy.

Colonel Hayne. TUESDAY, JAN. 24.— This distinguished senator made a long speech in the Senate on Monday, in reply to Mr. Clay's great speech in support of the following resolution offered by him: "That the existing duties upon articles imported from foreign countries, and not coming into competition with similar articles made or produced within the United States, ought to be forthwith abolished, except the duties on wines and silks, and that *they* ought to be reduced." The publication of Colonel Hayne's speech is commenced in to-day's papers. He comes out as usual with great force and eloquence against the whole protective system of duties, depicts in glowing colours the sufferings of the South, the inequality and injustice of the system in its operation upon them, and deplores the fancied evils which will result from it. He is certainly a great man, but has in my judgment the wrong side of the argument, and will have giants to contend against in the Senate.

WEDNESDAY, JAN. 25. — I attended a meeting this afternoon at Mr. Bucknor's office, to confer with Mr. Pugh, one of the canal commissioners of the State of Illinois, who has been appointed to visit New York in relation to raising funds to construct a railroad from the head of navigation on the Illinois river, a distance of ninety miles, to Chicago, near the southern outlet of Lake Michigan. This project would be of great advantage to the State of New York, as it would divert the trade of the new Western States bordering on the lakes from New Orleans to our seaport. The gentlemen present, brokers and practical money-dealers, did not seem disposed to trust their funds in an enterprise so far from home, and it is not likely that Mr. Pugh will succeed in his application.

I have been led by the discussions arising out of this conference to reflect upon the great prospects which the settlement of the new States holds out for this country. The tide of emigration sets in that direction with a force which has been hitherto unknown. The country is rich and productive; the settlers are a hardy, ingenious, and enterprising race of men, dependent upon their own physical resources, and uncontaminated by the curse of slavery, the deleterious effects of which are felt so severely in the Southern States. The chain of States, consisting of New York, and, stretching westward, embracing Pennsylvania, Ohio, Indiana, Illinois, Missouri, and the Washington Territory, seem naturally united by their geographical position and similarity of climate, productions and political policies, and the time may come when they will form a great empire and control the destinies of the Western world.

FRIDAY, JAN. 27. — The lot, corner of Wall and Broad streets, sixteen feet eight inches on Broad street and thirty feet on Wall street, was sold this day at auction for $17,750.

THURSDAY, FEB. 16. — I dined with James G. King, where I met Messrs. De Bourmont and De Tocqueville, the commissioners sent out by the French government to examine and report upon the prisons and prison discipline of this country. These gentlemen have just returned from a tour in the United States, and will sail for Europe in the packet of the 20th.

WEDNESDAY, FEB. 22. — This has been a jubilee in New York, the centennial anniversary of the birth of Washington, and the day has, no doubt, been observed in all other parts of the country. Here we had a firing of cannon and ringing of bells. A procession was formed under direction of a committee of arrangements of the Common Council. It left the City Hall, and thence to the new Dutch Church, under a military escort. I walked as a trustee of the college. The services in the church were opened and closed with prayers by Dr. Kuypers and Dr. Milnor. Two odes composed by Woodworth were sung, and an oration read by Gen. Morgan Lewis, which was written in good taste and well delivered, and rendered peculiarly interesting from the advanced age and great respectability of the orator, and from his being one of the small band remaining of the Revolutionary heroes who contributed to the success of the glorious struggle for independence in which Washington was the leader.

Washington's Birthday.

THURSDAY, FEB. 23. — The ceremony of breaking ground for the Harlem Railroad took place this day at Murray's Hill, three miles from town. The usual jollifications were observed. John Mason, vice-president, in the absence of C. P. White, the president, made a speech. He knows better how to make money, and that, as the world goes, is a more important talent.

SATURDAY, FEB. 25. — The following party dined with us: Mr. D. Lynch, General Fleming, Gen. J. J. Jones, Mr. Gibbes, J. A.

Hamilton, Robert Ray, Richard Ray, Mr. Charles King, T. W. Ludlow, S. Swartwout, Bucknor, Henry Hone, N. Low.

WEDNESDAY, FEB. 29. — We went to an evening party at Mrs. Henry Parish's, Barclay street. The house is new, everything stylish and elegant, and the company filled every part of the splendid mansion.

PHILADELPHIA, TUESDAY, MARCH 13.— We left New York at six o'clock, in the steamboat "Swan;" reached New Brunswick at half-past ten; thence we found the roads very bad, and when we came to Trenton ascertained that the boat was down at Bristol, having been prevented from ascending farther by a freshet in the Delaware. The river was swollen to a great height, and rushing with fearful rapidity past the bridge, bringing down with it branches of trees and great quantities of drift-wood. We took the boat at Bristol and came to the Mansion House at seven o'clock.

BALTIMORE, WEDNESDAY, MARCH 14. — Left Philadelphia at six o'clock this morning in the "Robert Morris," and came to New Castle at half-past nine, where we were transferred to the railroad; a pleasant ride, which brought us in an hour and three-quarters to Frenchtown. The railroad is just finished, and is an excellent substitute for the bad roads which travellers had formerly to encounter in crossing the peninsula. The cars are new, very handsome, and commodious, and are drawn at present by horses. At Frenchtown we took the "Independence," and arrived here this evening. The weather during the day had been extremely cold; the decks were covered with ice, and on the passage up the Chesapeake bay the wind blew so bitterly cold that the stoutest passengers were unable to remain upon deck.

WASHINGTON, THURSDAY, MARCH 15.— We left Baltimore at eight o'clock this morning, and came on the stage over a bad and somewhat dangerous road, but without accident, and arrived here at two o'clock.

I dined with Mr. Pendleton. The party consisted of Mr. Forsyth, of the Senate; Judge Wayne, of Georgia; Mr. Cambreling;

Colonel Drayton; J. A. Hamilton; Daniel Glover; Mr. Ewing, of Philadelphia; James J. Jones; and Jones Schermerhorn. After dinner we went to the President's; the rooms were all filled, and the company consisted, as usual, of all the varieties of rank and station, — foreign ministers and shopkeepers, heads of departments and dressers of heads, senators and office-hunters. The President was sociable and courteous, and the ladies of his family performed their parts with great propriety; on the whole, it was an affair not to be missed.

MONDAY, MARCH 19. — Mr. Hamilton and I had an agreeable visit this afternoon from Mr. Webster, who came in after dinner to drink a glass of wine with us. He was in a fine talking humour, and of course we were pleased and instructed. We went this evening to a ball at Mrs. Bankhead's. It is a delightful house to visit, but the New Yorkers say we have better evening parties at home. There were many great folk, some clever folk, and a fair proportion of queer folk.

WEDNESDAY, MARCH 21. — The girls and I dined with Mr. and Mrs. Bankhead. The party consisted of Mr. and Mrs. Johnston, of Louisiana; Mr. and Mrs. T. L. Smith; Miss Lewis; Messrs. Webster, W. P. Adams; Pageot of the French, and Khremer of the Russian, Legation; Mr. Letcher; Baron Stackelberg; and Colonel Washington. In the evening we went to a ball given by Mrs. White, of Florida, at which were all the distinguished men, and a large proportion of the fine women, of Washington.

THURSDAY, MARCH 22. — We passed five hours in the Senate to-day, and I do not think I was ever more interested in a debate. The subject was Mr. Clay's resolutions, and the whole strength of the Senate was brought out. Sprague, of Maine, made a beautiful speech. He is considered a man of fine talents, and is well listened to. Mr. Clay spoke several times; so did Mr. Forsyth, who is an exceedingly eloquent man, Mr. Webster, General Hayne, Governor Dickenson, Mr. Wilkins, General Smith, etc. Hayne was vehement, Forsyth graceful, Clay triumphant, Webster didactic,

Sprague argumentative, Wilkins confused, Marcey concerned, Holmes persevering. In the course of the debate General Hayne charged Mr. Forsyth with having deserted his cause, going over to the enemy, and pointing his guns against his friends. Forsyth, in reply, said he would go as far in opposition to the protective system as any man, *constitutionally* and *legally*, but not one inch farther. Hayne took fire, and demanded if the gentleman meant to insinuate that he and his friends would go farther. He was violently agitated. Forsyth replied with dignity and calmness. He did not allude particularly to the gentleman and his friends, but he did allude to a party who were disposed to redress their grievances at the risk of the Union and the Constitution. The girls sat during the whole debate, and left the Senate only when I was compelled to go away, at half-past five o'clock, to prepare for dinner. The Senate adjourned soon after we left the chamber. It was a great exhibition of talents, and we were fortunate in being present.

BALTIMORE, SATURDAY, MARCH 24. — We left Washington at nine o'clock, and came here to dine. A fine day, and the roads much improved. We had a pleasant ride. We had scarcely dined when we had a large number of visitors, and after they left us we passed an hour sociably at Mr. Meredith's. We found here most of the New Yorkers who left Washington before us, and Parish, who came from Philadelphia.

SUNDAY, MARCH 25. — Mr. Meredith called this morning, and we walked out to see the monument, the cathedral, and the Unitarian church, with a number of fine houses which have been lately erected in that improving part of the city. The Unitarian church is a far more beautiful edifice than the cathedral; indeed, I think it, as a single room, the finest in America. We returned to meet Mrs. Calvert, who was waiting to accompany us to St. Paul's church. The organ and church singing is very fine. The organist, a German, is a first-rate performer, and he made his instrument speak a language finer than I ever heard in one of our churches.

On our return from church the girls had a levee of visitors; they receive the kindest attentions from all the most distinguished persons, and our time is already appropriated during the whole week. Mr. and Mrs. Caton having called this morning to invite us, we passed an hour or two delightfully at their house this evening. The family were all present. Mr. Carroll was cheerful and talkative, and enjoyed himself very much until nine o'clock, when, according to his uniform practice, he took the arm of Mrs. McTavish, and quietly left the room. I feel while in the presence of this venerable man as if I were permitted to converse with one of the patriarchs, revisiting the land which, in days long gone, he had enriched with his patriotic counsels. He is in his ninety-sixth year; his hearing is defective, and his memory of recent events imperfect; but he presents a beautiful example of the close of a well-spent life, — serene, cheerful, and happy; prepared, it would seem, "to take his rest, with all his country's honours blest." It is very probable I shall never again see him after the present visit, and this reflection enhanced the value of the delightful hour I have just passed in his company. I made Mary take a seat by his side, and she has it to say that she conversed some time with the last surviving signer of the immortal Declaration of Independence. Would to God we had such a race of men in high places at this eventful period of our country's affairs! But Providence took care of us in their days, and as the Scottish ballad says, "it aye will again."

From Mrs. Caton's we went to Mrs. Swan's, where we had been invited to meet a party of the most agreeable people in Baltimore. This is pretty well for Sunday, and the Baltimoreans are rather strict, too; but these parties were rational, delightful, and void of offence. It is impossible to be received with a more frank and hospitable welcome than we have, and if our time does not pass agreeably the fault will be our own.

MONDAY, MARCH 26. — It rained all the morning, and I did not go out until one o'clock, when I called upon Mr. Oliver and Mr. Gilmor. The girls rode out with John Hoffman to see Chatsworth, his brother's place. I dined with a pleasant party at Dr. White's, and in the evening we went to a ball at Mrs. David Hoffman's, where we met all the agreeable people of the place, and more agreeable people are not to be met with anywhere.

TUESDAY. — Dined with Mr. Meredith, with a gay and pleasant party, consisting of Messrs. Gilmor, uncle and nephew, Oliver, Gibbes, Carroll, Harper, Donnell, two or three Hoffmans, etc. In the evening went to a beautiful party and supper at Mrs. George Hoffman's, where we met the whole array of Baltimore beauty and fashion. The party was given in honour of my girls, and I presume Mr. Hoffman's splendid house was never more splendidly filled.

THURSDAY, MARCH 29. — Mr. Oliver sent me a horse this morning, and at one o'clock we made an equestrian party, consisting of Messrs. Oliver, Meredith, Charles Carroll, and myself, and rode around the city, visiting the country-seats of Mr. Oliver and Mr. Carroll, and seeing what was worthy of notice.

FRIDAY. — In the evening we went to a leave-taking supper-party at Mr. Meredith's. As this is our last evening in Baltimore, Mr. and Mrs. Robert Gilmor, the ladies of Mrs. William Gilmor's family, and several young gentlemen were invited to meet us.

SATURDAY, MARCH 31. — At half-past six this morning we went on board the steamboat "George Washington." Besides our party we had Jones Schermerhorn, William Edgar, Hamilton Fish, and young McEwen, of Philadelphia; Mr. Meredith and his son, John Hoffman, and John Donnell politely accompanied us to the boat, and we started with their kind adieus. Thus ended our visit to Baltimore, during which we have received the most gratifying attentions and the kindest hospitality. I shall never forget them.

THURSDAY, APRIL 1. — The Historical Society having
Historical Society. lately removed their library to the spacious room in the third story of the new edifice belonging to Mr. Remsen at the corner of Broadway and Chambers street, over the one occupied by the Athenæum, it was opened this day, and an address was delivered to a respectable assemblage of ladies and gentlemen by

William Beach Lawrence. It was well written and interesting, but his delivery is somewhat painful, owing, apparently, to a difficulty of articulation. I presided as first vice-president in the absence of Gen. Morgan Lewis, the president. The room is fitted up with much taste, and the books and curiosities skilfully and scientifically arranged, for which the society has been as usual indebted to the exertions of Mr. John Delafield.

Ogden Hoffman's Address. MAY 2. — Ogden Hoffman made the annual address before the alumni of Columbia College. The high reputation of this gentleman as a scholar and an orator caused the college chapel to be filled with ladies and gentlemen, the fairest and best of our city, and no expectations had been raised which were not fully realized. I have never heard a production of more taste, purity, and appropriateness, or one delivered with greater grace and eloquence. Its principal subjects were a brief biography of the members of the faculty in the orator's time, and a dissertation on the several branches of education taught in the college. In the latter, Mr. Hoffman took a well-chosen occasion to enforce the claims of classical learning, when a host of utilitarians are springing up on all sides preparing the public mind for a desertion of those pure springs of knowledge, from which the great and the good in past ages have drawn their richest draughts, and who would annihilate for all future ages the glorious language in which Homer and Virgil sang and Demosthenes and Cicero declaimed. Columbia College is sufficiently orthodox on this subject; but when the floods of innovation threaten to destroy the foundations of learning, the strongest barriers must be opposed to their progress. On this subject Hoffman was clever, forcible, and touching, and all the power of the purest English was employed to protect the classical sanctity of the Greek and Latin.

I feel this subject deeply, for I am sensible of my own deficiency, and would give half I possess in the world to enjoy the advantages of a classical education. Oh that my sons knew how to appreciate their opportunities of acquiring knowledge, and would profit by their father's experience! The toils of eighteen would be then richly rewarded by the delightful experience of fifty, and the pleasures of prosperity enhanced, and the sorrows of adversity assuaged, by the stores of intellectual riches laid up in early life.

TUESDAY, MAY 15. — The annual exhibition has just been opened at the new rooms in Barclay street. There is the usual display of horrid portraits, like enough, in all conscience, to the originals, who I wish were hanged in their places. There are two most beautiful pictures by Carlo Maratti, belonging to an amateur named Dunderdale. He wants to sell them. I should like to buy them, but I will not. The Academy of Design are making great preparations for their exhibition, which will be opened in two or three days, and will be very good. They have six of my pictures: Bennett's "View of Castelamare," Heyle's "Landscape," Newton's "Greek Girl," "The Greek" and "The Toque" of Weir's, and Morse's "Thorwaldsen." Allston's new picture (I believe the subject is taken from the "Mysteries of Udolpho," or some such startling romance) has been obtained from the owner. This picture has made noise, and is certainly fine. There is also a noble full length of Colonel Varick, by Henry Inman, a splendid picture. Portraits, portraits enough, in all conscience!

Academy of the Fine Arts.

Arrival of Washington Irving.

TUESDAY, MAY 22. — The packet-ship "Havre" arrived last evening, having sailed from Havre on the 12th of April. Among the passengers is our distinguished countryman, and my old friend, Washington Irving, who visits his native country after an absence of seventeen years. I called to see him this morning at his brother's, Ebenezer Irving. He has grown very fat since I saw him in England in 1821, looks exceedingly well, and is delighted to be once more in his native city. I passed half an hour with him very pleasantly. He talks a great deal and is in high spirits, a thing not usual with him, except when under excitement, as he is at this moment.

Cholera in Paris.
This dreadful disease has increased to an awful degree in Paris, and the citizens are flying in every direction. Irving hurried away in consequence of it. Mr. Van Buren went to Holland immediately, and was to return to England, whence he should embark for America on the 1st of June. Brevoort and his family have gone to reside at Fontainebleau.

WEDNESDAY, MAY 23. — I have devoted nearly the whole day to Washington Irving. We were invited by a committee of the corporation to accompany them on a visit to Blackwell's Island and Bellevue, which has been made up for the purpose of exhibiting the public institutions to General Santander. Alderman Murray called for Irving and me at eleven o'clock, and we rode out and joined the party at the penitentiary on Blackwell's Island. We then returned with them to the almshouse, which, with the workshops, schools, etc., was exhibited to the company. Besides General Santander and his suite and ourselves there were Mr. LeRay de Chaumont and his son, Col. George Gibbs, Don Tomas Gener, Dr. Bronson, Mr. Hoyt, etc. At three o'clock, when they were preparing to go to dinner, Irving and I left them and came to town to meet friends whom I had engaged to dine with me. Our party at dinner consisted of Mr. Washington Irving, Dr. Wainwright, Mr. Charles King, James G. King, Ogden Hoffman, J. P. Giraud, Isaac S. Hone, James Paulding, Professor Renwick, and Captain Nicolson.

SATURDAY, MAY 26. — I dined with Dr. Wainwright, and met Irving and Newton, Mr. Gray, of Boston, and other agreeable persons. The return of Geoffrey Crayon has made old times and the associations of early life the leading topics of conversation amongst his friends.

Public Dinner to Washington Irving.
WEDNESDAY, MAY 30. — The dinner took place to-day at the City Hotel, and went off finely. About three hundred gentlemen sat down. It was a regular Knickerbocker affair. There were old New Yorkers and their

descendants in goodly numbers, who are seldom seen at such places, and among the invited guests were many distinguished men; viz., the bishops, Dr. Wainwright, General Santander, Baron de Behr, the new Minister from Belgium, Don Tomas Gener, General Scott, Commodore Chauncey, the Chancellor and Vice-Chancellor, the Lieutenant-Governor, Edward P. Livingston, Judges Hoffman, Oakley, and Irving, Mr. Gallatin, Mr. LeRay de Chaumont, Mr. James Paulding, Colonel Trumbull, and Mr. Newton.

SATURDAY, JUNE 9. — A great meeting was held last evening of persons avowedly friends to the union of the States and in favour of such a modification of the tariff as would serve to produce that effect, together with many violent free-trade men (as they call themselves), who would destroy the industry of the country and discourage all improvement to support their opinions and establish their theories. The meeting was called to order and organized by that mild, amiable, and reasonable gentleman, Preserved Fish. James Kent was chosen president, Stephen Allen and Gideon Lee, vice-presidents, Cornelius W. Lawrence and John A. Stevens, secretaries. The meeting was addressed and the resolutions moved by Peter A. Jay, and they are quite unexceptionable, as was to be expected from that gentleman, who is always wise, always honest, but sometimes a little prejudiced; but would to God the affairs of our country, tariff and all, were in the hands of such men! The meeting was so large that the room was insufficient, and all the approaches to it crowded to excess. Great tumult and disorder were occasioned by some tariff men who had better have stayed away. Party spirit has unhappily been mingled with the question. The excitement increases every day. Reflecting men who love their country and would preserve its institutions are full of alarm and serious forebodings. Both sides are wrong. It is vain to talk of conciliation. Prejudice on one side, interest on the other, and intolerance on both will prevent them from approaching nearer to each other. Mr. Adams's wisdom might do something if it were

Anti-tariff Meeting.

seconded by General Jackson's decision. Happy would our country be if those qualifications were united in one person, and he the chief magistrate!

FRIDAY, JUNE 15. — The Albany steamboat which came down this afternoon brought the alarming news that the cholera, which has of late been the scourge of the Eastern Continent, has crossed the Atlantic and made its appearance first in Quebec, and from there has travelled with its direful velocity to Montreal. It was brought to the former city in a vessel called the "Carricks," with a cargo of Irish immigrants, of whom many died on the way. In a few days fifteen cases and eight deaths were reported, principally in the narrow, dirty streets of the lower town, and the last report gave seventy cases. This dreadful disease has not been more mortal in any part of the world which it has visited. The proportion of deaths to the number of cases is dreadful. There can be little reasonable ground to hope for our exemption in New York from this dreadful scourge. It must come, and we are in a dreadful state to receive it. The city is in a more filthy state than Quebec and Montreal, and I do not know a European city which is worse. The alarm is great in Albany and Troy.

Cholera in Canada.

The accounts are confirmed. They have it bad enough at Quebec and Montreal, and there are reports of a few solitary cases at Plattsburgh, but they do not appear to be authentic. Mr. Bowne, our mayor, has published his proclamation interdicting the approach to the city of steamboats and other conveyances having passengers ill with the disease. Bishop Onderdonk has published a very sensible pastoral letter to the ministers of his diocese, urging them to make a spiritual use of the apprehended danger, and prescribing a form of prayers to be used in the service of the Church.

More of the Cholera.

MONDAY, JUNE 18. — Prayers were offered up yesterday in all the churches to avert the threatened visit of the cholera, and sermons preached to prepare the minds of the people for the affliction, which seems now to be considered inevitable. The weather is warm, but clear and pleasant; recent showers have refreshed the earth, and have been succeeded by pleasant southerly winds and a bright atmosphere. The reports of the day are that the disease has increased in Montreal and Quebec. The number of deaths in the former place is said to be two hundred and fifty, and great exertions are made to prevent the Canadian emigrants from being brought by steamboats or canal-boats into our State.

<small>The Indian War.</small> General Scott has received orders from the War Department to proceed forthwith to Fort Dearborn, at Chicago, on Lake Michigan, to take command of the army, and fight the Sacs and Fox Indians who have recently committed outrages upon the inhabitants of Illinois, and murdered some of the Menominee Indians friendly to the United States. Fourteen companies of United States troops equipped as infantry are ordered to rendezvous here and proceed by the North river, the Erie canal, and the lakes to their destination. The cadets from West Point who have just now graduated are ordered on this service. Henry Swartwout, who is one of them, called this afternoon to see us, and is delighted, as most of his class are, with the prospect of military distinction which this expedition promises. I saw the major-general this evening. He will wait for the arrival of the troops, five companies of whom are to come from Old Point Comfort, Va., and expects to embark the latter part of this week. He is ordered to demand the surrender of the murderers of the friendly Indians, to compel the hostile Indians to observe the treaty which was made with them by General Gaines last year, and to take their leader, the Black Hawk, dead or alive. This celebrated warrior is said to be as formidable as the famous Tecumseh, and peace cannot be restored to the frontier until he is captured or destroyed.

WEDNESDAY, JULY 4. — It is a lovely day, but very different from all previous anniversaries of independence. The alarm about the cholera has prevented all the usual jollification under the public authority. There are no booths in Broadway, the parade which was ordered has been countermanded, no corporation dinner, and no ringing of bells. Some troops are marching about the street, "upon their own hook," I suppose. Most of the stores are closed, and there is a pretty smart cannonade of crackers by the boys; but it is not a regular Fourth of July. The disease is here in all its violence, and will increase. God grant that its ravages may be confined and its visit short!

NEW YORK, MONDAY, JULY 23. — I left Rockaway after breakfast this morning, and came up to the city. Miss Lewis accompanied me. The alarm is very great, but the streets are more lively than I expected. I went to Wall street and transacted some business; there was a considerable number of persons on 'Change, and I saw but few stores closed in my walk. I hear many dreadful stories of cholera cases. The end of last week a man was found in the road at Harlem who had died of cholera. A coroner's inquest was called, and of twenty persons, jury and witnesses, who were present, nine are now dead. John Aspinwall told me this story, who had it from Alderman Murray, of the ninth ward.

JULY 25. — The Count Survilliers sailed from Philadelphia in the ship "Alexander" for London. His departure from his residence at Bordentown, on the Delaware, was marked by the regrets of his neighbours; among whom his hospitality and munificence have made him very popular, and he received on his embarkment at Philadelphia the marked attentions of the citizens.

AUGUST 8. — Joseph Jefferson, comedian of the Philadelphia Theatre, died at Harrisburg, Penn., on the 4th inst. This man's acting of comic parts on the New York stage is connected with the pleasing recollections of my early years. He was a great favourite at that time, and has preserved a high reputation ever since as a comic performer.

SUNDAY, AUG. 19. — Margaret has a letter from Helen Kane, accompanied by a present of a purse for me, which is the subject of the following neat remark: "Tell your father that, although, like my affection for him, my poor little purse as yet knows no change, I hope it may soon resemble my sad heart when absent from him, and prove heavy and full to overflowing."

WEDNESDAY, AUG. 29.— We set off to the railroad, and embarked in one of a train of carriages; arrived at Schenectady, breakfasted, walked a short distance to the commencement of the Saratoga road, and came in the same way to Saratoga Springs by the way of Ballston, where we arrived at eleven o'clock, and I am well accommodated at Congress Hall. This is a pleasant mode of travelling; not very rapid but free from fatigue or inconvenience of any sort. The Mohawk and Hudson road is travelled by the power of a steam locomotive engine; the Saratoga, by a horse-power. The latter road is scarcely in a state to be travelled, and has been in operation only a few weeks.

Saratoga Springs.

The Springs have been almost deserted this summer, but there are now some clever people here and at Sans-Souci. We have General Van Rensselaer and his sons, Mr. and Mrs. Wilkins, Oliver Kane and his wife, with Anna and Lydia, Mrs. Phil. Van Rensselaer, Mr. and Mrs. Dickenson; Judge Pendleton, Judge Woodworth, Mr. Dudley, William Laight, all with their wives; Mr. Huntington and his family from Troy, with a few beaux, etc., — in all about sixty persons. The house is clean, quiet, comfortable, and well attended. I rode this afternoon with Dr. McLean and Giraud to Riley's, at Saratoga lake. S. Van Rensselaer, of Albany, and Philip Schuyler, of Schuylerville, came this evening.

NEW YORK, THURSDAY, SEPT. 6.— The city appears as lively and the streets as full of people as it usually is at this season. If the cholera is still amongst us, it proceeds quietly, uninterrupted by municipal regulations, and apparently unheeded by those who are exposed to it.

The packet-ship "Pacific" arrived on Monday last, having on board Charles Kemble, the celebrated comedian, and his highly gifted daughter, Miss Fanny Kemble, who has lately created, by her fine acting, a great sensation in the theatrical circles of Great

Britain. They are engaged by the manager of the Park Theatre; and as the fame of the father has long since reached this country, and the daughter is said to inherit the talents of a family in which were numbered a Siddons and a John Kemble, there is no doubt that we shall be furnished with a theatrical treat of the highest order. Wallack made his first appearance since his arrival on Monday evening, and was well received. They ought to do well this season at the Park.

FRIDAY, SEPT. 7. — Mr. Kemble called this morning and left me letters of introduction from Mr. Vaughan, the British Minister to this country, who is now in England, and from Mr. Price. I returned his visit and saw his daughter (her father was not at home). She appeared deserving of all her reputation, — a good figure, easy manners, sprightly and intelligent, self-possessed, not very handsome, but with features animated and expressive, and calculated for great stage effect. Mr. Kemble is to make his first appearance in "Hamlet," and his accomplished daughter will come out on the 17th, most probably in the character of Juliet, in which she made her successful *début* at Covent Garden.

The Kembles.

Mr. Jones Schermerhorn called to see me yesterday, and I have sanctioned his engagement with Mary. His mother and other members of the family called to-day, and are heartily pleased with the intended alliance. Mr. Schermerhorn is confined to his country-house with indisposition. My beloved child could not have made a choice more pleasing to me. Schermerhorn is a young man of most amiable disposition, good morals, agreeable deportment, and a gentleman, of a family with whom I shall consider it an honour to be allied. As far as human foresight can penetrate, it is a union calculated to promote our happiness. May the Almighty smile upon it and realize our expectations!

Jones Schermerhorn, Mr. Gaston, and Isaac Hone dined with us. In the evening we went to the theatre and saw Wallack for the first time. He played the part of Martin Heywood in the new piece of " Rent Day,"—a very effective part, to which he gives great interest. He has been well received and is in good spirits, although his engagement will be somewhat interfered with by the arrival of the Kembles so soon upon his heels.

SATURDAY, SEPT. 15. — The following party dined with us: Charles Kemble, Miss Fanny Kemble, Miss De Camp, Mr. and Mrs. C. A. Davis, Dr. A. E. Hosack and Mrs. Hosack, Mr. and Mrs. Cornwall, of Nova Scotia, Mr. Charles Bankhead, Mr. Charles King, General Fleming, Mr. Gaston, D. Lynch, Jones and Aug. Schermerhorn, Henry Hone, and James A. Hamilton. Miss Kemble, like all young persons who have become celebrated, has many and strong admirers. But many dislike her on first acquaintance. Her manners are somewhat singular. Allowance should be made for the peculiarity of her situation, just arrived among strangers, with a consciousness that she is viewed as one of the lions of the day, and as such the object more of curiosity than of affection. Her behaviour would be attributed naturally to timidity, were it not that at times she appears to be perfectly self-possessed. She talks well, but will only talk when, and to whom, she chooses. She sat at my side at dinner, and I certainly had no reason to complain of her, for I lost my dinner in listening to her and in endeavouring to make myself agreeable. She has certainly an air of indifference and nonchalance not at all calculated to make her a favourite with the beaux. Indeed, Henry Hone and I think that she prefers married men. Her fault appears to be an ungracious manner of receiving the advances of those who desire to pay her attention. This may proceed from the novelty of her situation, and may be soon removed. But now is her time to make friends if she wants them. She sang and played for us in the evening. Her voice is not sweet, but has great force and pathos. I am confirmed in my opinion that she has astonishing requisites for the stage. Her features separately are not good, but combined they make a face of great and powerful expression. She is said to resemble her aunt, Mrs. Siddons. I am of opinion that she does not like her profession. It is not her favourite theme of conversation; necessity, rather than choice, has led her to adopt it. Her father is a gentleman of fine manners and dignified deportment, somewhat stiff, — for he is a Kemble, — but evidently well-bred and accustomed to good society.

SUNDAY. — Mr. and Miss Kemble and Miss De Camp were at Trinity Church, and sat in my pew. They are evidently accustomed to attend divine service, a practice which is not so frequent with persons of their profession as might be wished.

MONDAY, SEPT. 17. — Charles Kemble made his first appearance this evening at the Park Theatre, in the character of Hamlet, to a great house. He was well received, and listened to with great attention. There were not many ladies in the house, but the audience appeared to be critical and discriminating. It was precisely such acting as my recollection of Kemble and my opinion of his powers had led me to expect. The part was deeply studied and well understood; his reading is critically correct, his elocution distinct, and his manner dignified; but he is too formal, even for Hamlet. His pauses are too long and too frequent, so much so as to make the representation fatiguing; and for myself, I confess that, although my judgment is perfectly satisfied, his Hamlet falls far short of the power to interest me and give me pleasure of Kean's or even Wallack's, and he labours, moreover, under one great disadvantage, of which he has, unfortunately, no chance of amendment, — he is too old by thirty years for this part, and the expression of his face will do better for Lord Townly, Sir Edward Mortimer, King John, and other such parts. He is, on the whole, a fine actor, a good study for the younger men, and his visit to this country ought to improve the American stage. Fanny Kemble is to appear to-morrow evening in "Fazio."

TUESDAY, SEPT. 18. — Miss Fanny Kemble made her first appearance this evening in the character of Bianca, in Milman's tragedy of "Fazio." It is a fine part, well calculated for a display of the strongest passions of the female heart, — love, hate, and jealousy. I predicted before we went that it would be no half-way affair; she would make the most decided hit we have ever witnessed, or would fail entirely; and so it proved. I have never witnessed an audience so moved, astonished, and delighted. Her display of the strong feelings which belong to the part was great beyond description, and the expression of her wonderful face would have been a rich treat if her tongue had uttered no sound. The fifth act was such an exhibition of female powers as we have never before witnessed, and the curtain fell amidst the deafening shouts and plaudits of an astonished audience. She has some faults: her low tones are sepulchral and indistinct, — and yet her voice appears to me capable of anything which her judgment would lead her to execute, — and she is at times somewhat monotonous, particularly in the unimpassioned passages; but this may be the defect of education. It was the fault of John Kemble and of Mrs. Siddons, and is that of her father. It runs in the family. But on the whole I am quite satisfied that we have never seen her equal on the American stage, and England has witnessed none since Miss O'Neil.

Died on Monday, at Kinderhook, in the eighty-sixth year of his age, Peter Van Schaick, LL.D., one of the most distinguished lawyers and accomplished scholars in the United States. He was a contemporary and fellow-student of Governor Jay, Chancellor Livingston, Judge Benson, and other great men of former times. He has been blind for the last twenty years, but his intellectual faculties continued unimpaired, and he was considered to the last an oracle of legal wisdom and literary endowment.

THURSDAY, SEPT. 20. — Charles Kemble and his accomplished daughter appeared this evening in "Romeo and Juliet." Both parts were admirably performed. Mr. Kemble is too old for Romeo, — Mercutio is his part, — but this difficulty was overcome by his perfect conception of the character, the grace of his elocution, and the eloquence of his deportment. Juliet was something beyond my powers of description. I never saw a female performer at all to compare with her in this part, and I cannot imagine anything to exceed it. She is destined to fill the place of Mrs. Siddons, and make the finest performer in the world.

<small>European Emigrants.</small> The distresses of the lower classes in England and Ireland have caused emigration to America in numbers so great as to cause serious alarm. Besides the immense numbers which are daily arriving here and in other parts of the United States, it is stated that forty-nine thousand five hundred and sixty-nine emigrants have arrived at Quebec since the opening of the navigation of the St. Lawrence the present year. Of these, a large proportion find their way into the United States destitute and friendless. They have brought the cholera this year, and they will always bring wretchedness and want. The boast that our country is the asylum for the oppressed in other parts of the world is very philanthropic and sentimental, but I fear that we shall, before long, derive little comfort from being made the almshouse and place of refuge for the poor of other countries.

TUESDAY, SEPT. 25. — Died yesterday, at Throg's Neck, George Lorillard, aged sixty-six. He was an old bachelor, brother of Peter and Jacob Lorillard, and lost an immense sum of money by dying.

SATURDAY, SEPT. 29. — Miss Kemble drove out this morning with my daughters and me. The more I see of this wonderful girl the more I am pleased with her. She has rare talents in conversation, and in her profession she has already made an impression which will never be forgotten by the people of New York.

TUESDAY, OCT. 16. — I rode out this morning with Mr. Richard Caton, son-in-law of Mr. Carroll, and father of the Marchioness of Wellesley and the Countess of Carmarthen, who is here on a visit from Baltimore. We drove about the suburbs, and it was gratifying to me to hear the astonishment expressed at the magnificence of the city by one who has not visited it for upwards of twenty years.

FRIDAY, OCT. 19. — I went with the girls this morning to pay a bride's visit to Mrs. Jared Sparks, late Miss Allen, of Hyde Park. She is one of the most interesting women I ever saw, —

not what would be called a perfect beauty, but with a face expressive as one of Raphael's Madonnas, and a form of Grecian mould. This lady writes well, paints beautifully, and excels in music. She is going to Boston, where they know how to appreciate such characters.

MONDAY, OCT. 22. — Ball Hughes's monument to Bishop Hobart is ready to be put up in the chancel of Trinity Church, and we are preparing to alter the pulpit and desk to suit it. Mr. Hughes is also engaged in making a beautiful altar-table of white Italian marble, and I think the effect of the whole will be much finer than anything of the sort we have seen in this country.

WEDNESDAY, OCT. 24. — Miss Fanny Hamilton, daughter of James A. Hamilton, was married last evening to George Bowdoin.

THURSDAY, OCT. 25. — My birthday. I am fifty-two years of age. I am much older in feelings than I was last year at this time. Two or three attacks of illness during the last summer have left me weakly and subject to indisposition. If I indulge in the good things which are constantly tempting me I am sure to suffer for it, and am compelled to temperance *malgré moi*.

FRIDAY, OCT. 26. — I dined with Abraham Schermerhorn, where we had a clerical party, consisting of Bishop Bowen, Bishop Brownell, Dr. Wainwright, Mr. Creighton, and several laymen of the convention. This body has been engaged for several days in the discussion of an important subject; viz., the acceptance of the resignation of Bishop Chase, of Ohio, and the validity of the appointment of Mr. McIlvaine as his successor, the question being whether a bishop can vacate his see in any case. There has been a great deal of speaking, and the meetings of the convention daily at St. John's Chapel have attracted crowds of people to hear the debate. Mr. Jay, President Duer, and Dr. Wainwright, of the New York delegation, have each made long and eloquent speeches.

WEDNESDAY, Nov. 7. — The following gentlemen dined with us: Mr. Wallack, Charles Kemble, Mr. Truman, Mr. Moore, I. S.

Hone, J. Howard Payne, Mr. Buckland, Thomas W. Ludlow, Robert Emmet, and Henry Hone.

FRIDAY, Nov. 9. — This glorious light of literature, which has for some months been flickering in the socket of existence, is at last extinguished. The pride of Great Britain, the delight of all who can read the English language and enjoy its richest treasures, has closed his brilliant career, and increased the gap which the death of Byron occasioned to an extent so great that it cannot be filled during the present generation of mankind. Both were splendid luminaries in the world of letters; but the former passed over its firmament like a bright and transient meteor, while the latter, adding to the influence of his talents that of his excellent moral character and kind feelings in his intercourse with mankind, shed around his path the genial warmth of the sun, enlightening and vivifying like his rival, but not like him scorching and dazzling the eyes of beholders.

Death of Sir Walter Scott.

TUESDAY, Nov. 13. — Dined with Mr. Charles March. Mr. and Mrs. Henry Cary, Mrs. Wayne, Dr. A. E. Hosack and his wife, Mr. Van Buren, Cambreling, Lynch, etc., were of the party. After dinner I saw part of Fanny Kemble's Juliet, which she played admirably. I saw her Julia, in the "Hunchback," last evening, — her best part, and better than anything I have ever seen. The house was full as possible, and hundreds left the doors unable to get seats. I then went to the party at Mrs. Delafield's, Park place. The attractions of the evening were the bride, Miss Delafield, daughter of John Delafield, who has married a son of Cornelius Du Bois, and *The Pedrotti*, the *prima donna* of the Italian opera, wretchedly out of place, with her immense vulgar figure, staring eyes, and tawdry dress, amongst the lovely, modest, and graceful women with whom she was associated. And she refused to sing, too, after Mrs. Parish and Helen McEvers had kindly set her the example. If she did not sing, why was she there? And then the elegant amateurs of Italian music pretend to compare this woman to Fanny Kemble; nay, pretend to say that, independently of her singing, she plays better and has more grace! She is no more comparable to her than I to the Apollo Belvidere, a sunflower to a violet, a cart-horse to the Bussorah Arabian, an ale-house sign to a landscape of Claude, or Jane, our chambermaid, to Mrs. Gardiner Howland.

FRIDAY, Nov. 16. — The papers are clothed in mourning; the venerable Charles Carroll, of Carrollton, died at his house in Baltimore on Wednesday morning, 14th inst., at four o'clock, in the ninety-sixth year of his age. This aged patriot and most respectable man was born on the 8th of September, in the year 1737, at Annapolis, Md. His father died in 1782, aged eighty years. Mr. Carroll was a patriot in the days which tried men's souls. He was a member of Congress of respectable talents and great personal influence; but his celebrity of late years has arisen principally from the interesting position in which he has stood before the American people as the last of that immortal band of patriots who, in signing the Declaration of Independence, took all the responsibility of the measure upon themselves, and gave a noble pledge to work out the political salvation of America. He has been the sole survivor since Jefferson and the elder Adams died, on the 4th of July, 1826. Mr. Carroll was ninety-five years old in September.

[marginal note: Death of Mr. Carroll.]

His Excellency, William C. Rives, American Minister at the court of France, and his family arrived this morning in the packet-ship "Sully," from Havre. Amongst the passengers by this ship were Samuel F. B. Morse, the artist, and president of the National Academy of Design.

Dined at the navy yard with Commodore Chauncey. Mr. Van Buren was of the party. He is all the fashion at present. I think the pride of human nature must, in the case of this gentleman, be fully gratified. The late election is a prodigious triumph for him, and he must be more or less than man if he can avoid exultation when he assumes the Vice-President's chair, vacated by the man who gave the casting vote in the Senate which recalled him from his honourable station abroad.

NOVEMBER 27. — The anti-tariff convention of the State of Georgia assembled on the 15th inst., at Milledgeville. A long string of violent resolutions were reported, breathing the poison of nullification in every line.

DECEMBER 3. — The South Carolina convention have passed a number of resolutions, worse by far than the friends of union believed it possible for them to go. It is rank treason, and in my opinion the leaders deserve to be hanged. It is well, however, that these violent measures have been adopted before the meeting of Congress, which will take place to-morrow. It places the nullifiers at once in the wrong, and will remove the doubts in the minds of many good men in Congress as to the necessity of energetic measures in the commencement of this rebellion, for it can be called by no other name.

<small>South Carolina.</small>

DECEMBER 12. — Very much to the surprise of some, and to the satisfaction of all our citizens, we have a long proclamation of President Jackson, which was published in Washington on the 12th inst., and is in all our papers this day. It is a document addressed to the nullifiers of South Carolina, occasioned by the late treasonable proceedings of their convention. The whole subject is discussed in a spirit of concili-ation, but with firmness and decision, and a determination to put down the wicked attempt to resist the laws. On the constitution-ality of the laws which the nullifiers object to, and their right to recede from the Union, this able State paper is full and conclusive. The language of the President is that of a father addressing his wayward children, but determined to punish with the utmost severity the first open act of insubordination. As a composition it is splendid, and will take its place in the archives of our country, and will dwell in the memory of our citizens alongside of the farewell address of the "Father of his Country." It is not known

<small>President's Proclamation.</small>

which of the members of the cabinet is entitled to the honour of being the author; it is attributed to Mr. Livingston, the Secretary of State, and to Governor Cass, the Secretary of War. Nobody, of course, supposes it was written by him whose name is subscribed to it. But whoever shall prove to be the author has raised to himself an imperishable monument of glory. The sentiments, at least, are approved by the President, and he should have the credit of it, as he would the blame if it were bad; and, possessing those sentiments, we have reason to believe that he has firmness enough to do his duty. I say, Hurrah for Jackson! and so I am willing to say at all times when he does his duty. The only difference between the thorough-going Jackson men and me is, that I will not "hurrah" for him right or wrong. And I think Jackson's election may save the Union. If he is sincere in this proclamation he will put down this rebellion. Mr. Clay, pursuing the same measures, would not have been equally successful. He is considered the head of the American System Party, and his political opponents would have thrown obstacles in his way from party motives; whereas Jackson's opponents are generally men of more principle, and will not withhold their approbation from him when his measures, as in the present instance, are marked by wisdom and decision. A majority of the people would have gone with him, right or wrong; they all will when he is right. In this able State paper he addresses the deluded people of South Carolina with tenderness, but seems to be gathering up his wrath to let it fall heavily on the heads of the ringleaders.

DECEMBER 18. — The Camden and Amboy Railroad was opened on Monday on the whole line, and passengers who left New York in the steamboat for Amboy at half-past six were in Philadelphia about two o'clock. This is expected to be the best joint-stock property in the United States.

<small>South Carolina.</small> DECEMBER 20. — Gen. Robert Hayne has been elected Governor of South Carolina, in place of Governor Hamilton, whose term of office had expired.

One Hotspur in place of another. And John C. Calhoun, the present Vice-President of the United States, is elected to the Senate of the United States in place of General Hayne. These appointments prove the strength of the "Nullification" party. How I hate the word! It is a newly invented one, hard to write and horrid to think of, but the most expressive that can be adopted.

1833.

JANUARY 7.—A new periodical, called the "Knickerbocker," made its first appearance on the 1st of this month. It is to be a monthly publication, edited by Charles Hoffman, assistant editor of the "American," and published by Peabody & Co. Bryant, Paulding, the late Mr. Sands, and a number of other eminent literary men were engaged as contributors, and the work starts with a subscription list of eight hundred names. Public expectation has consequently been highly raised, and, in my case, much disapppointed. I do not know what other people may think about it, but in my judgment these great guns have grievously missed fire. The introduction by Hoffman is long, laboured, and dull; one of Paulding's stories is an unsuccessful attempt at quaint humour (not an unusual thing, by the by, in the works of that author), and the poetry a mere makeweight, written apparently just to fill up such a space on such a page, to which it has been allotted. The "New York Mirror," a neat weekly conducted by Morris, which is a welcome visitor at my house every Saturday, is worth a dozen of the "Knickerbocker;" but I am unkind in criticising so closely the first number; succeeding ones will, no doubt, be better, and I am so partial to the editor, and wish so heartily success to the concern, that I will not allow myself to doubt it.

WASHINGTON, MARCH 2.— I witnessed an interesting scene in the Senate this morning. Mr. Clay arose, and with great solemnity, and in that bland, engaging manner which in him is irresistible, adverted to an angry dispute which occurred a few weeks since, between Mr. Poindexter, of Mississippi, and Mr. Webster, at the conclusion of which the former said, " He felt the utmost contempt for the gentleman from Massachusetts." These expressions were attributed by Mr. Clay to the heat of debate and the excitement of opposition at a moment of peculiar interest, and he expressed the greatest anxiety that at the close of the session, when so much had been done to conciliate in other quarters, two gentlemen who had frequently acted together, and between whom the best feelings had heretofore existed, should not be suffered to part in anger. Mr. Poindexter immediately arose, disclaimed any intention to offend Mr. Webster, and made a gentlemanly sort of apology, which was received in the same spirit and acknowledged in a short speech by Mr. Webster. The parties then approached each other, shook hands, and the affair was settled.

MONDAY, MARCH 4. — The inauguration of Andrew Jackson as President, and Martin Van Buren as Vice-President, of the United States, took place at noon in the hall of the House of Representatives. I went up at eleven o'clock, and formed one of the immense crowd who thronged the approach to every door. The wind was very high, and the severity of the cold unmitigated, so that the time spent in waiting was not particularly agreeable. The President and Vice-President and their *cortège* arrived at twelve o'clock, and soon afterwards the doors were opened, when I was carried in with the ruffianly crowd, but never got farther than the little vestibule in front of the Chamber. I am told that the President delivered an inaugural address, and the oaths were administered by the venerable Chief Justice. The address is published in handbills. It is well done, not too long, and well adapted to the state of public affairs.

FRIDAY, MARCH 29. — The following party dined with us : Judge Wayne, of Georgia, and his lady; Mr. and Mrs. E. H. Pendleton, Mr. and Mrs. Peter Schermerhorn, Mr. and Mrs. Hamilton Wilkes, Mr. and Mrs. S. S. Howland, Sir Charles R. Vaughan, Mr. Bankhead, Mr. Thorn, Marquis Torrigiani, Mr. James J. Jones, Washington Irving, Commodore Chauncey, Mr. Granger, and Mr. D. Lynch.

SATURDAY, MARCH 30. — I dined with Mr. William B. Astor, and in the evening went for a short time to a party of distinguished literary gentlemen and others, at Dr. Alexander Stephens's.

MONDAY, APRIL 1. — Mr. Audubon, the celebrated ornithologist, called upon me a day or two since with letters of introduction from Mr. Quincy, President of Harvard College, and Colonel Perkins, of Boston. He is about setting out on one of his enterprising excursions to the coast of Labrador, in pursuit of information to illustrate his favorite science, to which he is devoted with the ardour of a lover to his mistress. He is an interesting man of about fifty-five years of age, modest in his deportment, possessing general intelligence, an acute mind, and great enthusiasm. His work on the birds of North America, on which he is now engaged, is probably the most splendid book ever published. I have seen several of the numbers in the library of Congress. It will require nine years to complete it, and will cost eight hundred dollars; all the drawings are executed by himself or under his special superintendence. Wilson's book on the same subject is deservedly celebrated, — beautiful, no doubt, but comparing with Audubon's as the Falls of Trenton to those of Niagara.

SATURDAY, APRIL 6. — Subscribers to the Marine Pavilion to be erected at Rockaway. The following persons have each subscribed five hundred dollars: Nathaniel Prime, Robert Ray, John A. King, Rufus Prime, Philip Hone, Alfred Seton, John Haggerty, Isaac S. Hone, Edward Prime, Thaddeus Phelps, John C. Cruger, Samuel S. Howland, Thomas Suffern, Charles A. Davis, Gerard H. Coster, Reuben Withers, Isaac Jones, Jr., John G. Coster, James Boggs, Goold Hoyt, Peter Schermerhorn, Lewis Curtiss, William B. Crosby, Benjamin L. Swan, Robert White, David S. Jones, John MacGregor, Jr., Stephen Whitney, Rupert L. Cochran, Isaac Carow, J. Boorman, Samuel Glover, George Newbold, William McLeod, James Monroe, John Mason, John Gihon, Henry Parish, Robert L. Patterson, W. N. Furniss, John Johnston, John W. Leavitt, William Wright, Herman Thorn, C. H. Russell, Joseph Walker, Asaph Stone, Samuel Alley, Moses H. Grinnell, Hendrick Booraem, Amos Palmer, Gideon Pott, Richard Suydam, Timothy T. Kissam, James Boyd, Jr., Charles A. Heckscher, Brockholst

Cutting, John F. Delaplaine, Charles Hall, Gideon Lee, Mortimer Livingston, James Heard, Peter J. Nevins, Henry Laverty, Peter G. Stuyvesant.

National Academy. WEDNESDAY, MAY 15. — The spring exhibition of the National Academy has just opened. I have paid it only a flying visit. It is a good exhibition, and if the smiling faces of sundry "fat and greasy citizens" and their self-complacent helpmates were turned to the wall instead of looking down from their canvas habitations to fright the spectators from "their propriety," it would be worth visiting half a dozen times. The president, Mr. Morse, and Cole have contributed the pictures which they painted and brought from Europe. The former are hard and cold as ever. The warmth of the sunny skies of Italy does not appear to have had any effect upon the worthy president. He is an excellent fellow, and is well acquainted with the principles of his art, but he has no imagination. He makes good portraits, strong likenesses. My portrait of Chancellor Kent, by Morse, is very good, and Thorvaldsen is excellent, but he cannot design. There is no poetry about his painting, and his prose consists of straight lines, which look as if they had been stretched to their utmost tension to form clothes-lines. Cole maintains his ground. His pictures are admirable representations of that description of scenery which he has studied so well in his native forests. His landscapes are too solid, massy, and umbrageous to please the eye of an amateur accustomed to Italian skies and English-park scenery, but I think every American is bound to prove his love of country by admiring Cole.

Excursion to the Fire-place. MONDAY, MAY 27. — Messrs. Charles L. Livingston, Phelps, Giraud, and I left home last Tuesday at one o'clock on an excursion to Long Island. The next morning we rose early, and started at five o'clock; a fine morning, the country on all sides looking bright and beautiful. We had a very agreeable ride, breakfasted at Timothy Carman's, and arrived at Sam Carman's, at the Fire-place, at four o'clock. The following day the wind got around again to the north-east, raw, cold, and rainy, and so it continued the remainder of the week, with occasional intervals, which allowed Giraud and me the opportunity of fishing every day for an hour or two, and we took trout enough to supply our table during the whole of our visit. They were very fine, not very abundant; but, on the whole, we had good sport, and we formed within doors a gay, pleasant party, and with the assistance of stores we took with us, we had quite as much to eat and drink as was good for us. On Sunday morning at eleven o'clock we left Carman's on our return. The Speaker and I brought with us a dozen trout which were taken on the morning we came away. The weather was fine during the whole of yesterday, and we came to Van Cott's, at Jamaica, where we lodged, and came away this morning after breakfast. This is the first day of the races, and there is a great match race between a colt of Walter Livingston's and a Southern colt of Colonel Johnson's. Livingston and Phelps remained at the race-course to see the race, and Giraud and I came to Brooklyn, where we arrived at nine. The road was crowded with vehicles of every description and pedestrians of every age and complexion. Brooklyn was a scene of bustle and confusion, and the sporting gentlemen eyed us with looks of compassion that we could have so little taste as to turn our backs upon so pleasant an affair.

Navy Yard. TUESDAY, MAY 28. — My excellent old friend, Commodore Chauncey, is ordered to Washington, to fill a place at the Board of Navy Commissioners, and Captain Ridgely is appointed to our navy yard. This will be deeply regretted by many in New York, for Chauncey has a vast number of devoted friends here. I shall be a heavy loser myself. He was ever a most welcome guest at my table, and I have partaken "many a time and oft" of his noble hospitality. We had a standing compact, that each of us was to stand ready to obey the other's summons at a day's notice, when not otherwise engaged. And then his fine, old sherry, too! he will have to give it to those who have not half so much regard for him.

Mr. Webster was at the Eagle Tavern the other day, on his way to the western part of the State, and was presented to Judge Buel, the celebrated agriculturist, by the loquacious landlord, Crittenden, in the following flowery style: "This is Judge Buel, who cultivates the finest flowers of the field, and this the Hon. Daniel Webster, who culls the choicest flowers of rhetoric." Mr. Webster then happily observed: "Your *flowers* produce *fruit;* mine, I fear, may prove abortive." To this Judge Buel, with great felicity, replied: "My flowers, sir, are *annual* and *evanescent*, while yours promise a perpetual bloom."

MONDAY, JUNE 3.— Died on Saturday evening, in this city, Oliver Wolcott, in the seventy-fourth year of his age. Mr. Wolcott was Secretary of the Treasury under Washington. His father was a patriot of the Revolution, and one of the signers of the Declaration of Independence. He was afterward a merchant of this city, president, successively, of the Merchants' Bank and the Bank of America, in which latter institution I was associated with him as a director. He then removed to his native State, Connecticut, of which he was elected Governor, and in which office he continued several years. He came recently again to New York, where he lived in bad health and in perfect retirement from society.

THURSDAY, JUNE 13.— The President is certainly the most popular man we have ever known. Washington was not so much so. His acts were popular, because all descriptions of men were ready to acknowledge him the Father of his Country; but he was superior to the homage of the populace,— too dignified, too grave for their liking; and men could not approach him with familiarity. Here is a man who suits them exactly. He has a kind expression for each,— the same to all, no doubt, but each thinks it intended for himself. His manners are certainly good, and he makes the most of them. He is a *gourmand* of adulation, and by the assistance of the populace has persuaded himself that no man ever lived in the country to whom the country was so much indebted. Talk of him as the second Washington!

President Jackson.

It won't do now. Washington was only the first Jackson. Poor Adams used to visit New York during his presidency. The papers, to be sure, announced his arrival; but he was welcomed by no shouts, no crowd thronged around his portals, no huzzas rent the air when he made his appearance, and yet posterity, more just than ourselves, will acknowledge him to have been, in all the qualifications which constitute his fitness to fill the office of a ruler of this great Republic, twenty times superior to Jackson. He wanted tact. He gave the toast of *Ebony and Topaz*, the ungracious offspring of a mind overloaded with study and unskilful in adaptation. And the other, in a moment when we were all anxious to save the country from the mad schemes of visionary theorists whose crude principles of government seemed to threaten the welfare of our federative institution, and when we doubted what his course would be, gave in a happy moment his toast, "The Union — it must be preserved." It made a difference of five hundred thousand votes. Adams is the wisest man, the best scholar, the most accomplished statesman; but Jackson has most tact. So, huzza for Jackson!

JUNE 15. — The celebrated Indian chief, Black Hawk, and his companions, the prophet and his son, now occupy the place in the public curiosity which General Jackson filled during his recent visit here. They arrived yesterday, and witnessed the ascension of the balloon from the steamboat in which they arrived. They are under the charge of Major Garland of the United States Army. The crowd was so great that they found it impossible to land and enter the garden, as was expected. They were afterward taken to their lodgings at the Exchange Hotel, in Broad street, and Black Hawk is now the order of the day.

SATURDAY, JUNE 29. — My estimable friend, Colonel Nicholas Fish, died during my absence, on Tuesday, 20th inst., in the seventy-fifth year of his age. He was a gallant and distinguished officer in the War of the Revolution, an accomplished gentleman of the old school, and in all respects an amiable and excellent man.

Col. Thomas H. Perkins, of Boston, made a short time since a donation to the New England Institution for the Education of the Blind of his house and lot of ground in Pearl street, worth $30,000, on condition that the further sum of $50,000 should be raised for the same object by voluntary contributions. The Bostonians went to work with their accustomed spirit, and collected in a very short time the sum of $51,117, of which $11,400 were the proceeds of a ladies' fair. This result having been announced to the Colonel by a committee appointed to receive the subscriptions, he made his offer binding by a conveyance of the splendid mansion which he formerly occupied, and which I should say from my recollection of it is fully worth the estimated sum.

Munificence of Boston.

JULY 1. — Married *suddenly*, on Saturday evening, Henry N. Cruger, of Charleston, to Miss Harriet Douglas, the American Madame de Staël.

WEDNESDAY, JULY 3. — The celebrated Colonel Burr was married on Monday evening to the equally celebrated Mrs. Jumel, widow of Stephen Jumel. It is benevolent in her to keep the old man in his latter days. One good turn deserves another.

THURSDAY, AUG. 22. — A very agreeable wedding took place this day at Jamaica. Henry Van Rensselaer, son of Gen. Stephen Van Rensselaer, was married to Miss Elizabeth Ray King, second daughter of John A. King. I was in company one evening last winter at a party with Mrs. King, Mrs. Abraham Ogden, and Mrs. Edward R. Jones, and was boasting of some fine Arrack more than sixty years old which I had obtained. I promised each of these ladies a bottle of it on the occasion of a marriage of a daughter. This is the first, and I have redeemed my pledge by sending Mrs. King a bottle on Saturday, with my compliments and congratulations.

MONDAY, AUG. 26. — Died at Jamaica, Long Island, on Saturday evening, Egbert Benson, aged eighty-seven years. This patriarch has held a conspicuous station in the affairs of this State, — a lawyer of eminence in the early part of his life, occupying a high judicial station at a more advanced period, a patriot and a staunch Whig during the Revolution. Few men have been more generally known and esteemed than Judge Benson. He has lived in retirement for many years, and dies at a very advanced age.

MONDAY, SEPT. 16. — The drawing for boxes at the Italian opera house took place this morning. My associates, Mr. Schermerhorn and General Jones, are out of town, and I attended and drew No. 8, with which I am well satisfied. The other boxes will be occupied by the following gentlemen: Gerard H. Coster, G. G. Howland, Rufus Prime, Mr. Panon, Robert Ray, J. F. Moulton, James J. Jones, D. Lynch, E. Townsend, John C. Cruger, O. Mauran, Charles Hall, J. G. Pierson, and S. B. Ruggles.

MONDAY, SEPT. 30. — We went this evening to see Mr. and Miss Kemble in the "Stranger." Mrs. Haller is thought by many persons to be Fanny Kemble's best part. She certainly played this evening with the most affecting pathos and tenderness; and so the audience appear to think, for I never saw persons more attentive and more deeply affected. This will probably be her last engagement, if the report is true that she is married already, or about to be, to Mr. Pierce Butler, of Philadelphia.

Abolition Meeting. THURSDAY, OCT. 3. — A notice appeared in the papers of yesterday, signed by Joshua Leavitt, William Goodell, William Green, Jr., John Rankin, and Lewis Tappan, calling a meeting of "the friends of immediate abolition of slavery in the United States" at Clinton Hall last evening. I expressed great dissatisfaction that the hall should be let without my approbation for any purpose not immediately connected with the objects of the institution, and my decided opposition to its being used for the agitation of this most mischievous question. A great crowd of people collected to oppose the object of the meeting, and hearing that they had become tumultuous, I went over and found that Mr. Leavitt and Mr. Olmstead, the former of whom had granted the use of the hall, had been there and countermanded the permission, and locked the doors. The assemblage of persons had adjourned to Tammany Hall, appointed Robert Bogardus chairman and M. C. Patterson and P. P. Parsells secretaries, and passed resolutions disapproving the objects of the meeting.

MONDAY, OCT. 7. — On the way to Rockaway my daughter and I stopped at Snedecor's to look at Eclipse. This noble animal, whose blood flows in the veins of all the finest horses in this country, was twenty years old last spring. His owner, Walter Livingston, has lately sold one-half of him for $4,500 to Colonel Johnson, of Virginia, who (after a year, during which time he is to remain on Long Island) will take him away to improve the blood of the South. Eclipse looks as fine as ever. He is under the care of a groom who has had nothing else to do for the past nine years but attend to the grand sultan, brush his coat, comb his mane, make his bed, and provide his meals; verily, the horse and his keeper have both an easy life of it.

FRIDAY, OCT. 18. — I regret exceedingly that the visit of my distinguished friend, Mr. Clay, should have been made during my absence. I knew he was expected, but hoped to be back before his arrival. He came on Tuesday, and was received with the most distinguished marks of respect. Crowds of people received him with enthusiastic cheers on his landing, and he was escorted by one hundred gentlemen on horseback to the lodgings which had been prepared for him at the American Hotel, the same which "the greatest and best" occupied during his visit. A public dinner was tendered to him, which he declined, as he had previously done a similar compliment in Philadelphia.

Mr. Clay's Visit.

NOVEMBER 2. — I dined with Mr. Bucknor, and met Commodore Chauncey there. Dr. Wainwright was of the party. He has determined at last to accept the call which has been strongly pressed upon him to become rector of St. Paul's, Boston, and will leave Grace Church and his congregation here — the most eligible clerical living, I believe, in the United States — from what he considers a sense of duty, it having been represented to him that his acceptance of the call is the only means of keeping the congregation of St. Paul's, the most respectable Episcopal church in New England, from falling to pieces. But I fear if they are such a set of nullifiers he will not have much comfort amongst them, and his departure from New York will occasion a severe loss to his congregation, and be deeply lamented by a large circle of devoted personal friends.

TUESDAY, Nov. 5. — James Fenimore Cooper and his family arrived to-day in the ship "Sampson" from London. This gentleman has acquired a high literary reputation during his residence in Europe as the author of several novels, but I doubt very much if the works which he published before he went away do not form a foundation for his fame, of which the superstructure he has subsequently erected is scarcely worthy. His late works have certainly not added much to his reputation on this side of the water.

<small>Opening of the Opera House.</small> MONDAY, Nov. 18. — The long-expected opening of the opera house took place this evening, with the opera, "La Gaza Ladra," — all new performers except Signora Marozzi, who belonged to the old company. The prima-donna soprano is Signorina Fanti. The opera, they say, went off well for a first performance; but to me it was tiresome, and the audience was not excited to any violent degree of applause. The performance occupied four hours, — much too long, according to my notion, to listen to a language which one does not understand; but the house is superb, and the decorations of the proprietors' boxes (which occupy the whole of the second tier) in a style of magnificence which even the extravagance of Europe has not yet equalled. I have one-third of box No. 8; Peter Schermerhorn, one-third; James J. Jones, one-sixth; and William Moore, one-sixth. Our box is fitted up with great taste, with light-blue hangings, gilded panels and cornice, arm-chairs, and a sofa. Some of the others have rich silk ornaments, some are painted in fresco, and each proprietor seems to have tried to outdo the rest in comfort and

magnificence. The scenery is beautiful. The dome and the fronts of the boxes are painted in the most superb classical designs, and the sofa-seats are exceedingly commodious. Will this splendid and refined amusement be supported in New York? I am doubtful.

MONDAY, Nov. 18. — The ill-advised and arbitrary step of the President in removing the deposits from the Bank of the United States has, as was predicted, occasioned a collision between the branches of that institution and the State banks which have been selected to receive the public money, producing an awful scarcity of money, with immediate distress and melancholy forebodings to the merchants and others, who require credit to sustain them. Stocks of every description have fallen, — Delaware and Hudson, from one hundred and twenty-five to one hundred and fourteen; Boston and Providence, from one hundred and fifteen to one hundred and three: in both of these I suffer. Money cannot be had on bond and mortgage at seven per cent., and I am told good notes will hardly be discounted at nine per cent.

TUESDAY, Nov. 19. — Mr. Clay told me this morning that he wished to visit Chancellor Kent, and I called for him and drove him to the Chancellor's, where we paid a delightful visit of about an hour, with which they were both highly gratified. It is a fine tribute to the character of my excellent friend that such a man as Mr. Clay, when he visits New York, is always desirous to see him. There is a virtuous simplicity about him which adorns the sterling qualities of his mind, and leaves us in doubt whether we are most fascinated by his good heart or his strong intellect.

I dined with Mr. Donaldson, where I met his distinguished father-in-law, Mr. Gaston, Chancellor Kent, Mr. Everett, Colonel Trumbull, Mr. Jay, Mr. David B. Ogden, etc. It was, of course, a pleasant dinner. I have seldom met a man with whom I was so much pleased as Mr. Gaston. He possesses a refined mind, cultivated understanding, and agreeable manners, and would be an ornament to public life, were it not that he adheres with honourable pertinacity to the unfashionable name and principles of Federalism. More's the pity for the country!

WEDNESDAY, Nov. 20. — Mr. Edward Everett, the distinguished member of Congress from Massachusetts, called to see me this morning, and sat half an hour with me. He is a man of fine talents, a good writer, and an eloquent orator; a little pedantic, but his manners are unaffected, and his conversation instructive and agreeable. He is to deliver, this evening, the introductory to the course of lectures of the Mercantile Library Association, at Clinton Hall. It will, no doubt, be a great treat. I ought to go, and would like to, but I have engaged company at home to meet Mr. Clay. The following gentlemen supped with me: Mr. Clay, Mr. C. L. Livingston, Mr. Lydig, Mr. Phelps, Mr. Moore, Mr. H. Suydam, Mr. D. S. Jones, Mr. Talman, Mr. Giraud, Mr. I. S. Hone, Mr. Wynkoop, Mr. Bowne, and Dr. McLean. Mr. Clay, as usual, was exceedingly agreeable, and some of my guests declared they had never spent a more agreeable evening.

WEDNESDAY, DEC. 4. — The language of the message in relation to the Bank of the United States is even more violent and intemperate than could have been anticipated; and in an important State paper, which is read with avidity in all parts of the world where our country and its institutions excite the least interest, it is undignified, because marked with strong personal feelings of hostility, and unjust, because it abounds in charges which cannot be proved, either by the President or the unworthy advisers who, influenced by paltry motives of pecuniary interest, avail themselves of the weakness of excited feelings and uncompromising obstinacy to promote their own objects.

MONDAY, DEC. 9. — The Bank of the United States has published an elaborate and able report in vindication of its measures, as a reply to the charges against it in the report of the Secretary of the Treasury. It concludes with a recommendation of the adoption of the following resolution: "That the removal of the public funds from the Bank of the United States under the circumstances and in the manner in which it has been effected, is a violation of the contract between the Government and the Bank; and that the President be instructed to present a memorial to Congress requesting that redress should be afforded for the wrong which has been done to the institution."

FRIDAY, DEC. 13. — The session of Congress has commenced in a stormy manner, and the President and his out-and-out supporters have been assailed in both Houses. The opposers of the administration are bold and determined, and its friends unprepared to stem the torrent. A resolution offered by Mr. Clay in the Senate to have the standing committees appointed by ballot instead of being nominated by the president of the Senate (the Vice-President not having taken the chair) was carried by a majority of five or six. This is understood to be an indication of the state of parties. Several questions have also come up in the House in relation to the removal of the deposits, the great question which is to agitate the country to its very centre, in which the vote has been so strong in opposition that there must be some awful quakings amongst those whose business in Washington is to sanction all rescripts from the seat of power and the source of patronage. Of our four representatives, White, Cambreling, and Lawrence have taken the bit kindly and drive very well; but Selden shows a strong disposition to restiveness, and the collar does not set easy upon him.

SATURDAY, DEC. 14. — I dined with Mr. Edward R. Jones. Peter A. Jay talks extremely well when he has a mind, and this day he was "in the vein." I do not know when I have been so well pleased, and we sat until ten o'clock.

FRIDAY, DEC. 27. — The holidays are gloomy; the weather is bad; the times are bad; stocks are falling; and a panic prevails which will result in bankruptcies and ruin in many quarters where, a few short weeks since, the sun of prosperity shone with unusual brightness. It will be worse before it is better.

MONDAY, DEC. 30. — The times are dreadfully hard. The supererogatory act of tyranny which the President exercised in removing the deposits has produced a state of alarm and panic unprecedented in our city. The friends of the United States Bank on the one side, and the whole array of Jackson men, together with the friends of the Pet Banks, on the other, mutually accuse each other of being the cause of the pressure; and so between them both, the community groans under the distress which these misunderstandings have created. "A plague on both your houses!" I say. The truth is, we are smarting under the lash which the vindictive ruler of our destinies has inflicted upon us as a penalty for the sin which Nicholas Biddle committed in opposing his election. My share of punishment amounts to $20,000, which I have lost by the fall of stocks in the last sixty days. Delaware and Hudson Canal Company stock has fallen suddenly from one hundred and twenty-five per cent. to seventy-five per cent.; Boston and Providence Railroad, from one hundred and fifteen per cent. to eighty-eight per cent.; Camden and Amboy, from one hundred and fifty per cent. to one hundred and twenty-five per cent. Delaware and Hudson fell twenty per cent. in two days, owing principally to the failure of Shipman & Corning, brokers, who have been gambling in the stock, and being caught with heavy contracts when the fall took place, were unable to fulfil them, and a great amount of hypotheticated stock was thrown at once in the market. The removal of the deposits I believe to be the great cause of the pecuniary distress, to which may be added the operation of cash duties on woollens, which brings a large amount of payments into the Treasury. The gambling in stocks which has been carried on by the brokers to an extent disgraceful to the commercial character of the city is another cause of the distress. It consists in selling out stocks ahead, as it is called, where a man buys and sells to the amount of millions, without owning a dollar of the stock, betting it will fall, and then taking pains by every kind of lying and chicanery to injure the reputation of the stock that he may win. This, the good sense of the merchants, aided by the endeavours of the honourable part of the brokers, may remedy in time, and the effect of double engagements at the Custom-House will soon end, for the old bonds are nearly run out. But the great cause of the evil, the opposition of General Jackson to the Bank of the United States, admits no ray of hope. He has said it. He takes the responsibility. His flatterers, the sycophants who crawl beneath his feet, impose upon his weakness and flatter his vanity; they persuade him that his obstinacy is firmness, and his vengeance Roman dignity.

TUESDAY, DEC. 31. — The year 1833 commenced with brilliant prospects of national prosperity and individual happiness, and during the greater part of the year those prospects continued unchanged, and the fair expectations of those who were reasonably sanguine appeared likely to be realized. The merchants were doing a good and profitable business, and the bounty of Providence, which gave plentiful crops to the farmer, and the state of foreign and domestic commerce, which afforded him a good and certain market, enriched the country and enabled the merchants in other States to meet their New York engagements with punctuality. Real estate increased in value, money was as plenty as it ought to be, and the improvement of the city kept pace with the enterprise and resources of the citizens. But the change is melancholy, and has fallen upon us so suddenly that men feel the blow and know not whence it comes. Public confidence is shaken, personal property has no fixed value, and *sauve qui peut* is the maxim of the day. Never in any year did the 31st of December fail so completely to redeem the pledges of the 1st of January.

1834.

JANUARY 1. — The year commences with a beautiful, mild, sunshiny day. May it prove ominous of a dispersion of the political clouds which hang over the country, and of the cheerfulness which will result from a restoration of confidence among our citizens and a return of good times!

WEDNESDAY, JAN. 8. — Anniversary of the battle of New Orleans. It was a proud day for America, and the chief who then "plucked up the drowning honour of the nation by the locks," well deserved the gratitude of the people. But, alas, how has he been overpaid, and at what a sacrifice have they rewarded his services! Any arm which has strength enough to wield a hammer and an axe may destroy the most beautiful work of a Phidias or a Michael Angelo; but where is the artist who can restore its desecrated remains to their original beauty, and where the power which can bid the delicate machinery of individual credit and public confidence to resume its harmonious functions when once deranged and put out of tune by the hands of ignorance and misdirected power?

TUESDAY, JAN. 21. — The commercial distress caused by the derangement of the relations between the Government and the Bank of the United States does not appear to be alleviated. On the contrary, the sacrifices which are necessary to support individual credit are becoming more oppressive, and there seems to be no quarter of the political horizon to which men are to look for a ray of sunshine. In both Houses of Congress the all-absorbing topic of the removal of the deposits occupies the time, and the members on both sides of the question seem determined to have their talk out. Mr. Webster stands on ground of his own. He belongs to none of the political parties, — the friend of his country and the supporter of the Constitution. As chairman of the Committee of

Finance, he is preparing to come out with a report from which much is expected. His chance of success in any measure to settle the present difficulty is better than that of any other man, from the nature of his position. It is not impossible that he may enjoy the triumph of saving his country. Mr. Clay had that triumph last season; the effect of his compromise of the tariff question is now apparent and acknowledged by all. For if that question had been left unsettled and suffered to mix with those other subjects which agitate the public mind and fill the hearts of good men with alarm for the future, it is impossible to say what would have been the consequences. But Mr. Clay can do nothing now; the bitter feeling of animosity which the President entertains toward that patriot forbids the possibility of his exercising any influence over the minds of the party which constitutes the majority in the lower House. Mr. Webster may succeed better. He does not stand so much in the way, and they may not be unwilling to adopt with him some terms of compromise. Of one thing we may be certain, — that the honour of the country and the security of its institutions are safe in his hands.

WEDNESDAY, JAN. 22. — The memorial to Congress, adopted at the meeting on Saturday, has received three thousand signatures, embracing nearly all the respectable merchants; and a meeting was called at the same place, No. 40 William street, but the numbers were so great that the meeting adjourned to the Exchange. Jonathan Goodhue was chairman, and John P. Stagg, secretary. The following gentlemen were appointed delegates to proceed with the memorial to Washington: James G. King, D. W. C. Olyphant, James Boorman, George S. Robbins, Pelatiah Perit, John Crumby, Sam. S. Howland, James W. Otis, Charles H. Russell, Robert C. Cornell, John A. Stephens, and G. P. Disosway.

THURSDAY, JAN. 23. — This was the most brilliant affair we have seen in a long time. "Mr. Ray at home, Thursday, 23d inst. Quadrilles at nine o'clock." The very cards gave promise of *quelque chose distin-*

<small>Mr. Ray's Party.</small>

guée. The fashionable world rushed with excited expectation to the gay scene, and none were disappointed. Mr. Ray has the finest house in New York, and it is furnished and fitted up in a style of the utmost magnificence, — painted ceilings, gilded mouldings, rich satin ottomans, curtains in the last Parisian taste, and splendid mirrors which reflect and multiply all the *rays*, great and small.

On this occasion all the science of all the accomplished *artistes* was put in requisition; decorators, cooks, and confectioners vied with each other, and each in his vocation seemed to have produced the *ne plus ultra;* and, unlike other entertainments of the kind, the spirit of jealousy and emulation cannot be excited to an inconvenient degree, for as no person possesses such a house, and very few the means to show it off in the same style, it will not be considered incumbent upon others to attempt to rival this splendid *fête,* and it will be no disgrace to play second fiddle to such a leader.

TUESDAY, JAN. 28. — The strong expression of public opinion which the circulation of the memorial to Congress has called forth occasions great alarm amongst the Jackson men, and orders have been issued from the "Republican General Committee" at Tammany Hall for meetings to be held in the several wards to-morrow evening and a general meeting on Thursday evening, not of citizens interested in the momentous question which occupies every mind, but of the *Jackson party*, who are to approve all that has been, or may be, done. The sufferings of the merchants from present evils, and the fearful apprehensions of the future, are of no moment compared to the preservation of party discipline. Many of the President's political friends regret the ill-advised and rash step which he took in removing the deposits, but they dare not advise him to make the only amends in his power, by retracing it. The pressure increases. Stocks fall every day; Delaware and Hudson sold to-day at sixty-eight per cent.; Boston and Providence Railroad, eighty-three per cent.;

Mohawk and Hudson, about the same. It was worth once, one hundred and ninety per cent. I believe Cambreling sold out at that, and now he is one of the set who laugh at our misfortunes, and refuse to take those measures for our relief which are within their power as representatives of the people.

Packets. WEDNESDAY, JAN. 29. — The old line of Liverpool packets originally established by Isaac Wright and Francis Thompson has been sold out, and Goodhue & Co. are to be the agents in the future; the house of Baring & Co., of London, is said to be concerned in the speculation. Six fine ships have been purchased for $216,000, or $36,000 each. The establishment of this line of packets and the punctuality with which it has been conducted served as a pioneer and pattern to all other lines which were subsequently established between this port and London, Liverpool, Havre, and la Vera Cruz, and has contributed more than any other cause to the commercial prosperity of New York, and her unrivalled eminence among her sister cities. The original proprietors, Wright & Thompson (both of whom are deceased), were well calculated for such an undertaking; bold and enterprising, they were distinguished for habits of industry and methodical correctness in business, peculiar to the religious sect (the Quakers) of which they were members; and notwithstanding the pecuniary difficulties which one of them, Mr. Thompson, had to contend with, and which terminated in his failure, the line of packets has been kept up in its original integrity, and its business has been always well conducted until now, when it has passed into other hands equally competent to its management, and possessing in a high degree the confidence and good opinion of the public.

FRIDAY, FEB. 7. — Out of forty-six packet-ships plying between New York and London, Liverpool, and Havre, but two are now in port, both of which, in the ordinary course of things, ought to sail to-morrow. Our latest advices from Liverpool are seventy-one days old, London seventy-two, and Paris seventy-five. This has never before happened since the establishment of regular lines of American packets, about forty years ago, it is said, when there were only British packets running between here and Liverpool, one leaving each port monthly. It happened on one occasion that the packets for December, January, and February all arrived here on the same day.

<small>Great Meeting.</small> A public meeting having been called by a notice signed by many respectable names of "the citizens who are opposed to the removal of the deposits from the Bank of the United States, and who are in favour of a sound currency by means of a national bank," an immense concourse assembled at twelve o'clock at the place of meeting, — the park. The number is computed at from twelve to fifteen thousand. I was waited upon by a committee and requested to officiate as chairman. When I came on the ground, precisely at twelve o'clock, I found an immense crowd already assembled, consisting principally of the most respectable mechanics and others in the city, — men of character, respectability, and personal worth, with a few miscreants who went, perhaps, of their own accord, but were more probably sent there to excite disturbance and disturb the proceedings. The rabble had gotten possession of the chair, and it required some hard thumps to clear the way sufficiently for me to come forward. I attempted to address the meeting, but the yells of the mob, and the noise of better-disposed persons in attempting to command silence, rendered all my efforts unavailing; so I put the question upon the resolutions, which were carried by an immense majority, and then adjourned the meeting; but the mob did not disperse for a considerable time afterward. This apparently organized outrage upon the freedom of the citizens cannot fail to strengthen our cause, for they will not consent to be muffled, and will convince their rulers that public opinion means something more than the drilled voices of certain political friends of General Jackson, who are pledged, body and soul, to support him at all events.

TUESDAY, FEB. 11. — The delegates who were appointed to carry the merchants' memorial to Washington having returned, a meeting of the signers was called this afternoon at the Exchange to receive their report. Such a meeting never before assembled in New York. When I reached the spot at the hour of meeting, the great room in the Exchange with all its avenues, the vestibule, and the porch were filled, and three or four thousand persons occupied the street in front, — all firm and enthusiastic, but orderly and decorous in the extreme. The meeting within doors was organized precisely at half-past four o'clock by the appointment of Jonathan Goodhue as chairman, and John P. Stagg, secretary. The report of the delegates, announcing the unsuccessful result of their mission, was read by James G. King. On motion of John A. Stevens, the following resolution was adopted unanimously: "That with a view to the importance of combining mercantile influence and opinions for commercial and not for party ends, and by the exercise of this influence to ameliorate present distresses and to avert future evils, that a Union Committee of twenty-five persons be now appointed, whose duty it shall be to confer with committees of the State and national banks, with a view to produce that entire concert and harmony of action essential to enable them to afford the greatest possible relief to the community." The following persons were appointed and constitute the Union Committee: Albert Gallatin, James G. King, Jonathan Goodhue, G. G. Howland, John Haggerty, Nathaniel Weed, James Boorman, John W. Leavitt, James Brown, David Lee, Rufus L. Lord, Fanning C. Tucker, Isaac Carow, Elbert J. Anderson, John G. Coster, Francis Olmstead, Thomas Brooks, Charles H. Russell, Herbert Van Wagenen, E. G. Fale, Joseph Kernochan, Philip Hone, John A. Stevens, John P. Stagg, and D. W. C. Olyphant. The meeting then adjourned into the street, and the vast body came pouring down the principal avenue like a mighty rushing river to mix with the multitudinous sea beneath. The whole street

Public Meeting.

from William street to a distance below the Exchange was a compact, solid mass of men. I was called upon from all parts of the crowd to read the report and resolutions for the benefit of the out-door part of the concern, and was placed in a conspicuous situation on one of the pedestals at the end of the steps forming the great entrance. I was received in the most flattering manner, and read them with considerable effect, notwithstanding the disadvantage I suffered from not having seen the papers or heard them read previously. I then adjourned the meeting, and the great, the sublime, the intelligent mass separated and retired with decorum and dignity. Such an assemblage has never before been witnessed in New York; the spectacle from the elevation on which I stood was extremely imposing, — a solid mass of heads with faces beaming with intelligence, actuated by one strong feeling, silent, attentive, decorous; every sentiment was understood, every patriotic expression in the report and resolution responded to with feeling and reflection. If this is not a public opinion, we may look in vain for it.

WASHINGTON, MONDAY, MARCH 3. — Our party, with the Kembles, left Baltimore at seven o'clock and arrived here at three, and I got a good room at Gadsby's, which had been previously engaged for me by Mr. Selden. At five o'clock I went to dine with Baron Behr. He has the apartments formerly occupied by Bankhead, and the cook also, an *artiste* of the highest grade. The Colonel and I went to the theatre to see the Kembles in " Hamlet ; " but Fanny Kemble in the Washington Theatre is like a canary-bird in a mouse-trap, and I soon came away and went to a delightful party at Mrs. Tayloe's. There I met many distinguished people and all the Washington belles.

MARCH 4. — I called this morning on the Vice-President, Secretaries McLane, Cass, and Woodbury, and several others. In the number was Sir Charles R. Vaughan, who, while I was so engaged, was at my lodgings, having with his usual kindness laid aside etiquette, and called as soon as he heard of my being in town to engage me for dinner to-morrow.

The terrible question which agitates the whole country is as far as ever from a happy termination. The late message of the Governor of Pennsylvania, attributing the financial distress of the country to the Bank of the United States, has thrown all aback, for better things were expected. The President is more obstinate than ever, and the Speaker (Stevenson), with whom I had a talk this morning, is as subservient as the most docile man at Tammany Hall. How is it possible that a high-minded Virginian like him should consent to administer to the vanity and prejudice of a weak, unreasonable old man? But my friend wishes to go to England. My first visit this morning was to Mr. Clay. He says our only hope is in the elections in our State and Pennsylvania. Let them go for us, and a sufficient majority will be found in Congress to set things right, in spite of the opposition of the *greatest and best.* Our only relief is in the ballot-boxes. Is it not worth fighting for?

MARCH 5. — I returned a number of visits, walked up to the Capitol with Mr. Webster and Mr. Chauncey, spent two or three hours in the two Houses (the ladies were too wise to go in, but pursued their walk), and afterward went to dine with Sir Charles R. Vaughan, where we had the Kembles, Commodore and Mrs. Chauncey, De Behr, Colonel McDougal, etc. Lynch dined with us, but he is on a pretty severe regimen, and looks poorly.

MARCH 6. — The proceedings in the House have been more interesting to me than heretofore. I was admitted upon the floor, a favour conferred so charily under the present rules as very much to enhance its value. This gave me a fine opportunity to converse with all the leading members. Among others I had a long talk about the state of affairs with that sagacious man, John Quincy Adams; and if I was not instructed, it was my own fault. He agrees with Mr. Clay that our only hope lies in the elections in New York and Pennsylvania, particularly our charter election. I heard Mr. Webster argue a cause in the Supreme Court. I say with the fair Venetian, "Would that Heaven had made me such a man!" Mr. Preston, the new senator from South Carolina, is a very interesting man. I had a long conversation with him at Major Smith's. He is ardent and romantic like his countrymen, and apparently well educated; an eloquent speaker (and saving the sin of nullification), a wise and patriotic statesman.

MARCH 7. — Contrary to my expectation, this has been a great day in the Senate. Mr. Webster made a glorious speech on the presentation of a memorial in favour of the bank and of a restoration of the deposits, and Mr. Clay introduced the proceedings on the same subject of a meeting of mechanics concerned in building in Philadelphia, in one of the most eloquent appeals to the feelings of his audience that I have ever heard. It was solemn, energetic, and impressive, especially in that part in which he addressed the Vice-President personally, and exhorted him to use the influence he possesses over the President to persuade him to a better course of measures. "And if I touch your heart," said he, "and persuade you to come to the rescue of your suffering country, I shall merit her gratitude and promote your glory." Touch Mr. Van Buren's heart, — good! Mr. Webster beckoned me out of the Senate into one of the committee-rooms, where we had more than an hour's talk. He unburdened his mind fully on the state of affairs and future prospects, explained all that has passed, and fully laid open his future plans. He will be in New York in a fortnight, for one night, when he wishes me to convene a few of our political friends to meet and consult with him. His plans for an extension of the bank charter will be laid before the Senate on Monday, where it will lie for a fortnight. He showed it to me, and explained his views and expectations in relation to it. I was exceedingly flattered by this mark of Mr. Webster's confidence, and certainly never heard a man talk so.

MARCH 8. — I dined with the Vice-President, where I met a large party of officers, diplomats, and members of Congress.

MARCH 9. — I called for Mrs. Webster this morning, and went with her to the Episcopal church on President's square, where Rev. Mr. Hawley preached; after which Commodore Chauncey and I drove out to the navy yard, where we made a pleasant visit to Commodore Hull and the ladies. The Commodore presented me with a box made from one of the original live-oak timbers of the frigate "Constitution." I dined with Judge Wayne and Mr. Cambreling, and passed the remainder of the evening with Mr. Clay.

NEW YORK, MARCH 15.— The President has renominated to the Senate the Government directors of the Bank of the United States whom they rejected the other day, with a threat, it is said, that he will appeal to the people if their nomination is not confirmed. It is difficult to tell what this means, but his hostility against the Senate will lead him into some extravagant acts of rage, which he relies upon his popularity to bear him out of. Selden has returned to Washington. He was received by the merchants at the Exchange with cheers and other marks of their approval of his conduct. Mr. Biddle returned yesterday to Philadelphia. Crowds of people followed him in Wall street, to gaze upon the man who has been made conspicuous by the unrelenting hostility of President Jackson. The merchants, however, expressed their approbation of his course by applause similar to that which they gave to Mr. Selden.

MARCH 18. — Washington Irving acquainted me with a circumstance to-day which occasions me the deepest regret. Stuart Newton, the eminent painter, his friend and mine, was, at the last accounts from London, a lunatic confined in a mad-house. His poor wife, the former lovely Miss Sullivan, with her child is in the greatest possible distress, and has written to her father to come out and bring her home when death shall have closed her husband's unhappy calamity. I am told there is a taint of madness in Newton's family; his uncle, Gilbert Stuart, the great portrait painter, had the character of a very eccentric man, at least. It is melancholy to observe how slight is the division line between the higher order of genius and the loss of intellect. Stupidity is a comfortable quality; men grow rich and fat and easy under it; they live out their days, and sleep sound at night, and do not scorch their brains by soaring into the bright regions of imagination. I saw Weir afterward, who told me that he has heard that Newton is dead.

MARCH 19. — The Committee of National Republicans appointed to nominate a mayor met last evening, and nominated for that office Gulian C. Verplanck. This gentleman was ousted from his seat in Congress by the Jackson party, because he would not go all lengths in his opposition to the United States Bank. In that point of view he is a good candidate, and his success will be a triumph for the bank party; but I do not think him a popular man, or by any means well qualified for the office. He is not a practical man; learned he certainly is, and an able writer on subjects connected with *belles-lettres* and the fine arts; but he knows little of mankind, and his political course has been unsteady as the wind. Still he must be supported. The Tammany men have sent a deputation to Albany to obtain Charles L. Livingston's consent to run as their candidate for the mayoralty. He is more suited for the office, and if he had not committed himself againt his judgment in the approval of the ruinous course of measures pursued by the administration in relation to the bank, I would have supported him with all my heart. As it is, I shall have to make some sacrifice of feeling in voting for Mr. Verplanck against him. But it cannot be helped; the salvation of the country depends in a great measure upon the defeat of the Jackson party in the struggle which will come on next month, and personal predilections must give way to the public good.

The Mayor. MARCH 21. — Mr. Livingston refuses, it is understood, to run as mayor. Mr. Cornelius W. Lawrence has been applied to, and consents to run as the candidate of the Jackson or Tammany party. This is a bold measure on the part of the Jackson men. Mr. Lawrence is now their congressman, and circumstances have placed him on prominent ground as an opposer of the bank and supporter of the measures of the administration (against his conscience, as I believe on mine). He has been vilified by the delegates of the merchants for refusing to present their memorial, and his name has been hissed when it occurred in their report. He is most heartily sick of his present situation, but he is compelled by his party to accept the nomination of mayor. This will be a fair trial of. the issue, — Mr. Lawrence, the man who has for the sake of party proved recreant to the interests of the merchants, of which profession he is a member, on the one side, and Mr. Verplanck, who lost his seat in Congress because he would not pursue the same course, on the other. The personal characters of both these gentlemen are irreproachable. Verplanck at first declined the nomination, but it is now understood that he consents to serve.

MARCH 25. — I availed myself of a regular rainy day to stay at home and prepare books for binding and file my letters. Such a day once in a while is a jewel beyond price.

APRIL 2. — Politics occupy all my time. Mr. Webster wrote me from Washington that he would be in New York this afternoon on his way to Boston, and agreeably to his suggestion when I saw him in Washington, I invited a number of our political friends to meet him at my house. James G. King, G. G. Howland, Giraud, and Isaac dined with us at three o'clock ; at four Mr. Webster arrived, and found the following gentlemen assembled to receive him : Jonathan Goodhue, Samuel Ward, James G. King, Charles H. Russell, David B. Ogden, John A. Stevens, Joseph Hoxie, Jacob P. Giraud, George F. Talman, Isaac S. Hone, G. G. Howland, David S. Jones, A. Chandler, Samuel Stevens, Charles King, Hugh Maxwell, John W. Leavitt, Philip W. Engs, and George Zabriskie. We had a full, free, and interesting conversation, in which the great Massachusetts senator detailed all his operations during the session, and confirmed in the most emphatic manner the declaration which he made to me at Washington, that the hopes of our friends there to bring about a favourable change in the affairs of the country rely mainly upon the success of the great struggle which is to take place in New York next week.

APRIL 3. — Mr. Webster left New York for Boston at five o'clock this afternoon; the wharf near the steamboat was crowded with people, who saluted him with repeated cheers. Thousands pressed forward for a sight of the defender of the people's rights and the supporter of the Constitution and laws of the country.

APRIL 4. — Mr. John Jacob Astor arrived yesterday in the packet-ship "Utica" from Havre. The news of his wife's death will be the first to meet him. He comes in time to witness the pulling down of the block of houses next to that on which I live, — the whole front from Barclay to Vesey street, on Broadway, — where he is going to erect a New York *palais royal*, which will cost him five or six hundred thousand dollars.

TUESDAY, APRIL 8. — The election for mayor and charter officers commenced this day with a degree of spirit and zeal in both parties never before witnessed. This is the first election for mayor by the people since the new law, and has acquired immense importance, since it is considered a test of the approval or disapproval of the people of New York of the arbitrary and unconstitutional measures of the President and his advisers, and as it will influence the politics of the State in the more important elections next fall. The number of votes will be very great (probably thirty-five thousand); the Whig party, whose candidate for mayor is Mr. Verplanck, are active, zealous, and confident of success. A great meeting was held yesterday at four o'clock, at the Exchange, at which Benjamin Strong presided, and John W. Leavitt and Edmund Penfold were secretaries. The meeting was addressed by John A. Stevens, George W. Bruen, James G. King, Charles H. Russell, and Chandler Starr, and several resolutions were passed, one of which recommends to the merchants and traders to omit their usual attendance at the Exchange, and to close their stores and places of business at noon on each of the three days of the election, in order to devote their undivided attention to the great business of reform at the polls. This last suggestion has been in part observed; many stores are closed to-day, and several have notices on the doors that the inmates are gone to the polls to vote for Verplanck. A very large meeting was also held last evening of adopted citizens at Masonic Hall to approve the course of Dr. MacNeven in joining our party. After the meeting adjourned they went to his house and cheered him, and he addressed them, wishing the party success. They came also before my door and gave me some hearty huzzas, but I was unfortunately absent, having gone to the theatre with my girls and Miss Kane. My wife was alarmed at the row, as I had a visit of another kind a few evenings since from a party of the retainers of Tammany Hall, and she was not able in her fright to distinguish between the shouts of enemies and the cheers of friends.

THURSDAY, APRIL 10.— Last day of the election; dreadful riots between the Irish and the Americans have again disturbed the public peace. The Mayor arrived with a strong body of watchmen, but they were attacked and overcome, and many of the watchmen are severely wounded. Eight of them were carried to the hospital, where I went to visit them. The Mayor has ordered out Colonel Sanford's regiment and a troop of horse, and proper measures have been taken to preserve order, but we apprehend a dreadful night. This outrage has been instigated by a few men in the sixth ward, — George D. Strong, Abraham LeRoy, Dr. Rhinelander, Preserved Fish, and a few like him. Let them answer for it.

FRIDAY, APRIL 11. — Such an excitement! So wonderful is the result of this election that all New York has been kept in a state of alarm; immense crowds have been collected at Masonic and Tammany Halls, but the greatest concourse was in front of the Exchange. The street was a dense mass of people. Partial returns were coming in every few minutes, and so close has been the vote that the Whigs at the Exchange and the small party for Jackson in front of the office of the "Standard" opposite shouted alternately as the news was favourable to one or the other; and up to the last moment the result was doubtful, when, at the close of the canvass, the majority for Mr. Lawrence, the Jackson candidate, out of the immense number of votes — thirty-five thousand one hundred and forty-one — was found to be one hundred and seventy-nine. There is no doubt, however, that we have elected a majority of aldermen and assistants. The Common Council is reformed, and we shall succeed in the great fall election. It is a signal triumph of good principles over violence, illegal voting, party discipline, and the influence of office-holders.

APRIL 12. — The following gentlemen dined with us, all Whigs, and most of them active men in the late contest; it was a feast of triumph for the result of the election, and we drank success to the cause in the best wine I had to give them: Francis Granger, John Greig, Bryant P. Tilden, of Boston, who has just arrived from Canton, Sydney Brooks, William H. Aspinwall, Simeon Draper, Jr., Charles King, Charles H. Hammond, Isaac S. Hone, Charles H. Russell, and James Monroe.

APRIL 15. — This was the day of the great *fête* at Castle Garden to celebrate the triumph gained by the Whig party in the late charter election in this city, and it went off gloriously. Tens of thousands of freemen, full of zeal and patriotism, filled the area of the castle; every inch of ground was occupied. Tables were spread in a double row within the outer circumference; three pipes of wine and forty barrels of beer were placed in the centre under an awning, and served out during the repast. Many speeches were made, regular and volunteer toasts were drunk, and the beautiful little frigate "Constitution," which has borne so conspicuous a station in the late struggle, was placed upon the top of the building which forms the entrance to the garden, from which she fired a salute during the *fête*. All was enthusiasm, and the shouts from time to time rent the air. But on a signal given the immense concourse broke up in good order, and no excess or rioting marred the pleasure of the day. Six or eight thousand men formed a procession, and marched off the Battery, preceded by a band of music. Of these, a large number went into Greenwich street. Having learned that Mr. Webster (who had declined the invitation of the committee to unite in the celebration at Castle Garden) was on a visit to Mrs. Edgar, they formed in a solid body before the house, and called for him. He made his appearance at one of the windows, and was received with shouts that rent the air. I was admitted through the basement, and having passed through the kitchen, came into the front room as Mr. Webster began to address the multitude. His address was full of fire, and was received with rapturous shouts. After he retired, he was called again, and spoke a few words more, when the mighty mass moved off as they came, with order and propriety. I walked up with him as far as my house. He was engaged to sup with Mr. Samuel Stevens, where I was also invited, but did not go.

<small>Fishing Excursion.</small> APRIL 16. — Giraud and I started this morning on a fishing excursion to Long Island. We dined at Timothy Carman's, where we met John Suydam, Garrit Storm, Edmund Smith, and Augustus Wynkoop. We went on to Snedecor's after dinner, where we found the house so full that if we had not taken the precaution to write in advance for beds, we might have lain on the floor. There was Hamilton Wilkes, William E. Laight, Mr. Kortright, Thomas Morris, Clinton Norton, and several others, some of whom were on their return from the Fire-place. The weather was fine, with southerly wind — a good prospect for fishing.

We came to Sam Carman's at eleven o'clock, and took a good mess of trout. Mr. Suydam and Mr. Storm came to dine with us, Mr. Smith and Mr. Wynkoop having gone down to the bay brant-shooting. They returned to Patchogue after dinner; easterly wind and cold, but the fish are plenty.

SATURDAY. — Cloudy weather and rain part of the morning and a severe thunder-storm in the afternoon. Giraud and I went down the creek with Joe in the boat to fish, and I took some of the largest trout I ever saw. One weighed two pounds seven ounces, and one two pounds. Joe Carman took the largest, weighing two pounds twelve ounces. They were a beautiful sight. We have been rather unfortunate in weather, but I have never seen the fish so fine and so plentiful.

At Home.

WEDNESDAY, APRIL 23. — What a pile of newspapers to read and what a bundle of letters to answer, and how much news to record in this journal! The Whigs of Philadelphia had a grand celebration yesterday at Powelton on the Schuylkill of our late victory. Philadelphia is not the only city which has celebrated our victory. The Whigs of Albany fired one hundred guns. Buffalo made a great affair of it with guns and illuminations. Portsmouth, N.H., received the news with one hundred guns, had a town-meeting, and made speeches. There was also a grand affair at Goshen, which brought all Orange County together. Baltimore is making preparations.

Mr. Leslie, the painter, sailed for England on Wednesday, having resigned the office of professor of drawing in the Military Academy at West Point. On the evening before his departure he met a large party of artists and literary gentlemen, at the rooms of the Academy of Design. I was invited, but it was the evening of the day on which I left town. Weir is an applicant for the office which Leslie has left. I wrote in his behalf to the Secretary of War, who replied to me in the most frank manner, that if the place became vacant Mr. Weir should have the appointment.

MAY 1. — Mr. Astor commenced this morning the demolition of the valuable buildings on the block fronting Broadway from Barclay to Vesey street, on which ground his great hotel is to be erected. The dust and rubbish will be almost intolerable; but the establishment will be a great public advantage, and the edifice an ornament to the city, and for centuries to come will serve, as it was probably intended, as a monument of its wealthy proprietor. I am sorry to observe since Mr. Astor's return from Europe that his health is declining. He appears sickly and feeble, and I have some doubt if he will live to witness the completion of his splendid edifice.

MAY 12. — Cornelius W. Lawrence, the mayor-elect, made his triumphal entry on Saturday. The Tammany party determined to make the most of the little they gained in the late charter election, mustered all their forces, hired a steamboat, and went down to Amboy, where they received their mayor, elected by a majority of one hundred and eighty-one out of thirty-five thousand votes, with colours flying and loud huzzas; had a dinner on board, when Jackson toasts were drunk and Jackson speeches made; and on his landing at Castle Garden he was placed in a barouche with four white horses, and attended by Walter Bowne, Stephen Allen, Preserved Fish, and two or three hundred of their followers, paraded through the streets. I pity poor Lawrence sincerely. He is not suited to such things, and will not be suited to the office into which they are about to thrust him. He was uncomfortable in his seat in Congress: there was (as my late venerable friend Dr. Stanford once told me) a pin in the cushion; but he will find pins and thorns enough in that which he is to assume to-morrow, and I am mistaken in the man if he will not consider the shouts of a set of mere party demagogues a poor compensation for the forfeiture of the good opinion of that part of his fellow-citizens with whom he has hitherto associated.

MAY 13. — The following gentlemen dined with us: Lord Powerscourt, Jacob Harvey, Mr. Parnell, George Barclay, Captain Campbell, John Laurie, Capt. H. Hamilton, Henry Cary. Lord Powerscourt, who has just arrived in the United States, is a young Irish lord only nineteen years of age. He appears to be modest and intelligent. We were much pleased with him at dinner. His travelling companion, Mr. Parnell, also a young man, is a nephew of Sir Henry Parnell.

MAY 15. — The unsightly wooden railings in the park have been removed and chestnut posts erected in their place, from which iron chains are to be appended, which will improve the prospect from my house. Mr. Astor's buildings are nearly all removed; the dust from the immense mass of rubbish has been almost intolerable for the last fortnight, and the crowds who promenade Broadway are compelled, like many of the politicians of the present day, to change sides, with this difference, that the one comes over to my side and the other leaves it.

MAY 20. — Something in Major Downing's style. Two or three of us were talking together yesterday morning on board the steamboat and, as is the fashion now-a-days, abusing General Jackson, and marvelling at the undeserved popularity which he still enjoys in some parts of our country, when the subject was illustrated by Colonel Worth in the following story: On the arrival of the stage in one of the towns in the interior of Pennsylvania, during the President's far-famed journey to the East, the crowd assembled in the bar-room of the tavern collected around the driver with the usual inquiry, " What news? " — " Why, haven't you heard ? " said the waggish driver. " The General made his grand entry into Philadelphia yesterday in a barouche drawn by four gray horses; and the crowd pressing around him so as to obstruct his progress, he just stepped out of the carriage, drew his sword, and run one fellow clean through the body." — " The darned fool," exclaimed one of the auditors, " why didn't he stand out of the General's way ! "

MAY 31. — Having been invited with a number of the stockholders of the Boston and Providence Railroad Company to attend the opening of a part of the road and the meeting for the election of directors on Wednesday, I availed myself of the occasion to carry into effect an excursion to New Hampshire, Maine, and the White Hills. I brought with me my daughter Margaret and Joanna Anthon, and we embarked on board the fine steamboat " Boston," the accommodations of which are at least equal to any on the Hudson river. She has a round-house and pleasant staterooms on the upper deck, one of which was occupied by the girls.

BOSTON, JUNE 1. — The position of Newport is superb, and I was surprised to find it so large a town. The ride to Boston is beautiful; we came through Dedham, by Roxbury and the Neck, and could not avoid being delighted with the view of the fine country, good roads, magnificent country-seats and neat cottages, notwithstanding it rained the whole afternoon. We got to Boston at seven o'clock, and dined at the Tremont House, where excellent quarters had been provided by the attention of Mr. Belknap, who called immediately to see us, and my reverend and excellent friend Dr. Wainwright sat half an hour with us.

JUNE 2. — The storm is over, and this morning we assembled in our pleasant parlour which overlooks the extensive cemetery of Park-street church and its ancient elms. We arrived at Sharon, where we met the railroad party, consisting of Messrs. Woolsey, Townsend, and Russell, of New York; Jackson, Wales, Thomas, and George Perkins; Loring, Moran, Rivière, and others from Boston; and Ives and Potter from Providence, with the gentlemen of the engineer department. We sat down to a good dinner provided for the occasion, with excellent wines, which had been brought from Boston. We left Sharon, and after viewing several important points on the railroad, returned to Boston at nine o'clock. I then went to the Mayor's, General Lyman, who gave a *soirée* to the civil and military characters on the occasion of the annual election of the artillery company, where I met the Governor of the State, Mr. John Davis, a distinguished man, and Mr. Armstrong, the Lieutenant-Governor, with whom I was much pleased; and many others whom it was well to know. Mr. Davis has been recently elected, and the State lost a most excellent and valuable representative in Congress when they gained in him a good governor.

JUNE 3. — The railroad party assembled at the depot to make an excursion on the road; but there was some deficiency in the locomotive engine, and the affair was postponed until to-morrow. Many of our friends called upon us during the morning, and after dinner Mr. William Appleton called in his carriage, and we took one of those beautiful drives with which the environs of Boston abound. We crossed the bridge to Cambridge, saw the colleges, and went to Mount Auburn, the great cemetery of Boston, from which it is distant about five miles. After leaving Mount Auburn we drove to Bunker's Hill. The monument which was begun with so much spirit eight or nine years ago on the spot where Warren fell, and where Great Britain was first taught to respect the energy and devotion of a people determined to be free, is still unfinished. It was commenced, as such things usually are in this country, upon too large a scale; the funds have run out, and it will require fresh exertions and a new impulse to finish it upon the original plan.

JUNE 4. — The directors and a number of invited gentlemen met at the depot of the company at nine o'clock and made the first trip on the railroad, under the direction of Captain McNeill, the chief engineer, and his assistants. The train of carriages was attached to a locomotive, and we went on very well to within a short distance of Dedham, where a collation was provided, with champagne, punch, etc. While we were partaking of this, the engineers indulged the country folk, — men, women, and children, — by riding them on the road a few miles, after which we returned at an accelerated speed, and came in town, ten miles, in twenty-five minutes.

JUNE 6. — The girls and I dined with Mr. Harrison G. Otis and Mrs. Ritchie, his daughter. They had an exceedingly agreeable party to meet us, and our dinner was pleasant as possible. We went from Mrs. Otis's to a party at Mr. William Sullivan's, where we found pleasant company and good music. Mr. Sullivan got a bottle of Eclipse wine for my special benefit, of which I had to drink two or three glasses, notwithstanding the copious libations to which I had been tempted where I dined. This Eclipse wine was imported into Boston in 1806, and arrived at the moment of the great solar eclipse, to which circumstance it owes its name, although it might claim it upon the ground of its eclipsing almost all other wines. I think it is perfection.

DOVER, N. H., JUNE 9. — We finished our delightful visit at Boston, and came away in the stage at eight o'clock this morning. Came to Newburyport, by Salem, thirty-five miles, to dinner. Then to Portsmouth. The Rockingham House has been lately fitted up. It was formerly the residence of Mr. Woodbury Langdon, father of the gentleman who married Miss Astor.

JUNE 14. — The old Yankee character appears to me to be nearly extinct. I have taken pains to bring out some originals among the persons I have met since we left Boston; I have found them generally civil and obliging and disposed to be communicative, but there are no oddities such as we used to meet in former days. The march of refinement and the progress of improvement which has substituted cotton-mills and railroads for mountains and cataracts has made men ashamed of those broad lines of national character which became them so well.

NEW YORK, JUNE 21. — The mail brought the "Journal of Commerce" of yesterday, which announces the arrival of the packet-ship "Silas Richards," bringing news from England to the 24th of May. My venerable friend Lafayette died at his house, Rue d'Anjou, a few minutes before five o'clock in the morning of the 20th of May, in the seventy-seventh year of his age.

Death of Lafayette.

JUNE 25. — The ceremonies in honour of Lafayette took place to-day under direction of a joint committee of the Common Council. It was the last tribute of New York to the last major-general of the Continental army, the hero of the American Revolution, the ardent apostle of liberty, the benevolent, the virtuous Lafayette, and everything was done as it should have been. An urn, covered by the wings of the American eagle, well done in bronze plaster, was drawn by four white horses in the centre of a hollow square formed by the Lafayette Guards and followed by the pall-bearers in barouches. These were members of the Cincinnati, associates of Lafayette in the War of the Revolution, and their selection was left with delicacy and good taste, by the committee, to the society. They consisted of the following: Major-General Morgan, Col. John Trumbull, Col. Simeon DeWitt, Maj. Samuel Cooper, Col. William North, Maj. William Popham, Col. John Van Dyke, and Capt. Nathaniel Norton.

JULY 10. — Our city last evening was the scene of disgraceful riots. The first was at the Bowery Theatre. An actor by the name of Farren, whose benefit it was, had made himself obnoxious by some ill-natured reflections upon the country, which called down the vengeance of the mob, who seemed determined to deserve the bad name which he had given them. An hour after the performance commenced the mob broke open the doors, took possession of every part of the house, committed every species of outrage, hissed and pelted poor Hamblin, not regarding the talisman which he relied upon, the American flag, which he waved over his head. This they disregarded, because the hand which held it was that of an Englishman, and they would listen to nobody but "American Forrest." He assured them that the object of their rage, Mr. Farren, had made a hasty exit, and the mob retired to enact a more disgraceful scene in another quarter.

Abolition Meetings.
There has been of late great excitement in consequence of the proceedings of a set of fanatics who are determined to emancipate all the slaves by a *coup de main*, and have held meetings in which black men and women have been introduced. These meetings have been attended with tumult and violence, especially one which was held on Friday evening at the Chatham-street Chapel. Arthur Tappan and his brother Lewis have been conspicuous in these proceedings, and the mob last night, after exhausting their rage at the Bowery Theatre, went down in a body to the house of the latter gentleman in Rose street, broke into the house, destroyed the windows, and made a bonfire of the furniture in the street. The police at length interfered, rather tardily, I should think; but the diabolical spirit which prompted this outrage is not quenched, and I apprehend we shall see more of it.

JULY 18. — Edmund Charles Genet died on Wednesday last at his residence at Schodack, Rensselaer County. He was at one time an important personage. He came as minister of the French Republic to this country, and acted as became the representative of the madmen who, under the name of liberty, were destroying their country and crushing the people. Nothing but the firmness of Washington prevented Genet from enlisting the people of this country in the cause of the French mob, and nothing but the personal character of the saviour of his country could have availed to check the madness of the people. Genet was recalled on the downfall of his party; but as he had no fancy to risk the separation of his head from his shoulders, he stayed where he was, married a daughter of Governor Clinton (the elder), and became an American citizen, and, I suspect, from his visionary notions, rather a troublesome one to the neighbourhood in which he resided.

JULY 22. — Mr. Frelinghuysen has been received with distinguished honours on his return to his own State; and Mr. Sprague, of Maine, another of the worthies of the Senate, has made a triumphant journey through Portsmouth, N.H., and was received in the most flattering manner at Portland; and his entry into his own town, Hallowell, was marked with the ringing of the bells, firing of cannon, and patriotic addresses; flags and streamers were displayed from the houses, and among the mottoes the following prevailed, "I am no man's man."

AUGUST 22. — The spirit of riot and insubordination to the laws which lately prevailed in New York has made its appearance in the orderly city of Philadelphia, and appears to have been produced by causes equally insignificant, — hostility to the blacks and an indiscriminate persecution of all whose skins were darker than those of their enlightened fellow-citizens. A most disgraceful riot also occurred on the night of Monday, the 11th, at Charlestown, near Boston. The populace having been deceived by ill-designing persons into an erroneous belief that a young lady was confined against her will in the Ursuline Convent, a highly respectable seminary under the charge of the Roman Catholics, made an attack upon the convent, a noble edifice near Charlestown, and the other buildings belonging to the sisterhood, and burned them to the ground with all the valuable

Riot in Boston.

furniture, desecrated the cemetery, and committed every species of outrage. This act has caused great excitement in Boston. A meeting was immediately held in Faneuil Hall, at which the most distinguished citizens of all parties attended. Resolutions were adopted reprobating in the strongest terms the unworthy conduct of their neighbours. The Mayor presided, and all the magistrates assisted in the proceedings. Large rewards were offered for the apprehension of the persons concerned in the riot. The venerable Bishop Fenwick of the Catholic Church succeeded in casting the holy oil of his eloquence upon the furious waves which were about rising in his excitable congregation, and the consequences were less serious than at first apprehended. The active and prompt measures which were adopted led to the apprehension of several of the ringleaders, who await their trial.

Rockaway. We had on Sunday last a visit from a party of gentlemen in the new steam-brig belonging to Mr. Cunard, of Halifax, which lately came out from England. She anchored abreast of the Pavilion, and Messrs. Cunard, Cochran, Charles McEvers, Brooks, and Dennistoun came ashore in the boat, and landed in the surf.

HYDE PARK, SUNDAY, SEPT. 14. — We left Albany at half-past six this morning in the steamboat "Champlain." There is a violent opposition between two lines of boats. The fare to New York is fifty cents. We were contending with the "Nimrod" all the way down, and for five or six miles before we reached Hyde Park landing, the boats were in contact, both pushing furiously at the top of their speed, and we and our trunks were pitched ashore like bundles of hay. The people at the landing being all in favour of the opposition, except Dr. Hosack himself, nobody would take a line, and we might have drowned without an arm being reached to save us.

At Home. SEPTEMBER 16. — We left Hyde Park and came on board the "Champion," an opposition boat, at half-past twelve o'clock. The "Albany" passed the landing a few minutes in advance, but did not stop. Our boat had three or four hundred passengers, and such a set of ragtag and bobtail I never saw on board a North-river steamboat — the effect of the fifty-cent system. If the people do not rise in their might and put a stop to the racing and opposition, it will be better to return to the primitive mode of travelling in Albany sloops. I would rather consume three or four days in the voyage, than be made to fly in fear and trembling, subject to every sort of discomfort, with my life at the mercy of a set of fellows whose only object is to drive their competitors off the river.

OCTOBER 3. — Party-spirit runs exceedingly high in every part of our country. Timid people begin to be afraid of the consequences of the struggle which is soon to take place, by which the question will be determined whether General Jackson, by the aid of his interested advisers, can sustain himself in his unconstitutional assumption of power, and perpetuate it in the election of his favourite, the heir presumptive, Mr. Van Buren, or whether the people, by a great and simultaneous effort, shall burst their shackles, rescue the Constitution, and stand once more erect in their majesty, free and disenthralled.

OCTOBER 4. — The country is on the eve of a great political contest. The party in power, consisting of office-holders and their dependants, supported by the public moneys over which they have usurped the control, and relying upon the personal popularity of the President, — impaired certainly, but still exercising an unaccountable influence over the minds of the people, — will fight hard and take many hard blows before they surrender their power. On the other hand, the Whigs are cool, determined, and willing to go all lawful and reasonable lengths to bring about a state of things more honourable to the country and advantageous to the people. This month and the next the elections will take place by which this important question will be decided. Pennsylvania elects in a few weeks, and our general election in this State comes on in November. We have little or no hope of the former, but New York looks well, and the Whigs have good hopes of success.

SUNDAY, OCT. 12. — I went this morning with my daughter to the Church du St. Esprit at the corner of Church and Leonard streets, the first service since its consecration. The corner-stone of the old church in Pine street was laid one hundred and thirty years ago. It was originally a Calvinist church, and continued so until Mr. Elias Desbrosses, a member of the church, left it a rich legacy, on condition of its joining the Protestant Episcopal communion, since which it has been Episcopal.

Matthews.
OCTOBER 14. — Matthews made his first appearance last evening at the Park, in his entertainment of the "Comic Annual" and "Mons. Morbleu," and was well received by one of the greatest houses I have ever seen. There was a design to make a row, and a number of disorderly fellows collected for that purpose, instigated by placards which had been placed during the day on the corners of the streets, denouncing Matthews as a libeller of our country and as having ridiculed us in one of his pieces performed in England after his last visit to America. This ridiculous attempt of some enemy of the Park Theatre to excite the bad feelings of a set of disorderly young men, who stand ready for any kind of mischief, whether it be to attack theatres, desecrate churches, assault Whigs, or murder negroes, was met with a determined spirit of opposition by a most respectable audience, who received Matthews on his return to our stage with such a burst of applause, that the instigators of mischief had not a chance to put in a single hiss in abatement, and the performance went off without interruption.

OCTOBER 18. — The election in New Jersey has gone against the Whigs, notwithstanding our shouts on the receipt of the first returns. All the counties nearest to New York returned large Whig majorities, and those were of course first heard from; but the news has been different from that part of the State bordering on Pennsylvania, so that the whole result gives something more than one thousand majority for the Jackson worshippers. We have lost the State, it is said, from the opposition of the Hicksites, one of the contending sects of the Quakers with whom that part of the State abounds. They have recently been engaged in a lawsuit with the orthodox party for the possession of certain property belonging to the Society of Friends, in which Mr. Frelinghuysen was professionally engaged against them. His term in the Senate of the United States is about to expire, and the Legislature now elected will have the appointment of a successor. Mr. Frelinghuysen would have been reappointed if the Whigs had succeeded, and these Hicksites, in a spirit unworthy of their professions of meekness and disregard of worldly politics, have deprived the State of the services of one of its most virtuous and enlightened statesmen, and prevented the success of a party who seek only to restore to the country its just rights and preserve the purity of our republican institutions. When these people are called upon to perform the civil duties required of them in common with other citizens, they are restrained by the rules of their order. When the country is in danger they cannot fight because their religion forbids them to carry arms, and yet, forsooth, they may interfere in elections, and bringing their petty squabbles to the polls, decide the contest in favour of a party who have no object but to strengthen the power of a *military ruler*, and blindly support his arbitrary measures.

OCTOBER 23.— The Whig nominating committee agreed last evening upon their tickets, but the rank and file out-of-doors object to one or two of the nominees for Congress; not that they are not good enough, but too good. The proceedings are to be reviewed this evening; the times are critical; a tremendous struggle is at hand, and most important consequences will result from the approaching election, and all personal feelings and predilections must be sacrificed for the success of our party, which we say involves the public good. We must discard all other considerations, and without committing ourselves to vote for unworthy persons, run only such as will obtain the most votes. Our folks are not so well drilled as their opponents; they will think for themselves, not, like them, go straight forward, right or wrong, as they are bidden.

Jackson Triumphs and Merchants' Meeting. MONDAY, OCT. 27. — Both parties have been hurrahing to-day at the top of their voices, — the Whigs for the victories they have won, and the Jackson men that they have lost no more. The latter rallied their forces in the upper wards from Brooklyn and all other places where numbers without regard to quality could be obtained, and marched them down to Castle Garden, where a feast (not of reason) was prepared, and a flow of whiskey (not of soul) was served out gratuitously to the well-drilled troops of the regency. They fired guns and exhibited fireworks, and all in the way of rejoicing for victories *not* won, or rather, "to keep their spirits up by pouring spirits down." Among other causes of rejoicing, as set forth in the summons to attend, was the triumph of the administration party in Ohio; but, unfortunately, the news of the day seems to leave little doubt of the Whigs having gained the election in that great and patriotic State; but the guns, nevertheless, were fired, the whiskey drunk, the congratulatory speeches made, and the hurrahs for Ohio rent ·the air, exactly according to the programme prepared at Tammany Hall.

The merchants had a great meeting at the Exchange, — a great Whig meeting in numbers, respectability, enthusiasm, and zeal, equal to any of those which were held in the same place previous to the Spring election, and which led the way then to such encouraging results. There was no falling off there, " my countrymen." I was unprepared to speak, but was compelled to go forward by a loud and unanimous call from all parts of the room; but I did not regret it, for it was one of the few cases in which I succeeded in satisfying myself, and judging by the applause I received I was not alone in my opinion. What a comforting thing it is to have a good opinion of one's self!

OCTOBER 30. — The following gentlemen dined with us: Mr. Charles Matthews, George Blake, of Boston, F. G. Halleck, Charles A. Davis, Washington Irving, William H. Maxwell, Thomas W. Moore, James Monroe, Isaac S. Hone, Henry Hone. Matthews was exceedingly agreeable. He did not sing or recite, as he was wont to do at dinner-parties, but he talked a great deal and with great enthusiasm, and introduced occasionally some good stories and amusing imitations, particularly of Curran, Shiel, O'Connell, and other eloquent Irishmen, in order to illustrate the different kinds of Irish brogue. He is admirable in his Irish and French characters in such a company as we had this evening. His intonations, so rich, the versatility of voice to suit his different characters, and the admirable expression of his countenance, all tell with powerful effect at my round-table, but are spread over too large a surface in the theatre, and lost to a large proportion of the audience. He complains of this himself. The Adelphi Theatre in London, where he performed, is not more than one-third of the size of the Park, and he acknowledges the difficulty he has in giving proper effect to his good sayings in so large a space and before so numerous an audience.

OCTOBER 31. — The Whigs are raising liberty-poles in all the wards. I went to one of those ceremonies yesterday in the tenth ward, at the corner of the Bowery and Hester street. The pole, one hundred feet high, with a splendid cap and gilt vane with suitable devices, was escorted by a procession of good men and true on horseback, and was received at the place of its destination by an immense collection of good-looking Whigs, each of whom appeared inspired by patriotic feelings and a fixed determination to do his duty in the approaching contest. I came away before the affair was over, finding that it was expected of me to make a speech, which would have interfered with my engagements at home.

NOVEMBER 3. — First day of the great election in the State of New York, which is to decide whether the principles of General Jackson are approved and ratified by the people, and whether Mr.

Van Buren is to be his successor; for these important questions are left to the decision of this State, and the test will be the result of the election. Both parties here are confident; but the confidence of the Whigs has gained strength daily for the last two or three weeks, and our success in Ohio, which is now certain, has conduced much to it.

TUESDAY, Nov. 4. — The election continues with spirit. The weather is fine, as it was yesterday, and contrary to the apprehensions of many of our citizens, we have had no riots or serious disturbance as yet. This is principally owing to the excellent arrangement of the inspectors, a majority of whom, in each ward, are Whigs; to the precautionary measures of the Mayor; and above all to the awe with which the mob have been impressed by the determination of the better sort of people of all parties to prevent, at all hazards, a repetition of such scenes as disgraced our city in the Spring, and more recently and to a greater degree, our neighbours in Philadelphia. In the course of the evening an immense collection of Whigs from Masonic Hall went in a body to Washington Hall, where Mr. Webster lodges, and saluted him with cheers; after some time he came out and made them a short and eloquent speech.

WEDNESDAY, Nov. 5. — The election closed this evening. The Governor's votes were canvassed in all the wards except the sixth, and by nine o'clock enough was known to satisfy us to our heart's content that we are beaten, — badly beaten; worse than the least sanguine of us anticipated. The majority in our wards (with the exception of the 15th) have fallen off grievously, and theirs have increased in an equal ratio; the third ward has fallen off two hundred from the Spring election. The Tories will have between two and three thousand majority.

THURSDAY, Nov. 6. — The triumph was celebrated last night by the worshippers of Jackson with the refinement and forbearance which might have been expected. I had been taken in the morning with an attack of vertigo and headache, which confined me to the house nearly the whole day, but I made out to walk up in the evening to Masonic Hall, where the news I received was not calculated to make me feel better. I returned home much indisposed, and retired to bed at an early hour, where I was kept awake during the greater part of the night by the unmanly insults of the ruffian crew from Tammany Hall, who came over to my door every half-hour and saluted me with groans and hisses. This continued until past three o'clock, and for what? Because I have exercised the right which, in common with every American citizen, I enjoy (or have enjoyed until this time), of expressing my disapprobation of a course of measures which I conceive to be dangerous to the liberties of the people, and inimical to the free institutions of my native land. This I have done with truth, zeal, and firmness, but always, I trust, with decorum and propriety; and for this I have been insulted and annoyed. I have for many years sacrificed my comfort, exhausted my time, and abridged my enjoyments by a devotion to the service of my fellow-citizens. A member of all the public institutions, charitable, public-spirited, or patriotic, where time was to be lost, labour performed, and no pay to be had; my own affairs neglected, and my money frequently poured out like water; the friend and patron of the working-men, without regard to party; — and now my reward is found in the revilings of a mob of midnight ruffians, among whom, I have no doubt, were some of the very men whom I have assisted to support, to the exclusion of others who are proud to acknowledge themselves my personal and political friends. I believe I am rightly served.

I dined with Mr. David S. Jones. Mr. Webster was one of the party, and notwithstanding the sad disappointment which, in common with his political friends (but in a greater degree), he has just now experienced, he was in the vein to be exceedingly pleasant, and I have not in many a day enjoyed a more delightful conversation.

NOVEMBER 10. — I apprehend that Mr. Van Buren and his friends have no permanent cause of triumph in their victory. They have succeeded by the means of instruments which may work their own destruction; they have mounted a vicious horse, who, taking the bit in his mouth, will run away with him. The agrarian party, who have had things pretty much their own way, will not stop at Martin Van Buren, — they will dig deeper into the swamps of political depravity, and the good men of our community, the supporters of the Constitution, and the true friends of civil liberty may be soon called upon to unite in his favour, against a worse man and principles more dangerous than his. This battle had been fought upon the ground of the poor against the rich, and this unworthy prejudice, this dangerous delusion, has been encouraged by the leaders of the triumphant party, and fanned into a flame by the polluted breath of the hireling press in their employ. In the saturnalian orgies with which our streets have been disgraced, the unmannerly epithets which were so liberally bestowed upon myself and other peaceable citizens for having exercised the privilege of freemen in opposing a party whose political doctrines we thought unfavourable to the true interests of the nation, the cry of "Down with the aristocracy!" mingled with the shouts of victory, and must have grated on the ears of some of their own leaders like the croaking of the evil-boding raven. They have succeeded in raising this dangerous spirit, and have gladly availed themselves of its support to accomplish a temporary object; but can they allay it at pleasure? Will their voices be heard when they cry "Thus far shalt thou go and no farther"? Eighteen thousand men in New York have voted for the high-priest of the party whose professed design is to bring down the property, the talents, the industry, the steady habits of that class which constituted the real strength of the Commonwealth, to the common level of the idle, the worthless, and the unenlightened. Look to it, ye men of respectability in the Jackson party, are ye not afraid of the weapons ye have used in this warfare? It is idle to plead the necessity of the case, the force of what you call regular nominations. How came this power so strong among ye? Where was the influence of the Allens and the Bownes, the Bloodgoods and the Alleys, the Phelps and the Van Schaicks, when the disciples of this man came among ye, and made the walls of old Tammany resound with his appalling dictum? The dose was unpalatable, but you swallowed it.

NOVEMBER 12. — I went to the opera, where I saw the second act of "La Straniera," by Bellini. The house is as pretty as ever, and the same faces were seen in the boxes as formerly; but it is not a popular entertainment, and will not be in our day, I fear. The opera did not please me. There was too much recitation, and I shall never discipline my taste to like common colloquial expressions of life, "How do you do, madam?" or, "Pretty well, I thank you, sir," the better for being given with an orchestral accompaniment.

NOVEMBER 13. — There is some salt left in the land, — the late general election in Massachusetts has gone for the Whigs by unprecedented majorities. Governor Davis will be reëlected by an immense vote. Abbott Lawrence goes to Congress from Boston.

Massachusetts.

NOVEMBER 21. — The President, since he came into office in 1829, has had four secretaries of state, two of war, five of the treasury, three of the navy, and three attorney-generals. Tyrants are fickle in the choice of servants.

NOVEMBER 22. — Power had his benefit last night. He appeared in Rover, in "Wild Oats," and a piece called "Botheration." It was a good house. In the last piece a little row was raised by accident. Ritchings, speaking of a lady who wore a wig, says wigs are out of date. This touched a sore place, and was received with applause by one party in the pit and disapprobation by the other, and the clamour became so long and loud that Ritchings was under the necessity of coming forward and disclaiming all intention of alluding to the political party called Whigs, who, although defeated, are not willing to acknowledge themselves "out of date."

NOVEMBER 24. — The fine old frigate "Constellation" arrived at Norfolk on Thursday, in thirty-eight days from Gibraltar, after a cruise of several years in the Mediterranean. She was one of the

three ships built in the year 1797, "Old Ironsides" and the
"United States" being the other two. She is now commanded by
my gallant friend, George C. Read. Commodore Patterson, in the
"Delaware," was on the coast of Syria, and Ballard, in the
"United States," at Smyrna, giving convoy to American vessels.
The "Constellation" has brought over two fine marble statues, by
Louis Persico, emblematical of peace and war, intended to ornament the Capitol of the United States, accompanied by the artist,
who has also a bust of the hero, General Jackson, who can regulate both peace and war, and carry the Capitol away in his pocket,
or set fire to it with his pipe, if he chooses. The "Constellation"
is ordered around to Washington with these sculptural trophies. I
would advise the "greatest and best" to have his counterfeit representation set up in one of the high places to receive the homage of
his liege subjects, a majority of whom are unhappily more willing
to bow to him or his image than even his own vanity may prompt
him to exact from them.

NOVEMBER 29. — The refusal of the French Chamber of Deputies to vote the supplies necessary to carry into effect Mr. Rives's
treaty of indemnity for spoliations committed under the reign of
Napoleon, begins to cause an apprehension that our government
may find it necessary to pursue a course of hostility to coerce
France into the performance of obligations freely entered into by
her, and the stipulations of which on the part of this country have
been carried into effect with good faith. Congress is to meet on
Monday, and the expectation of a hostile tone of the President's
message is so great that the sailing of the Liverpool packet of the
first of December is delayed until the third, to enable her to carry
out that document. Restrictions on the trade between this country and France would be agreeable news for John Bull. The
American ladies must have silk dresses to exhibit in Broadway and
Chestnut street, and if France should be interdicted from supply-
ing us with the material it would occasion an accelerated motion
of the shuttles of Spitalfields. It is to be hoped, however, that the

matter may be settled without a serious misunderstanding. Mr. Rives's five millions are hardly worth going to war about, unless there should be some point of national honour so deeply involved as to forbid a calculation of dollars and cents. Louis Philippe does not seem to have sufficient power over the Chamber of Deputies. He is only a king; it would be well for him to take advice from our President touching the manner of rendering the representatives of the people, so called, subservient to his wishes.

DECEMBER 3. — Yesterday at noon the President's message was communicated to both Houses, and it was in New York at two o'clock this morning, having been brought on by express, in little more than twelve hours, two hundred and thirty miles. This is a great performance, and shows what money can do; but *cui bono?* the game is not worth the candle. There is not one reader of the daily papers out of a hundred who would give sixpence to read this document four hours earlier than he otherwise might, and the express in this instance is said to have cost seven hundred dollars. The message is, as usual, too long; but the people have become accustomed to take these annual outpourings of executive wet-nurses in pretty large doses, and rely more upon the efficacy of a bottle of Congress water than on the concentrated virtue of a Seidlitz-powder; and so Dr. Jackson, who can make his patients swallow anything, has, by the aid of his regular-bred practitioners in the study, and the green-apron boys below, managed to give the body politic enough to insure tolerable regularity until his next regular visit. This message is interesting principally from the view it takes of our relations with France, with whom we have a knotty question which may ultimately lead to something serious, and I must say that on this subject the message is quite satisfactory; its explanations are clear, its language dignified, and its sentiment manly and patriotic. The negotiations of Mr. Rives, for indemnification for the spoliations of France committed during the reign of Napoleon, resulted in a treaty signed at Paris on the 4th of July, 1831, by which France agreed to liquidate all our claims by the payment of twenty-five millions of francs, in six annual payments. This treaty was duly ratified in Washington on the 2d of February, 1832, and acts were passed by Congress to reduce the duties on French wines, agreeably to the stipulations on our part, which have been continued in good faith. In the mean time the Chamber of Deputies delayed from time to time to make the necessary appropriations for carrying the treaty into effect; the draft of the government for the first annual instalment which was negotiated through the Bank of the United States was returned protested, and finally the last action of the Chamber of Deputies, in the month of April last, nearly three years after the signing of the treaty, resulted in their refusal to make the appropriation. And so the matter stands. All this is fairly laid down in the message in a manner creditable to the President and his Cabinet; but I do not approve the conclusion he comes to. He asks Congress to give him power to issue letters of marque and reprisals which cannot fail to be considered by the French Government as a menace, and will, I fear, counteract the good effects of the firm but courteous style in which our claims for justice are set forth in the message, and weaken our cause with the lookers-on in other countries. Besides, I am not one of those who wish to place power in the hands of the President, and I almost wonder that he should have thought it necessary to ask for it, after some of his late experiments, which must have satisfied him that he may take what power he pleases and the people will bear him out in it. The Constitution and the laws may stand in his way, to be sure, but those are trifles. Andrew Jackson, depending upon his popularity with the Jackson party, is superior to the petty trammels which restrained the Washingtons, the Jeffersons, and the Madisons of former times. The Jackson party are in the majority. They will support him right or wrong, and it was very pretty behaved, but altogether supererogatory to ask the leave of Congress, to do this or anything else he may think proper. William III. or Louis Philippe may require legislative sanction; they are only kings; give me the president of a republican people for a bold stroke of power. General Jackson's *coup d'état* would not endanger his standing with the people, much less cost him his crown, as it did that loving, but less fortunate brother, Charles X. The language of the message in relation to the Bank of the United States is disgraceful to the President and humiliating to every American. It smells of the kitchen, and resembles no more that in which the foreign relations of the country are laid before the people than a scullion does a gentleman. The language is intemperate, the charges against the bank false and disingenuous, and the measures recommended injurious to the public interest.

DECEMBER 6. — Chancellor and Mrs. Kent and some other friends took tea with us. They came soon after six o'clock, and we passed a most delightful evening. The Chancellor was gay, cheerful, and talkative, and not restless as he is wont to be. I would "that Heaven had made *me* such a man." This excellent man is in his seventy-second year, having been born July 31, 1763, with his mental faculties unimpaired and still improving, by a constant but not laborious employment of them in pursuits which constitute his greatest pleasure and recreation. His constitution sound, the happy result of good habits and a cheerful disposition, and the consciousness of purity of heart and uniformly virtuous intentions. I do not know so perfect a model as Chancellor Kent, or a man so much to be envied. I wonder how he came in these artificial days to hit upon so sensible a way to pass an evening.

1835.

THE new year commences auspiciously so far as the weather is concerned. There has never been a finer New Year's Day; the air is clear and pleasant, and just cool enough to preserve the snow, which gives facility to the visiting part of the population. I went out in the sleigh at twelve o'clock, and visited until four, leaving several of my visits unpaid, which delinquency my wife and I made up in the evening. Broadway, from morning until night, and in the night too, was crowded with pedestrians, and the music of sleigh-bells was heard without the least intermission. Smiling faces were seen on all sides, and all the cares and troubles of 1834 appear to have been forgotten in the joyful anticipations of 1835. The year which has commenced seems destined to be an eventful one, at home and abroad. The administration of General Jackson and the continuance of his popularity will test the strength of our political institutions. If the people continue to support him in his most unwarrantable assumption of power, it will be idle to talk about the republican principles on which the government is founded. But among other difficulties which he has to encounter during the coming year is that of the quarrel with France, in which his unnecessary threats have involved us. The king is disposed to do us justice; but the Chamber of Deputies, composed of men who like bullying themselves, will not submit to the bullying of others, and I fear that our government has been committed by the President too far to admit of any peaceable compromise. The wisdom of Congress may save us, and it certainly would, if party-spirit had not more influence than a regard for the true interest of the country. But to the Senate we may yet look for patriotism and public virtue, and there we rest our cause.

JANUARY 5.—Extracts from the commonplace-book of this lady (now Mrs. Butler) are published in one of the Boston papers and copied occasionally into the "Commercial Advertiser" of this city. How they got there it is impossible to say. Cary & Lea, of Philadelphia, say in an advertisement that if they are genuine they must have been stolen, for they are the only legal proprietors of the work in this country. At any rate, if she has any good feelings, and is at all tenacious of her good name as a lady or an authoress, it must be "a sorry sight" to see herself thus served up to the public gaze. There is all the light gossip, the childish prejudice, the hasty conclusions from erroneous first impressions, in which the diary of an imaginative youthful traveller in a country in which all things are new and untried may be supposed to abound; and the style is sometimes bad; and the remarks she makes on the private habits of persons who received her and her father kindly, and treated them hospitably, are all in bad taste. As a literary production it is unworthy of the character of Fanny Kemble, and its publication, now that she has become the wife of an American gentleman and is to remain among us, injudicious in the extreme. I cannot believe that she ever intended it should see the light, and should be led to believe it a fabrication were it not that the facts related are true (many of them within my own knowledge), and of a nature to preclude the possibility of their becoming public without her knowledge and consent. For instance, she gives the following account of the dinner I gave to her and her father on the 15th of September, 1832, — the first occasion on which she was introduced into American society. It was evidently written on the evening of the very day, and with all the flippancy and want of reflection that one might expect to find in the commonplace-book of a giddy girl who had just returned from a dinner-party in which herself was the principal object of notice and attention, and from which, I can tell her, she went away leaving no very favourable impressions behind her. Now, if Mrs. Butler participated in the publication of all this tittle-

[margin note:] Fanny Kemble.

tattle she is a greater fool than ever I expected it would fall to my lot to record her. Well was it said, " Oh, that mine enemy would write a book !" Mrs. Butler says:

"Saturday, 15th.— At five dressed and went to ——, where we were to dine. This is one of the first houses here" (thank you, madam !), "so I conclude that I am to consider what I see as a tolerable sample of the ways and manners of being, doing, and *suffering* of the best society in New York. There were about twenty people. The women were in a sort of French demi-toilette, with bare necks and long sleeves, heads frizzled out after the very last petit-courier, and thread-net handkerchiefs and capes, the whole of which, to my English eye, appeared a strange marrying of incongruities. . . . The younger daughter of our host is beautiful, — a young and brilliant likeness of Ellen Tree ; with more refinement, and a smile that was, not to say a ray, but a whole focus of sun-rays, — a perfect blaze of light ; she was much taken up with a youth, to whom, my neighbour at dinner informed me, she was engaged."

I can excuse many of her impertinences for this glowing and just eulogium upon my sweet Mary. The following contrast between the delicate and interesting appearance of the ladies and the ruddy looks of English women are, unhappily, not far from the truth : —

" The women here, like those of most warm climates, ripen very early and decay proportionately soon. They are, generally speaking, pretty, with good complexions, and an air of freshness and brilliancy, but this, I am told, is very evanescent ; and whereas, in England, a woman is in the bloom of health and beauty from twenty-five to thirty, here they scarcely reach the first period without being faded and looking old. They marry very young, and this is another reason why age comes prematurely upon them. There was a fair young thing at dinner to-day who did not look above seventeen, and she is a wife." (Mrs. Alexander Hosack, I presume.) " As for their figures, like those of

French women, they were too well dressed for one to judge what they really are like; they are, for the most part, short and slight, with remarkably pretty feet and ankles; but there's too much pelerine and petticoat and *de quoi* of every sort to guess anything more. The climate of this country is the scape-goat upon which all the ill-looks and ill-health of the ladies is laid; but while they are brought up as effeminately as they are, take as little exercise, live in rooms like ovens during the winter, and marry as early as they do, it will appear evident that many causes combine with an extremely variable climate to sallow their complexions and destroy their constitutions."

Now for the portrait of my friend, Dom. Lynch. "There was a Mr. ——, the Magnus Apollo of New York, who is a musical genius, sings as well as any gentleman need sing, pronounces Italian well, and accompanies himself without false chords, all of which renders him the man round whom (as round H. G., Lord C., and pretty Lord O., in our own country) the women listen and languish. He sang the 'Phantom Bark.' The last time I heard it was from the lips of Moore, with two of the loveliest faces in all the world hanging over him, Mrs. N. and Mrs. B. By the bye, the man who sat next to me at dinner was asking me all manner of questions about Mrs. N., among others whether she was as 'pale as a poetess ought to be.' Oh, how I wish Corinne had heard that herself! what a deal of funny scorn would have looked beautiful on her rich brown cheek and brilliant lips. The dinner was plenteous (that is the word) and tolerably well dressed" (Peter Van Dyke ought to make her *half* a bow for that compliment), "but ill-served; there were not half servants enough to do the work" (John Stokes is not very ornamental, but tolerably useful, and the others are rather smartish, I think, but I have no servants in orange-coloured inexpressibles with tinsel epaulettes; when she comes again, I will endeavour to procure a bevy of them from Colonel Berkeley, or some other of her distinguished countrymen), "and we had neither water-glasses" (in this I think she is mistaken, we are never without them), "nor, oh, horror! that absolute indispensable, — finger-glasses. Now, though I don't eat with my fingers (except peaches), whereat, I think, the aborigines" (oh, for shame, Miss Kemble, to compare Mrs. Davis, General Fleming, and Dominick Lynch to wild savages!), "who were pealing theirs like so many potatoes, seemed to me rather amazed. Yet I do hold a finger-glass, at the conclusion of my dinner, a requisite almost to my digestion. However, as it happened, I digested without it."

With all submission I disagree with my fastidious guest. I don't eat with my fingers, and therefore do not require finger-glasses. We have them in the house, but do not frequently use them. I think it unseemly to see a company at the dinner-table, particularly the female part, washing their hands, rinsing their mouths, rubbing their gums with the finger, and squirting the polluted water back into the vessel, as was formerly the fashion in this country, a fashion which prevails yet in England in the higher circles.

"After dinner we had coffee, but no tea, whereat my English stomach was in high dudgeon. The gentlemen did not sit long, and when they joined us Mr. ——, as I said before, uttered sweet sounds. By the bye, I was not a little amused at Mrs. ——" (my wife takes this to herself), "asking me whether I had heard of his singing, or their musical *soirées*, and seeming all but surprised that I had no revelations of either, across the Atlantic. Mercy on me! what fools people are all over the world! the worst is, they are all fools of the same sort, and there is no profit whatever in travelling. Mr. B——" (Bankhead, the British secretary of legation), "who is an Englishman, happened to ask me if I knew Captain ——, whereupon we immediately struck up a conversation, and talked over English folk and doings together, to my entire satisfaction. The —— were there; he is a brother of that wondrous ruler of the spirits whom I do so dislike in London, and his lady is a daughter of Lord ——." (These are Mr. and Mrs. Cornwall, and she is welcome to say what she pleases of them. We had better folk than they in our party that day.) " I was very glad to come home. I sang to them two or three things, but the piano was pitched too high for my voice; by the bye, in that large, lofty, fine room they had a tiny, old-fashioned, becurtained cabinet piano, stuck right against the wall, unto which the singer's face was turned, and into which his voice was absorbed." (I'm afraid she is right about the piano. I wish she knew that I bought it upon Dr. McLean's recommendation, who has some conceit of himself in these matters, and that it cost me seven hundred dollars.) " We had hardly regained our inn, and uncloaked, when there came a tap at the door, and in walked Mr. ———" (Cornwall again), " to ask me if we would not join them, himself and the ———, at supper; he said that, besides five being a great deal too early to dine, he had not half dinner enough " (the Turk ! he ate like an ox), " and then began the regular English quizzing of everything and everybody we had left behind. Oh, dear ! oh, dear ! how thoughtfully English it was, and how it reminded me of H———; of course we did not accept their invitation, but it furnished me matter of amusement. How we English folk do cling to our own habits, our own views, our own things, our own people ; how, in spite of all our wanderings and scatterings over the whole face of the earth, like so many Jews, we never lose our distinct and national individuality, nor fail to lay hold of one another's skirts, to laugh at and depreciate all that differs from that country which we delight in forsaking for any and all others."

JANUARY 6. — Mr. Adams delivered on Wednesday last, at the Capitol, a eulogy upon the character of Lafayette, to which duty he was appointed by a vote of Congress at their last session. It is agreed on all hands and by all parties to have been a masterly production. It was a subject to call out the fine talents of the accomplished scholar and orator, and it was precisely the kind of "labour" which Mr. Adams "would delight in." It would appear, however, from the following gossip of the "Spy" in Washington that the "greatest and best" and "New York's favourite son" do not consider it good policy to bestow unqualified praise upon the man whom they have heretofore united to pull down: "After Mr. Adams had delivered, on Wednesday last, his masterly eulogy on General Lafayette, a gentleman asked the President (Mr. Van Buren being present) how he was pleased with the address. The venerable Christian, pausing a few seconds, coolly replied, 'There are some good things in it, but Mr. Adams *fails very much;* don't you think he does, Mr. Van Buren?' 'Very much,' repeated echo."

JANUARY 10. — The following gentlemen dined with us: Bishop Onderdonk, Dr. Hosack, Bishop Smith, of Kentucky; Mr. Peter A. Jay, Mr. Harrison G. Otis, Mr. W. Johnson, Chancellor Kent, Mr. D. S. Jones, President Duer, and Mr. P. Schermerhorn.

JANUARY 14. — The rage for speculating in lands on Long Island is one of the bubbles of the day. Men in moderate circumstances have become immensely rich, merely by the good fortune of owning farms of a few acres of this chosen land. Abraham Schermerhorn has sold his farm of one hundred and seventy acres at Gowannes, three miles from Brooklyn, at $600 per acre; four years ago, having got out of conceit of it as a residence, he offered it for sale at $20,000, and would have taken $18,000; to-day he pockets $102,000, and regrets that he sold it so cheap!

FEBRUARY 12. — Died on Saturday last, in Baltimore, Mr. William Patterson, in the eighty-third year of his age. He was formerly a distinguished merchant of that city, the father of Jerome Bonaparte's wife, who was separated from her husband by order of Napoleon, who did not think it becoming when he placed a crown on his brother's head that his throne and royal honours should be shared by the daughter of an American republican. It is not unlikely that about these times the *ci-devant* king of Westphalia would have no objection to return to the object of his first love. There is a son by this marriage, who married a Miss Williams, a handsome girl with a large fortune. They live in Baltimore, in very good style. I have partaken of the hospitality of this gentleman. It is somewhat remarkable that the three men who held the most distinguished place in the great community of merchants which imparted wealth, splendour, and character to Baltimore have all died within about a year, leaving good names and large fortunes to their children. Alexander Brown, Robert Oliver, and William Patterson might at one time have been considered the royal merchants of America, as the Medici of old were of Italy.

FEBRUARY 14. — Dr. Mott's dinner took place on Tuesday last, at the City Hotel. Dr. David Hosack presided, and made a good speech, which was well replied to by the respectable recipient of the compliment. The vice-presidents were Doctors McLean, Stearns, MacNeven, A. L. Anderson, S. W. Moore, and Francis. The toasts, regular and volunteer, were given in small doses, and as the gentlemen of the faculty had to take them themselves, they were neither unpalatable nor violent in their operation. They toasted each other *brown*, and said many pretty things, all but Dr. Rhinelander; this gentleman is not in very good odour with some of his brethren, from the circumstance of his having intrigued with his political friends in the board of regents to get Dr. Augustine Smith removed and himself appointed to a professor's chair in the College of Physicians. So when his turn came to give a toast, he did certainly infuse a dash of wormwood into the draught, which the sons of Esculapius had to swallow. Sheridan himself would have been gratified at this new application of his joke, — " The medical profession, when they all agree, their unanimity is wonderful." By Dr. Gilford : " Dr. Mott, by *cutting* an acquaintance, he often saves a friend." Not so bad.

I attended this evening a meeting at Washington Hall of a number of New Yorkers, with a design to form a regular Knickerbocker society, as a sort of set-off against St. Patrick's, St. George's, and more particularly the New England. The meeting was large and exceedingly respectable; there were the Irvings, Moores, McVickars, Renwicks, Rapelje, Stuyvesant, Laight, Fish, Wilkins, the

Schermerhorns, Brinckerhoffs, Costers, Colden, etc., — a goodly show of good fellows who will not disgrace their ancestors. Bloodgood was chairman and Washington Irving secretary. A committee was appointed, consisting of Peter Schermerhorn, Judge Irving, Alexander Wyckoff, Hamilton Fish, Dr. Manley, and the president and secretary, to report a constitution and by-laws to a future meeting. I suppose we shall have a few annual dinners, which will be pretty much all that will grow out of this project.

FEBRUARY 17. — The proceedings in the Senate of the United States have become very interesting within a few days. During the discussion of a bill brought forward by Mr. Calhoun to restrain executive patronage, which has brought out the most virulent opposition of the friends of General Jackson, Benton, the fiercest tiger in the den, insulted Mr. Calhoun by charging him with falsehood. The accomplished Carolinian was compelled to notice it, and Benton was called to order. The Vice-President, by some casuistical definition of parliamentary practice, pronounced the gentleman not out of order. Mr. Webster appealed from this decision, and his appeal was sustained by a vote of 24 to 20. There is some talk about Mr. Calhoun challenging Benton; but it cannot be. I would as soon think of challenging one of the hyenas in the zoölogical institution for snapping at me as I passed his den.

MARCH 14. — The packet-ship "Rhone" arrived yesterday from Havre, bringing Paris accounts to 11th ult. They are highly favourable to amicable settlement of our affairs with France. Mr. Clay's able report, with the resolution which accompanied it and was passed unanimously by the Senate in January last, was received in Paris on the 7th of February, and had precisely the effect which I predicted. It healed the wounded pride of the French government and people; it convinced them that the menacing proposal to grant letters of marque and reprisal was only the act of the President, and would not be sanctioned by the legislature of the nation, and there was little doubt that the Chamber of Deputies would pass the Indemnity Bill. Thus has the patriotic majority in the Senate once more interposed to save the country from a vexatious and unnecessary war, without the slightest sacrifice of national honour, although it is quite likely that Jackson will get the credit of it.

MARCH 16. — The frigate "Constitution," under
Old Ironsides. command of Commodore Elliot, got under way yesterday morning, and went to sea. She goes to France, from which place, if the Indemnity Bill should not have been passed, she will receive on board the American Minister and his family and return to the United States, but if the bill should have become a law she will join the squadron in the Mediterranean. Commodore Elliot went on Saturday evening to the Bowery Theatre to receive the homage of his suburban admirers, and as some opposition was apprehended from those who were opposed to the worship of the golden calf, or of him who set it up, he was accompanied by a guard of forty marines with side-arms; but it proved unnecessary: not a Whig was to be seen, and nothing occurred to mar his triumph, or interrupt the shouts of those who went to cry, Huzza for Jackson! Huzza for Elliot!

I went to the Book Club with Charles King and
Book Club. Davis at nine o'clock. This is a club which meets every other Thursday evening at Washington Hotel, where they sup, drink champagne and whiskey punch, talk as well as they know how, and run each other good-humouredly. I have been admitted a member after having refused several applications, for I have already more engagements than I wish; but this is a very pleasant set of fellows. They sit pretty late, however, for I came away at one o'clock and left the party seated at the supper-table. I don't exactly understand why this is called a Book Club, for the book of subscription to the expenses is, I suspect, the only one in the library. Our party this evening consisted of about twenty; viz., Davis, President Duer, Charles King, Wilkins, William Kent, Harvey, Arthur Barclay, Isaac Hone, Halleck, Ogden

Hoffman, Patterson, Blunt, Dr. Francis, Baron Behr, Mr. Trelawny, author of the "Younger Son," Beverly Robinson, etc.

MARCH 23. — This great work, which is to cost millions of dollars, was undertaken by a company who applied to the present Legislature for a loan of the credit of the State to the amount of two millions, to aid in the accomplishment of their undertaking. This application occasioned a warm debate; promises were freely made previous to the late election that the bill should pass, whereby the votes of the middle and southern counties were secured to the dominant party, but after a severe struggle the question was decided on Friday evening by a vote of sixty-one to forty-six. The majority may have had good reasons, for aught I know, but it is understood that the most prevailing one was that James G. King was one of the leading men in the enterprise, and he is a Whig; liberal he certainly is, and public-spirited and enlightened, but he is a Whig, and does not wear the Jackson collar, and it was exceedingly simple in the projectors of this great work to ask favours of the present Legislature with such an encumbrance; if the State-House was on fire they would not allow it to be extinguished by a Whig fireman. I wonder the statesmen at Albany do not pass a law to deprive all but Jackson men of the privilege of voting at elections, or holding real estate, and making it treason for the butchers and bakers to sell them meat and bread.
[New York and Erie Railroad.]

MARCH 28. — Mr. and Mrs. Webster arrived in town last evening from Philadelphia. He is going home to Boston on Wednesday, and she will remain here with her friends for a week or two. Mr. Webster came this evening and drank tea with us, and delighted us for an hour with his conversation. He talked about trout-fishing, Plymouth, Cape Cod, and Nantucket, and his eloquence made those trifling subjects interesting as those of more serious import, which it so ably illustrates and adorns. He and I agreed to make an excursion together in the month of June next, from Boston to New Bedford and Nantucket, in which I promise myself great pleasure. Mr. Webster's description of that part of the State of Massachusetts; the primitive manners of the people of Nantucket; the homogeneous nature of the institutions and social customs, and the isolated pride of their sea-girt territory, — has awakened in me a curiosity which will be gratified in this proposed excursion, and I shall enjoy in perfection the delightful society of a man who, in his hours of relaxation, is playful and agreeable as he is great in the discharge of his public duties.

APRIL 2. — I dined with Mr. Abraham Ogden. We had a very pleasant dinner. Mr. Webster was there, and Mr. H. G. Otis, and Meredith. The great senator has been more uniformly cheerful during his present visit than I have ever seen him, and he is, when "in the vein," one of the best talkers in the world. Mr. Otis, when the tyrant of the limbs allows him to dine out, is always a most delightful companion; his voice is perfect music, his choice of words scrupulously nice, and talent gives a charm to his narrative, which makes his hearers regret that his longest stories should ever come to an end. He appears to me sometimes a little pedantic and too studious of effect, but no man of taste and feeling can listen to him during the social hours of a dinner-party without improvement and delight. My friend Meredith is also an excellent diner-out, of a more joyous temperament than either of the above-named persons. He laughs louder, and his flashes, if not brighter, are sharper. He is a fine scholar, a good dramatic critic, and Shakesperian to the very letter. He was to have gone with me to the reading club this evening, but was not very well, and had to make preparation for his departure to-morrow morning.

APRIL 8. — The political aspect of the country is worse than ever: "In the lowest depth, a lower still is found." General Jackson's star is still in the ascendant, and shines brighter than ever; the returns of the election in Connecticut, which was held last week, prove, as far as they have been received, that his party have succeeded in that Yankee State. Our charter election comes on next week, and I presume we shall be beaten. The Jackson people have renominated Mr. Cornelius W. Lawrence as Mayor, and the Whigs will not oppose him. I am glad of it, for if we do not take him we shall have a worse man; indeed, I have been well pleased with his conduct during the first year of his mayoralty, and he would have had my cheerful support but for the circumstance of his having recently vetoed a resolution of the Common Council which recommended to the Legislature the passage of a law to register the votes. This is a measure so obviously proper to secure the purity of our elections, and so loudly called for, especially in this city, by all who desire to preserve the peace and good order which ought to prevail at such times, that nothing but a blind devotion to party could have influenced the Mayor in his opposition to a measure so salutary. I hoped better things from that gentleman. Notwithstanding this untoward state of political affairs, the country generally is in a prosperous state, and the city of New York peculiarly so. All descriptions of property are higher than I have ever known them. Money is plenty; business brisk; the staple commodity of the country (cotton) has enriched all through whose hands it has passed. The merchant, mechanic, and proprietor all rejoice in the result of the last year's operations.

APRIL 10. — The weather being fine and spring-like, I walked for an hour before dinner with my wife on the Battery. Strange as it is, I do not think that either of us had done such a thing in the last seven years; and what a beautiful spot it is! The grounds are in fine order; the noble bay, with the opposite shores of New Jersey, Staten and Long Islands, vessels of every description, from the noble, well-appointed Liverpool packet to the little market craft, and steamers arriving from every point, give life and animation to a prospect unexcelled by any city view in the world. It would be worth travelling one hundred miles out of one's way in a foreign country to get a sight of, and yet we citizens of New York, who have it all under our noses, seldom enjoy it. Like all other enjoyments, it loses its value from being too easily obtained.

I have passed a few hours delightfully in reading Washington Irving's "Tour on the Prairies." It is of the very best kind of light reading; like the violet of the spring, it exhales a refreshing mental fragrance, which soon passes away and leaves the mind conscious only that it was something very sweet. The charm of the book is the easy, graceful manner of describing the events of a tour of great interest, certainly to such persons as Ellsworth, Irving, and Latrobe, because such people seldom undertake expeditions of the kind. Killing buffaloes, hunting wild horses, sleeping every night on the ground for a whole month, and depending from day to day for the means of subsistence on the deer, wild turkeys, and bears which the rifles of their own party alone can procure, — all events of ordinary occurrence to the settlers of the great West, but matters of thrilling interest to comfortable citizens who read of them in their green slippers, seated before a shining grate, the neatly printed page illuminated by a bronze astral lamp; or to the sensitive young lady who, drawing up her delicate little feet on the crimson damask sofa, shudders at the hardships which the adventurous tourist has undergone, "and loves him for the dangers he has passed." The introduction to this little bijou affords the author the first opportunity he has had since his return from Europe to speak of himself, his success abroad, the doubts which filled his mind as to the unchanged affection of his countrymen, and to the removal of those doubts, and the overflowing of his heart by the kind reception which awaited him on his arrival.

The Crayon Miscellany.

APRIL 23.— Francis B. Cutting and Robert Bayard bought two or three years ago the country-place, as it then was, of the late William Bayard, for a sum between $50,000 and $60,000 (a great price at that time), and sold it at auction in lots the day before yesterday for $225,000. David S. Jones sold yesterday at auction, in lots, the former country-seat of Mr. Harrison, which he bought about two years since, and made a profit of $85,000. Real estate is high, beyond all the calculation of the most sanguine speculators. Immense fortunes have been made and realized within the last three months, and everything is dear but money. There must come a change; and when it does, woe to those who are caught! This distribution of property, however, by small lots, will divide the losses when the evil day comes, and they will not be felt in the same degree by any, as the profits are now by a few.

APRIL 24. — A great foot-race, which has occupied the mind of the fancy for several months past, took place this day on the Union Race Course, Long Island. It originated in a large bet between John C. Stevens and Samuel L. Gouverneur, that the former would produce by a given time a man who should run ten miles within an hour, for which he offered a reward of one thousand dollars, and three hundred more if it was performed by one only. This was the day fixed for the exploit, and without intending it by any means, when I arose this morning I found myself, with Robert, in the barouche, enveloped in clouds of dust, and our faces lacerated by a north-west wind which came loaded, not with ambrosial sweets, but with a sort of concentration of razor-blades, on the road to the race-course, jostled by every description of vehicle, conveying every description of people. The crowd on the ground was as great, I think, as at the famous Eclipse race, and immense sums were betted by men who find it difficult to pay their honest debts, and by hopeful boys, who have to square the amount of their losses from the reluctant pockets of fathers who, had they been thriftless and improvident as their progeny, would have brought them up to qualify them for holding the horses which they now proudly drive.

At one o'clock nine men started for the prize. They all came around the first three miles, each within six minutes, and the first five miles were performed by five of the number within half an hour. They then began to give in, and three only ran the whole ten miles. One man alone won the race, performing the ten miles in fifty-nine minutes forty-eight seconds. His name is Henry

Stannard, a farmer, aged twenty-four years, born in Killingworth, Conn., tall and thin, weighing one hundred and sixty-five pounds. He appeared to me exactly of the size and form for such an undertaking, with much bone and muscle and very little fat. He was not distressed by his effort, made a speech to the populace, who cheered him with loud applause, sprang upon a horse and rode around the course on which he had gained his laurels.

APRIL 25. — A man named Clayton made an ascension a few days since from Cincinnati in a style of adventure more splendid than any hitherto attempted. He gave notice that he meant to remain in the air as long as his supply of gas continued. He started at five o'clock P.M., went to sleep at a good regular hour in his car, travelled four hundred miles, made fast his balloon at two o'clock to the top of a tree on one of the mountains of Virginia, and then returned leisurely home to relate his adventures. We run faster, sail smarter, dive deeper, and fly farther than any other people on the face of the earth.

Ballooning.

APRIL 30. — The following gentlemen dined with us: Mr. Armour, Dom. Lynch, Washington Irving, Robert Ray, Peter Schermerhorn, Jonathan Goodhue, G. G. Howland, James G. King, and Isaac Hone.

The return of May brings with it its usual accompaniment of pulling down and altering houses. The streets are beginning to be filled with rubbish, and to increase the troubles of our locomotive citizens a new easterly storm is setting in, in which beds and bookcases, chairs, carpets, and crockery, will be exposed to damage.

The rise of lots in the upper part of the city goes on without interruption from any cause, foreign or domestic. Mr. Kane has sold his large house, corner of St. Mark's place and the Second avenue, to Charles Graham, for $35,000. He called this morning to offer it to me for the last time, before he closed the sale; but I do not want it, nor indeed would I consent to remove to any other situation, unless I was compelled to do so, by selling my house in Broadway. Mr. Boardman offered me, about two months since, the price I asked for my house, $55,000; but I was to take in part payment seven lots of ground on the Second avenue, below St. Mark's place, at a valuation of $35,000. This I declined, for I could not imagine then, nor can I now, that they are worth so much money. He has, however, sold them since for $38,000, and the speculators say they are a bargain.

MAY 12. — I went this morning to the Exhibition at Clinton Hall. There is a manifest improvement in the works of several of our old favourite artists. Ingham has some splendid portraits; Durand has several very good, three in particular, of President Jackson, Mr. Adams, and Charles A. Davis, are admirable. Inman has several fine paintings, the best the "Bride of Lammermoor," which he painted for a Southern gentleman; and Mount has three pictures which would do credit to Wilkie. Weir has, as usual, some good pictures, but his last does not please me. It is a picture painted for Mr. Verplanck; the subject is "The Landing of Hendrick Hudson."

National Academy.

MAY 18. — Yesterday was a pleasant day, the first, I think, this spring, and being Sunday the streets presented a gay and cheerful appearance. The ladies' new French hats and the gentlemen's white pantaloons were exhibited with impunity from staining shower or biting blast, and the air was redolent of the tender grass and opening lilacs. During the day and evening the fire-engines were exercised by the boys with their accustomed alacrity, and a few houses here and there in the upper part of the city were burned for their especial gratification.

MAY 21. — How beautifully expressive are the Indian proper names! Comprehensive in meaning, as they are lofty and musical in sound. I honour the towns, the rivers, and the mountains to which the good taste and patriotic feeling have left the names by which the sons of the forest designated them before the white man became their proprietor, much more than I do the Baths, the Bristols, the Frankforts, and the Orleans, for which we are indebted to the exhausted gazetteers of

Indian Names.

Europe; or even the Homers, the Virgils, the Solons, or the Manlius, albeit they have been raked up from the ashes of classical lore. Our lakes and rivers have been less despoiled of their original Indian designations than the towns which they irrigate and beautify, and they differ as much in name as they do in grandeur from those of Europe. What can be more expressive than "Alleghany," clear water; " Ohio," most beautiful of rivers; " Connecticut," long river; " Winnipiseogee," the smile of the Great Spirit; "Canandaigua," place of rest, etc.! Such words as Ontario, Onondaga, Tallahassee, and Michigan are full of poetry as of magnificence, and the spirit of the American people should guard them with as much jealousy from the innovations of European refinement as they would the hardy maxims of their republican institutions from the insults of courtly forms of government or the errors of modern philosophy.

MAY 22. — The Jackson Convention, convened by orders from Washington to nominate Mr. Van Buren for the presidency, assembled at Baltimore on Wednesday, and appointed Andrew Stevenson, late Speaker of the House of Representatives, and rejected Minister to England, to preside over them. No other business was done on Wednesday; there are some difficulties in the way, such as a double set of delegates from Pennsylvania, true-blue both, but hating each other nearly as much as they do honesty and the Whigs, and a little insubordination about the choice of Vice-President. Mr. Rives and Richard M. Johnson have each friends in the convention, who will at first make a little show in support of their respective candidate, but will soon fall into the ranks of "passive obedience and non-resistance," and ratify unanimously the edict which has gone forth from Washington and been countersigned at Albany. So "God help the people" ! This farce is over, and their *deliberations* have terminated as was previously arranged. On Friday the convention proceeded to the nomination of candidates for the offices of President and Vice-President of the United States. Martin Van Buren was unanimously nominated as President, and Richard M. Johnson was nominated as Vice-President by the following vote: for Richard M. Johnson, 178; for William C. Rives, 87.

MAY 26.—The packet-ship "Napoleon" arrived yes-
French News. terday from Liverpool, bringing news to the 25th of April. The Indemnity Bill passed the French Chamber of Deputies on the 18th by a larger majority than was anticipated. The whole amount of 25,000,000 francs, with interest from the date of the treaty, was agreed to be paid. The Ministers assented to the introduction of a clause in the bill forbidding the payment of the money until after the French Government shall have received satisfactory explanations with regard to the President's message of Dec. 2, 1834.

What will "Old Hickory" say to this? Apologize? He certainly will not, for his flatterers have told him and told the people, and they all believe it, that his firmness, his vigour, his dare-deviltry have extorted from the fears of the French that which we should never have gained from their justice, but *la grande nation* will be satisfied with a few unmeaning words: "Our old allies," "Our faithful friends," "The compatriots of our Lafayette;" they cannot suppose, not they, that any affront was intended, etc., etc., and so the matter will be settled: the louis will jingle in our pockets, Jackson will get all the credit for the success of a negotiation which his arrogance had well-nigh defeated, the "Hurrah for Jackson!" on our shores will be responded on those of France by "Vive Louis Philippe!" saltpetre will be used only for the peaceful purpose of curing hams, and the star-spangled banner will wave as heretofore over cargoes of cotton and potashes, or serve to give an impulse to the Fourth-of-July celebrations of General Morton's division of artillery.

MAY 27.—I went last evening to a grand supper at Washington Hall, given by the members of the Book Club to the Rev. Dr. Wainwright, who is considered the founder of the club. The party was larger than usual, and comprised several of the *élite* of the city.

There were President Duer, Dr. Wainwright, Dr. Jarvis, Henry Brevoort, Colonel White, of Florida, General Scott, Joseph Blunt, Charles King, Ogden Hoffman, John Duer, Jacob Harvey, Arthur Barclay, James J. Jones, Dr. Francis, Beverly Robinson, Charles A. Davis, Dr. A. E. Hosack, Isaac S. Hone, P. Hone, Washington Irving, M. C. Patterson, and two or three more whom I do not recollect.

JUNE 1. — All the world (our world) is going to Europe. The packet-ship "Europe" sailed this morning for Liverpool with thirty-five passengers; among the number were Professor Ticknor and family, of Boston, and Lord Powerscourt, who has been travelling in the United States. His friend and companion, Mr. Parnell, remains behind, having been married yesterday in Grace Church to Miss Delia Stewart, daughter of Commodore Stewart. He will follow in a short time, and take his Yankee bride with him to Ireland.

JUNE 17. — The Boston and Providence Railroad is completed except a viaduct, and the passengers by the New York steamboats were carried over for the first time one day last week. The time was two hours and a half, and the Lexington steamboat goes from New York to Providence in twelve hours, so that leaving this city at six in the morning travellers can unstrap their trunks at their lodgings in Boston by daylight on a summer's day.

JUNE 23. — The U.S. frigate "Constitution" arrived yesterday afternoon, having on board Mr. Livingston, our late Minister to France, and his family. Mr. Livingston comes back in a bad humour, and it is much to be feared that he may infuse some of it into the mind of the obstinate and weak old man at the head of our government, and so prevent an amicable arrangement of the difficulty with France, — a consummation devoutly to be dreaded, if it should lead to war. The only hope is that Mr. Van Buren's influence will be stronger in that quarter than that of the Minister, and that his chance of a succession to the presidency may be promoted by keeping the peace.

Old Ironsides.

We saw the noble ship "Constitution" plainly from Rockaway yesterday afternoon, under a full spread of canvas, on her way up to the city. She sailed from Havre on the 5th, and from Plymouth England, on the 16th ult. I do not think much of her commander, have little respect for the effigy on her bow or the manner of its being placed there, and am not exceedingly proud of the country's representative which she now bears in her bosom; but I love her for her name, and honour her for the share she has had in the preservation of her country's glory. She is still "Old Ironsides."

WEDNESDAY, JULY 1. — On Saturday evening last, during a severe gale in Baltimore, Mr. Marshall, son of the Chief Justice, having taken shelter in a building partially destroyed by fire, was killed by the falling of a chimney. He had just arrived from Philadelphia, where he had been to visit his venerable father. There is great reason to apprehend that the shock of this calamity, added to his bad state of health, will prove too much for this most excellent of men. I know of no greater misfortune which our country could sustain at this time than the death of Chief Justice Marshall. He is the sheet-anchor of the Constitution; pure, enlightened, and patriotic; the loss of such a man would be a national calamity at any time, but it is a fearful thing to think of his place being filled by a man who is willing to sacrifice everything we hold sacred to the gratification of his personal feelings and the aggrandizement of his party.

JULY 4. — I dined with the honourable the Corporation. These dinners are never very refined nor very intellectual, but this was even less so than usual. The constituents of the members, who, like some of themselves, are rather queer sort of folk, must be invited, and as the dinner and diners are abundant, they feed enormously, and, in utter disregard of the good temperance rules so much in fashion, lay in large stores of present hilarity and future headache, and, as in duty bound, they pay for their share of the municipal banquet by lauding their liberal entertainers, and shouting, at the top of their excited voices, "Huzza!" to all their party sentiments, no matter how violent or unreasonable. The President's health was received with all the fire and vivacity which brandy or champagne can inspire, but the great burst of feeling was reserved for New York's favourite son, "the Vice-President." The "three times three" which succeeded the announcement of this toast made the very cupola on the top of the hall tremble over our heads; the deep-toned bell which is suspended under the queer-looking canopy, like a toad under some enormous mushroom, to utter the sounds of fearful vibrations, and the four-and-twenty pounders of "Old Ironsides," which were at the same moment keeping 4th of July on the North river, could scarcely be heard in the patriotic din which spontaneously burst forth to waft the glorious sentiment to the responsive heavens. There, I am sure the "Times" cannot make more of the toast than I have done. I sat at the table on the right hand of the Mayor, between Commodore Elliot and Governour Troup. A chair was left in the place of honour on the immediate right of the Mayor for Mr. Livingston, who was so ill that he could not attend the dinner; but the place was pertinaciously kept by the Commodore, who is a great glorifier of President Jackson and all that appertains to him, and when the cloth was removed and the champagne, like a poker, had begun to stir up the latent flame of patriotism in the bosoms of the faithful, the name of the Minister was announced, and he was led up with all due formality to the vacant chair. This was the signal for three glorification cheers, which he would not have gotten in a regular way. His health was given; he made a speech; all his actions, past, present, to come, were fully approved, and "No explanation," "No apology," resounded through the room, and divided the echoes of the spacious dome with the equally inspiring shouts of "Hurrah for Jackson!" and success to the nominee of the Baltimore Convention. This may all have been accidental, but it appeared to me exceedingly like management. It was passing strange that a person should be too ill to go out to dinner at five o'clock, but able to calculate his recovery with so much nicety that a chair should be kept for him to occupy at seven. I crossed the path of the glorification toasts with the following sentiment, out of place, to be sure, but they dared not express any disapprobation, — "John Marshall: may his valuable life be spared to his country, while his mental and physical faculties remain, to elucidate and to defend the Constitution."

Death of Chief Justice Marshall. JULY 8. — The calamity which has for some time past threatened our country has happened at last, and every man who admires talents and venerates virtue mourns over the loss we have sustained. John Marshall, the wise, the virtuous, the patriotic, died on the afternoon of Monday the 6th inst., at six o'clock, in Philadelphia, in which city he has been for some time, to avail himself of the best medical advice. Take the Chief Justice for all in all, he combined in his character more good and great qualities than any other man in the United States during his or any other time, with the exception of his friend and associate, Washington; and his death at this time is a greater national calamity than Washington's was when it occurred, for reasons which I have stated at a former page of this journal, in noticing the melancholy death of his son at Baltimore. Would it had pleased Divine Providence to delay the stroke for a few years! Less danger would be apprehended if the successor of General Jackson had had the filling of this most important office, even if that successor were (as it most probably will be) Mr. Van Buren. He will be governed less by personal predilections, and if he has no more virtue than the present incumbent, he has more policy and less reliance upon his own infallibility. At any rate, I would rather trust him.

In 1797 Marshall was appointed by President Adams, with General Pinckney and Elbridge Gerry, to negotiate with the French Directory. They were not received by the French, and it was in this embassy that the famous X. Y. Z. correspondence was instituted, in which the envoys were invited to bribe the Directory as the means of obtaining justice for this country. It was this infamous proposal which gave rise to the celebrated expression so frequently quoted, "Millions for defence, not a cent for tribute." In 1799 he was elected and took his seat in Congress. Here his talents became immediately so conspicuous that in 1800 he was appointed Secretary of War, and on the 31st of January, 1801, he became Chief Justice of the Supreme Court of the United States, which distinguished position he continued to fill with unsullied dignity and preëminent ability until the close of his mortal career. All newspapers are, as they ought to be, clad in mourning.

JULY 10. — Charles King gave me, on board the steamboat, yesterday morning the "Evening Post" to read an infamous editorial notice of the death of Chief Justice Marshall. They say he was a man of *considerable talents!* but an enemy to Democratic principles, and used his influence in the court over which he presided to subvert them, and on the whole his removal is a cause of rejoicing. This is absolutely a species of impiety for which I want words to express my abhorrence. It is of a piece with Duane's celebrated article published in the "Aurora" on the death of Washington, beginning with the scriptural quotation, "Lord, now lettest thou thy servant depart in peace, for mine eyes have seen thy salvation;" and the painful recollection of these two great national bereavements will ever be accompanied in the minds of all good Americans by their detestation of the sentiments of the two compeers in infamy, who have thus acquired a most unenviable notoriety. The "Times," another of our Jackson papers, on the other hand, has noticed the Chief Justice's death in the most feeling manner, and consecrated his memory by eulogiums which none but a fool would deny, or a knave withhold.

JULY 18. — The papers contain a report that the President has appointed Roger B. Taney Chief Justice of the United States in the place of the lamented John Marshall. Mr. Taney is a lawyer of high reputation, and except in his slavish devotion to General Jackson and his party, which led him during his short career as

Secretary of the Treasury to perform an act of subserviency which must "damn him to everlasting fame," he was always esteemed a respectable man. The act alluded to, the acceptance of office solely to do the President's dirty work of removing the deposits, was sufficient to entitle him to this or any other office in his gift; and as none but a person possessing that sort of qualification would be appointed, it is fortunate, on the whole, that the ermine has not fallen upon less worthy shoulders. If this appointment has been made, and Mr. Van Buren should be elected President (of which I think there is very little doubt), the remarkable fact will be disclosed of the two most exalted offices in the country being held by individuals whose nominations for other offices of greatly inferior importance have been rejected by the Senate.

BUFFALO, TUESDAY, JULY 21. — We arrived here in the canal-boat at three o'clock this afternoon. The boat was not crowded, the weather was cool and pleasant, the accommodations good, the captain polite, our fellow-passengers well-behaved, and altogether I do not remember to have ever had so pleasant a *ride* on the canal. My hammock, to be sure, was rather narrow and not very soft, and my neighbour overhead packed close upon my stomach; but I slept sound as a ploughman, and did not wake until tapped on the shoulders by the boy, and told to "clear out."

JULY 29. — At the moment of my arrival I found
Saratoga Springs.   the ladies dressed for a ball at Congress Hall and just entering the room. At the solicitations of some of my fair friends, whose solicitations are a matter not to be disregarded, I went down to look at the gay assemblage. There is a large company at Congress Hall, but not many New Yorkers. The Patroon and old Mrs. Philip Van Rensselaer, Mrs. Wilkins, Mr. and Mrs. Henry Phelps, Mr. and Mrs. Davis, Mr. and Mrs. James W. Otis, Mr. and Mrs. Post, lately married (she was Miss Church); Mrs. Otis's sister, another newly married couple; Mr. and Mrs. Rupert Cochran, Mr. and Mrs. DePau, Mr. and Mrs. Washington Coster, Giraud, McLean, Buckland, McLeod, Laight, Pringle,

Edward Heckscher, Governor Wolf, of Pennsylvania, and many others, as Lord Duberly says, "too tedious to enumerate."

AUGUST 2. — A terrible system prevails in some of the Southern and Western States of late, which consists in the people taking the law in their own hands and inflicting summary punishment upon persons who have made themselves obnoxious to their high mightinesses, beating, tarring and feathering, and in some cases hanging the unhappy object of their vengeance, and this is generally called "Lynch's law." At Vicksburg, in the State of Mississippi, from the 6th to the 10th of July, scenes were enacted which are calculated to make humanity shudder, and to bring disgrace upon the country. The same inflammable spirit in our part of the country has caused excitement and tumult in a less dangerous degree. Finding more combustible matter in the South and West, it has kindled a flame which may in time endanger the safety of our institutions throughout the Union. There is an awful tendency toward insubordination and contempt of the laws, and there is reason to apprehend that good order and morality will ere long be overcome by intemperance and violence, and "Lynch's law" be made a substitute for written law and the regular administration of public justice. God forbid that the fair inheritance of our fathers should be laid prostrate by the lawless hands of their degenerate sons, in this early stage of its existence! As for me, I have no desire to be ruled by the maxim of government so fashionable in the extreme south and west part of our country, and I say, give us no more Tennessee presidents.

AUGUST 3. — The prices of property in and about this city and Brooklyn keep up astonishingly; unimproved lots on this island are higher than ever. Several great sales have been made at auction during my absence, but I think the greatest is the property of the late Mrs. Ann Rogers, which goes principally, I believe, to her grandchildren, the children of her daughter, Mrs. Heyward. It consisted of her proportion of the Rose Hill estate left by her first husband,

Nicholas Cruger, and the country-seat at Bloomingdale, about six miles from the city, on the banks of the Hudson river. The amount of the sales of these two pieces of property was $688,310. Fifteen years ago they would not have brought $40,000. The money goes into good hands.

Death of Matthews. AUGUST 4. — Charles Matthews, the comedian, died in England, on the 29th of June, of an ossification of the heart. His health was bad during his last visit to the United States, and he had a dangerous fit of illness while in Boston. He dined with me once during that visit, was very agreeable, but not the man he was when here before. Even while amusing the public by his ludicrous performances on the stage, he was moody, fretful, and dissatisfied, and left the country for the last time in a very bad humour. Few men of the present age have contributed so much to the amusement of others, but in his best days he was subject to fits of discontent and lowness of spirits, and I have seen him at my own table delighting and surprising the company with stories, songs, and imitations, himself the only person whose heart was not light and joyous by the merriment he caused.

Chief Justice Marshall. The following distinguished gentlemen have been appointed and have consented to pronounce eulogiums upon the character and services of the late illustrious Chief Justice: Judge Story, of the Supreme Court of the United States; Daniel Webster, of Massachusetts; James Kent, of New York; Horace Binney, of Philadelphia; and Walter Jones, of Washington.

ROCKAWAY, THURSDAY, AUG. 6. — We left home this afternoon in the Rockaway omnibus, with Miss Lydia Kane. Mr. Nicholson drove Miss Helen Kane.

The house is not so full as it ought to be, but the company is exceedingly agreeable. Mr. and Mrs. R. Bayard; Mrs. Carroll; Mr. and Mrs. Jackson (Mrs. Carroll's other daughter); two beautiful Misses Willing, daughters of Richard Willing, of Philadelphia; Dr. and Mrs. McAuley, of Baltimore; Mrs. Davis; Miss E. Callender; and an excellent lot of beaux.

AUGUST 7. — The weather is delightful this morning, and we have had a day of amusement and pleasure. It was the birthday of Miss Elizabeth Willing, one of the handsomest and loveliest girls I ever saw. Count Streliski, who is chief manager and the best beau at the Pavilion, issued a programme of the amusements, which consisted of a trotting match, a champagne dinner, birthday ode, ball, and supper. The trotting match took place at ten o'clock, on the beach, and the company from all the houses assembled to witness it. Three one-mile heats were trotted. The race was won by Robert Goelet, who was regularly invested by the queen of the day on the ground with the prize, which was a beautiful embroidered scarf. This part of the day's sport went off well and afforded much pleasure. At the dinner, toasts and speeches in honour of the occasion went their jocund round. The ball in the evening was unusually splendid, for there never were a dozen handsomer girls assembled in one cotillion. A part of the arrangement consisted in my promising a birthday ode, which was set to music by Kendal and sung with great effect by the Count. It was well received, for the good-humour which prevailed rendered the company indulgent critics. Amongst the other delights of the day I had a most luxurious bath at noon. Why do people go to Saratoga to mix in a crowd of queer strangers, dragging out a tiresome day of artificial enjoyment, when they might come here and enjoy pure air, invigorating bathing, and refined society? *Chacun à son goût.* I prefer this.

NEW YORK, AUG. 11. — My beautiful namesake, the brig "Philip Hone," arrived on Sunday, from the Pacific ocean, to Howland and Aspinwall.

<small>Riots in Baltimore.</small> My poor country, what is to be the issue of the violence of the people and the disregard of law which prevails in all parts of it? On Friday night a mob collected in Baltimore, instigated by inflammatory handbills, to take vengeance upon several persons who had been directors of the Bank of Maryland, — an institution which stopped payment something

more than a year ago, and by which many persons had lost money. They attacked and broke the windows of the house occupied by Mr. Reverdy Johnson, which was built by James A. Buchanan, next door to Mrs. William Gilmor, near to Barnum's Hotel, and within a short distance of Meredith's house. The Mayor interfered, and the mob was addressed by several gentlemen, and dispersed without doing a great deal of damage, but only to renew the attack with increased numbers and greater ferocity. The same scenes were repeated on Saturday night and on Sunday, when the house was pulled down, as well as that of Mr. Glenn, another of the bank directors, who lived in North Charles street. All the furniture of both these houses was thrown into the street, burned, and destroyed. The troops fired upon the mob, several were killed, and a large number wounded.

The accounts published in the papers of this afternoon are up to yesterday morning, at which time the work of destruction was still going on. The scene is represented as horrible in the extreme, but the accounts are vague and contradictory. About twenty persons were killed and one hundred wounded. The house of the Mayor, who had done his duty well, was destroyed; the troops had refused to act any further, and the mob appears to have completely got the ascendency. This is Lynch's law, or Club law, or Beelzebub's law, or Jackson's law. It is the state of things which the editor of the "Evening Post" must have anticipated and wished for when he congratulated his fellow-ruffians that the sheet-anchor of the law and the Constitution was lost; that the wise and the virtuous Marshall no longer lived to control the bad passions of the people. Where will it end?

ROCKAWAY, WEDNESDAY, AUG. 12. — My feelings are
Dreadful Fire. excited and my heart is sick at the scenes I witnessed this morning; but I am glad I happened to be in town, for it was better to see the work of destruction than to hear it described. At two o'clock a fire broke out in the large new brick building No. 115 Fulton street, occupied by a number of

bookbinders, etc. I saw the fire from my bed, and knew, from the direction and the reflection of the light on the steeple of the North Church near, about where it was. I did not arise for some time, until I concluded, from the progress of the flames, that Clinton Hall might be in danger. I then went out and witnessed the awful scene until seven o'clock. It has been the most destructive fire which has ever occurred in New York, with the exception, perhaps, of the great fire, thirty or forty years ago, at the Coffee House Slip; because in this case most of the buildings were new, five and six stories high, and of brick. This part of the city was the Paternoster Row of New York, in which two or three thousand persons were employed daily in the various departments of book making, binding, publishing, etc. Fifteen or twenty newspapers and other periodicals were published within its precincts, and the stock of books, most of which was destroyed, was immense.

The building in which the fire originated, with six others, occupying the whole ground on that side of Fulton street, including Bliss & Wadsworth's splendid book and stationery store and Abraham Bell & Co.'s counting-house, from the Dutch church minister's house to the North Church, were entirely destroyed, and nearly all the houses on the opposite side of Fulton street. The flames passed through the block to Ann street, and swept away all the new lofty buildings on both sides of the street, including Holbrook's store, Fuller's gymnasium, six stories high, and the Catholic church, which was the extent of the devastation in that direction. From Ann street it communicated to Nassau street, where ten or twelve buildings on the east side were destroyed; two of these, Nos. 110 and 112, were large new warehouses filled with books and paper, all of which was lost. The houses on Nassau street were the last destroyed, and at this period the immense establishment of the American Bible Society, Clinton Hall, and my property, Clinton Hotel, were in considerable danger; but happily the progress of the flames was arrested and all this valuable property escaped uninjured.

Five persons are known to have lost their lives: Mr. Blanchard, a respectable bookbinder, and two printers in the building where the fire originated. The former jumped out of a window in the fourth story and died in ten minutes; the others were burned, and two more were killed by falling walls. I witnessed the conflagration from the upper story of Clinton Hall, and it was astonishing to see the rapidity with which it progressed.

<small>The Abolitionists.</small> AUGUST 13.— Great excitement prevails in all parts of the country on the subject of the attempts made by the friends of immediate emancipation to excite the slaves of the South to resist the authority of their masters; at least, such is the alleged tendency of the indiscreet measures of those fanatical persons who have engaged in that cause. Inflammatory publications have been circulated in the slaveholding States by means of the mails, and the people of those States have resorted to violent measures to counteract their effects; among others, application was made to the Postmaster-General to prevent their distribution. The reply of that important functionary (the notorious Amos Kendal) contains the following sentiment, which embodies all the essence of the abominable doctrines on which the Vicksburgh and Baltimore riots were founded; viz., that the people are to be governed by the law just so long as it suits them, and constitutes them the judges of the time when they may release themselves from the obligation of obedience, and the manner of substituting " Lynch's law " for the written law of the land. The letter is addressed to the Postmaster of Charleston, S.C. "We owe an obligation to the laws, but a higher one to the community in which we live, and if the former be perverted to destroy the latter, it is patriotism to disregard them." Every petty postmaster in the country is thus made the judge of the cases which justify his interposition, and he may stop the circulation of pamphlets, newspapers, and letters too, for aught I can see to the contrary. These postmasters are to a man the subservient tools of Jackson, Kendal, & Co., and may consider it " patriotism to disregard the laws " by preventing the

circulation of all publications opposed to the reigning dynasty and the legitimate succession.

The abolitionists, Arthur Tappan and his fanatical coadjutors, are certainly engaged in a most mischievous undertaking, which may bring destruction upon their own heads and civil war into the bosom of our hitherto happy country; but the remedy is worse than the disease. If they are punished, if their dangerous career is arrested, it must be done according to law. I do not choose to surrender the power of executing justice into the hands of the slave-owners of South Carolina.

AUGUST 14. — That affair is over. The mob have dispersed after pulling down five or six fine houses, burning the furniture, and drinking the old wine. The number of persons killed was exaggerated in the first accounts. It does not exceed seven. This was one of Amos Kendal's cases, in which the people determined that the "laws were perverted, and it was patriotism to disregard them."

Baltimore Mob.

AUGUST 19. — The "Constitution" sailed this morning on a cruise in the Mediterranean, with Jackson's head disgracing her bow, and Commodore Elliot her quarter-deck. The vile sycophancy which caused the former to be placed where it is, obtained for the latter a distinction which would not have been awarded to him by any brother officer in the navy.

Old Ironsides.

A meeting has been called in Boston for 21st instant, signed by fifteen hundred persons, at the head of whom is Harrison G. Otis, to express their disapprobation of the proceedings of the fanatics who are seeking to sow the seeds of discord among our fellow-citizens of the South, and to excite the slaves to revolt against their masters. This may be good. It will serve to convince the slave-owners that the number of those who seek to do them harm is too inconsiderable to give them uneasiness. I should approve of such a meeting in New York, if it could be conducted without violence and party-spirit.

Anti-Abolition Meeting.

AT HOME, WEDNESDAY, AUG. 26. — The abolition question continues to agitate the public mind, and acquires hourly a most alarming interest. A great meeting is to be held to-morrow afternoon, in the Park, of those opposed to the incendiary proceedings of the abolitionists. The call is signed by several hundred persons, of different political parties, headed by the Mayor. One object of my coming to town is to attend this meeting, for I am desirous that persons of character should be present in the greatest possible numbers, with the twofold object of convincing the people of the South that the incendiaries constitute an inconsiderable proportion of our citizens, and to prevent any violence which might possibly be attempted by turbulent persons ever on the lookout for a row, for it is certain that in the present state of feeling the least spark would create a flame in which the lives and property of Arthur Tappan and his associates would be endangered.

AUGUST 27. — The public meeting of citizens opposed to the abolition society, and the interference of individuals between the masters and the slaves in the Southern States, was held this afternoon, at four o'clock, in the Park. The following were the officers, and if wisdom is found in a multitude of counsellors this must have been an eminently wise assemblage: President, His Honor the Mayor. Vice-Presidents, Thomas L. Oakley, William T. McCoun, David B. Ogden, Henry Parish, Peter Crary, Walter Bowne, John L. Morgan, Luman Reed, Isaac S. Hone, Campbell P. White, Prosper M. Wetmore, Philip Hone, Edward Curtis, Thaddeus Phelps, Joseph Cowdin, Daniel Jackson, Charles A. Davis, George L. Robbins, Charles L. Livingston, Reuben Withers, John D. Wolf, Seth Geer, Egbert Benson, John L. Graham, Isaac H. Varian, Robert Center, William L. Johnson, Joseph D. Beers. Secretaries, John R. Marshall, George Sharp, Robert Pitts, John L. Bailey, Isaac Townsend, Morgan L. Smith, R. C. Wetmore, James Lee, Henry H. Elliott, Seneca Stewart, Thomas C. Doremus, George L. Easton. The preamble and resolutions were all very temperate and proper, the proceedings orderly, and the large assembly broke up without the least indecorum.

AT HOME, TUESDAY, SEPT. 1. — The marine Pavilion is now "a banquet-hall deserted." This establishment, gotten up and supported at so great an expense, has been neglected by the New Yorkers, with the exception of my family and connections and a few others. The house has been encouraged only by Philadelphians and other strangers. The fashionable people of our city have preferred the Virginia Springs, Saratoga, Newport, and a place they call Sachem's Head, to a house of their own possessing advantages greater than any other.

Packets.

We had a pretty sight at Rockaway. Shortly before we came away, the three outward-bound packets were all in sight in a line with the beach, about a mile apart; viz., the "Toronto," for London; "Caledonia," for Liverpool; and "Utica," for Havre. The wind was light, but fair, and these noble vessels, under full sail, passed, slowly, steadily, and gracefully on to their several destinations. May they arrive in safety to "the havens where they would be"!

Trip to Boston.

BOSTON, SATURDAY, SEPT. 5. — We landed the Newport passengers, of whom Mrs. Ritchie was one, at five o'clock. Mrs. James W. Otis came on to Providence. At eight o'clock we left Providence on the railroad and arrived here at three-quarters past ten. Dr. Wainwright was our fellow-passenger from New York. We got a tolerably good bed-chamber at the Tremont House, and were regularly installed into the comforts of Mr. Belknap's pleasant parlour. I found, among the inmates of the house, Mr. and Mrs. Richard Bayard, Mr. and Mme. Podestad, Francis March, John C. Hamilton, Mr. and Mrs. DeWitt Bloodgood, Miss Mary Van Schaick, and many other acquaintances.

Speculation in real estate has reached as great a height as in New York, pulling down and rebuilding in the fashion of the day, and it seems as if all the world had entered into a combination to exhaust the quarries of granite in the neighbourhood. A company, consisting of Patrick T. Jackson, Abbott Lawrence, and William Appleton, have bought the ancient house and grounds of the late

Gardiner Greene, on Court street, and the adjoining property of Deacon Philips, at enormous prices, pulled down the houses, levelled a hill sixty feet in height, and made fifty or sixty building lots, of which they will make maps and sell the whole at auction, and, availing themselves of the present rage, will no doubt make a great deal of money.

SEPTEMBER 6. — In the afternoon I visited and had a delightful talk of two or three hours with Mr. H. G. Otis, where I drank tea, and went in the evening to Mr. Peter Parker's, Mr. Samuel D. Parker's, and Mr. Sullivan's, at each of which places I had been invited to those agreeable Sunday-evening parties for which the Bostonians are so celebrated, and which I enjoy so much.

TUESDAY, SEPT. 8. — The Legislature is in session. I went this morning, first to the Senate and afterward to the House of Assembly. In the latter chamber, Mr. George Blake, who is a member, placed me in a most conspicuous seat, near the Speaker, and close to the clerk's table, in view of the whole House, where I received the attentions of several of the members with whom I was acquainted. This is an extra session for revising the laws of the State. The number of members is too great. The House consists of upwards of six hundred, of whom four hundred were present this morning. They are a good-looking, orderly body of men, and their business is conducted in a decorous, gentlemanly manner.

In the evening I went to a party at Mrs. Augustus Thorndike's. A prettier party, a more tasteful house, I have never seen. Madame Podestad and the Count sang delightfully. Mrs. Thorndike's sisters, Mrs. Delprat and Mrs. Calvert, and their father, Dr. Stuart, of Baltimore, are here on a visit.

SEPTEMBER 9. — At eleven o'clock precisely we started on the railroad for Lowell; arrived at a quarter-past twelve. Started on our return at two, and got to Boston at half-past three. The distance is twenty-five miles. There is a prodigious deal of travelling on the road. They take seventy-five minutes to perform the distance, and the punctuality is astonishing. There was not a variation of half a minute in starting and arriving either way. Our time was rather short in Lowell, but long enough to see this lion of New England; this Manchester of America; this city of enormous brick factories, of canals and waste-gates, of billies and jennies, of jacks and spindles.

I dined at Mr. H. G. Otis's, and had, as is always the case in the house of this agreeable and hospitable gentleman, a most capital dinner. Mrs. Ritchie (who came with her mother yesterday from Newport) presided at the dinner, and imparted to it the charm which always attends her presence. The company, besides myself, consisted of Mr. and Madame Podestad, Mr. and Mrs. Bayard, Messrs. Belknap, F. Grey, Sears, Middleton, J. G. Pierson, of New York, and Allyn Otis.

SEPTEMBER 10. — This day has been devoted to a sailing and fishing party, in the beautiful bay of Boston, on board the " Dream," — a pleasure schooner belonging to a company of gentlemen of this place. She was formerly owned in New York by Hosack, Center, and my son Robert and others. We left Boston at ten o'clock, the party consisting of Messrs. Brooks, Belknap, Whitwell, Isaac P. Davis, Colonel Freeman, Philip, and myself. After we had proceeded twenty miles down the bay, and were engaged in fishing, we were joined by the celebrated sloop (formerly Mr. Cushing's boat), whose passengers, Messrs. Forbes, Bryant, and Sturgis, joined our party. We sailed in company during the remainder of the day, which was passed in joviality and good-humour. We caught about three dozen codfish and haddock, ate our chowder, drank any quantity of punch, champagne, and old Madeira. The weather was fine as possible, the wind fair both going and returning, and we got home about eight o'clock.

SEPTEMBER 11. — I passed this morning in returning visits. Mr. Sears called to see me, and took me to his house to see a number of capital pictures which he has lately brought from Italy. They are copies from celebrated pictures, and possess great merit. Mr. Sears's house is certainly the finest in the United States. The front, on Beacon street, is one hundred feet. They say it cost $175,000; and this noble house is filled with treasures of art. Among the pictures are the "Miriam" and another of Allston's. Mr. Sears went to Europe for his health, which was much impaired, and returned quite well in July last.

Concord Jubilee. SEPTEMBER 12. — This day must be marked with a white stone. It was one of the most pleasant of my life. I expected much from it, but my expectation has been more than realized. At six o'clock Philip and I went, by previous arrangement and breakfasted with the acting governor, Samuel T. Armstrong. After breakfast we started in his carriage, the party consisting of the Governor, his military staff, Adjutant-General Dearborn, Colonel Winthrop, and ourselves. The morning was lowering, but it soon cleared, and the weather during the day was peculiarly favourable. On arriving at Lexington, eleven miles from Boston, we left the carriage, and visited the celebrated spot behind the meeting-house where the first blood was shed in the glorious cause of American independence, on the 19th of April, 1775. A granite monument has been erected on the spot where the bones of the first martyrs in that cause were interred. No description nor drawing of the spot could convey to my mind so full an idea of the events of that important day in the history of my country as a view of it, with the detailed account I received from my companions.

We proceeded to Concord, seven miles farther by the same road which the British took after the skirmish at Lexington, where they were opposed by the militia, and where the first regular battle took place. At Concord, therefore, the revolution commenced.

We found the whole population in motion, waiting to receive us; proceeded, agreeably to arrangement, to the house of Mr. Hoar, member of Congress from the district, from whence we went to the hotel, where a grand procession was formed, escorted by a company of troops. The procession passed through a line of ladies and children (the latter pupils of the schools), and entered the meeting-house in which the exercises of the day were to be performed. These exercises were introduced by prayer from the venerable pastor, Dr. Ripley, a hearty old gentleman eighty-four years old, as he informed me himself. Several odes were sung, and an excellent oration spoken by the Rev. Ralph Waldo Emerson, a young clergyman of distinguished talents and eloquence. It was full of interesting details relative to the first settlement of Concord, the first inland town settled in the colony. The grant which was made to the Rev. Peter Buckley and Major Simon Willard was dated 2d Sept., 1635, old style. The history of the sufferings and privations of the first settlers and their immediate descendants, their wars and adventures with the Indians, and many facts illustrative of those primitive times carefully collated from the ancient town records up to the time when this little republic of honest Yankees was called to act an important part in the revolution which separated the western world from the dominion of the mother-country, gave a vivid interest to the oration, the reading of which occupied two hours. The services all partook of the spirit of the olden times; amongst them was the "107th Psalm, tune St. Martin's," "from the New England version used in the New England churches in 1640," which was sung by the whole assemblage, the deacon giving it out line by line.

The exercises in the meeting-house concluded at two o'clock, when the procession formed again and marched to a great pavilion on the green, where tables and a cold collation were spread, and about four hundred as honest-looking Yankees as ever sat down to eat cold roast pig were assembled. Never have I seen anything of the kind so decidedly American; no foreign influence; no grating brogue; every man looked and acted as if the honour of his virtuous ancestors was in his sole keeping. Mr. Keyes, member of the General Court from Concord, presided with great ability. There were no regular toasts, but the president gave them, prefaced by some apt remarks calculated to draw out in succession the distinguished guests. We had speeches from Lieutenant-Governor Armstrong, Mr. Everett, Mr. Philips, member of Congress from Salem; General Dearborn, and Colonel Winthrop, of the Governor's staff; Judge Davis, Mr. Bradford, and Mr. Emerson, the orator of the day. I also was called out by a toast from the Chair, complimentary to myself and the city of New York, and replied in a speech which must have been pretty good, unless I mistook the expressions of kindness to a stranger for an approval of his sentiments and his manner of conveying them to the audience. I closed my address with the following toast: "Concord and Boston, the birthplace and cradle of American liberty; good nursing has made the babe healthy and vigorous, but she requires watching more now than ever."

Our party went from the dinner-table to visit the ladies, who had invited us to drink coffee with them at their banquet. The court-house was beautifully fitted up with festoons and wreaths of flowers and evergreens, and tables were spread at which all the ladies of Concord had dined. There was not a house in the whole town probably at which dinner had been provided this day, and not one which contained an inhabitant who was able to leave it, and here I was, talking to fine Yankee women and blooming Yankee girls until the Governor's carriage was announced, which carried us unwillingly away, and we arrived in Boston at nine o'clock. I have been delighted with this affair, for it was precisely one of those which I have long desired to witness; and the honour which has been conferred upon me on this occasion I shall remember with gratitude.

I had forgotten to remark that we had amongst us, in the meeting-house and at the dinner, eight or ten old gentlemen who were soldiers of the battle of Concord on the 19th of April, 1775. They were eloquently alluded to by the orator of the day, and verbal laurels were showered upon their hoary heads in abundance by several of the gentlemen who spoke at dinner.

SUNDAY, SEPT. 13.— We went this morning to the King's Chapel, and heard a good sermon from Dr. Greenwood, the Unitarian pastor of that congregation.

One of the pillars intended for the portico of the new courthouse was brought into the city this evening from Quincy. It weighs between twenty-eight and thirty tons, and was drawn by forty-two yoke of oxen.

SEPTEMBER 14. — We went this morning to see the pictures at the Athenæum, principally a head by Allston, "Isaac of York," which, notwithstanding the praise so liberally bestowed upon it by the Bostonians, I do not like. But there are some fine pictures belonging to the Academy which required more time to examine than I had to bestow, for I had to return to my lodgings to take a luncheon preparatory to my departure.

SEPTEMBER 15. — The Legislature of Mississippi have passed a law offering a reward of $5,000 for the arrest and conviction of any person "who shall utter, publish, or circulate within the limits of that State, the 'Liberator,' or any other paper, circular, pamphlet, letter, or address of a seditious character."

SEPTEMBER 23. — The plan for macadamizing the street before my house not having fully answered public expectation, the corporation have been trying a new experiment in Broadway, in front of the block between Warren and Chambers streets, copied from a plan of paving in St. Petersburgh, Russia. The street is excavated to the depth of about two feet; a layer of broken stone is placed, such as is used for macadamizing, on the top of which a regular pavement of round stones, the whole covered by a compact course of wooden blocks, sexagonal, one foot in length, and placed vertically. These are made to fit very nicely, the interstices (which of course are small) filled with liquid tar, and covered with a thin coat of gravel. The street was used yesterday for the first time, and the multitudinous train of omnibuses, carriages, carts, and wagons which infest Broadway appeared to pass over the new Appian way "pretty tolerably slick." But it remains to be seen whether hemlock timber is less destructible than Nyack stone, and whether three distinct layers of road may not peradventure cost more than one.

Paving Broadway.

SEPTEMBER 30. — I took Mr. Brevoort, Mr. Louis McLane, and Washington Irving out in the carriage to dine with old Mr. Astor, at Hell-gate. We had a pleasant, easy, sociable dinner, and returned home at nine o'clock.

Jones Schermerhorn and Mary came in town this morning to stay with us until they sail. The day of their departure, alas! approaches very fast. This day week my dear girls leave me; it would be nothing to part with them if Mary's health were not precarious. If she were the gay, jocund, bright-eyed, and cherry-cheeked creature she formerly was, her voyage would be a pleasure to me as to herself; but Heaven will hear my prayers, unworthy as I am, and return in due time my beloved child to me, looking and acting and talking as Mary Hone used to do.

OCTOBER 5. — The penny papers and the two-penny people of our slander-loving city have nuts to crack in a spree which took place last night, in which the performers were the young noblemen who are here. The Marquis of Waterford, Lord John Beresford, Lord Jocelyn, and Colonel Dundas dined yesterday on board the yacht belonging to the Marquis, got drunk, came on shore, made a row, had a battle with the watch, were overcome, taken to the watch-house, and kept in durance vile until this morning, when they were liberated by the Mayor. The papers, with their usual veracity, charge upon the Mayor the offence of entertaining these gentlemen at dinner yesterday and making them drunk; but it is not true. Some of them dined with him on Tuesday, as I know, for I was there; but he is not chargeable with this Sunday's entertainment.

OCTOBER 8. — This has been a day of severe trial for me and my family. My daughters, Mary and Catharine, with Mary's husband, J. Jones Schermerhorn, and Gen. James J. Jones, sailed for Havre in the packet-ship "Poland," Captain Anthony. Everything was propitious. She is a noble ship, has admirable accommodations, and a first-rate

<small>Departure of my Daughters.</small>

commander. The weather, which has been stormy the first of the week, cleared up, and a more beautiful morning never broke upon the eyes of anxious travellers and their friends. The wind, too, was quite fair, and it would have been a holiday for us had not my dear Mary's health been so delicate that fears, anxieties, and forebodings dashed the cup of enjoyment from their lips and ours. All the relations and intimate friends of the family called in the morning, and the anguish of parting and the excitement caused by the number of persons present was too much for poor Mary, and I thought at one time it would have overcome her, but she went off tolerably well.

OCTOBER 12. — The friends of General Harrison, the Whig candidate, got up a festival and dinner on the 5th, the anniversary of the battle of the Thames, in which he was the commanding general. This affair took place twenty odd years ago, and this is the first time it has been celebrated in this part of the country; but as glorification is the order of the day, the Harrisonites thought it was better late than never. But the best of the joke is, that the Van Buren men determined to have a glorification of the same event, in honour of their candidate for the Vice-Presidency, Richard M. Johnson, who fought in the same battle, and, as they say, killed Tecumseh; but he didn't. So they had a dinner at Tammany Hall on the same day. The Mayor presided, as a set-off against General Bogardus, the president of the other party; and amongst the regular toasts, and the one hundred and one volunteers, of which Johnson was the oft-repeated burthen, not a single man had the grace to mention the name of Harrison. The play of Hamlet was performed, the part of Hamlet (by particular desire) left out.

Harrison's Festival.

OCTOBER 13. — Miss Helen Kane was at our house last evening, and went home attended by Robert. A long time afterward a messenger came to inquire about her. Nicholson, her lover, met them on the way, took the lady from Robert, and one of those moonlight walks so dear to lovers was the consequence.

OCTOBER 14. — The gambling in stocks in Wall
Gambling. street has arrived at such a pitch, and the sudden
reverses of fortune are so frequent, that it is a matter
of every-day intelligence that some unlucky rascal has lost other
people's money to a large amount, and run away, or been caught
and consigned to the hands of justice. It is one taken from the
mass; there is some swearing among the losers, some regret on the
part of the immediate friends of the defaulter, but the chasm on
the face of society which his detection and removal occasions is
filled up in a day or two. They go to work again to cheat each
other, and the catastrophe of Monday is forgotten by Saturday
night.

The Count Survilliers (Joseph Bonaparte) arrived yesterday at
Philadelphia, in the ship "Monongahela," from Liverpool. His
visit to Europe was said, at the time of his departure from this
country, to be in consequence of certain revolutionary movements
in France, which indicated a chance for the restoration of the
Bonapartes to the throne. If such was his motive he has been
disappointed, and it is likely he will pass the remainder of his life
in the United States.

OCTOBER 24. — The excitement about abolition
Abolition
Meetings. meetings is increasing, and, as I feared, the remedy
is becoming worse than the disease. The abolition
convention was to have assembled at Utica on Wednesday, and the
Common Council had granted to them the use of the court-room
in which to hold the meeting. This was highly disapproved by a
large proportion of the citizens; the consent was withdrawn, and
the convention procured one of the churches. An opposition
meeting was held on the same day, which succeeded in preventing
the convention from meeting, and compelled the members to leave
the city, although in their number were reverend divines and sage
judges, and a speech of that ass Lewis Tappan was cut short in the
middle.

OCTOBER 25. — My birthday. I am fifty-five years of age. My

health is tolerably good, my faculties unimpaired, my mind capable, I believe, as ever it was, but less disposed to exertion; my temper, I fear, a little more irritable than it should be, and I cannot jump so high, nor run so fast, as I did twenty years ago; but, on the whole, I have not much reason to complain, and am better off in all respects than I deserve to be.

OCTOBER 26. — Mr. Van Buren has been in town about ten days. I called to see him and invited him to dine, but others had the start of me, and he was engaged for the whole of his stay in the city. He leaves town to-morrow. He looks very well, and, from his ease of manner and imperturbable good temper, it might be supposed that he had less to occupy and trouble his mind than any man in New York. His outward appearance is like the unruffled surface of the majestic river which covers rocks and whirlpools, but shows no marks of the agitation beneath.

Democratic Meeting. The general meeting took place last evening, at Tammany Hall, to approve of the nomination of a member of Congress in place of Campbell P. White, and the Assembly ticket. Great opposition was expected from the anti-monopoly agrarian and pledge party, and one of these rows for which Tammany Hall is famous took place, and great was the confusion and dire the din which prevailed in the wigwam. The opposition was directed principally against the nomination of Gideon Lee for Congress. He is thought to be a little too much of a gentleman. The regulars, however, having previously made their arrangements disregarding the opposition, declared the nominations agreed to, adjourned the meeting, and put out the lights. The malcontents, however, were not content to grope thus in the dark, but each producing from his pocket a tallow-candle, ten to the pound, and a loco-foco to ignite it, soon brought matters to light again, reorganized the meeting by placing the noted demagogue, Joel G. Seaver, in the chair, passed resolutions condemning banks and other monopolies and approving the system of legislative pledges, substituted Charles G. Ferris for Congress in place of Mr.

Lee, put Job Haskell and three or four others on the Assembly ticket, and marched up to the Bowery to the music of their own throats and the light of their own candles.

In the mean time the Native American Association, made up of different parties, and having no other bond of union than the total exclusion of foreigners from office, have had a meeting and nominated an Assembly ticket, of whom I do not know an individual; but I like the ostensible object of this association, and am of the opinion that times may come and cases occur in which its influence may be favourably exercised.

OCTOBER 31. — The Native American Association have nominated James Monroe for Congress. The split among the Tammany folks is so wide, and their animosity against each other so bitter, that Monroe may very easily be elected if the Whigs can be interested sufficiently in the event to induce them to go to the polls.

Oratorios.

NOVEMBER 11. — I went this evening to the Chatham-street chapel to hear the oratorio of the "Messiah" performed by the Sacred Music Society, and was astonished at the magnificence of the scene; the audience, of whom a large proportion were ladies, must have amounted to between two and three thousand. Mr. and Mrs. Wood, Mrs. Franklin, Brough, and Pierson were the principal singers. The chorus consisted of upward of a hundred; the females, all dressed alike in white and arranged on the opposite sides of the music gallery, formed a beautiful and interesting *coup d'œil*. The ground-floor, which is very capacious, and two large galleries were so crowded that I could scarcely find standing-room behind the benches, and I came away before this rational and delightful entertainment was finished.

How little do the people of such a city as New·York know what is passing around them! These oratorios have been going on for a long time, and I have never heard them spoken of; while if I had attended such an exhibition in a foreign country it would have been the theme of a glowing and animated description, and very probably I should have lamented the want of such things in my own country. So every night we have four theatres open, and one at least, the Park, full at every performance, and making money fast enough, I should say, to satisfy even Mr. Simpson, the proprietor.

The avidity with which people crowd to hear these oratorios, and the immense houses which Mr. and Mrs. Wood bring nightly to the Park, prove that the New Yorkers are not devoid of musical taste, notwithstanding that the Italian opera does not succeed, and the proprietors are about selling their opera-house (the neatest and most beautiful theatre in the United States, and unsurpassed in Europe) ; but there are two reasons for this, both of which savour much of the John Bullism which we have inherited from our forefathers. The first is, that we want to understand the language ; we cannot endure to sit by and see the performers splitting their sides with laughter, and we not take the joke ; dissolved in "briny tears," and we not permitted to sympathize with them ; or running each other through the body, and we devoid of the means of condemning or justifying the act. The other is the private boxes, so elegantly fitted up, which occupy the whole of the second tier. They cost six thousand dollars each, to be sure, and the use of them is all that the proprietors get for their money ; but it forms a sort of aristocratical distinction. Many people do not choose to occupy seats (more pleasant and commodious than they can find in any other theatre) while others recline upon satin cushions, and rest their elbows upon arm-chairs, albeit they are bought with their own money. These causes have prevented the success of the Italian opera, and I do not wonder at it. I like this spirit of independence which refuses its countenance to anything exclusive. "Let the proprietors," say the sovereigns, " have their private boxes and satin cushions ; they have paid well for them and are entitled to enjoy them. We will not furnish the means of supporting the establishment, but go to the Park Theatre, where it is 'first come, first served ; ' where our dollar will furnish us with 'the best the House affords,' and where the Woods will provide us with that dollar's worth of something we can understand without the aid of a bungling translation.

NOVEMBER 13. — This gentleman (who, by the bye, I have never seen) has been playing at the Bowery Theatre. He is a great actor in high, strongly-marked tragedy parts, such as Richard, Iago, Sir Giles, and Sir Edward Mortimer. He is also remarkable for his eccentricities, and there seems to be little doubt that at times his mind is alienated; he gave a proof of this on Monday night. He was to play Iago. When all was ready, the play begun, and Othello (Hamblin) waiting for him, he stalked across the stage, made an irregular exit by a back door, and was seen no more that night and for two or three following days. Some of the audience got their money back, and the play went on with a substitute in the part. Poor Booth now comes out with a humble apology for the "sad and unconscious act," the excuse for which he says " is a serious visitation, affecting and enfeebling my nerves, and a long deprivation of sleep, acting on a body debilitated by previous illness, and a mind disordered by domestic affliction, occasioning a partial derangement." He prays to be permitted to appear again, and says very affectingly, "If I find by your reception that I have offended beyond forgiveness, I will immediately withdraw from that stage where I have ever been treated, both by the public and the manager, with kindness and liberality." Mr. Hamblin has by this apology been prevailed upon to consent to his appearance to-morrow evening in the part of Sir Giles Overreach, and there is no doubt that public sympathy will be excited to fill the house and give the poor fellow not only the forgiveness of the audience, but a kind and generous reception.

Booth, the Tragedian.

A meeting of the friends of General Harrison was held, on Thursday evening, at Constitution Hall, to recommend him as the candidate for the Presidency in opposition to Mr. Van Buren. I did not attend this meeting, nor do I intend to commit myself to the support of General Harrison, Judge White, or any other man, until it is clearly ascertained that

Harrison Meeting.

there is no chance for Mr. Webster. A meeting of his friends is soon to be called in this city. That meeting I *will* attend. Daniel Webster's claim is incomparably stronger than that of either of the other candidates. He is entitled to the people's votes, for he is their true friend, and not the friend of a party or a section. He merits the support of his country, for his patriotism is not of those scanty proportions which will cover only a part of his country, and the Constitution can never be so safe in any other hands as in his who has proved himself its ablest expounder and firmest supporter. I go, therefore, for Webster until it is made manifest that he has no chance of success, and then for the next best man, Harrison or whoever it may be.

<small>Webster Meeting.</small> NOVEMBER 26. — The following notice is published this morning with one thousand one hundred signatures:
"Liberty and Union, now and forever, one and inseparable. The citizens of the city and county of New York, friendly to the election of *Daniel Webster* to the Presidency, are requested to assemble at Masonic Hall, on Friday evening, the 4th of December."

There are now three candidates fairly in the field in opposition to Mr. Van Buren, very much to his satisfaction, no doubt; the more the merrier, the greater the division amongst his opponents the more certain his chance; such things do not happen in the party which supports him,— they are too well drilled, and, right or wrong, they "go ahead." Judge White, of Tennessee, General Harrison, of Ohio, and Daniel Webster, of Massachusetts, are the Whig candidates in opposition to the nominee of the Baltimore Convention; the friends of each seem at present indisposed to abandon their favourite, but I should not be surprised if, in the end, they should give up their own *ground* and take to *Clay*.

<small>Musical Taste.</small> NOVEMBER 27. — The good people of New York are certainly not fairly chargeable with a want of taste in music, or liberality in rewarding musical talent, notwithstanding the failure of the Italian opera. That failure arose

from causes inherent in its own construction, which I have explained in a former part of this journal; but the citizens of New York, not those alone who constitute what is called "good society," but respectable persons in the middle walks of life, who select with careful deliberation the kind of amusement which suits them best, are fond of music, and patronize it in preference to any other public or theatrical entertainment. This description of persons constituted a large proportion of the audience at the performance of Mr. Horn's oratorio on Wednesday evening, and it is said that the proceeds amounted to $1,600. In corroboration of my opinion on this subject, the engagements of those beautiful singers, Mr. and Mrs. Wood, have been more profitable than any former one in this country.

Dear Living. Living in New York is exorbitantly dear, and it falls pretty hard upon persons like me, who live upon their income, and harder still upon that large and respectable class consisting of the officers and clerks in public institutions, whose support is derived from fixed salaries. I can raise my rents, if the tenants are able and willing to pay; but the increase of their pay depends upon others, who in their turn are precluded from the exercise of liberality by the fact of their being the stewards of others, who cannot be consulted, and who as individuals may be liberal enough, but collectively are very apt to verify the adage that "corporations have no souls." Marketing of all kinds, with the exception of apples and potatoes, is higher than I ever knew it. The sweat of the brow of New York all runs into the pockets of the farmers. I paid to-day $30 a ton for hay, and not an old-fashioned ton of 2,240 lbs., but a new-fangled ton, invented to cheat the consumer, of 2,000 lbs. This is a cent and a half a pound, nearly three times the ordinary price. I paid also for my winter butter, 400 to 500 lbs., $2.14 per pound. In the long course of thirty-four years' housekeeping I never buttered my bread at so extravagant a rate. Good butter is almost an indispensable article in the family; but there are many persons in New York as good as myself who must be content to eat dry bread this winter, or at least to spread the children's slices confoundedly thin.

Governor McDuffie's Message. DECEMBER 2. — The message of the Governor of South Carolina to the Legislature is published in the "Commercial Advertiser" of to-day. It is altogether worthy of the redoubtable champion of nullification, it "out-Herods Herod;" it is made up of gunpowder bombs, blunderbusses, and hand-grenades. He has worked himself up into an exterminating passion, and it is impossible to read his speech without shivering with apprehension and looking around to see a fiery dragon issuing from the crater of a volcano; and all this rage is excited on the subject of the silly abolitionists, who, from mistaken views of moral and religious duty, have been meddling in things which did not concern them. See now, infatuated men, what you have done! Crittenden, of the Eagle Tavern, used to tell a story of a Yankee militia captain, who, in addressing his troops to "screw their courage to the sticking place," depicted in glowing terms the awful consequences which would result from the success of the enemy. "They will, gentlemen," said he, "lay your towns in ashes, ravish your wives, murder your children, and pull down your fences." So it may be said to the abolition meddlers, only the subject is almost too serious to joke about, and the application is only to be excused by Governor McDuffie's rhodomontade : —

"See, you abolitionists, ye Tappans, ye Thompsons, see what you have done, — you have sown the seeds of discord amongst friends and brethren of different sections of our hitherto happy land; you have sought to break down the solemn compact into which our fathers entered on the adoption of the Constitution; you have caused your countrymen of the South to tremble for their safety and their lives, and — you have made Governor McDuffie angry."

But in truth the temper of this document is ridiculous, and its arguments absurd. "It is my deliberate opinion," says the Governor, "that the laws of every community should punish this species of interference by *death without benefit of clergy,* regarding the authors of it as enemies of the human race." He demands of the non-slaveholding States that they shall pass laws to punish, in the most exemplary manner, this nondescript and non-enumerated crime against the peace and dignity of South Carolina; and they had better be pretty quick about it. Governor Marcy, when he reads the following sensible passage, will be derelict of duty if he does not anticipate the meeting of our Legislature, and call them together to pass laws for the hanging instanter all the vile miscreants who have offended Governor McDuffie: —

"As between separate and independent nations the refusal of a State to punish these offensive proceedings against another, by its citizens or subjects, makes the State so refusing an accomplice in the outrage, and *furnishes* a *just* cause of war." A pretty pickle we of the North are going to be placed in! Louis Philippe on one side, and Governor McDuffie on the other. We shall have to apologize to both; the same formulæ will do for both, with the alteration of "the State of New York" for "the United States."

The course of reasoning in this message is not to prove that slavery is unavoidable, and cannot be abolished in the Southern States. Oh, no! he scouts that idea. He goes the whole hog. Slavery an evil? By no means. It is a positive benefit to the community, sanctified by God and man in all ages; it promotes religion and morality, and, what is more wonderful still, it proves incontestably the existence of liberty in its most fascinating shapes. The Governor does certainly work himself up into this absurd conclusion, and winds up his argument, like the stars which coruscate on the explosion of a sky-rocket, with the following magnificent paragraph: —

" Domestic slavery, therefore, instead of being a political evil, is the corner-stone of our republican edifice. No patriot who justly estimates our privileges will tolerate the idea of emancipation at any period, however remote, or on any conditions of pecuniary advantage, however favourable. I would as soon think of opening a negotiation for selling the liberty of the State at once, as for making any stipulation for the ultimate emancipation of our slaves.

So deep is my conviction on this subject, that if I were doomed to die immediately after recording these sentiments, I could say, in all sincerity and under all the sanctions of Christianity and patriotism, 'God forbid that my descendants in the remotest generations should live in any other than a community having the institution of domestic slavery as it existed among the patriarchs of the primitive church and in all the free states of antiquity!'"

This Hotspur of the South having let off his steam by the safety-valve of this last flourish, and recovered his breath, turns suddenly around and vents the residuum of his vial of wrath upon poor Jackson. What he says upon the subject, "though I most powerfully and potently believe," adds materially to the ludicrous wrath of this furious message. After telling the Legislature that he has not much to say on national affairs, and giving them the comfortable assurance that the corruption of the government will soon become incurable, he adds: "The chief magistrate of our imperial Republic is at this moment more independent of public opinion, and wields a more despotic power, than either the King of Great Britain or the King of France, and it remains to be seen whether the people of the United States, like the degenerate Romans in the time of Tiberius, will recognize his right to nominate his successor, by raising to the throne the imperial, though not very youthful, Cæsar, who has been already clothed in the purple with due solemnity, and formally presented to the people as the anointed and rightful heir to the succession."

DECEMBER 8. — I have seldom been so much shocked
Death of Judge Smith. by the sudden announcement of a death, or have realized so fully the uncertainty of life, as in the case of Judge Smith, — Nathan Smith, Senator of the United States from Connecticut. Exactly a week ago I met him at Nevins and Townsend's office in Wall street, was introduced to and conversed with him a few minutes. I have always been struck with his appearance when I saw him in the Senate, and was much pleased to be made acquainted with him.

When I went home I described him to the family, — a fine, handsome, healthy-looking gentleman, aged sixty-six years, of great personal dignity, and of the old school in his dress; a remnant of that race of men, the very form and fashion of whose clothes are a passport to deference and respect; his white hair well powdered; a handsome blue coat with shining gilt buttons; drab kerseymere breeches and top-boots, the clean white tops of which were well contrasted by the elaborate black polish of the legs. Now that this worthy man has gone, I know of but one such pair of boots in American occupancy, and they are at present the admiration of Europe, on the well-formed legs of my learned and excellent friend, Dr. Mott, of this city.

I dined to-day with Mr. Charles March; a very pleasant party, but its crowning feature was Daniel Webster. I have never seen him so agreeable; for five hours he was the life of the company; cheerful, gay, full of anecdotes, and entirely free from a sort of gloomy abstraction in which I have sometimes seen him, as it were, envelop himself. He amused us with anecdotes of his early life, stories of down-East and descriptions of down-East men and manners; talked wisdom enough to let us see that he was wise, but evidently preferred the light gossip in which he delights to pass the social hour. On public affairs Mr. Webster avowed his determination to support the government in its stand against France. He says the President cannot make any explanation, and the honour of the country is concerned in his being borne out in his refusal. I inferred, however, from what he said on this subject (and he was quite free and communicative), that he does not apprehend any immediate difficulties of a serious nature, and appears to think that the French will yet do right.

Weddings.

DECEMBER 10. — Married last evening, December 9, Peter Augustus Schermerhorn, second son of Peter Schermerhorn, to Adeline Emily, youngest daughter of the late Henry A. Coster. The wedding took place at Dr. Hosack's. We were all there; a large company was assembled. The Schermerhorns, the Costers, the Hosacks, and the Hones, all the links of several long chains, form a goodly number when they are collected together on such an occasion. The ceremony was performed by the Rev. Mr. Sherwood, the respectable pastor of the Episcopal church at Hyde Park. The wedding supper was sumptuous, but no part of it so superb as the products of the doctor's greenhouse, which graced the upper end of the table.

Mrs. Hosack has now married the last of her daughters, and I am released from the guardianship of the last of my seven wards. I have had the principal management of their property for the last fourteen years, and am now preparing my accounts for a settlement with the last heir. The bride is very young, only seventeen years old on the 18th of May last.

DECEMBER 11. — The prevalence of westerly winds during the present cold weather has deprived us of news from Europe. The packet from Havre of the 24th of October has not arrived. This delay, though not unusual at this time of the year, occasions some anxiety in the present excited state of the public mind with regard to the dispute with France. It is understood that Mr. Barton has orders to make a formal demand of the indemnity, and in case of refusal, to break off the negotiation by returning home, in which event Mr. Pageot, the French *Chargé d'Affaires* at Washington, will hand in his P.P.C., and both parties will draw off their diplomatic forces. Mr. Barton is expected to arrive in one of the first packets. I have, however, a more interesting reason to note the non-intercourse with France occasioned by storms and head-winds. It is sixty-four days since my daughters sailed, and we begin to be anxious for news from them. The first change of wind will bring it.

Duelling.

DECEMBER 15. — The practice of duelling has increased to such a degree in the South and West, and is marked with such savage ferocity and deadly determination, as to form a stigma upon the national character. It seems impossible to carry on a political election, which is in any degree warmly contested, without an excitement of feeling leading to quarrels amongst the most active partisans, and most frequently between the candidates themselves, which nothing but blood will settle. Scarcely a day passes that our newspapers do not contain accounts of some of those sanguinary semi-barbarous conflicts, and these Southern and Western men, like the brant shooters of Long Island, do not like to waste powder and ball for nothing. The order of combat is such as to preclude the chance of both the combatants escaping; it is not children's play; one at least, and frequently both, seal their political faith and write their title to fame in blood which could be better employed in defending their native soil and supporting the liberties of their country; and this practice unhappily prevails amongst the finest fellows in the community, the choice spirits possessing all those high qualities required to develop the resources and establish the institutions of a new country. But the vitiated taste of the people seems to require that a man in that part of the country should fight his way up to public notice, and his claim to serve his fellow-citizens is not so well established by talents, virtue, and patriotism, as by having "killed his man." The foregoing remarks have been suggested at this time by the publication in the "National Intelligencer" of a letter from Florida, giving an account of a desperate duel, fought on the 21st of November, between Captain Everett White, brother of Colonel White, the delegate to Congress from Florida, and Colonel A. Bellamy, late president of the legislative council, arising out of the circumstances of an election in which they were rival candidates, and White had been elected. The regulations of this combat were such as to render a fatal result inevitable. "The parties were to stand sixty feet apart, each with four pistols, and to advance and fire. Captain White advanced and received three shots without injury, and then fired at a distance of fifteen paces. His first shot passed through Colonel Bellamy's arm, the next through his body, and in the act of advancing with the other two pistols he received a mortal wound from Colonel Bellamy's fourth pistol. Colonel Bellamy is not yet dead, but must certainly die of his wounds."

In this manner have the gentlemen proved themselves men of honour and courage, and their fellow-citizens sanction the act which has deprived them of one, at least, of their distinguished men, by their expressions of sorrow, unmingled with the slightest disapprobation of the savage practice which occasioned the catastrophe. The letter goes on to say: "I yesterday performed the painful office of following Captain White to the grave. The Court adjourned, and the funeral was attended by the Bar and the grand jury in a body. Every testimony of respect and deep-felt interest was evinced by the whole population of the place. All the stores were shut, and I have seldom witnessed a more general and sincere exhibition of sorrow than was manifested on this solemn occasion."

<small>Unparalleled Calamity by Fire.</small> DECEMBER 17. — How shall I record the events of last night, or how attempt to describe the most awful calamity which has ever visited these United States? The greatest loss by fire that has ever been known, with the exception perhaps of the conflagration of Moscow, and that was an incidental concomitant of war. I am fatigued in body, disturbed in mind, and my fancy filled with images of horror which my pen is inadequate to describe. Nearly one-half of the first ward is in ashes, five hundred to seven hundred stores, which with their contents are valued at $20,000,000 to $40,000,000, are now lying in an indistinguishable mass of ruins. There is not, perhaps, in the world the same space of ground covered by so great an amount of real and personal property as the scene of this dreadful conflagration. The fire broke out at nine o'clock last evening. I was writing in the library when the alarm was given, and went immediately down. The night was intensely cold, which was one cause of the unprecedented progress of the flames, for the water froze in the hydrants, and the engines and their hose could not be worked without great difficulty. The firemen, too,

had been on duty all last night, and were almost incapable of performing their usual services. The fire originated in the store of Comstock & Adams, in Merchant street,—a narrow, crooked street, filled with high stores lately erected and occupied by dry-goods and hardware merchants, which led from Hanover to Pearl street. When I arrived at the spot the scene exceeded all description; the progress of the flames, like flashes of lightning, communicated in every direction, and a few minutes sufficed to level the lofty edifices on every side. It crossed the block to Pearl street. I perceived that the store of my son was in danger, and made the best of my way, by Front street around the old Slip, to the spot. We succeeded in getting out the stock of valuable dry goods, but they were put in the square, and in the course of the night our labours were rendered unavailing, for the fire reached and destroyed them, with a great part of all which were saved from the neighbouring stores; this part of Pearl street consisted of dry-goods stores, with stocks of immense value, of which little or nothing was saved. At this period the flames were unmanageable, and the crowd, including the firemen, appeared to look on with the apathy of despair, and the destruction continued until it reached Coenties Slip, in that direction, and Wall street down to the river, including all South street and Water street; while to the west, Exchange street, including all Post's stores, Lord's beautiful row, William street, Beaver and Stone streets, were destroyed. The splendid edifice erected a few years ago by the liberality of the merchants, known as the Merchants' Exchange, and one of the ornaments of the city, took fire in the rear, and is now a heap of ruins. The façade and magnificent marble columns fronting on Wall street are all that remain of this noble building, and resemble the ruins of an ancient temple rather than the new and beautiful resort of the merchants. When the dome of this edifice fell in, the sight was awfully grand; in its fall it demolished the statue of Hamilton, executed by Ball Hughes, which was erected in the rotunda only eight months ago, by the public spirit of the merchants.

It would be an idle task to attempt an enumeration of the sufferers; in the number are most of my nearest friends and of my family; my son John, my son-in-law Schermerhorn, and my nephew Isaac S. Hone, and Samuel S. Howland were all burnt out.

The buildings covered an area of a quarter of a mile square, closely built up with fine stores of four and five stories in height, filled with merchandise, all of which lie in a mass of burning, smoking ruins, rendering the streets indistinguishable.

All the property within the following limits is destroyed: south side of Wall street from William street to East river, including the Merchants' Exchange, and excepting three or four unfinished buildings above Pearl street; Exchange street, both sides, from Broad street, crossing William to Merchant street; Merchant street, both sides, from Wall street to Hanover square; Pearl street, both sides, from Wall street to Coenties Slip, with the whole sweep of Hanover square, Stone street, and Beaver street, nearly to Broad street; Water street, Front street, and South street, with all the intersecting streets and lanes from Wall street to Coenties Slip, including the south side of Coffee House Slip. A large portion of the valuable estates of the Jones and Schermerhorn families was within these limits, and is not now to be found. The fire has been burning all day in the direction of Coenties Slip, and was not fairly gotten under until towards evening.

A calculation is made in the "Commercial" this afternoon that the number of buildings burned is 570, and that the whole loss is something over $15,000,000. The insurance offices are all, of course, bankrupt, their collective capitals amount to $11,750,000; but those down-town have a large proportion of the risks, and will not be able to pay fifty per cent. of the losses. The unfortunate stockholders lose all. In this way I suffer directly, and in others indirectly, to a large amount.

The Mayor, who has exerted himself greatly in this fearful emergency, called the Common Council together this afternoon for the purpose of establishing private patrols for the protection of the city; for if another fire should break out before the firemen have recovered from the fatigues of the last two nights, and the engines and hose be repaired from the effects of the frost, it would be impossible to arrest its progress. Several companies of uniformed militia and a company of United States marines are under arms, to protect the property scattered over the lower part of the city.

I have been alarmed by some of the signs of the times which this calamity has brought forth; the miserable wretches who prowled about the ruins and became beastly drunk on the champagne and other wines and liquors with which the streets and wharves were lined, seemed to exult in the misfortune, and such expressions were heard as, "Ah! they'll make no more five per cent. dividends," and "This will make the aristocracy haul in their horns." Poor, deluded wretches! — little do they know that their own horns " live, and move, and have their being " in these very horns of the aristocracy, as their instigators teach them to call it. This cant is the very text from which their leaders teach their deluded followers. It forms part of the warfare of the poor against the rich, — a warfare which is destined, I fear, to break the hearts of some of the politicians of Tammany Hall, who have used these men to answer a temporary purpose, and find now that the dogs they have taught to bark will bite them as soon as their political opponents.

These remarks are not so much the result of what I have heard of the conduct and conversations of the rabble at the fire as of what I witnessed this afternoon at the Bank for Savings. There was an immediate run upon the bank by a gang of low Irishmen, who demanded their money in a peremptory and threatening manner. At this season there is usually a great preponderance of deposits over the drafts, the first of January being the day on which the balances are made up of the semi-annual dividend. All the sums now drawn lose nearly six months' interest, which the bank gains; these Irishmen, however, insisted upon having their money, and when they received it were evidently disappointed and would fain have put it back again. This class of men are the most ignorant, and consequently the most obstinate, white men in the world, and I have seen enough to satisfy me that, with few exceptions, ignorance and vice go together. These men, rejoicing in the calamity which has ruined so many institutions and individuals, thought it a fine opportunity to use the power which their dirty money gave them to add to the general distress, and sought to embarrass this excellent institution, which had been established for the sole benefit of the poor; but they have not the sense to understand, nor hearts to respond to, the benevolent feelings which prompt the managers of the savings-banks to devote their whole time and labour for the benefit of others. Now comes the most painful of all the reflections which arise out of this unnatural state of society. These Irishmen, strangers among us, without a feeling of patriotism or affection in common with American citizens, *decide the elections in the city of New York.* They make presidents and governors, and they send men to represent us in the councils of the nation, and, what is worse than all, their importance in these matters is derived from the use which is made of them by political demagogues, who despise the tools they work with. Let them look to it; the time may not be very distant when the same brogue which they have instructed to shout "Hurrah for Jackson!" shall be used to impart additional horror to the cry of "Down with the natives!"

Dr. Hosack. DECEMBER 18. — I went out this morning with my wife to view the scene of the recent conflagration; but we had proceeded only a short distance when we met Robert Benson, who informed us that Dr. Hosack, the elder, had been seized a few moments previous with a fit of apoplexy. We of course returned, and I went immediately around to his house; and what a scene was there! What an awful instance of the uncertainty of life and the instability of human happiness! Here was the doctor laid upon a sofa, insensible to all around him, his limbs paralyzed, his faculties suspended, and his large and estimable family surrounding his couch, with despair and anguish depicted in every countenance. Two days before, the very room in which he lies was the scene of festivity. The bride (Mrs. Schermerhorn) was receiving the visits of her friends, and I was there, a joyful witness of the happiness of both families. Since that time, in a space of less than forty-eight hours, Mrs. Berryman, the daughter of Mr. John G. Coster, has died suddenly. The calamity under which the city now suffers so severely has fallen heavily upon every branch of the connection. The splendid estate of the bride, which I was about to transfer to her husband, has been most seriously encroached upon by the same cause; and the highly respected head of her family, from being in the full possession of his bodily and mental faculties, lies extended on his bed of death, prostrated in an instant, in a situation which seems to preclude all hopes of recovery.

Further Particulars of the Fire. DECEMBER 19. — I went yesterday and to-day to see the ruins. It is an awful sight. The whole area from Wall street to Coenties Slip, bounded by Broad street to the river, with the exception of Broad street, the Wall-street front between William and Broad, and the blocks bounded by Broad street, Pearl street, the south side of Coenties Slip and South street, are now a mass of smoking ruins.

It is gratifying to witness the spirit and firmness with which the merchants meet this calamity. There is no despondency; every man is determined to go to work to redeem his loss, and all are ready to assist their more unfortunate neighbours. A meeting of citizens was held this day, at noon, at the Session Court-room, on the call of the Mayor. A committee of one hundred and twenty-five was appointed, which met in the evening at the Mayor's office and appointed sub-committees on each branch of duty submitted to them. I am of the committee to make application for relief to the State government. That committee is to meet to-morrow evening at my house. The utmost spirit and harmony prevailed at the meeting, which embraced all the best and most influential men in the city. During the evening intelligence was brought in of the proceedings of a great meeting held yesterday in Philadelphia, at which the Mayor presided. Amongst other things a resolution was passed calling upon the general government to appropriate the sum of $12,000,000 to our relief. This is an important step, for it will tend to remove the only objection to such a measure, — that of its being exclusive and partial in its operation. A body of four hundred Philadelphia firemen came on yesterday to relieve our firemen. They are to be seen about the streets and in the neighbourhood of the fire, in their peculiar uniform. This is truly a brotherly kindness and charity, and will never be forgotten.

Companies of soldiers are on guard all the time, and patrols of citizens are formed in each ward, who are on duty during the night; the exhausted state of the firemen and the disabled condition of their apparatus render these extraordinary measures necessary. A fire would be awful at this moment. The insurance offices are all bankrupt, and every man is his own underwriter.

The Merchants' Exchange is held at the Mechanics' Exchange in Broad street; the post-office removed to the rotunda in Chambers street. The printing-offices, of which a large number are burned out, are distributed into different places, and it is amusing to see the holes and corners into which the merchants have stowed themselves.

Mr. Biddle, President of the Bank of the United States, came on to-day to see what that institution could do for us. The first step must be to turn the bonds and mortgages held by the insurance companies into cash, to enable them to pay as much as they can of their losses. But the unfortunate stockholders, what is to become of them?

The following are the sub-committees appointed at the meeting of the general committee this evening: 1. Committee to ascertain the extent and probable value of property destroyed, and how far the sufferers are protected by insurance: Nathaniel Weed, Gabriel

P. Dissosway, Brittain L. Woolley, George S. Robbins, Walter R. Jones, Isaac S. Hone.

2. Committee on application to Congress for an extension of credit on duty bonds, and remission of duties, and on such other aid as it may be expedient to ask of the general government: Albert Gallatin, Preserved Fish, George Griswold, John T. Irving, Louis McLane, James G. King, Reuben Withers, Cornelius W. Lawrence, Samuel Jones.

3. Committee on application to the State and city government: Enos T. Throop, John L. Graham, John A. Stevens, Charles H. Russell, Thomas J. Oakley, Philip Hone, Daniel Jackson, Benjamin L. Swan.

4. Committee on the origin and cause of the fire: James B. Murray, George Douglass, James Lee, David Bryson, Marcus Wilbur.

5. Committee on change in the regulation of the streets: Samuel B. Ruggles, Jonathan Goodhue, David S. Jones, John Haggerty, John S. Crary.

6. Committee on the erection of buildings and the arrangement of the fire department: Stephen Allen, Peter G. Stuyvesant, John Leonard, Benjamin Strong, Charles A. Davis, George D. Strong, Prosper M. Wetmore, Seth Geer, George Ireland, James J. Roosevelt, Jr., Dudley Selden, and Stephen Whitney.

7. Committee on relief, with power to receive and distribute contributions: Samuel Cowdry, Jacob Lorillard, Samuel S. Howland, Benjamin McVickar, M.D., John J. Boyd, William T. McCoun, Ogden Hoffman, William L. Stone, Jacob Harvey, Thaddeus Phelps, John W. Leavitt, James Boorman, Edward Prime.

DECEMBER 21. — The sub-committee on the subjects of applications to the State and city governments met last evening at my house and agreed to a report recommending an application to the Legislature to issue a State stock, under the guarantee of the corporation, of six millions of dollars, and the appointment of a committee of five to go to Albany and confer with the Governor on the facts to be laid before the Legislature. The general committee met this evening; our report was accepted, but the resolutions amended so as to call upon the corporation to issue their bonds for $6,000,000, to create a fund for the purpose of buying up the bonds and mortgages held by the insolvent fire insurance companies, and thereby enable them to pay their losses as far as they may be able.

DECEMBER 22. — The weather since the fire has become more mild. This day is very pleasant. This is a happy circumstance, for it facilitates the labors of an immense number of workmen who are employed in removing the rubbish. Goods and property of every description are found under the ruins in enormous quantities, but generally so much damaged as to be hardly worth saving. Cloths, silks, laces, prints of the most valuable kinds, are dug out partly burned, and nearly all ruined. A mountain of coffee lies at the corner of old Slip and South street. The entire cargo of teas, arrived a few days since in the ship "Paris," lies in a state not worth picking up, and costly indigo and rich drugs add to the mass of mud which obstructs the streets.

Crowds of spectators (amongst whom are many ladies) have been perambulating the streets in the neighbourhood, lost in wonder and absorbed in horror at the awful scene of destruction. Many curious facts are now coming to light in relation to the fire. A note of hand of fifty-seven dollars, in favour of the Ocean Insurance Company, was blown, during the fire, from a store in South street to a garden at Flatbush, Long Island, five miles distant. A gallant effort was made to save the statue of Hamilton by a young officer from the Navy-Yard, with a party of four or five sailors. They had actually succeeded in removing it from the pedestal, when the danger of the approaching fall of the dome compelled them to abandon it. The fire was seen at New Haven and at Philadelphia; the firemen turned out, supposing the fire was in the suburbs of the city.

DECEMBER 23. — Hopes have been entertained that Dr. Hosack might survive his attack. There was an appearance of consciousness and a slight improvement

Death of Dr. Hosack.

in his symptoms during the whole of yesterday; but it would have been better otherwise, for it excited false hopes in his anxious family, which were doomed to be destroyed, for at eleven o'clock last night he died. He has never spoken since his attack, and it is quite doubtful if he has at any time recognized those about him. Thus has the house of joy been suddenly turned into the house of mourning.

Dr. Hosack was born on the 31st of August, 1769. He has passed an active and useful life, and filled a large space in society. In his profession he was learned, skilful, and bold, and, in my opinion, the best physician in the city. I remember him from my earliest years; the physician of my father's family, and he has always been mine. His literary acquirements were of a high order, and although not a man of great genius, his industry and acquirements had rendered him a good writer. His style was correct and strong, without elegance, and his great experience will render his works respectable authorities to professional men. He retired a few years ago from general practice, and resided two-thirds of the year on his splendid estate at Hyde Park. His wife, the widow of Henry A. Coster, is my first cousin, by whom he became possessed of a large estate. She had seven children, of whom I was appointed guardian on the death of Mr. Coster.

CHRISTMAS DAY, but not by any means "a merry Christmas." The recent calamity bears so hard upon the whole community that it seems unfeeling to be joyful. Philosophy enables many of us to bear our own misfortunes without repining, and hope spreads its buoyant wings over the future; but as all are not equally consoled by the former, or encouraged by the latter, respect for individual loss restrains all the appearance of mirth which belongs to this otherwise happy season.

Dr. Hosack's Funeral. I attended, as a relation, the funeral of Dr. Hosack, at one o'clock. The service was read in Grace Church by the Bishop and Dr. Ducachet. It was very impressive; the large family connection and the great number of friends which attended filled the church. The pall-bearers were, Colonel Trumbull, Mr. John Watts, Herman LeRoy, Edward W. Laight, Edward Livingston, Charles McEvers, Chancellor Kent, and Gen. Morgan Lewis.

1836.

ALBANY, JAN. 1. — It makes me somewhat melancholy to reflect that this is the first New Year's Day, except one, that I ever passed from home, and that one was passed at sea, on my return from Europe. I am here against my will. I would much rather have spent this day with my family and in the society of my friends; but, alas! it is not a happy day in New York.

The year 1835 is passed; it began well; the city prospered, and all went on swimmingly until its close. But now many aching hearts are in our borders. What blighted prospects, what disappointed hopes! The calamity of the night of the 16th has reduced thousands from comparative independence to cheerless poverty. Not the poorest class, for if they were burned out, and exposed to the inclemency of the biting blasts of winter, a good fire, a warm bed, and plenty to eat and drink, as a temporary relief, would make them as well off as they were before: "take nothing from nothing and nothing remains;" but this loss falls upon those who were accustomed to enjoy the comforts and little elegances of life, which must now be given up.

JANUARY 4. — I went yesterday morning with Mr. Stevenson to St. Peter's Church, and was so much pleased with the sermon from the Rev. Mr. Potter that I was induced to go again in the afternoon, although the hour, two o'clock, affords but a brief allowance of time for dinner. The church has been repaired and new modelled; has a new organ and pulpit, and the handsomest, most comfortable, and best-arranged pews I have seen in any of our churches. There is a large and respectable congregation, and if their pastor is in the practice of giving them such sermons as I heard yesterday, they have no reason to be dissatisfied.

JANUARY 4. — Whilst I was writing in my room this evening

there was an alarm of fire. Two or three wooden houses were burned in the upper part of Market street. It was quite a refreshing sight, for it reminded me of home. It was a mark of civilization in a strange country, as the traveller said, who saw a man hanging on a gibbet.

Relief Bills. The bills authorizing the city loan of six millions, and for enabling the fire-insurance companies to settle their concerns and to resuscitate their businesses, have passed the Legislature with great unanimity.

NEW YORK, JAN. 16.— I went, this morning, to dine with Mr. John C. Stevens at his place on Long Island, about eleven miles from Brooklyn, and three miles from the race-course on the South road. Charles King, General Fleming, and Cornelius Low went with me in my sleigh. We arrived at Stevens's about three o'clock; had a most capital dinner, fine wine, good fires, and plenty of laugh, joke, and joviality. We found, on our arrival, John A. King, Commodore Ridgely, Mr. Botts, and Robert L. Stevens.

At half-past eight we started to return. It was very dark and had become excessively cold, and the road, being but little used, was hard to be distinguished. John soon planted us in a snowbank, from which we extricated the sleigh and horses with some difficulty. King then undertook to drive, and had not proceeded above a mile when the darkness of the night, the narrowness and indistinctness of the road, and John Stevens's good wine combined to bother the skill of our new driver, and over went the sleigh. I was slightly scratched in the face and bled a little, but the rest of the party were uninjured. The sleigh was broken a little. We now held council of war, and concluded to return to the "place whence we came." This was accomplished without difficulty; our friends were still assembled, and a few hickory logs added to the fire, a renewal of the bottles and glasses, a reproduction of the remains of the dinner to serve as supper, and a cigar afterward, brought us to the sensible conclusion that it was better to be there than in a snow-bank. After a few hours passed in pleasant conversation John A. King went home to Jamaica, taking with him General Fleming, Mr. Low, and Mr. Botts; Charles King, Commodore Ridgely, and I were well accommodated with good beds in the house of our hospitable host.

We had breakfast this morning at eight o'clock, and started for home. A fine, bright morning, but very cold. Charles King was sick; the Commodore had an unwelcome visit from an old acquaintance, — the gout, — which prevented him from putting on his boot, and I, who was the only sick man who went upon this pleasant frolic, returned the only well one. We left the Commodore at the Navy-Yard and arrived in town at eleven o'clock.

The following party dined with us: Mr. and Mrs. Boreel, Mr. and Mrs. Charles Brugiere, Miss Helen Kane, Captain Anthony, of the "Poland," Mr. Nicolson, Henry Hone, and Edward Schermerhorn.

JANUARY 20. — I went over to dine with Mr. John A. King, at Jamaica. Charles and James A. King and General Fleming went with me, in my sleigh. Besides ourselves, the party consisted of Robert Ray, Jacob LeRoy, Robert L. and John C. Stevens, and Mr. Nicholas. The weather was very fine and the sleighing admirable. On our return we came to Brooklyn ferry at ten o'clock, but found two steamboats there, blocked in by the ice, which detained us nearly three hours, and I did not get home until one o'clock.

The "Herald." There is an ill-looking, squinting man called Bennett, formerly connected with Webb in the publication of his paper, who is now editor of the "Herald," one of the penny papers which are hawked about the streets by a gang of troublesome, ragged boys, and in which scandal is retailed to all who delight in it, at that moderate price. This man and Webb are now bitter enemies, and it was nuts for Bennett to be the organ of Mr. Lynch's late vituperative attack upon Webb, which Bennett introduced in his paper with evident marks of savage exultation. This did not suit Mr. Webb's fiery disposition, so he attacked

Bennett in Wall street yesterday, beat him, and knocked him down. In the mean time Webb and Lynch maintain a relative position something like that of France and the United States: they carry clubs, but do not strike; and look fierce at each other, but do not speak. They cannot adjust their pecuniary differences in an *honourable* manner, for each considers the other unworthy of his notice. None but men of acknowledged honour and good character are entitled to the privilege of having their brains blown out. If Lynch and Webb are both men of truth they are liars, and if neither is to be believed they are both honourable men.

Opera House. The Opera House was offered this morning for sale at auction, under the direction of Gardiner G. Howland and Robert Ray, trustees. It was set up at $100,000; but there was no bid, and the sale was postponed. The articles of association designated the Merchants' Exchange as the place of sale, if ever it should be found necessary to dispose of the property. As there is unfortunately no such edifice at present, it was deemed necessary to have the sale on the porch, which is all that remains of that edifice. It was a melancholy illustration of the decay of commerce and taste to witness the auctioneer, mounted on the ruins of the Merchants' Exchange, endeavouring to sell the Italian Opera-House to the highest bidder.

JANUARY 21. — I dined with Mr. Henry Cary. We had Irving, Paulding, Brevoort, Gouverneur Kemble, Doctor Stevens, Professor Renwick, and such literary and learned men; and, as is always the case, it was excessively stupid. There were more brilliant things said at John Stevens's the other day, when it was a party of no pretension, than could be elicited from these learned pundits in the course of a long life, and one of any of the thousand hearty laughs which we had on that occasion was worth all the wisdom of such a reunion. Washington Irving was the only man who ventured to say a good thing.

JANUARY 26. — The "Poland," Captain Anthony, sails to-day for Havre. In her go Monsieur Pageot, his lady, and their little son

Andrew Jackson, Mr. Saligny, *attaché*, and all the odds and ends of the French Mission. We are no longer on speaking terms with our dear friend and sister, France, and like two rival dames, who are desperately affronted without exactly knowing the cause, we stand pouting, turning up our noses, and tossing our disdainful heads at each other. The Lord knows who is to speak first now, and woe betide the one who first treads on the other's corns. What a ridiculous and unnatural position!

Madame Pageot is an American lady, daughter of Major Lewis, who is in one of our public departments in Washington. Her father being one of the kitchen Cabinet and a glorifier of "the greatest and best," and everything being sweet as sugar-candy between the two countries at the birth of her boy, it was determined to fill the measure of his infantile glory by giving him the august name of "Andrew Jackson." This was honour enough as long as the parents continued in this country, and affairs went on smoothly; but now, when the mighty brow of the warrior statesman is kindled with rage against our Gallic neighbours, and the presence of France in the person of her representative's representative is about to be removed from amongst us, the name of this young American Frenchman may not sound so pleasantly in the ears of his father's compatriots as in the land of his birth, and Andrew Jackson Pageot will not be the best possible name by which to be ushered into the regal halls of Louis Philippe d'Orléans.

Indian Massacre.

JANUARY 27.—Reports have prevailed for the last two or three days of the massacre of two companies of United States troops in Florida, by the Seminole Indians. It was hoped that they might not be true, but the account is confirmed to-day by intelligence from Mobile. Major Dade had started with two companies from Tampa Bay, for Camp King, to join General Church, when on the morning of 28th of December, at eight o'clock, they were surrounded by a large body of Indians, supposed to number from eight hundred to one thousand men, and were *cut to pieces;* only three men escaped, and they returned, badly wounded, to the station at Tampa Bay, to give the lamentable history of the fate of their comrades.

It is also reported that General Scott is to be sent immediately to take command of the forces in Florida; the result of all this will be that, after some hard service and destruction of the lives and property of the whites, the Indians will be exterminated, and the government saved the expense of transporting them out of our territories and providing for their maintenance. Humanity may deplore the fate of the *red men*, and philanthropists talk as they will about equal rights and the oppression of power, but it is inevitable; the Indians cannot live amongst, or in the immediate neighbourhood of, the whites, and this very battle in which temporary success has been won by their savage arms will be the ultimate cause of their destruction; the blood of the gallant men who have fallen in this sanguinary encounter will not sink unrevenged into the sands of Florida, and the speculators in Florida lands will be consoled for this national disaster by the confirmation of their titles in the final removal of the original owners of their lands.

Peace.

FEBRUARY 1. — The war of etiquette between the United States and France is in a fair way now of being averted, and the trusty sword of "the hero of two wars," there is good reason to hope, will be permitted reluctantly to remain in its scabbard. John Bull, like a good, honest fellow, who never likes any fighting to go on and he not have a hand in it, has interposed his good offices and proffered his mediation to settle the silly dispute. He says there is nothing to quarrel about, and he does not want his commerce, flourishing as it is at present, to be knocked about by new belligerents, nor does he wish to have the trouble and expense attending the preservation of an armed neutrality between the two most important maritime powers. So the King of England, the sailor king, writes a loving letter to his brother, the soldier king (we call him President), begging him to think a little better of the affair; and I suppose that noble old cock, Sir Charles Vaughan, has added a postscript, telling his Yankee friends (of whom he has great store) that they must not make damned fools of themselves. (I use this expression, not that I think it looks as pretty on the page of a book as a rose does in a flower-garden, but to preserve the verisimilitude; for I should hardly recognize my excellent friend, Sir Charles, even when drawn by myself, if he was not ushered in by one of those harmless, but very characteristic, expletives.) So the king and Sir Charles send over a king's ship in midwinter, "The Pantaloons" (in former times she ought to have gone to the other side first, the French being then *sans-culottes;* her very name would have made them feel comfortable), and she brings a messenger, who confers with my good friend Bankhead. He delivers the pacific missives. The "greatest and best," albeit full of fight, his "ever-pointed" hair bristling defiance against Louis Philippe and all that belongs to him, cannot find it in his heart to disgrace such friendly wooing, or in his conscience to send the messenger "back as he came;" so he becomes for the first time in his life amenable to reason, sends back a favourable answer, without consulting anybody. (Why should he? How can consultation and advisement enlighten the focus of America's glory?) The vessel returns forthwith, the business will be settled, France will pay the twenty-five millions of francs and America pocket it, without any wear and tear of national honour and dignity on either side, and England will have the credit of acting like a kind friend and good neighbour, and keep clear of a contingent scrape in the bargain.

Nothing certain is known about this business, for our guardian angel with upright hair holds it derogatory to his dignity to share "responsibility" with anybody. The people need not know anything about such matters until it suits him to tell them, and he is sure of their hurrahs in every supposable case; but public opinion seems to have settled the question; men have taken counsel from their hopes, and cry Peace! Peace! God send that it may be so; and I cry Hurrah for William the Fourth and Andrew Jackson, the mediator and the *mediatee!*

FEBRUARY 6. — The following gentlemen dined with us, and sat honestly, like good fellows, until the "noon of night:" Mr. J. W. Wallack, George Barclay, Samuel Hay, Charles A. Davis, James G. King, Benjamin E. Bremner, Robert Ray, William L. Miller, Frederick Norton, Washington Irving, Henry Brevoort, and Henry Hone.

FEBRUARY 12. — The "Erie" and the "Rhone" arrived to-day from Havre, the latter bringing letters to the 9th of January. The President's message had arrived in Paris. It was received with joy and exultation by the Americans, and is considered by the government and the chambers as removing all the obstacles in the way of carrying into effect the treaty of indemnification. These arrivals bring us letters from Paris, which we have been without for three weeks, owing to the horrible weather, which has kept all vessels from entering the harbour. The Americans in Paris are elated at the *éclat* which attended the reception of the message. Mary writes that she intends to shout "Hurrah for Jackson!" as long as she lives. His usual good luck has attended him throughout this whole affair, wrong as he may have been in the commencement. The French have managed so badly as to place him on the vantage-ground in every succeeding step, and circumstances have conspired to give him the power to trump the last trick and win the game whenever he pleased, without compromising his own pride or the national character.

FEBRUARY 13. — By the bye, I think the merchants are wrong in opposing so strenuously the wishes of the up-town people to have the Post-Office somewhere in the vicinity of the City Hall park. The Custom-House and the Exchange are properly located in Wall street, for they are exclusively devoted to the merchants, and their wishes should alone be consulted on the subject; but it is not so with the Post-Office. Many persons in the upper wards are in the habit of receiving letters, — not so many, certainly, as the Howlands and the Griswolds, but enough to give them a right to a say in the matter. But the strongest argument is one of policy, and in disregarding it the merchants are short-sighted; the numerical strength of the upper wards is so great that they control our elections, and have on all municipal questions a controlling voice. They have been foiled in one or two affairs of this kind, and are somewhat savage at this determination of the "moneyed aristocracy" (for that is the term which the cant of the demagogues applies to the merchants) to keep the Post-Office to themselves; they would consent to a compromise which would place this establishment near the park (the site of the present Bridewell would be a grand place, and a building similar to the Record Office would make a splendid finish), and that location would be permanent; whereas there is danger that, if Wall street is now agreed upon, the pertinacity of the people of the first ward would be punished by its removal, before five years, to the Bowery or Union place.

FEBRUARY 18. — The following fact, proving the unprecedented severity of the present winter, and (I should say) the folly of the persons concerned in the exploit, I copy from one of the newspapers, as worthy of being preserved amongst the records of the weather in this vicinity: "A friend at Cow Neck informs us that two gentlemen (Thomas and Adam Mott), on the 7th of this month, crossed Long Island Sound on foot, — a distance of seven and a half miles, — on the ice, from the mouth of Hempstead Harbour to Rye Point, in Connecticut, and then returned, making a distance of fifteen miles."

FEBRUARY 19. — Mr. Biddle has foiled his implacable enemy, General Jackson. The United States Bank has been incorporated in the State of Pennsylvania. Every effort was made to defeat it and the stale charge of bribery brought against some of its friends; but it passed both Houses, and the Governor, Rittner, having signed it, "the monster" is on its legs again, and the President must seek his retreat "in the deserts of Arabia," where he swore he would go whenever the bank was incorporated. I have no interest in the matter, and doubt much if the institution of so great a bank in a neighbouring

United States Bank.

State may not prove injurious to New York; but if it is the cause of Jackson going to Arabia to stay, I rejoice.

FEBRUARY 23. — Twenty lots in the "burned district," the property of Joel Post, deceased, were sold at auction this day, by James Bleecker & Son, at most enormous prices, greater than they would have brought before the fire, when covered with valuable buildings. This, at least, is the opinion of the best judges of the value of down-town property. The settlement of the French question has had much to do in producing this result, aided by the spirit of speculation and the sanguine hopes of the merchants of a great business this year. The lots were formed principally out of the property bought by Mr. Post from the guardians of Mr. Coster's children, for which he gave $93,000. They fronted on Wall, William, and Merchant streets, and Exchange place, in the immediate vicinity of the site of the old Merchants' Exchange, and where a new one is to be built, on a larger and more magnificent plan. The whole brought $765,100.

Sale of Lots.

FEBRUARY 24. — The trades-union people have been trying for some time past to get up a row, and succeeded yesterday. The journeymen and labouring men of different occupations have struck for wages, and their employers, in most instances, have resisted them with firmness. The stevedores and other labourers employed along-shore made a demand for an increase of wages, which the employers consented to, in consideration of the severity of the weather, the increased expense of living, and the abundance of work; but this concession encouraged further demands, and they would not go to work without a promise of the new wages for a year in advance. This was resisted; an immense body of the malcontents paraded the wharves all yesterday and attacked the men who refused to join them. Several vessels were armed to protect the men who were willing to work. Captain Waite, of the ship "United States," loaded a four-pounder with grape and canister shot, determined to

Riots.

oppose their boarding the vessel. The Mayor and police magistrates repaired to the spot; some of the officers were attacked by the rioters, one of whom, named Brink, had his skull fractured, and his life is despaired of. While this disgraceful scene was acting on the wharves, a large body of labourers assailed the men who were at work removing the rubbish from the ruins of the fire, with clubs and brickbats; the police were sent for, and succeeded, after a battle, in capturing four or five of the ringleaders.

The Mayor, who acts with vigour and firmness, ordered out the troops, who are now on duty with loaded arms, ready for action. These measures have restored order for the present, but I fear the elements of disorder are at work; the bands of Irish and other foreigners, instigated by the mischievous councils of the trades-union and other combinations of discontented men, are acquiring strength and importance which will ere long be difficult to quell.

New Exchange.

The subscription for the new Exchange, on the enlarged plan, has been filled with a liberality which does great honour to our merchants. It will embrace the whole front on Wall street from Exchange place to William street, taking in the whole block, and will cost from $1,000,000 to $1,200,000. The certainty of the accomplishment of this magnificent project was one of the causes of the high prices of Mr. Post's property at the sale yesterday. The location of the Exchange in Wall street has made princely fortunes for the proprietors of lots in the first ward. If it had been originally placed in the park (as was strongly urged by many at the time) my house would now have been worth more money than all the property of Post's, which has been sold for $765,100; without that I do not think that it would have brought the odd $65,100.

MARCH 2. — The Fire-king reigns supreme in this devoted city; what with alterations, pulling down and burning up, the city in the aggregate is rebuilt, I should think, about once in seven years.

The Hon. John Tyler, member of the Senate from Virginia, a leading Whig and an influential member of that patriotic party, resigned his seat, on Monday last, in a very handsome letter addressed to the Vice-President. It is understood that this gentleman has withdrawn his valuable services from the public at this important crisis when such men are so much wanted, from his view (a mistaken one, I humbly conceive) of his duty to his constituents, who have instructed him and his worthy colleague, Benjamin Watkins Leigh, to vote for the expunging resolutions (as they are called), in which they are to condemn their own act when they voted that the President, in certain of his rash measures, had transcended his powers and violated the constitution. This, of course, they cannot do, as honourable men, and Governor Tyler, maintaining the doctrine that the representative is governed by the instructions of his constituents, has no alternative but to resign his seat, and, to the gratification of the administration party, leave it open for one of their own men; the Legislature of Virginia having at present (temporarily, perhaps) a small majority of that sort of folks.

Thus it ever is. The honourable, high-minded men, viewing personal consistency as of greater importance than party fidelity, do not hesitate to maintain the one at the expense of the other, and persons less scrupulous usurp their stations in the government. Who ever knew a Jackson man to give up his seat one day before he was forced to, because the body of his constituents, much less an evanescent Legislature, held political opinions different from his? This change will, it is to be feared, place the Websters, the Clays, the Prestons, the Calhouns, and the Leighs in a minority, and the arm of power will be extended unchecked over this great, but hardly ridden, country. It is hoped the opinions of Governor Tyler's colleague do not coincide with his, and that he will not resign. If my view of his constitutional obligations is correct, he ought not.

MARCH 7. — The following gentlemen dined with us: Mr. Alexander Duncan of Canandaigua, Mr. George Griswold, Samuel Hay,

S. S. Howland, J. B. Fleming, Mr. B. L. Swan, I. S. Hone, and Charles Clinton.

MARCH 8.— I have this day sold my house in which
<small>Sold my House.</small> I live, No. 235 Broadway, to Elijah Boardman, for $60,000, to be converted into shops below, and the upper part to form part of the establishment of the American Hotel, kept by Edward Milford, in which I imagine Mr. Boardman to be interested. I bought this property on the 8th of March, 1821, after my return from Europe. I gave Jonathan Smith $25,000 for it. I make a large profit; but the rage for speculation is at present so high that it will prove an excellent purchase. The house belonging to the Phœnix Insurance Company, two or three doors above Warren street, was sold this day at auction, for $40,000. The building is worth little or nothing, and the lot only twenty-five feet by one hundred and six feet; mine is thirty-seven feet by one hundred and twenty feet, and is very cheap compared with the other.

I am to retain possession until the 15th of October, unless I choose to give it up before. I shall leave this delightful house with feelings of deep regret. The splendid rooms, the fine situation, my snug library, well-arranged books, handsome pictures, what will become of them? I have turned myself out of doors; but $60,000 is a great deal of money.

WEDNESDAY, MARCH 9.— After the breaking up of the Board of the Savings-Bank, Mr. Swan and I walked out to the Second avenue, St. Mark's place, Tompkins square, and Lafayette place. I am turned out of doors, and he expects soon to be. Almost everybody down-town is in the same predicament, for all the dwelling-houses are to be converted into stores. We are tempted with prices so exorbitantly high that none can resist, and the old down-town burgomasters, who have fixed to one spot all their lives, will be seen, during the next summer, in flocks, marching reluctantly north to pitch their tents in places which, in their time, were orchards, corn-fields, or morasses a pretty smart distance from town, and a journey to which was, formerly, an affair of some moment, and required preparation beforehand, but which constitute at this time the most fashionable quarter of New York. We did not see any lots which appeared to us so desirable as some on Lafayette place.

MARCH 12. — The winter is not yet over; the wind came out from the north-west last night; the thermometer is down to 18° this morning, and the high banks of ice in the streets have the appearance of solid walls of black marble. I make these remarks so frequently about the weather, because I imagine the winter of 1835–6 will stand hereafter recorded in our annals as the *hard* winter of modern days. I saw it mentioned in the papers that the ice has been sawed through in Connecticut river, opposite Hartford, and found to be forty inches in thickness.

Everything in New York is at an exorbitant price.
High prices. Rents have risen fifty per cent. for the next year. I have sold my house, it is true, for a large sum; but where to go I know not. Lots two miles from the City Hall are worth $8,000 or $10,000. Even in the eleventh ward, toward the East river, where they sold two or three years ago for $2,000 or $3,000, they are held now at $4,000 and $5,000. Everything is in the same proportion; the market was higher this morning than I have ever known it, — beef twenty-five cents per pound, mutton and veal fifteen to eighteen cents, small turkeys a dollar and a half. This does very well for persons in business and speculators, who make, as the saying is, "one hand wash another;" but it comes hard upon those retired from business, who live upon fixed incomes, particularly public officers, clerks in banks and counting-houses, whose salaries are never raised in proportion to the increased expense of living.

MARCH 19. — I dined with Mr. Louis McLane. He
Mr. McLane. occupies the house No. 1 Greenwich street, formerly Dominick Lynch's, and more recently Abraham Schermerhorn's, who owns it still. Mr. McLane is one of the ablest and

most agreeable men I ever knew, and has a delightful family. He has occupied several of the highest stations in our government; originally member of the House of Representatives for the State of Maryland, then in the Senate of the United States; in both houses he was one of the most distinguished members. In April, 1829, he was appointed Minister to Great Britain. On the breaking up of General Jackson's first cabinet, in April, 1831, he was appointed Secretary of the Treasury, and subsequently, on the retirement of Mr. Livingston, he was made Secretary of State, which office he held until the *old chief* made the place too hot for him. He resigned, as was pretty well understood at the time, because he disapproved of the removal of the deposits; but he went quietly out of office, without assigning that as the reason. He was soon afterward elected president of the Morris Canal Company, with a salary of $6,000, and became a citizen of New York, to the sincere gratification of all the New Yorkers who have the pleasure of his acquaintance.

MARCH 24. — I dined with the members of the Reading Club, at Washington Hotel. There were about twenty; some bright spirits: the Duers, Irving, Hoffman, Charles King, Davis, Harvey, Colonel White of Florida, Fleming, Patterson, Halleck, etc.

I bought this day, from Samuel Ward, for $15,000, the lot corner of Broadway and Great Jones street, twenty-nine feet wide and one hundred and thirty feet deep. It is my intention to build a house on this lot for my own residence, after I shall be turned out of the house I now occupy.

Albany Tunnel. MARCH 26. — The Legislature of the State have granted an act of incorporation to a company to construct a tunnel under the Hudson river, from the city of Albany to the east side. The directors named in the bill are: Joel N. Note, Stephen Van Rensselaer, Jr., James Stevenson, James Vanderpoel, and John Townsend. The charter is in perpetuity, without a reservation of the power to modify or repeal. The width of the tunnel is to be twenty-four feet and the height twelve feet, the crown of the arch eighteen inches below the bed of the river. This is, I believe, the first tunnel under water in this country. New York is ever first in works of improvement and enterprise.

Mr. Webster in Massachusetts. MARCH 29. — The Legislature of Massachusetts on Thursday last in convention, renominated Mr. Webster for President, and nominated Mr. Granger for Vice-President. Their resolutions are patriotic and uncompromising. They go for principle, not for expediency. A letter from Mr. Webster was read at this convention worthy of himself. He prefers to retire from the contest, but will stand by his friends and by the Constitution, to use his own words, "whether in majorities or minorities, in prosperous or in adverse fortune."

APRIL 4. — I went this evening to a party given at Mrs. Frederick Sheldon's, Bowling Green. Everything was in admirable taste, and the pictures and other works of art which were collected by the host and hostess during their late visit to Europe were displayed to great advantage.

Miss Martineau. APRIL 5. — This celebrated lady is now in New York. She arrived here last autumn, and has been travelling in the Southern States. She brought me a letter from Mr. MacCready. Margaret and I called upon her. She has been at our house, and this morning I called again to see her. I was apprehensive, from her high literary reputation, that I should find her a little too blue to be agreeable. But it is not at all the case; she is pleasant and unaffected, has great vivacity, talks well upon all subjects, and is fond of laughing; with these qualifications she is, of course, an engaging companion. The only difficulty in conversing with her arises from her great deafness, which is obviated (at least so far as one speaker at a time is concerned) by the use of a trumpet formed of a tube of gum-elastic, one end of which she places in her right ear, while the mouth of the person conversing with her is applied to the other.

APRIL 7. — The Reading Club gave a dinner, at Washington Hotel, to Mr. John Duer, on the occasion of his departure for

Europe. My engagement prevented me from going until nine o'clock, at which time I joined the party, and I have seldom passed so agreeable an evening. I was too late for a speech from the distinguished guest, which was agreed on all hands to have been admirable, but the whole time until the hour of breaking up (half-past twelve o'clock) was a scene of joviality, wit, and brilliancy. Many excellent speeches were made, and innumerable good things said, which literally "set the table in a roar."

Henry S. Hoyt, eldest son of Mr. Goold Hoyt, was married at the college, this day, at noon, to Frances, eldest daughter of Wm. A. Duer, LL.D., President of the college.

APRIL 8. — We had a dinner-party to-day consisting of the following ladies and gentlemen: Mrs. and Miss McLane (Mr. McLane is absent), President and Mrs. Duer, Mr. and Mrs. Davis, Mr. and Mrs. Edward R. Jones, Mr. and Mrs. James A. Hamilton, Mr. Washington Irving, Mr. Chas. McEvers, Jr., Mr. and Mrs. Peter Schermerhorn, Miss Sarah Duer, Mr. and Mrs. Isaac S. Hone, Miss Elizabeth Jones, Miss Mary Hamilton, Mr. Hay, Mr. Nicholas Low, Edward Schermerhorn.

APRIL 22. — I this day hired the house belonging to Mr. Bloomer, the upper one of the two marble houses with porticos in Broadway, opposite Washington place, for $1,600 per annum. It is a fine house, delightfully situated, and quite convenient to the place where I intend to build.

Mexican Affairs. MAY 9. — There is much excitement in relation to the revolt of the people of Texas against the Government of Mexico. These people, fugitives and renegades from the United States, having raised the standard of rebellion (or revolution, I suppose they call it) against the Government under which they have chosen to live, and, having been unsuccessful thus far, now claim the protection of the Government of this country. They abandoned America as citizens, and General Jackson, having failed in getting up a French war, seems determined to recognize this sort of paternity, and have a tilt of some kind before he doffs his knightly armor as Grand Master of the Columbian Order. Instructions have been given to General Gaines to protect the United States frontier bordering on Texas, at all events. This is very well as far as it goes, but his orders will warrant him in leading his forces over the Mexican line, if, in his opinion, there should be indications of a hostile intention; in other words, giving him authority to commence a war without the sanction of Congress, and I have no doubt the "old chief" has intimated to him that that course would "break no squares" at Washington. These facts came out in the House of Representatives, on Friday last, on a resolution of Mr. Cambreling to appropriate a million of dollars for the protection of the Mexican frontier. Colonel White is in town; he told me on Saturday that he considers a Mexican war as a very probable event. The Western speculators will be all in favor of it.

MAY 14.— This has been a busy week for me. I have done more work than in any other week since I quitted business. On Monday morning I commenced the removal of the library; the bookcases were taken to pieces, carried to the new house, and are now nearly ready to receive the books, which are all there lying on the floor, tied up and labelled with the numbers of the shelves. Having had two wine-closets and a part of the cellar shelved and prepared, we began on Thursday morning to remove the wine from the garret and wine-room of the old house, in which a great part of it has remained untouched fourteen years. It went away in fifteen cartloads of baskets. I received it, stowed it away nicely, and took an inventory of two thousand one hundred and eighty quarts and two hundred and fifty-four half-gallon bottles of Madeira and sherry; so that job is done.

MAY 28.— There has been another disgraceful riot at the Park Theatre. Mr. Wood, notwithstanding he sings so well, is the cause of this breach of harmony. Music may have "charms to soothe the savage breast," but not the breast of the pugnacious Mr. Webb, editor of "The Courier and Enquirer." This important personage charged Wood with unkind-

Row at the Theatre.

ness and a want of gallantry towards Mrs. Conduit, a little woman who sings well and is pretty, and has been associated with the Woods in some of their operas. This occasioned Mr. Wood to be hissed; he came forward and denied the charge. Webb reiterated it; Wood challenged him; the audience on a subsequent evening again expressed their disapprobation, and were not satisfied with his explanation. In yesterday morning's "Courier and Enquirer," Mr. Webb, in a most reprehensible article, calls upon the populace to go that evening to the theatre and drive Wood off the stage. This, of course, had the desired effect; for when was there a difficulty in finding ruffians enough not only to break into a theatre when thus instigated, but to pull down, set fire to, and destroy the city if they had a chance? Mr. Webb succeeded; an immense mob collected about the theatre, forced an entrance, and compelled Mr. Simpson to withdraw the Woods and promise that they would not again appear. This was the last engagement of those charming singers previous to their return, and I and others must be deprived of the pleasure of hearing them because Mr. Webb charges Mr. Wood with impoliteness, and he denies it. As well may this presumptuous newspaper editor exert the power of the press which he conducts to the gratification of personal pique or private resentment, and the public, the orderly part of the public, must acquiesce, and relinquish a rational amusement, or engage in a disgraceful contest with the loafers and Five-pointers who are ever ready to respond to such a call as they received on this occasion.

MAY 30.— I called yesterday to see an old friend, Dr. Peter Irving, who arrived on Saturday, in the ship "Erie," from Havre. He has resided in France twenty-seven years, during which time I have not seen him, for I missed him in 1821 when I was in Havre, owing to his absence from home. He expresses some surprise at my gray hairs, but he will find other changes equally astonishing. How strange must be the feelings of a New Yorker, absent so long, in witnessing the changes which have taken place; for no description can give the same idea of it as actual observation.

MAY 31. — I am a great lover of flowers. They furnish at all times, and particularly in the spring, enjoyment of the most refined and delicate nature, — a species of enjoyment which ranks with reading of poetry, looking at a fine picture, and drinking a glass of Château Margaux, in which the senses are gratified without sensuality.

JUNE 2. — There arrived at this port, during the month of May, 15,825 passengers. All Europe is coming across the ocean; all that part at least who cannot make a living at home; and what shall we do with them? They increase our taxes, eat our bread, and encumber our streets, and not one in twenty is competent to keep himself.

JUNE 3. — The following gentlemen dined with us: Chancellor Kent, Luther Bradish, Wm. H. Seward, Samuel B. Ruggles, Charles King, Charles H. Russell, John Van Buren, Murray, Isaac S. Hone, Charles A. Davis.

JUNE 6. — In corroboration of the remarks which I have occasionally made of late, on the spirit of faction and contempt of the laws which pervades the community at this time, is the conduct of the journeymen tailors, instigated by a set of vile foreigners (principally English), who, unable to endure the restraints of wholesome law, well administered in their own country, take refuge here, establish trades-unions, and vilify Yankee judges and juries. Twenty odd of these were convicted at the Oyer and Terminer of a conspiracy to raise their wages and to prevent any of the craft from working at prices less than those for which they struck. Judge Edwards gave notice that he would proceed to sentence them this day; but, in consequence of the continuance of Robinson's trial, the Court postponed the sentence until Friday.

Journeyman Tailors.

This, however, being the day on which it was expected, crowds of people have been collected in the park, ready for any mischief to which they may have been instigated, and a most diabolical and inflammatory hand-bill was circulated yesterday, headed by a coffin.

The Board of Aldermen held an informal meeting this evening, at which a resolution was adopted authorizing the Mayor to offer a reward for the discovery of the author, printer, publisher, or distributor of this incendiary publication. The following was the hand-bill: —

"THE RICH AGAINST THE POOR!

"Judge Edwards, the tool of the aristocracy, against the people! Mechanics and working men! A deadly blow has been struck at your liberty! The prize for which your fathers fought has been robbed from you! the freemen of the North are now on a level with the slaves of the South! with no other privilege than labouring, that drones may fatten on your life-blood! Twenty of your brethren have been found guilty for presuming to resist a reduction of their wages! and Judge Edwards has charged an American jury, and agreeably to that charge, they have established the precedent that workingmen have no right to regulate the price of labour, or, in other words, the rich are the only judges of the wants of the poor man. On Monday, June 6, 1836, at ten o'clock, these freemen are to receive their sentence, to gratify the hellish appetites of the aristocrats!

"On Monday, the liberty of the workingmen will be interred! Judge Edwards is to chant the requiem! Go! Go! Go! every freeman, every workingman, and hear the hollow and the melancholy sound of the earth on the coffin of equality! Let the court-room, the City Hall, yea! the whole park, be filled with *mourners;* but remember, offer no violence to Judge Edwards, bend meekly, and receive the chain wherewith you are to be bound! Keep the peace! Above all things, keep the peace!"

JUNE 7. — I had a letter to-day from the accomplished author of the "Ayrshire Legatees" and "Annals of the Parish" and "Eleven Strokes and Aggravations of Paralysis." The latter, he says, "Have disabled me from taking part any longer in the uses of the world"; but his
[John Galt.]

mental faculties appear to be unimpaired, and he does me the honour to say, that unless I forbid him he intends to inscribe to me a "little book," for which he has been arranging materials, "that I may have an opportunity," he adds, "of stating my own impressions of the United States, for the topic now begins to be popular here, and favourable opinions begin to be appreciated."

JUNE 9. — Among the fleet of vessels which sailed yesterday and to-day were the "Havre," having as passengers Mr. and Mrs. Cottenet and children, Mr. and Mrs. Boreel, and Miss Langdon; the "Montreal," with Mr. Stevenson, the new Minister to England, his lady and Miss Coles and Allyn Otis. The "Sheffield," in which Mr. Wallack went; she was ready for sea on the 24th of May, and was prevented from day to day by the easterly storm. The "Montreal" was the packet of the first instant. Arrived yesterday, from Liverpool, the "Orpheus." Temple Bowdoin was one of her passengers.

Arrivals and Departures.

JUNE 13. — Yesterday morning was clear, bright, and beautiful, and we enjoyed in our new residence up town all the pleasures of the country. The air was refreshing, the trees in full verdure, the birds sang sweetly, and when I walked down to Trinity Church (where I shall continue to go at least once a day), I met and overtook crowds of well-dressed persons on their way to the several places of divine worship. It looked indeed as the morning of the Christian Sabbath always should.

JUNE 17. — A new club is about being established, at the head of which are a number of our most distinguished citizens, to consist of four hundred members, and to be similar in its plan and regulations to the great clubs of London, which give a tone and character to the society of the British metropolis. A meeting was held this evening, at the Athenæum, to organize the club, at which I was earnestly invited to attend, but I could not get away from Mr. Griffin's in time.

Union Club.

JUNE 20. — In the ship "Samson," arrived yesterday from London, came passengers Charles Parish, N. P. Willis and his new English wife, and the Right Hon. Edward Ellice. Greenough the sculptor arrived here a few days since, and went to Washington. I did not see him. His talents are an honour to his country, and his fellow-citizens should be proud of him. He is engaged in a great work by order of Congress, a statue of Washington, which I presume is the object of his visit at this time.

Delaware Senator. Mr. Naudian having resigned, his place in the Senate of the United States has been filled by the appointment of Richard H. Bayard, by a vote of seventeen to ten.

This is the gentleman whose society and that of his charming wife afforded us so much pleasure last summer at Rockaway. He is a thorough Whig, but the party gains nothing in their number by his election, his predecessor being equally so. The little State of Delaware is a precious jewel in the political diadem. She has always been governed by good principles and represented by talents.

Excursion in the "Novelty." ALBANY, JUNE 23. — A party of gentlemen consisting of the managers of the Delaware & Hudson Company, together with Matthew St. Clair Clarke, Colonel McKinny, Mr. Bradley of Washington, the Collector, Elisha Townsend, and others, went on board the "Novelty" this morning at six o'clock, at the foot of Chambers street in New York, and came to Albany in twelve hours.

This was the first voyage ever made from New York to Albany by a steamboat propelled by anthracite coal. Dr. Nott has been engaged for several years in contriving machinery to accomplish this important object, and has now succeeded completely. The great desideratum was to contrive the means of igniting the coal, and producing a flame sufficient to create the steam. This has been effected by condensing hot air, which, by injection into the bottom of the furnaces, accomplishes this object, and forces the flame into a chamber in which are a great number of iron tubes of the size of gun-barrels, placed vertically. There are four of these furnaces. The quantity of coal consumed on this trip was about twenty tons, which at five dollars per ton amounts to one hundred dollars. The same voyage would have consumed forty cords of fine wood, the present price of which is six dollars, making a difference of more than one-half. Dr. Nott, who was on board, has made experiments the result of which is that the difference of expense on board the " Novelty " during one season will amount to $19,000. The " Erie " left New York an hour after us, and arrived two hours after our arrival, but she made the usual stops, and we came directly on, so that their speed was probably nearly equal. The tide was against us all day, and there is a great freshet in the river. Dr. Nott has succeeded completely in this invention, which establishes the certainty that coal will supersede wood in all our steamboats, and the Delaware & Hudson Company will hereafter be able to sell all the coal they can bring down the canal at an advanced price.

Death of Mr. Madison. JUNE 30. — This enlightened statesman and illustrious citizen, James Madison, former President of the United States, died on Tuesday last. He had been gradually sinking for some time past. It is a pity he had not lingered six days longer, that his death might have occurred, like those of Jefferson and the elder Adams, on the anniversary of the political birthday of the country over which they had severally ruled.

Count Survilliers. JULY 2. — Joseph Bonaparte, formerly King of Naples and afterward of Spain, now bearing the title of Count Survilliers, after a residence in this country of twenty years, yesterday took his final leave and sailed for London in the packet ship " Philadelphia." During his residence in the United States he has conciliated the favourable opinions of all who knew him, and has left an exceedingly good name amongst his immediate neighbours at Bordentown, where he has a fine estate, on which he has lived for a great portion of the time of his residence among us.

JULY 11. — The discouraging accounts of Mary's health, and the uncertainty we are in respecting the movements of my children, have determined me to go to Europe on Saturday next, unless we should receive letters before that day rendering it unnecessary. My daughter Margaret will be my companion. I went on board the ship "England" this morning and engaged our staterooms.

AT SEA, JULY 16. — We went on board the steamboat this morning at eleven o'clock. Many of our friends attended to take leave of us, and several accompanied us to the ship, which was lying below Governor's Island. The party partook of a luncheon on board, and leaving us off Fort Hamilton, with three cheers of encouragement and kind wishes, we commenced our voyage to Liverpool on board the good ship "England," commanded by Captain Waite, an able seaman and a gentlemanly man. The "England" is a noble, fast-sailing ship of 731 tons' burden.

The weather was bright at the time of sailing, but the wind northeast, as it has been for so great a portion of the time during the present summer, and the departure of our friends in the steamboat seemed to be the signal for its increase, for by two o'clock it blew a gale from that inauspicious quarter directly on shore, with a rough sea, and our ship pitching heavily.

JULY 18. — The wind north-east, blowing hard and cold, with a heavy cross-sea. The passengers generally sick, but I have recovered, and eaten my allowance. I dined heartily on a fresh salmon, and drank my usual quantity of wine at dinner. Margaret, the only lady at the table. She is a famous sailor; she sits on the bulwarks, to which lofty station she is assisted by me, or some other of the gentlemen, and enjoys the wild scene as the gallant ship makes her way through the mountain billows.

JULY 19. — We have had one of those incidents to-day which sometimes break in agreeably upon the monotony of a sea voyage. A sail ahead was descried early in the morning, which we soon made out to be a large ship steering the same course. We gained steadily upon her, until it was ascertained to be the "Charlemagne" under a great press of sail. How she got ahead so far to windward I could not make out. She must have gotten a streak of more favorable wind, but we came fast up with her. Captain Waite "whipped up," and to his great satisfaction passed her to windward at four o'clock and hoisted the "star spangled banner," which was returned by the "Charlemagne." This is certainly very interesting, and proves the perfection of the art of navigation. Here were two ships, starting together from New York, after three days sailing nearly five hundred miles, in gales of wind, come in sight of each other so near that every person on board can be distinguished and almost hear each other's voices. The "Charlemagne" sails fast, but we have certainly beaten her handsomely. It was a glorious sight, when we were abreast of her, and saw her swelling canvas — royals, studding-sails and all — and her bright, high sides, rising from the waves like a walled city and plunging again into the glittering abyss of waters.

JULY 28. — At four o'clock we were called from dinner to see a large ship which was nearly abreast of us to windward. She proved to be the ship "Kensington" from Liverpool bound to New York. The passengers exchanged cheers, and the captain might as well have come down to speak to us as not. We were as close to the wind as the ship could possibly steer, and, of course, could not have gone nearer. This appears to have been excessively churlish. It would have been a great satisfaction to us to hear news, but a much greater to send our greetings to those dear ones we had left at home. But the "Lexington" cannot well avoid reporting us on her arrival, and our friends will know that on this day, twelve days out, we have made about two-thirds of our voyage.

It was a glorious sight to witness these two splendid ships passing each other, both close-hauled, on different tacks. The "Kensington" rose and sank on the waves with the majesty of the eagle and the calmness of the swallow. This is always an interesting incident on a voyage, but there was something more beautiful in this view than in any of the kind I have ever witnessed.

JULY 29. — We have two ladies, passengers, who exemplify the two extremes in the American female character. Mrs. May, of Boston, is a regular Yankee, quick of apprehension, intelligent, handy, self-confident, a person qualified to take care of herself in every situation in which circumstances could place her. She is (I undertake to say) in all respects a helpmate to her husband. Mrs. Hammond is soft, languishing, and inert, and her listlessness of manner proclaiming her at once a South Carolinean, with more feminine loveliness than the lady just described. She appears to be incapable of the least exertion, and would starve, I verily believe, if she had nobody to help her to food. She and her husband (who is a member of Congress from South Carolina) lounge all day on sofas in the cabin and a mattress on deck, and neither of them have been at the table during the voyage, except once that the lady made an effort and dined with the passengers. This may be accounted for by the bad health of both the husband and wife. But Mrs. May would require to be a great deal worse than either before she would consent to give up. There does not seem to be much congeniality between these two ladies. There is too much dissimilarity in their habits and dispositions to admit of it. The one must despise the other for her business-like qualities, and she in return wonders how a lady can submit to be served by slaves in matters which she ought herself to attend to. My daughter Margaret, from having been brought up on neutral ground, is nearer right in those particulars than either, and I am greatly mistaken if all the passengers are not of the same opinion.

JULY 31.— I arose early and went upon deck. It was a fine morning; the ship sailing ten knots an hour; the sea bright and blue, with that sort of crispness in the curling of the waves and the sparkling of the white foam which is usually a concomitant of westerly wind. We shall make a better run during this twenty-four hours than any since we left New York. Captain Waite says she sailed faster during the night than he ever saw her before, and he thinks her the fastest sailer in the American merchant navy.

Why is it that the Sabbath morning always appears more solemn to me than any other? There are many things on shore to produce that effect. The hum of business is hushed ; the streets deserted ; the world reposes in a sort of conventional quietude, but here on the ocean there are no such marks to denote the return of the day of rest; and yet when I went on deck this morning I felt myself influenced by the consciousness that this day was set apart from the others, and that I was enjoined " to keep it holy." It is indeed a holy institution. No man who acknowledges a dependence upon the Almighty Governor of the universe can avoid feeling that upon this day of rest he is more immediately brought in the presence of his Maker. I hope I do not mistake my own sensations, and attribute to an innate principle of right the consciousness that one cannot help feeling of helplessness and reliance upon the Almighty when exposed to the dangers of a sea voyage, but I certainly felt this morning my mind elevated by the knowledge that this was the Sabbath of the Lord. At the request of the passengers, I read the morning service of our church, and I trust the manner was not less acceptable for the reflections of the morning, the result of which I have given above.

Our accommodations are excellent. The most abundant provision has been made, and we have every day as good a table as the most fastidious gastronome could desire. A sheep and a pig were killed last evening, and plenty of poultry; and our larder presents a most inviting appearance. The passengers are good-humoured, accommodating, and jovial, and if I were not anxious to see my children I should not have any great objection to prolong our voyage a week beyond the time at which we may expect to arrive, if the wind hold on.

AUGUST 3. — At noon, however, the wind died away, and it became perfectly calm and continued so during the remainder of the day. Not a breath of air was stirring to agitate the sails, and the waters of the variable Channel were smooth as a mirror. Oh, for a steamboat at such a time ! Genius of Fulton ! if ever thou art dear to the memory of thy countrymen it must be when, at the close of a long voyage, they become suddenly becalmed within a few hours of the port of their destination. Wind and sails are nothing now compared to steam and paddles, and we had the mortification of realizing this fact this afternoon, by seeing a large steamer (I am in England now, and must talk as the English talk) puffing and wheezing and smoking rapidly on her course towards the Irish shore, while we were flapping and rolling and making no headway.

AUGUST 6. — And I once more set my foot upon English ground.

BOOTLE, SUNDAY, AUG. 7. — Mr. Heyworth took us to town this morning, where we attended divine service in the chapel of the Blind Asylum, which is the fashionable church. We sat in Mr. Brown's pew. Coming out of church Mr. William Rathbone brought Capt. Basil Hall to shake hands with us. He and his wife both expressed themselves in the following terms: "We are happy to see again a gentleman to whose kindness in America we are so greatly indebted." Pretty well, considering Mr. Rathbone asked me to meet Captain Hall yesterday at dinner at his house. After paying a few visits in town, we returned to dine and sleep at Bootle. I am charmed with all I see here. Our sweet friend, Charlotte Kane, has gotten a charming fellow for a husband.

LIVERPOOL, AUG. 12. — Having been honoured by an invitation from the mayor to meet the judges at dinner, Mr. Rathbone called for me at seven o'clock, and we went to the Town Hall. The doors of my hotel (The Waterloo) were beset by a crowd to see the egress of the high sheriff, a splendid, fierce-looking fellow, in full dress, with *chapeau bras* and a long black wand. He rode in a superb stage coach-and-four, with two dashing postilions. This gentleman's name is Standish of Standish Hall, a person of large fortune and high standing in the County of Lancashire. When we alighted at the door of the Council Hall, we were ushered by a train of servants in livery, by the beautiful staircase and vestibule to the splendid suite of rooms in which the mayor received his guests, the rich furniture being uncovered and everything arranged to suit the

Dinner at the Town Hall.

occasion. The *coup d'œil* was perfectly magnificent. The ballroom, with the splendid chandeliers, was not in the dining part of the palace, but I was taken to see it.

My reception by the mayor (Mr. Corrie) was not only flattering but marked by extreme kindness, and the judges, Mr. Justice Park and Mr. Justice Coleridge, to whom I was introduced immediately on their arrival, were particular in their attentions to me during the whole of the evening. The company consisted of about fifty gentlemen, principally members of Parliament, country gentlemen, and barristers connected with the assizes which are now being held. A Mr. Alexander seemed to be considered the most eminent lawyer in the company. The courts, both criminal and civil, are open at the same time, Justice Park presiding in the former and Justice Coleridge in the latter.

The dinner-table was richly set out with a splendid plateau the whole length, and the services of china and glass suited to a banquet of kings, and as good a dinner, too, as I ever saw. Turtle soup, turbot, grouse (this is the first day for shooting them), and a great variety of pine-apples and peaches, were among the varieties, and the wines were capital. I was seated on the right of the mayor, next but two. One of the judges sat on each side of him, next on the right the high sheriff, and then myself. This latter dignitary and myself were soon good friends, and he pressed me with great apparent sincerity to visit him in London. These folk seem much pleased to come in contact with a Yankee.

August 13. — Our first visit was to this princely
Chatsworth. mansion and grounds. I do not know how to describe it. It surpasses the highest reach of my imagination. Eton Hall is, I think, a handsome exterior, but the grandeur, the sublimity, the solid magnificence of Chatsworth, induce me to give it a preference. It stands rather low, embosomed in an amphitheatre of hills, with the river Derwent passing close to the walls. The view from every part of the grounds is beautiful. This is one particular in which it has the advantage of Eton; then there are

a number of fountains and cascades, supplied by reservoirs on the adjacent mountain, all of which were made to play for us. One of these is a tree, which looks so much like nature that it did not attract my attention, until all of a sudden, hundreds of jets from the ends of the branches began a spirited cross-fire which made us jump with surprise. The Italian Gardens below the terraces are beautiful. Herds of red and fallow deer are seen sporting over the grounds, and the conservatories and hot-houses and stables are all fine.

Haddon Hall. The next object of curiosity was a visit across the country four or five miles to Haddon Hall, an old baronial castle belonging to the Duke of Rutland. The contrast between this and the place we had just left was singularly striking. This was erected before the Conquest, and displays all the rude, grotesque style of architecture of those days of feudal power. Towers and turrets, covered with the ivy of ages. The banqueting hall, kitchens, with fireplaces in which wild boar and the red deer were roasted whole for the iron-handed baron and his faithful dependents; the armory, the dungeons, and the antiquated bed-chambers hung with tapestry, the figures of which resemble nothing in the heavens above nor in the earth beneath, — are all preserved in spite of the ravages of time, to show Englishmen how their fathers lived a thousand years ago.

We visited this ancient place at a peculiarly favorable time: at the close of such a day as the poets of England delight to describe, when the last rays of the setting sun throw the long, deep shadows of the moss-covered turrets and lofty pines over the bright green sward, and the beautiful river crept silently along, as if afraid to disturb the solemn stillness of the scene. It was an incident of my life never to be forgotten to have seen Chatsworth and Haddon Hall on the same afternoon.

LEAMINGTON, AUG. 16. — Warwick is handsome, clean, and dull as ever, but the castle is even more glorious than my recollections of it. Its situation, the views up and down the Avon; its ancient towers, lofty hall, superb wainscotted apartments; the venerable trees in the park; and the Warwick vase, the beau ideal of beauty, are all there in their former state, and some of the apartments (particularly the great hall of entrance and the dining-hall) have been recently repaired, and the ornaments retouched with great taste and delicacy. The part of Warwick Castle which most exceeded the recollection of my former visit is the pictures, which ornament the walls in every part; this arises probably from my having more taste for pictures now than at that time.

LONDON, AUG. 18. — The forenoon of this day was passed in visiting some of the most interesting objects in Oxford, the glorious metropolis of learning and literature. It was delightful for me to refresh my recollections of this magnificent city. This day's visit has realized all I have thought and said of it since I was there before.

At seven o'clock this evening, just as they were lighting the gas lamps, we were set down at the famous White Horse Cellar, Piccadilly; amidst coaches innumerable, lords and chimney sweeps, ladies and blacklegs. Our luggage was placed in one of those detestable vehicles, a hackney coach, in which we came to Mrs. Friedman's boarding-house. A comfortable establishment, No. 12 Devonshire street, one door west of Portland place.

Visit to Parliament.

AUGUST 20. — Having been introduced yesterday to Lord Palmerston, the minister for foreign affairs, he politely sent orders to Mr. Duer and me to go into the House of Lords to witness the prorogation of Parliament by the King in person, and we were fortunate enough to obtain very good places. The ceremony was very interesting to me, and the spectacle exceedingly magnificent. The attendance of the lords was greater than I expected. I saw several distinguished noblemen, the Archbishop of Canterbury, Duke of Wellington, Duke of Norfolk, Lords Melbourne, Westminster, etc., in all I think nearly a hundred. A great attendance of foreign ministers and a handsome display of ladies elegantly dressed. The king arrived at half-past two o'clock, attended by a numerous and brilliant cortege, and ascended the throne. He is much altered in appearance since I saw him at the coronation of his brother. He was then a stout man and walked erect; he is now old and bent, with a tottering gait, and has all the marks of advanced age. The young Princess Victoria will not, from his appearance, have long to wait for her exalted inheritance. As soon as the king was seated, the Commons were summoned, the Speaker (Abercombie) read the address in a very clear and distinct tone of voice, so that, notwithstanding, from his situation under the gallery, I could not see him, I did not lose a word. The king then read his speech, with a little prompting, which I also heard distinctly. Parliament was then prorogued until October, and the king retired as he came, amidst a discharge of artillery and the sound of trumpets. We got out in time to see the procession leave the House. The stage coaches, with the horse and foot guards, made a grand appearance, and everything went off well. I should have regretted exceedingly not to have witnessed this splendid pageant.

The manner of announcing the king's assent to the several bills is very singular, and the bows of the clerks in their robes and wigs, and the formal, quaint "*le roi le veut*" which accompanies each, had a ludicrous effect to such of us as had not before witnessed the ceremony.

We paid a few visits before dinner, which does not take place until six o'clock, one of which to Mrs. Jameson, the authoress of "Characteristics of Women," gave me great pleasure. This gifted lady is to sail for New York next month to meet her husband who has a legal appointment in Upper Canada.

AUGUST 21.— Margaret, Mr. Duer, and I went to pass the evening with Mrs. Jameson, where we met our kind and attentive friends, Mr. and Mrs. Stevenson, and other nice persons, amongst whom was an old lady seventy-two years of age, Lady George Murray, and her daughter, distinguished equally for rank and talents, preceptress and governess of the Princess Charlotte, the lamented "rose and fair expectancy of the state." The young lady is the bosom friend of Lady Noel Byron, the widow of the immortal *roué* poet. I talked much with her on the subject of their separation. She describes Lady B. as a perfect angel, and although it may be necessary to make some allowances for the exaggeration of warm female friendship, the high character and intelligence of Miss Murray forbids the possibility of her coming to very erroneous opinions on a subject so important and so much disputed. Lady Byron mixes very little in society, but is much engaged in doing good.

AUGUST 23. — I took Margaret this morning to Westminster Abbey. She was much pleased, and I experienced anew and in a greater degree the awe and pleasure which the first view of this sublime and interesting edifice occasioned me.

This has been a busy day. Mr. Duer and I went to breakfast with Mr. Rogers, the poet, an agreeable, kind-hearted old gentleman. He is very rich, although a poet, and lives in handsome style; has a fine collection of pictures and other pretty things. After we left him he sent me a beautiful copy of his poems with illustrated vignettes.

DOVER, AUG. 30. — We left London at eleven o'clock on the top of the Dover coach. There was a crowd about the door, attracted by the Duke of Wellington's carriage. He appears to be popular here at any rate, whatever the London radicals may think of him.

AUGUST 31. — Colonel Cockburn introduced me this morning to Colonel Arnold, commander of engineers and of the garrison at Dover. This gentleman is son of the infamous Benedict Arnold. He appears about my age; a short, handy little man, and apparently a gentlemen of good manners. It seems to be hard to apply the severity of the Levitical law to innocent men in these enlightened times, but I felt, while in his company, as if my prejudice was busied in " visiting the sins of the father upon the child."

[margin note: Benedict Arnold.]

PARIS, SEPT. 3. — We started much earlier than yesterday, and having less distance to go, arrived in Paris at eight o'clock P.M., and came to lodge at the boarding-house of Madame Bonfils, superbly situated in Rue de Rivoli, opposite the gardens of the Tuilleries, of which I have a fine view from my chamber windows. Soon after we came, a storm of thunder and rain announced to the people of Paris that we had arrived.

SUNDAY, SEPT. 11. — Horse race at the Champs de Mars at one o'clock, and afterward to the *fête* of St. Cloud. I am ashamed to record it, Sunday as it was; but what is to be done? If such scenes are witnessed at all it must be on the day which *Christians* call Sabbath. We intended to go to church this morning to hear an eloquent Protestant clergyman, Mr. Athanèse Coquerel, who is preaching in the churches of our faith at present; but until one o'clock it rained very hard, notwithstanding which the races took place, and the queen and royal family were there, and a tolerable concourse of people. It stopped raining at one o'clock, and the men came out; but the course and all the grounds around were an ocean of mud. The horses running looked like the wizard horse of Leonora, only their halo was of a less luminous nature. We came away after the first two heats, and pursued our way to St. Cloud. A horse race in Paris is not by any means the same thing as an English one, nor even one of ours. I do not think it a favourite amusement of the French. It is the only one which does not appear to excite them. *Ils sont gais à la messe, et grave à la course.* The principal race to-day was won by a horse of the Duc d'Orléans, beating Lord Seymour, who has been in the constant habit of carrying away the purses from the natives. One would have thought there was something exhilarating in this, but there was no shouting, no triumph amongst the men, or flashing of bright eyes amongst the women.

The weather by this time had cleared, and the sun came out bright, so that when we arrived at St. Cloud the immense little world was congregating fast. Men, women, and children in their newest finery crowding to the long avenue, in which booths are erected. Such chattering, such a variety of queer noises, such singular exhibitions, so many lures to attract customers to buy their wares, to witness their spectacles, or to eat their pâtés, were almost an excuse to break the Sabbath for once to visit the *fête* de St. Cloud. I shall not probably see another. We passed the first hour in viewing the apartments of the palace; the state apartments are open to everybody on Sunday. These we saw, of course, but were further permitted to pass through all the other apartments. Nothing can be more magnificent; the pictures are exceedingly fine, and there are several vases of Sèvres porcelain superb beyond imagination.

I remember that the king's bed, and those of all the family, even the princesses, are hard mattresses, a few inches thick, with no paillaisses, and the bedsteads only about a foot from the floor.

The French are certainly Sabbath-breakers, and their religious habits do not set as close as ours, but one thing I will remark in their praise: In all this concourse of people to-day, formed principally of the lower classes, assembled for pastime and enjoyment, when eatables of all kinds were exhibited, such as cakes, hot waffles, pâtés, etc., I did not see a drop of spirituous liquor, nor do I believe there was one on the ground. No drink but lemonade, carried about by old women who carry as much acidity in their faces as on their backs.

SEPTEMBER 12.— Having determined to leave Paris for Geneva to-morrow, we have been employed in making preparations. Mr. Chazournes and I went in pursuit of a carriage, and succeeded in getting a commodious travelling callèche of a Mr. Panhard, Rue Bergue, for which I am to pay him two hundred francs. We take post horses, and go by the Dijon route across the Jura mountain. George W. Lafayette is in town. I did not know it until yesterday, when I called and left my card. I received a note from him this morning stating that he was engaged with lawyers to-day in an affair of family business, but would be with me to-morrow. This I interdicted, and requested him to postpone his visit until after our return.

Well, I have seen Taliogni. She danced this evening at the French Opera, in the ballet of the Sylphide. It was a single performance, and, fortunately, fell upon our last night in Paris. The immense theatre was crowded in every part. Bradford obtained excellent places for us in the course of the day. The opera was the "Siege of Corinth," which, did not interest me; but the ballet was certainly the poetry of motion and the sunlight of beauty. I never saw anything of the kind before which is not routed horse and foot out of my recollection by the force of this fascinating spectacle. Not only the calypso of the night, but her attendant nymphs all danced and moved and floated like beings of another world. The piece is exactly the same as that gotten up in New York as an opera when Mrs. Austin was there, under the name of the "Mountain Sylph"; but, fortunately, there was no singing or speaking here. It would have been too much, when one of our senses was completely absorbed, to have another invaded, and in danger of being captured; it might have ended in *nonsense*. The whole affair was so nicely managed, the machinery worked so well, the sylphs flew in the air, as if their little delicate feet had never touched the ground, and when their lovely sister died, four of them enveloped her in a net of gold and, each taking a corner, flew up with her into the air, where, I take it for granted, the Sylphic Père la Chaise is situated. Or, perhaps, the beauteous beings of their race, when defunct, are taken up to exhale in the regions above, and return to us in the form of dew-drops to sparkle on the leaves of the newly blown rose, or hide in the velvet recesses of the fragrant violet. Taliogni is small, delicate, and, I think, pretty, and her dancing excels that of any other woman as much as Mrs. Wood's singing does Mrs. Sharp's. It is not only in great agility and dexterity, but it is the perfection of grace and beauty, and addresses itself to the imagination, as it is, in fact, half the time something *between earth and heaven*. When this pleasant affair was ended, we went to Tortoni's and took our ices. This is the most fashionable house in Paris.

EN ROUTE, SEPT. 13. — We left Paris this morning in our carriage, with a number of little comforts, and put ourselves fairly *en route* for Geneva. The weather was bad; it rained with short intervals during the day, and the uninteresting country through which we passed, rendered more gloomy by the dark clouds which hung over it, and the cheerless, uncomfortable villages, with more mud and dirt even than usual, gave us frequent occasion to laugh at the absurdity of the application of the term " *la belle* France " to such a country. It is worse in every particular than when I was here before, and we are travelling through the very heart of France, and its most celebrated provinces. Formerly the cheapness of living in the country was more commensurable with its value (I speak not of Paris); but now the extortion, the cheating of all kinds with which the traveller comes in contact, is greater than in England, and you are not so well served. The porter at Madame Bonfils made a regular charge of fifteen sous for every trifling errand he performed for me. At one of the towns, this evening, I sent a boy for two candles to put in the lamps of the carriage. The young rascal said they cost him a franc, and I had to pay him ten sous for his trouble. It is so in everything. There is a gang of female harpies stationed in the lobbies of all the theatres in Paris to prey upon strangers. I suffer from being *prima facie* a John Bull, and he is fair game in France. They have a double motive in swindling him: their cupidity and the dislike they bear to him. France is fattening upon the food she loathes. These polite, disinterested ladies make me pay twenty sous for opening the box door, and demand the same sum for a little programme which is sold at the door for three sous.

GENEVA, SEPT. 17. — This place is filled with English and Americans. Our hotel is the fashionable resort of the latter, of whom there were thirty-four a few days since. There are now here, besides our party, Abraham Schermerhorn and family, Mr. George Ticknor and family, of Boston; Horace Binney, of Philadelphia, and his daughter, Mrs. Otis; General Jones, Charles McEvers, Mr.

and Mrs. Brinkerhoff, Mr. and Mrs. Ashurst, of Philadelphia; Charles C. King and his brother, James T. Irving, Jr., Mr. Whitney, the Rev. Henry Morton, Mr. and Mrs. Hammond, our fellow-passengers in the "England," and others, perhaps, whom I have not met. From my recollection of what Geneva was like when I was here before, I was surprised, until I came now, that it should be made a place of so great resort. It was then a dull, confined place with dirty, narrow streets, and nothing but the beautiful lake to recommend it. I find it now a splendid, agreeable town; streets of handsome houses have been erected on grounds which were formerly the marshy shores of the lake, and the course of the clear, blue, rushing waters is confined in massive stone docks, with a splendid bridge; a pretty island has been formed, in which is a bronze statue of Jean Jacques Rousseau; spacious public gardens ornament the part of the town remote from the lake. Immense hotels have been erected for the accommodation of the hosts of travellers who pass through on their way to Italy, and the whole has an air of splendor and gayety which must surprise the rigid, formal descendants of the reformers of John Calvin's severe days.

I am here with my three daughters and son-in-law, and surrounded by friends and acquaintances, my window overlooking the brightest blue waters the sun ever shone upon (except, perhaps, those of Lake George); splendid new edifices on the one hand and the green shore of the lake, with a majestic perspective of snow-clad mountains, on the other. I think I may say with the patriarch of old, "It is well to be here." One look out of Mary's bright eyes (and oh! how much brighter than I expected to see them), with her whole heart mixed up with mine, conspire to render the few days of my sojourn in Geneva among the happiest of my life — but how to get away!

The English swarm so on the Continent. They are generally vulgar people, without taste, and with their pockets well filled, and the French and Swiss do love so dearly to handle their money that the market is spoiled for us Americans, who can better appreciate the value of the articles offered for sale. This place has benefited more by the intercourse of foreigners than any on the Continent. It is on the direct road to Italy, and so pleasant that travellers in transit linger here as long as possible, besides which, many pass their summer here, and several English families have delightful villas on the banks of the lake, cultivated so much in the English style that the country around Geneva has greatly the appearance of England, which makes it a Paradise compared with the adjacent country which the traveller must pass to reach it. This all comes from John Bull; the substantial stone docks and lofty edifices, the sight of which from my window affords me so much pleasure, are all based upon English guineas. I have heard it estimated that four millions of pounds sterling are annually spent on the Continent, and Geneva gets a fair share of it; the Americans, too, are spending a great deal of money in Europe, and unfortunately there is no reciprocity in the trade (except as relates to England). How few of the dollars which we expend in France, Switzerland, or Italy, ever find their way back again. The people of those countries do go out to America sometimes, it is true, but for what? Not to enrich the country, but themselves; to carry on business and make their fortunes, if they can. Latrobe and Pourtalais and a few others are exceptions to these remarks, but it is the general course of the business.

SEPTEMBER 24. — The day of parting arrived at last. It is amusing to see how shy travellers (the English particularly) are of each other. They regard fellow-travellers, not as persons thrown in their way, whose society and conversation may afford pleasure and instruction, but who may rob them of their breakfast, or anticipate the post-horses. How different in our country, where travellers meeting on the road ask and answer questions, give and receive information, compare notes, and often form agreeable associations; and these Europeans have the impudence to curl their disgusting mustaches and ridicule those amiable traits in the American character. Yankee inquisitiveness forsooth! that's the way we come to know so much more than they.

FONTAINEBLEAU, SEPT. 25. — We were *en route* at eight o'clock in the wake of a carriage and four horses with a Count " Quelque Chose," his wife and child, which the etiquette of the road forbade our postilion to pass. Whilst we were changing horses at Joigny, I scraped acquaintance with our antecedent count (addressing him first, of course), and found him a sociable little man, and his wife an agreeable person. " Don't, father," said Margaret, but I was determined to give him a specimen of Yankee freedom of manners, and quite certain am I that neither of us were losers by the experiment. We travelled in company all day, and are at the same hotel.

Sunday brings no holiday for France. Everything goes on the same as on another day; the labors of the husbandmen are not suspended; the hammer rests not on the anvil; the shops are open, and carts loaded with wine and other merchandise pursue their wonted course on the roads where workingmen are employed in breaking stone. You see no groups of well-dressed people, as in England and our own blessed land, responding willingly to the summons of the cheerful village bell. I should like to know how this suits our reverend gentlemen who are so fond of visiting the Continent of late — the Springs and the Wainwrights, the Taylors and the Mortons. They cannot convert the Frenchmen, that's certain. I suppose they pray for them.

PARIS, OCTOBER 3. — George W. Lafayette made us a long visit this morning. He came in town last evening from La Grange. The family are very desirous that we should go out to see them, but our time is too short to permit it. He looks very well, talked much of his father, and gave us a great deal of information about the Trois Jours, the trial of the Carlist ministry, and other interesting events in which the general and himself bore conspicuous parts. Our meeting was quite tender; the style of greeting was somewhat amusing to Mr. Ludlow and Margaret. We kissed each other on both cheeks.

HAVRE, OCTOBER 7. — It rained with little intermission all the morning. The prospect of our sailing to-morrow is not encouraging. We went on board the ship, the "Sylvie de Grasse," and a splendid ship she is. My bosom swells and my heart warms to see my beloved stars and stripes floating over vessels in this port, superior to those of any other nation. They are so trim and neat, so beautiful and yet so majestic; they hold the same station in the commercial marine which their nation is destined to hold amongst the nations of the earth. This is not bravado nor prejudice, everything tends to it, and I do "most potently believe it."

HAVRE, OCTOBER 10.— The storm continues with unabated violence, and we are still detained in this *triste* vestibule of "*la belle France.*" I am punished now for having occasionally used this term when I wished to ingratiate myself with Frenchmen to whom I was writing or talking. We have certainly found nothing "*belle*" about it, except Paris and two or three of the royal palaces. We have found very little comfort or enjoyment. French politeness went out of fashion with the Bourbons, and "*place aux étrangers*" means nothing more now than a struggle amongst all classes and professions to cheat the English and Americans out of as much money as possible. The best thing they have is their noble king, and his amiable family; and Louis Philippe can no longer go abroad amongst his *loyal* subjects in the confidential manner to which his manly frankness would prompt him, from the constant apprehension that some vile assassin may be lying in wait to blow him up or to plant the parricidal steel in his bosom.

I repeat that France is not the country which I formerly knew. Perhaps I am changed myself. The eyes of fifty-six may not see things *couleur de rose* like those of forty; but it cannot be. I found England improved, as I fancied, and I know of no reason for my being prejudiced in my preference. My opinion may be influenced, too, by the constant bad weather I have experienced in France. I think there has not been a day since I crossed the Channel that it has not rained some part of the time, except on those five delicious ones which I passed with my children in

Geneva; then, indeed, the heavens seemed to smile in unison with the joyous feelings of my heart. The wind here blows an unrelenting hurricane from the westward. Oh, for one of those northeasters which have so often caused me to fret while at home! Here they come "with healing in their wings," if ever they do come, which my experience causes me to doubt.

AT SEA, OCTOBER 12. — I was not so much pleased as might have been expected, when we were summoned on board the "Sylvie de Grasse" this morning; for, although we were about to be released from our tedious detention, the prospect was not by any means encouraging. The wind had changed a little to the southward, but the sky was black and stormy in the west, and there was evidently only a temporary suspension of the terrible storm which has raged for a long time. We came on board a little before noon, and the ship was towed out of the narrow harbour by a steam-boat. By the time the pilot left us, the gale recommenced with increased fury, and a more miserable set of people were never congregated together. Every hole and corner of the ship is filled with passengers. A dozen women and as many children of all ages, and men of all nations, speaking every language. Sea-sickness in its direst aspects attacked us all and sent us to our staterooms before night.

OCTOBER 20. — We amuse ourselves so well that the time does not pass heavily. Eating and sleeping, the two great occupations of a sea life, are carried on with *amazing* spirit, and I perform my part of both without the least defalcation. Besides these, I read a great deal, and confine my reading to French, in which I think I am greatly improved; there are a great many good books on board. Then we play whist, several parties of which are formed. Mons. Tavout, Mr. Niles, Professor Longfellow, and I make one. We all play pretty well, and our bet never exceeds a franc a game. Some of the passengers play on the violin and other instruments, and on Thursday evening we got up a cotillion on deck — *Ainsi va le temps.*

OCTOBER 28. — After a night of fine sailing, with the wind at north-east, which enabled the passengers to make up the arrears of sleep of which the gale of the previous night had deprived them, I went on deck this morning at sunrise, and never did the sun rise on a more beautiful morning. We were on the edge of the banks of Newfoundland, in about 49 degrees of longitude, the thermometer at 50, immense numbers of aquatic birds, including ducks, hovering over our heads or resting on the waves. Amongst the other wonders of the deep a whale gave us a call and passed off astern. It soon fell calm, and the boundless ocean presented a smooth expanse of untroubled waters. The horizon in the west has a singular appearance. There is a fog which has an astonishing resemblance to land. I can almost fancy that the shores of our own Long Island lie exposed to my longing eyes.

NOVEMBER 3. — At eleven o'clock last night I went upon deck. The ship was sailing finely, at the rate of ten knots, before the wind, with studding-sails all standing. At one I was awakened by the noise and confusion upon deck, occasioned by a dreadful squall, which commenced at about one o'clock and continued four hours. Fortunately, the studding-sails had been taken in before the storm commenced, but it came on so suddenly and with such violence that the main top-gallant-sail and the mizzen-top-sail were torn away from the masts. I was alarmed, for I supposed the wind had changed to the south-west, and I knew we were not far south of George's bank; but this was not the case, the wind during the whole time was aft. The night was very dark, and the wind furious beyond description; but we have made nearly four degrees in the last twenty-four hours.

After the gale of last night had subsided the wind came out ahead, which was succeeded by a calm until five o'clock, when it began to blow again, and there was another violent gale which lasted all night. The motion of the ship was so disagreeable that I went to my birth. At ten I went on deck for a short time. The ocean appeared to be on fire. I have never seen this luminous appearance to so great a degree; not only the spray from the ship's bow, but every crested wave, as far as the eye could reach, appeared to be formed of myriads of bright stars. The pitching of the vessel was so great that I could not remain on the deck, but returned to roll again in my berth. These have been two dreadful nights in succession, and so near the shore too.

NOVEMBER 6. — The wind is still most obstinately ahead. We are within half-a-day's sail of our port, with no more chance of getting in until the wind changes than we had a week ago. We have fallen more than a degree south of Sandy Hook. It is like being locked out-of-doors on a stormy night, without a night-key and all the family asleep.

NOVEMBER 8. — This morning found us in the same position. I packed up my concerns and made all ready for going ashore. The pilot came on board at eight o'clock, but it became nearly calm, and the wind we had was nearly ahead. The news-boat boarded us, and took off several of our passengers at noon, but they gained nothing by it, for there was not a breath of wind during the remainder of the day. The spacious bay lay all around us without a ripple to disturb its bosom. Vessels of every description were to be seen immovable like our own, and so we continued until the steam-boat came down with the "Charlemagne" in tow, and after separating from her was attached to our ship. Another steam-boat with the "Pennsylvania," the Liverpool packet of this day, took the "Oxford" (which had come up with us with the fair wind while we were lying to). It was a splendid illustration of the power of steam. Our noble ship was lying like a log on the water when the little steam-boat took her by the arm, and cantered off with her at the rate of eight miles an hour. We arrived at the dock, foot of Rector street, at seven o'clock, where we found Charles Brugiere, who had heard accidentally of our arrival from Mr. Saligny (one of our renegade passengers), who arrived only an hour before us. Margaret and I, with Brugiere, took a carriage, and at eight o'clock I was in my own house. I entered the room in which my wife and son were without their having the least intimation of our arrival; for the packets of the 24th of September and the 1st of October, in both of which were letters announcing our intention of sailing in the "Sylvie de Grasse," have not arrived, and if they were, the case would not have been different, for no intelligence of our arrival had reached the city until an hour before we came to the dock.

The surprise and the joy of this unexpected meeting were almost too great, but we were soon the happiest little group in New York. My family and immediate friends are all well; there is a great deal of gossip which must find a place in this journal, but not now. I am once more at home by my own fire-side, — in my domestic circle, — doubly dear to me from a four months' absence.

Cole's Pictures.

NOVEMBER 18. — The series of five pictures by Cole, which he calls the "Course of Empire," I have seen in their progress, but the pleasure of seeing them finished was reserved for me until this morning. I went with my wife to the Gallery of the National Academy, where they are exhibited. My expectation, great as it was from the parts I saw before, has been more than realized. The conception is sublime and the execution admirable. Cole has immortalized himself; he has executed the greatest work, in his department of the arts, which our country has produced, and one which would take high rank in the best collection of Europe.

Ellen Tree.

NOVEMBER 23. — This charming actress arrived to-day in the "Roscoe" from Liverpool. I saw her twice at the Haymarket in August, and was much pleased with her acting, and, while I was in London, Mr. Price informed me that he had engaged her for the United States. She was playing in a new tragedy by Sergeant Talfourd, which had a great run at the Haymarket during the summer vacation at Drury Lane and Covent Garden. I fancied I could perceive in Miss Tree the resemblance to Mary Schermerhorn which Fanny Kemble notices so beautifully in her pretty budget of impertinences.

DECEMBER 6.—In the evening I attended the anniversary meeting and dinner of the St. Nicholas Society. Gulian C. Verplanck, the newly elected President, presided, with Washington Irving and John A. King as Vice-Presidents. There were not more than sixty who sat down to dinner, and it was rather a forced concern. I doubt if there will be another anniversary. There is great difficulty in keeping up the other societies, even with the advantage they have in forming a rallying-point for their respective countymen lately arrived, a sort of home abroad, affording strong claims upon national sensibility; but in our society there is no such bond of union, and the zeal with which some of its founders entered into the undertaking has visibly subsided.

DECEMBER 7.—I dined with the governing committee of the Union Club at Windust's. There were twenty-three present.

The committee consists, when full, of thirty-five, to whom all the concerns of the club are intrusted; there are two hundred and fifty members, not a sufficient number to organize properly, but it was resolved to procure a house and commence immediately. A sub-committee of seven was appointed to carry the plan into effect and to admit members. I am on this committee, much against my will. If this club can be gotten up like the English clubs, it may succeed; little short of that will meet the views of the members.

Massachusetts. DECEMBER 9.—The electoral vote of good old Massachusetts has been given, as of right it should be, for Daniel Webster, President, and Francis Granger, Vice-President. These electors have done their duty, and may carry with them a good conscience. The very thought (wild and hopeless as it is) of having Daniel Webster President of the United States should make the heart of every American leap in his bosom and cause him to dream of the days of George Washington.

The Woods and the Forrests are no longer to be found in this country, but we have had the *Groves* for some time, and now a *Tree* has been transplanted on our shores, and never did a sweeter or a lovelier exotic grace our dramatic soil.

But to quit bad punning and descend to sober history, Miss Ellen Tree made, this evening, her first appearance in America, at the Park Theatre, in the character of Rosalind in "As You Like It," and Pauline in a sort of melo-drama called "The Ransom." Her Rosalind was a most fascinating performance, full of grace and refinement and the part well adapted to her style of acting. The play, admirable as it is, and abounding in Shakespeare's finest passages and most touching sentiments, is usually tiresome in the performance, and can be best appreciated in the closet; but on this occasion sweet Rosalind was so ably supported by all the other characters that it went off delightfully. The charming *débutante* was well received by a prodigiously crowded house, and was saluted by cheers and waving of hats and handkerchiefs. I was struck again, as in London, by the great resemblance of Ellen Tree to my daughter Mary. Her profile is much like hers, and her smile so like that it almost overpowered my feelings; they are both pretty well off for nose, neither being of the kind called "snub" by any means; "quite to the contrary, I assure you," as Temple Bowdoin says; but Mary's eyes are finer and more expressive than Miss Tree's. Fanny Kemble was right in this matter.

Mr. Biddle.

DECEMBER 14.—This gentleman has written two letters, addressed to the Hon. John Quincy Adams, on the subject of the derangement of the currency, in which he has exposed the fallacious arguments of the President and his Secretary of the Treasury, and exposed in language most eloquent, and reasoning the most conclusive, the mischief resulting from the gratuitous interference of these functionaries in matters which they evidently do not understand, and with which they had no concern. These letters are published, and have created a lively interest with all those who have read and can understand them; but, alas! how small a proportion of those whose voices control the affairs of the country are of this number.

If any man in the United States has reason to be proud of his standing in the community it is Nicholas Biddle. Assailed, as he has been by the malice and ignorance of unworthy men in high stations, he has performed his course with dignity and forbearance, illuminating his official path as by a sunbeam, and without the exultation of little minds, overcoming and placing under his feet all his opponents. If any man but Andrew Jackson had been at the head of the government, the Bank of the United States would still have been in existence, and the check which commercial and national prosperity has received would not have overwhelmed individuals in its operation, and occasioned the present unexampled embarrassments.

DECEMBER 16.— The anniversary of the great fire. It is just a year since the desolating calamity took place, which destroyed property to the amount of more than twenty millions of dollars. To the honor of the merchants, and as an evidence of the prosperity of the city, the whole is rebuilt with more splendor than before. No pecuniary engagements have been broken in consequence of the losses attendant upon it, and all this with no actual, effectual relief from the general or State governments, who, instead of extending their protecting arms over their worthy children, are at present occupied in throwing embarrassments in the way of trade, and checking, as far as they can by impertinent interference, the course of public improvement and individual enterprise.

DECEMBER 30. — I went this evening to a party at Mrs. Charles H. Russell's, given in honor of the bride, Mrs. William H. Russell. The splendid apartments of this fine house are well adapted to an evening party, and everything was very handsome on this occasion. The house is lighted with gas, and the quantity consumed being greater than common, it gave out suddenly in the midst of a cotillon. This accident occasioned great merriment to the company, and some embarrassment to the host and hostess, but a fresh supply of gas was obtained, and in a short time the fair dancers were again " tripping it on the light fantastic toe." Gas is a handsome light, in a large room like Mr. Russell's, on an occasion of this kind, but liable (I should think) at all times to give the company the slip, and illy calculated for the ordinary uses of a family.

1837.

JANUARY 1.—The beginning of another year. That of the last was inauspicious; the ruins of the great fire were still smoking, to remind our merchants and other citizens of the twenty millions of dollars which they had lost, and of which those melancholy ruins were the gloomy monument; but the indomitable spirit of the merchants soon recovered from the loss, and although they bent severely under the burden of their affliction, they were too proud and too honest to break, and if they had been let alone by General Jackson and the crew who surround him and minister to his vanity and humour his prejudices, they would have recovered their losses and been easy in their affairs; but the close of 1836 has been hard, indeed, to those who owed money, and depended upon others for the means of meeting their engagements; money is very scarce, and the usurers are fattening upon their two and one-half and three per cent. a month, which they make indirectly by the medium of bills of exchange. The poor borrowers are forced to pay for the ingenuity of the lenders in avoiding the penalties of the usury laws, and the price of money is talked of as familiarly as that of bank stock or cotton.

During the last year I, too, have had my troubles; my property nominally is worth as much as ever it was, but I am largely in debt, and cannot convert anything I have into money but at a sacrifice which I am unwilling to make. So I am compelled, like other poor devils, to bow to the men who have the money in their hands. This comes a little hard to me, who am not used to it; but I must put my pride in my empty pocket and hope for better times.

I have crossed the broad Atlantic,—an event which I little dreamed of at the commencement of the year; saw Old England to great advantage; enjoyed *les délices de Paris;* passed through France and a small corner of Switzerland; spent a few happy days with my dear daughters on the border of the lovely Lake Leman; had a short, and tolerably agreeable, voyage back to New York, escaping thereby many storms and tedious weeks endured by all those who sailed after us; and arrived again in the midst of my friends, confirmed in my opinion that home is the best place for a man of fifty-six years of age. On the whole, I have great reason to be thankful for the blessings I enjoy. My health is good, my family happy, and my position in society respectable. I am not too old to have a taste for the enjoyments of life, and my circumstances admit of a reasonable indulgence in them. I am fond of literature, have a sort of smattering in the fine arts, and perceive no failure in those faculties which are required for their enjoyment. The year 1837 has commenced; my prayers for better times are, I trust, sufficiently mingled with thanksgivings for the undeserved blessings I enjoy.

JANUARY 3. — Mr. Lawrence, the Mayor, kept open house yesterday, according to ancient custom; but the manners, as well as the times, have sadly changed. Formerly gentlemen visited the Mayor, saluted him by an honest shake of the hand, paid him the compliments of the day, and took their leave; one out of twenty taking a single glass of wine or cherry bounce, and a morsel of pound-cake or New Year's cookies. But that respectable functionary is now considered the mayor of a party, and the rabble, considering him " hail fellow well met," use his house as a Five-point tavern. Mr. Lawrence has been much annoyed on former occasions, but the scene yesterday defies description. At ten o'clock the doors were beset by a crowd of importunate *sovereigns*, some of whom had already laid the foundation of *regal* glory and expected to become royally drunk at the hospitable house of His Honor. The rush was tremendous; the tables were taken by storm, the bottles emptied in a moment; confusion, noise, and quarrelling ensued, until the Mayor, with the assistance of his police, cleared the house and locked the doors, which were not reopened until every eatable and drinkable were removed, and a little decency and order restored.

I called soon after this change had taken place; the Mayor related the circumstances to me with strong indignation, and I hope the evil will be remedied hereafter. But this comes of Mr. Lawrence being the mayor of a party, and not of the city. Every scamp who has bawled out "Huzza for Lawrence!" and "Down with the Whigs!" considers himself authorized to use him and his house and furniture at his pleasure; to wear his hat in his presence; to smoke and spit upon his carpet; to devour his beef and turkey, and wipe his greasy fingers upon the curtains; to get drunk with his liquor, and discharge the reckoning by riotous shouts of "Huzza for our Mayor!" *We* put him in, and *we* are entitled to the use of him. Mr. Lawrence (party man as he is) is too much of a gentleman to submit to this, and sometimes wishes his constituents and his office all to the devil, if I am not greatly mistaken; and if he rejects (as he has now done) their kind tokens of brotherly affection, they will be for sending him there ere long, and will look out for somebody of their own class, less troubled than he with these aristocratical notions of decency, order, and sobriety.

JANUARY 7. — The venerable Abraham Van Vechten died yesterday in Albany, in the seventy-fifth year of his age. He was one of the descendants of the Dutch settlers of Albany. A lawyer of the highest class, a statesman of the glorious old Federal school, honest in his politics and in his private character as the sun which shone above him, of a mind strong and vigorous as the winter of his native city, and a heart soft as the early summer breeze of the South.

Mr. Van Vechten.

JANUARY 12. — The arrangement which was so happily effected a few years since by the public spirit of Mr. Clay, which was understood by all parties to be inviolable, and which healed the wounds of Southern feeling without sacrificing the great manufacturing interests of the country, has now been assailed by the ruthless hand of party, and our little

A Compromise Disturbed.

representative, Mr. Cambreling, was the chosen instrument to sharpen the weapon, and give its direction. He has introduced into the House of Representatives, as Chairman of the Committee of Ways and Means, a bill to alter the tariff duties upon foreign manufactures, so that the reduction which, by Mr. Clay's compromise, was to be made gradually, is anticipated four years. Another section of the act takes off immediately the duties upon salt and coals. If this high-handed measure is sanctioned by the President-elect (of which there is very little doubt, for Cambreling is his acknowledged mouth-piece), a flame will be raised which may in time endanger the union of the States, prostrate the active industry of the East and North, and render the whole country dependent upon foreigners. No wonder General Jackson and his administrators, executors, and assigns are popular in England. They are an admirable party for the interest of John Bull. Huzza for Jackson and Van Buren! Down with the New York Whigs who opposed the "commercial representative," and were so near sending an honest man to take his place! These cries will be mighty popular in the "old country," and have more weight and unction than even "God save the King!" or "Down with the Bishops!"

JANUARY 14. — The ship "Wellington," of 740 tons burden, was launched this day from Bergh's ship-yards. She is intended for Grinnell, Minturn, & Co.'s London line of packets. The *great duke* (as the Spaniards used to call him) ought to be highly gratified at this compliment from republican America. How things are changed! A supposed predilection for Old England, charged upon the Federal party thirty years ago, lost them their political ascendency. At that time men were afraid to wear a red watch-ribbon, lest it might be taken for a symbol of Toryism and bring the wearer a broken head; but now the two old women who govern England and America are great cronies, and their subjects better friends than they were before the battle of Concord; and the name of the Prince of Conservatives, the greatest aristocrat in Europe, graces the bows of one of the noble ships of which America has reason to be proud.

FEBRUARY 16. — This terrible old man, whose term of office (happily for the country) will expire in a little more than a fortnight, has been committing one of those acts of violence in which he habitually indulges, toward a senator whose high character has hitherto preserved him from the personal insults of black . . . of meaner rank than his present assailant. The "old General," as he is affectionately called; the "greatest and best," as he is foolishly called; or the "second Washington," as he is profanely called by the band of sycophants who have made him what he is, — is determined to die game; or, to use an expression which was brought into the American vocabulary about the same time that he assumed the crown and sceptre, he goes "the whole hog" in insulting the feelings of that part of the American people who have yet remaining some veneration for their country's institutions. Mr. Calhoun laid before the Senate a letter which he had received from the President, calling him to account for remarks made in debate in regard to that most mischievous measure, the removing the national deposits from the late Bank of the United States. The Executive arraigning a senator who represents a sovereign State, and that the proud State of South Carolina, and abusing him for the exercise of a constitutional right, — the free expression of opinion on the conduct of another branch of the government, delivered, it is to be presumed, in a decorous and orderly manner, or his brother senators would not have permitted it. William of Orange would never have worn the crown of England had Parliament and the people been equally subservient to the dictates of power as are my dear, gullible countrymen. What would the Hancocks, the Adamses, and the Quincys; the Jays, the Clintons, and the Hamiltons; the Henrys, the Randolphs, and the Madisons, — have said at the bare suggestion of such a radical defect within the space of fifty or sixty years in the fair fabric which their patriotic labours contributed to erect, as could by

President Jackson.

possibility permit such a usurpation on the part of the executive magistrate? He could not wait until his time was out to vent his spleen against a political opponent. It was more convenient to "assume the responsibility" (a hateful Jackson term) before the fourth of March should have taken from his shoulders the mantle of official impunity. Or, perhaps, as "the old cocks teach the young ones to crow," this act was intended to instruct his successor and favourite in the art of governing upon patent Jackson principles, and to give him the exact length and breadth of the forbearance of the American people; but, thank God! Mr. Van Buren, although a wiser and a better man, does not enjoy the baneful popularity, at least in any important degree, of the present chief magistrate, and cannot (even if he were so disposed, which I am far from believing) ever trifle with the feelings of his countrymen with the same indulgence. Mr. Calhoun, on presenting the letter to the Senate, repeated the remarks which had occasioned it, and with great eloquence, dignity, and self-possession appealed to that body to protect their privileges.

MARCH 4. — This is the end of General Jackson's administration, — the most disastrous in the annals of the country, and one which will excite "the special wonder" of posterity. That such a man should have governed this great country, with a rule more absolute than that of any hereditary monarch of Europe, and that the people should not only have submitted to it, but upheld and supported him in his encroachments upon their rights, and his disregard of the Constitution and the laws, will equally occasion the surprise and indignation of future generations. The people's indifference will prove that the love of liberty and independence is no longer an attribute of our people, and that the patriotic labours of the men of the Revolution have sunk like water in the sands, and that the vaunted rights of the people are considered by them as a "cunningly devised fable."

This is also the commencement of Mr. Van Buren's reign, the first New York President. He has said that it was "honour enough to have served under such a chief," and will no doubt for a time speak with reverence of the ladder by which he has risen to the summit of ambitious hopes; but I do not despair of him. He will be a party President, but he is too much of a gentleman to be governed by the rabble who surrounded his predecessor and administered to his bad passions. As a man, a gentleman, and a friend, I have great respect for Mr. Van Buren. I hate the cause, but esteem the man; and, although I differ in my expectations from some of my political friends, I am disposed to give him a fair chance. What a tide there is in the affairs of men! The refusal of a Whig Senate to confirm his appointment as Minister to England made him President of the United States.

MARCH 6. — The new President was sworn into office at the Capitol, on Saturday, at noon. The ceremony was conducted as usual, in the presence of the "high dignitaries" of the nation, foreign ministers, etc., and as many of the "sovereigns" as could gain admittance to the presence of their "servant." Mr. Van Buren made an inaugural speech, which I think is very good. The principles on which he promises to govern are unexceptionable, and if he had not committed himself unnecessarily, and I think improperly, on the subject of slavery, by saying that he intends to veto any bill which may be passed by Congress to regulate that knotty subject in the District of Columbia, and if he could only have kept himself quiet about the old lion, who is now about to drag his reluctant steps away from the den, I should have said, Hurrah for Martin the First! His glorification of the "hero of a considerable number of wars" is too good to be lost.

Inauguration.

MARCH 15. — This has turned out a great affair; everything went like clock-work. I arose at six o'clock. The morning was raw and looked stormy, but soon became bright, and it proved a pleasant day. At seven o'clock the committee of arrangements, consisting of myself, Messrs. Draper, Barstow, Leavitt, Johnson, Smith, and Benson, started in the steam-

Mr. Webster's Reception.

boat and arrived at Amboy at half-past nine. On the arrival of the cars from Philadelphia we received Mr. Webster. The flags which had been prepared were hoisted on his coming on board, and we started immediately. We arrived at the steamboat wharf near the Battery at three o'clock; here the crowd was immense; the dock-houses, sheds, and that part of the Battery nearest the place of landing were covered with people. Mr. Webster was placed in my barouche, in which also D. B. Ogden, Peter Stagg, and myself were seated. An escort of horsemen, to the number of one hundred, preceded the barouche, and the carriages with the members of the committee followed. Broadway was filled with people from the Battery to the American Hotel (Mr. Webster's quarters), and he was cheered by the crowd on his whole progress with great enthusiasm. On his arrival at the hotel he addressed them briefly from a front window. The committee escorting Mr. Webster, with Mr. Granger, Mr. Abbot Lawrence, and a few others, went, at six o'clock, to Niblo's saloon, where an immense concourse was assembled by previous notice. The meeting was organized by the appointment of David B. Ogden, chairman, Robert C. Cornell, Jonathan Goodhue, Nathaniel Weed, and Joseph Tucker, vice-presidents, and Hiram Ketcham and Joseph Hoxie, secretaries. The resolutions passed at the first meeting were read, together with the correspondence. Our committee then ascended the stage with Mr. Webster, and I introduced him with a brief speech.

The chairman then read an address to Mr. Webster, to which he replied in a speech of two hours and a half, — one of those glorious exhibitions of talent for which he stands unrivalled in America. He gave a clear and forcible history of the administration for the last eight years; laid open his views and the course of his political conduct; told the Whigs, in glowing and animated terms, the duty they owed the Republic, even while in a minority; and sent home four or five thousand as good-looking men as I ever saw assembled, delighted and instructed, and unconscious that they had been standing in one position for nearly four hours. The use of the Governor's room in the City Hall has been obtained for Mr. Webster, where he will receive visitors to-morrow from twelve until two o'clock.

MARCH 18. — Notwithstanding the hard times and my participation in their effects, I could not resist the temptation of having Mr. Webster to dine with me to-day; so I had a nice little party, and an exceedingly pleasant one. "The man whom every true American delights to honour" (there is no harm in stealing out of my own pocket) was more at his ease than I ever before saw him at dinner-table; he was talkative, cheerful, full of anecdote, and appeared to enjoy himself as much as he caused others to enjoy themselves, and we made a very gay termination of an exceedingly sorrowful sort of a week. Our party consisted of the following: Mr. Webster, Mr. David B. Ogden, Chancellor Kent, Robert Ray, Mr. Granger, Charles King, Mr. James Brown, Simeon Draper, Mr. George Griswold, President Duer. The troubles in Wall street kept away James G. King and Morris Robinson. A number of failures have taken place to-day; only the forerunners of greater disasters. The names are not worth recording, for such events will soon cease to be worthy of remark

MARCH 20. — The prospects in Wall street are getting worse and worse. The Josephs do *not* go on. The accounts from England are very alarming; the panic prevails there as bad as here. Cotton has fallen; the loss on shipments will be very heavy, and American credits will be withdrawn. The paper of the Southern and Western merchants is coming back protested. Why should I be in such a scrape?

MARCH 28. — The general meeting of the Whigs was held this evening at Masonic Hall, to receive the nomination of Aaron Clarke for mayor. I was there for a short time. The great hall was filled, and great enthusiasm prevailed. I hope it will not evaporate. A much greater object is to be attained than the mere personal triumph of Aaron Clarke over John J. Morgan. This will be the first important election which has been held since Mr. Van Buren assumed the reins of government, and it will be well to let him know whether the people approve of his driving (as he has intimated he intended to do) according to the Jackson plan.

A meeting of merchants was held this day at the Merchants' Bank, Wall street, for the purpose of agreeing upon a letter to be presented to Mr. Biddle, requesting the Bank of the United States, at Philadelphia, to step forward in this most appalling crisis and save the commercial community of New York. Mr. Biddle and the cashier, Mr. Jaudon, have come on purpose to ascertain the true state of things, and, if possible, to afford relief.

I was invited to attend this meeting; never was seen such an assemblage of woe-begone countenances. Despondency had taken place of that indomitable spirit which usually characterizes the merchants of New York, and Nicholas Biddle, the insulted and proscribed of Andrew Jackson and his myrmidons, is the sun to which alone they can look to illumine the darkness. Did ever man enjoy so great a moral triumph? He is the only man, and the bank over which he so ably presides the only institution, in the country which has stood erect before the implacable hostility of Andrew Jackson. Mr. Biddle, placing himself upon the firm base of honour and integrity, has retaliated the wrongs which he has received from a portion of his fellow-citizens, by serving them whenever a suitable occasion occurred, and now he comes forward in the day of their adversity to relieve them to the extent of his ability. He can do so much, and most assuredly will.

Booksellers' Dinner. MARCH 31.— This was the greatest dinner I was ever at, with the exception, perhaps, of that given to Washington Irving on his return from Europe. I had the honour of being an invited guest. The Association of Booksellers in the principal cities of the Union have a great annual or semi-annual feast, at which eminent literary and scientific men are invited to join the trade. This, I believe, was the first in New York; it was given at the City Hotel, and was gotten up, arranged, and conducted in admirable style. At five o'clock yesterday, the Association, with their guests (I should think to the number of fifty), began to assemble, and when the company was seated the large dining-room was quite full. Mr. Crittenden told me this morning that two hundred and seventy-seven persons sat down to the table. Mr. David Felt presided in handsome style, assisted by F. Harper, Charles Carvill, W. Jackson, and James Conner, as vice-presidents, George Dearborn, master of ceremonies, and John Keese as toast-master.

Among the guests whom I noticed were Rev. Mr. Schroeder, Rev. Orville Dewey, Professor Follen, President Duer, and Professors McVickar, Anderson, and Renwick, of Columbia College, Chancellor Kent, Mr. Gallatin, Colonel Trumbull, Judge Irving, Washington Irving, Halleck, Bryant, Paulding, Hugh Maxwell, Dr. McMurtrie, Dr. Gray, Leggett, Herbert, Grenville Mellon, Inman, Weir, Chapman, Drs. Ticknor, Gilman, DeKay, and Francis, besides many gentlemen connected with literature in Philadelphia and Boston.

APRIL 10. — One of the signs of the times is to be seen in the sales of rich furniture. Men who a year ago thought themselves rich, and such expenditures justifiable, are now bankrupt.

Markets continue extravagantly high; meat of all kinds and poultry are as dear as ever. The farmers (or rather the market speculators) tell us this is owing to the scarcity of corn; but the shad, the cheapness of which in ordinary seasons makes them, as long as they last, a great resource for the poor, are not to be bought under seventy-five cents and a dollar. Is this owing to the scarcity of corn, or are the fish afraid to come into our waters lest they may be caught in the vortex of Wall street? Brooms, the price of which, time out of mind, has been twenty-five cents, are now sold at half a dollar; but corn is scarce. Poor New York!

APRIL 21. — An evidence of the pecuniary distress which pervades the community is to be found in the reduced price of stocks and unimproved real estate. All the local bank stocks have fallen below par. Railroads and canals will not bring in many instances more than half their value a year ago. The Delaware and Hudson, which is now in a more prosperous condition than at any former period, is selling at sixty-five per cent., and Mohawk and Hudson Railroad about the same. As to lots which have been the medium of enormous speculations, the following fact will tell their story: Lots at Bloomingdale, somewhere about One Hundredth street (for the whole island was laid out in town lots), which cost last September $480 a lot, have been sold within a few days at $50. The immense fortunes which we heard so much about in the days of speculation have melted away like the snows before an April sun. No man can calculate to escape ruin but he who owes no money. Happy is he who has a little, and is free from debt.

APRIL 25. — This volume commences at the most gloomy period which New York has ever known. The clouds which have been for six months hovering over us have become darker than ever, and no eye can perceive a ray of hope through their obscurity. I participate personally, to a great degree, in the distress and embarrassment of the time. The difference in my situation and prospects between the commencement of the last volume of this journal and the present time is so great that it requires a good share of philosophy and resignation to keep up under the reflections which flow from the contrast, and I would throw down this steel pen (which don't write over and above well) and give up the task of journalizing on the threshold of this volume, if I had not a lingering hope that I may yet, one of these days, have cause to write in a more cheerful strain.

APRIL 26. — A meeting of merchants was held last evening at Masonic Hall, "to take into consideration the present distress, and to devise suitable measures of relief." I took the chair of the largest and most respectable assemblage I ever witnessed.

Great Meeting of Merchants.

The resolutions are pretty well spiced, and some softening alterations were made at my suggestion; as they are, they contain nothing but the truth, and the truth which in such an emergency ought to be spoken. But I understand some of the Wall-street gentlemen (particularly the few who owe no money) are opposed to the meeting, or any other which may express the feelings of the suffering merchants and traders. But those who attended the meeting must have perceived a spirit there which cannot be quenched. The following committee was appointed, under one of the resolutions, " to repair to Washington and remonstrate with the Executive against the continuance of the specie circular, and in behalf of this meeting, and in the name of the merchants of New York and the people of the United States, to urge its immediate repeal."

I attended last evening the dinner of the governing committee of the Union Club, at Windust's. Nineteen present. The Executive Committee are engaged in preparing the house and laying in stores and furniture. They expect to be ready in about three weeks. This club will be well suited to the times. A single gentleman will be able to get a good dinner and his wine for half the price he would have to pay at a hotel.

I attended this evening an extra meeting of the directors of the Bank for Savings, called in consequence of applications from the Bowery and the Greenwich Savings-Bank to help them in their present difficulties. The poor and the labouring classes of the community, who constitute a large proportion of the depositors in those institutions, urged by their necessities, or by a want of confidence in all money institutions, are withdrawing their funds in a most alarming manner. The two banks above named will not be able to keep up, and I fear that even our great bank, with a deposit account of upward of three millions of dollars, will find it extremely difficult to meet the run which will be occasioned by the suspension of the others. Our funds have been safely and judiciously invested in State stocks bearing five and six per cent. interest, — good, if anything in America may be so considered in these times; but the run has already been dreadful. Up to yesterday the drafts in the present month amounted to $280,000. We have sold a large amount of stocks at a very heavy loss, and every exertion is making by as discreet and able a set of men as ever had the control of a public institution; but there is reason to fear that the State stocks of New York, Pennsylvania, and Ohio will not much longer command money at any price, so entirely has confidence been destroyed in the community. A panic amongst such people as the bulk of depositors in savings-banks cannot be restrained; it goes on to the destruction of themselves as well as the sources on which they depend for support. But there is no reasoning with them. Like the wild and frightened horse, their onward career cannot be checked by a curb or bridle, and reason might as well be employed to arrest the stormy waves of ocean.

APRIL 28. — Mr. Webster's great speech, delivered at Niblo's on the 15th of March, is published in the Whig newspapers, beside many thousand copies in pamphlet form. If the people would read this admirable address, it could not fail to produce the most salutary effects; but they dare not put themselves in the way of having their faith in their idols shaken; they heed not the charmer, "charm he ever so wisely." Mr. Webster did not aim at a display of eloquence in this address. His object, as he avowed it at the time, was to make a plain statement of the measures of the late administration, and a history of the causes which led to the present unparalleled state of distress and embarrassment here, and in all parts of this once prosperous country. Still it contains occasional flashes of eloquence in the most brilliant style of the accomplished orator.

Mr. Webster's Speech.

MAY 2. — The number of failures is so great daily that I do not keep a record of them, even in my mind.

MAY 6. — The committee of merchants met at five o'clock to receive the report of the sub-committee, who returned this morning from Washington. Their interview with the President, as was expected, produced nothing. He insisted upon a written communication, to which he sent a reply. He will do nothing in regard to the specie circular, will not call an extra session of Congress, and will not take into consideration the subject of the government forbearance to enforce the payment of bonds. The committee are under strong excitement, and I fear the consequences of a meeting which is to be held on Monday to receive this report. But there was no resisting it. It is a dangerous time for such a meeting; combustibles enough are collected to cause an awful conflagration; men's minds are bent upon mischief; ruin and rashness, distress and despair, generally go together, and a spark may blow us up. I must preside at this meeting, for it would be dishonourable to desert these men now. If I have influence, I will exert it to prevent violence.

MAY 8. — The Dry Dock Bank stops payment to-day. There was a meeting yesterday at the Mayor's office of the presidents and cashiers of the other banks in relation to the subject of helping the Dry Dock Bank. I saw the Mayor in the afternoon, who told me that they refused unanimously to come forward, on his representation that it was out of the question. This bank, with a capital of $200,000, has discounted to the amount of $1,200,000. It is not a safety-fund bank, but one of the pets selected by the government as a safer depository of the public money than the Bank of the United States, and has a government deposit of $280,000, which will go in part payment of the cost of the fatal *experiment.*

But three banks at Buffalo, all safety-fund banks, are under injunction and their doors closed. The Legislature immediately passed an act directing the bank commissioners to assume the payment of their notes, which will consequently be received and paid at the Manhattan Bank. This will probably sweep away the famous safety-fund. The bubble will burst, and the public creditors of rotten banks will look in vain hereafter to that delusive hope for protection from loss. Where will it all end? In ruin, revolution, perhaps civil war.

MAY 9. — The meeting of merchants took place last evening, at Masonic Hall, in pursuance of a resolution adopted at the meeting of the 25th of April, to receive the report of the committee appointed to go to Washington. Great anxiety prevailed throughout the city in relation to this meeting;

Great Meeting.

fears were entertained that in the present excited state of the public mind, particularly of that part of the community of which the committee were a part, violent proceedings might take place, and tumult and disorder destroy all chance of producing good by the meeting, — proceedings which would be an example and sanction to the lower orders of the people when bent (as they will soon be) upon mischief of some sort. I partook largely of these feelings, and determined to exert all my powers and influence to give a proper direction to the action of the committee of arrangements for the great meeting, and a hard time I have had of it. We met at three o'clock, at Delmonico's. The report of the Washington committee, which was prepared by Isaac S. Hone, is exceedingly well done. It was adopted, with some amendment; resolutions were proposed, true enough and very good ; but, having been prepared under strong excitement and a sense of injuries inflicted by the government, were so strong, in my judgment, as to defeat the object we have in view, viz., to raise up a party opposed to the men who have brought us into our present unhappy situation. One in particular charged the President with statements "unfounded in fact;" to this I made serious objections, but without avail, until I was compelled to declare that I would not preside at the meeting unless the language I objected to was stricken from the resolution. I prevailed, and was allowed to alter the resolution, which was then adopted.

The great meeting took place at half-past seven. The same officers were appointed ; the report and resolutions were read by Isaac S. Hone, who made an excellent address, explaining and elucidating some points in the report. Mr. Bryan was loudly called for, and made a good speech. The report was accepted, the resolutions adopted, the meeting adjourned, and the immense multitude retired without the slightest act of indecorum, much to the mortification of some of the adherents of the party in power, who hoped that this assemblage of the finest fellows in the State of New York would, by some act of violence, destroy the influence which the justness of their cause begins already to produce in the minds of men of all parties, and which will undoubtedly rend the State from Mr. Van Buren at the next election. I am thankful that the situation in which I was placed enabled me to infuse a spirit of moderation into the proceedings. As they are, they do us credit, and will have a favourable influence over the minds of men in other parts of the country.

A constant run was made to-day for specie on all the other banks, which will inevitably drain them all in a week. *The banks will be compelled to suspend the payment of specie,* and the Legislature must pass an act, before they adjourn, to suspend, for a given period, the operation of the law forfeiting the charters of banks refusing to pay specie. Mr. Van Buren's precious safety-fund cries " Enough ! " on receiving the first blow; the rotten fabric falls like the walls of Jericho on the first blast of the trumpet.

The Crisis,— Banks suspended.

MAY 10. — The *experiment* has succeeded; the volcano has burst and overwhelmed New York; the glory of her merchants is departed. After a day of unexampled excitement, and a ruthless run upon all the banks, which drew from their vaults $600,000 in specie yesterday, nearly as much having been drawn on Monday, the officers held a meeting last evening and resolved to *suspend specie payments.*

It was inevitable; and the banks will be sustained in this measure by all good citizens. The Legislature must pass an act immediately, suspending the operation of that part of the safety-fund law which annuls their charters on a refusal to pay specie; otherwise we shall be worse off than ever, having no circulating medium at all. They must also repeal the law which forbids the issuing of bank-notes under five dollars. I regret the necessity for the latter measure, having been always in favour of the law. It worked well, and would have continued to do so but for the accursed Jackson and Benton *experiment* (the word makes me sick. I wish it could be drummed out of the English language).

The savings-bank also sustained a most grievous run yesterday. They paid three hundred and seventy-five depositors $81,000.

The press was awful; the hour for closing the bank is six o'clock, but they did not get through the paying of those who were in at that time until nine o'clock. I was there with the other trustees, and witnessed the madness of the people, — women nearly pressed to death, and the stoutest men could hardly sustain themselves; but they held on as with a death's grasp upon the evidences of their claims, and, exhausted as they were with the pressure, they had strength to cry, " Pay ! Pay ! "

While we were in session intelligence was brought that the banks had suspended specie payments. Great fears were entertained that these measures would produce serious consequences when they became known, particularly those adopted by the Bank for Savings, where there are twenty-five thousand depositors, and those generally of the poorest and most ignorant classes. I went down this morning; the notice was hung out at the door of the bank. A crowd was collected, which continued during the day, but I do not think there were at any time more than one hundred persons. Some were a little savage, but they seemed to require explanation only. It was a sort of recompense for their disappointment, which they were entitled to; and when I addressed them, and some of the other trustees who were present made the explanations they wanted, they were easily pacified, and went away, by the tens and twenties, tolerably well reconciled to their disappointment, and two hours before sunset the street was cleared.

In the afternoon the trustees met in the Mayor's office. I was mortified to be there, and expressed myself freely in reprobation of the pusillanimity which led them to give up the ship of which they had the command. I do not know by whose order the place of meeting was changed at this interesting moment; but it was a sneaking affair, and most of the trustees thought so.

During the day Wall street was greatly crowded; but there was no riot or tumult. On the contrary, men's countenances wore a more cheerful aspect than for several days past. The suspension of specie payments will restore confidence, the men of capital will suffer by the deterioration of the value of the circulating medium, and John Bull (if he, too, has not been compelled to adopt the same measure ere this) will scold furiously, and stigmatize the Yankees as a nation of swindlers; but honest men who are in debt and wish to pay, and mechanics who are willing to work, will have cause to rejoice. As for myself, I am in the first predicament, and cry, *Laus Deo!* The limb is amputated, the symmetry of the body spoiled, but the life of the patient is saved. The new mayor has done his duty like a man. The troops were out during the day, and Major-General Hays, with his regiment of *Clubadiers*, have shown themselves at various points in strong force. Thus ends this most eventful day.

MAY 11. — A dead calm has succeeded the stormy weather of Wall street and the other places of active business. All is still as death; no business is transacted, no bargains made, no negotiations entered into; men's spirits are better, because the danger of universal ruin is thought to be less imminent. A slight ray of hope is to be seen in countenances where despair only dwelt for the last fortnight, but all is wrapped in uncertainty. Nobody can foretell the course matters will take. The fever is broken; but the patient is in a sort of syncope, exhausted by the violence of the disease and the severity of the remedies.

MAY 12. — The banks of Philadelphia suspended specie payments yesterday, except the Bank of the United States, and that must follow. It is impossible that that institution, mighty as it is, and reluctant to enter into the measure, can stand alone.

The Baltimore banks have also suspended. It cannot fail to become general. The commercial distress and financial embarrassment pervade the whole nation. Posterity may get out of it, but the sun of the present generation will never again shine out. Things will grow better gradually, from the curtailment of business, but the glory has departed. Jackson, Van Buren, and Benton form a triumvirate more fatal to the prosperity of America than Cæsar, Pompey, and Crassus were to the liberties of Rome.

News from England. The London packet-ship "Wellington" arrived yesterday, bringing news to the fourteenth of last month.

Everything in England is tending to a commercial crisis like that in which we are placed. The great American house of George Wildes & Co. has been sustained by the Bank of England. They owe the enormous sum of two million pounds. The bank sustains them, because, if they fall, they must carry all the others with them. The United States must ruin all the American houses, and they in their turn will cause such general embarrassments that even the Bank of England will not be able to stand.

MAY 19. — A Baltimore paper, after stating the report (which does not distress me as much as some things which I have heard, seen, and felt) that General Jackson "has lost by the recent commercial reverses so large a sum as to render it possible that his old age may be one of poverty even, instead of ease and opulence," introduces the following beautiful extract, than which nothing can be imagined more appropriate : —

> " So, the struck eagle, stretched upon the plain,
> No more through rolling clouds to soar again,
> Views his own feather on the fatal dart
> That winged the shaft that quivers in his heart.
> Keen are his pangs, but keener far to feel
> He nursed the pinion that impelled the steel."

MAY 20. — The part of Beatrice is, I think, the best of her acting. *Ellen Tree.* She played it last night, for her benefit, to a full house. There is a refinement, a grace, about her which suits the character. Miss Tree has not the force of Fanny Kemble, but more sweetness. She has less genius, but more nature. The Beatrice of the former is a virago ; the latter makes her a spoiled child ripened into a wayward, fascinating coquette, but a lady always.

My daughter and I called the other day upon Miss Tree, and left an invitation to dinner for to-day. She declined, pleading a promise to play this evening for Hill's benefit. She returned our visit yesterday. I was not at home. My daughters were exceedingly pleased with her, and enjoyed her visit greatly. All who know this lady, at home and here, speak of her in warm terms of commendation. She is intelligent, modest, and agreeable, and wholly uncontaminated by her profession.

The following party dined with us: Captain Marryat, I. S. Hone, Bankhead, Dr. McLean, Hay, President Duer, William Johnson, R. Freeman, Henry Brevoort, and Stevenson.

The lion, Captain Marryat, is no great things of a lion, after all. In truth, the author of "Peter Simple" and "Jacob Faithful" is a very every-day sort of a man. He carries about him in his manner and conversation more of the sailor than the author, has nothing student-like in his appearance, and savours more of the binnacle lamp than that of the study. He appears pleased with the little he has seen of this country, and very desirous to see more; but the bad times will deprive him of much of the attention and hospitality to which his talents and celebrity entitle him.

MAY 22. — The loss of life by steamboats in this country, and especially on the Western waters, is shocking in the extreme, and a stigma on our country; for these accidents (as they are called) seldom occur in Europe, where they do not understand the art and mystery of steam devices, or, indeed, of ship-building, better than we do. But we have become the most careless, reckless, headlong people on the face of the earth. "Go ahead" is our maxim and pass-word; and we do go ahead with a vengeance, regardless of consequences and indifferent about the value of human life. What are a few hundred persons, more or less? There are plenty in this country, and more coming every day; and a few years in the life of a man makes very little difference in comparison with the disgrace of a steamboat being beaten in her voyage by a rival craft.

Steamboat burned.

MAY 25. — The English writers indulge themselves greatly of late in quoting out-of-the-way words and queer sayings peculiar to the people of this country. "I reckon," as Brother Jonathan says; "go the whole hog," to use

Americanisms.

a Yankee expression; and other phrases of that kind which occur frequently in the novels and stories with which the British press abounds, prove that they begin to take a little notice of us, and we shall soon become as proud as the happy individual who boasted that the prince on a certain occasion had honoured him by his notice, and ordered him to stand out of the way.

MAY 26. — A deadly calm pervades this lately flourishing city. No goods are selling, no business stirring, no boxes encumber the sidewalks of Pearl street; stocks have fallen again, but not back to the prices at which they were before the suspension of specie payments. No remittances come from other States, and even where debtors are able and willing to pay, there is no means of getting the funds to New York. The French and English packets are greatly behindhand, as if to give us all the bad news they will bring in one *grand coup*. In the upper part of the city we shiver under the chilly blasts of a backward spring, and burn more coal than we can afford to pay for. Very few houses are being built, except in some cases like mine, where we began before the "evil day" came, and must go on. Lots which a year ago were like "rough-edge guineas," and brought any price for fear they might run away, stand now in the same places, and do not look nearly so pleasant nor so valuable as they did then. "Gold and silver we have none," and there is no change either in our prospects or our currency. No man has anything to comfort him unless it is he who is out of debt, and has no sympathy for the misfortunes of his neighbours.

MAY 27. — I dined with the governing committee of the Union Club, the first dinner in the club house, No. 343 Broadway. The house will be open to the subscribers on Thursday next. It is well fitted up, the furniture neat and handsome; the servants are good, and, above all, there is a most *recherché chef de cuisine*. Subscribers will get a better dinner and pay less for it than at any hotel in town. It is a great resource for bachelors and men "about town;" but I do not see how we married men can be induced to leave our comfortable homes and families to dine "*en garçon*" at the club, even under the temptation of Monsieur Julien's *bon diners à la Paris*.

MAY 29.— Captain Marryat called to see us this morning. I like him better than I did at first; but he has very little refinement of manner, and his conversation does not partake of the ease and fluency which characterize his writings.

MAY 30.— Mr. Webster, accompanied by his wife, is making a tour of the Western States. He has been received in all the principal towns with great demonstrations of respect. Public dinners and barbecues have been tendered to him in great profusion, and speeches made and answered at every place where there was a town-house or hotel large enough to hold the people. Even in Nashville, Tenn., General Jackson's own dunghill, a public meeting of the citizens was held, and a deputation appointed to invite him to partake of the hospitalities of the town. It would be amusing to see Mr. Webster at a Tennessee barbecue, with General Jackson as one of his entertainers,— the man who has done more mischief to the country than any other, proposing the health of him who has done the most to avert it.

Mr. Webster is boldly nominated in many of the Whig papers for the next President after the curse of Jacksonism shall have been removed from the land. This is premature; but it may be the means of keeping out of the field second-rate men, on whom the party cannot unite. I am clear for using the best materials we have. Webster or Clay,—nothing short of this. If we cannot have either, then let the dear people have another dose of Van Buren.

MAY 31.— We rode out this afternoon to Mr. Schermerhorn's. The weather is now warm and pleasant and the country beautiful. The grass will grow, though desolation stalks through the streets of our city; the trees will put forth their leaves and blossom, notwithstanding the suspension of all profitable business; the flowers are dressed in all their gaudy and smiling array, as if to mock the melancholy faces of the suffering merchants; and the birds sing merrily, regardless of the sighs and groans of the lords of creation.

JUNE 2.— My wife and I drove out this afternoon to visit Mr. and Mrs. Henry Hoyt, who are living very pleasantly at Mr. Post's place, at Manhattanville, which belonged once to Lord Courtney. It is one of the finest places on the Island. President and Mrs. Duer were of our party.

Prince Louis Napoleon Bonaparte. JUNE 12.— This youthful scion of the Bonaparte stock, who was exiled for ten years from France for a silly attempt at revolt made by him at Strasburgh, after walking Broadway during the last three or four weeks, sailed to-day in the "George Washington" for Liverpool. The ill-health of his mother is the alleged cause of his sudden return. He will go from England to Germany. He had better have stayed where he was, for he is likely to get into new scrapes where he is going. His formal attempt was not of a nature to create much alarm, or Louis Philippe would not have let him slip through his fingers when he had him.

New Books. JUNE 23.— The number of new books coming out every day from the English press, as well as ours, sets at defiance the hope of keeping up with those, even, whose merits, or the circumstance of a personal acquaintance with the author, or other local or individual interest, render it incumbent upon one to read. Besides the standard French and English works which my late visit to Europe leads me to peruse, I am now reading Bulwer's "Athens,"— a new work highly spoken of,— when down comes the second volume of Lockhart's "Life of Walter Scott," which (as I have read the first) is irresistible. Then comes the funny "Pickwick Papers," which, though lighter, shoves aside the others. Then, Miss Martineau's "Society in America," which some say is very saucy, and others very good, cannot be neglected if one would be in the fashion; and every feeling of good taste and friendship and patriotism calls upon us to lay everything else aside and read Washington Irving's "Adventures of Captain Bonneville."

JULY 4. — The anniversary of the birth of our country was marked by most delicious weather. I wrote until noon, then walked down to see the crowd as far as St. Paul's Church. The bells were ringing a merry peal in honour of the day. Their sounds proclaimed the liberty and independence of my country; but now, for the first time, there appeared to me mockery in those sounds. The glory seemed to have departed. We are nominally in the enjoyment of the liberty which was bequeathed to us by the men of the Revolution; we have the glorious Constitution which they framed for us, but eight years of misrule has left us nothing but the empty name. Independent, too, we are of foreign control, — and long may God preserve us so! — but the tyranny of public opinion, supporting measures of the most oppressive character, has destroyed that proud and manly personal independence which was heretofore the characteristic of my countrymen, and men are governed by self-interest, or bound down by a strong, but invisible, chain of party-spirit, a badge of slavery like that of Wamba, or the Serf of the North.

AUGUST 1. — The packets which sailed to-day took out a million and a half of gold and silver, and no American passengers; this is as it should be. We must not buy any more goods or spend any more money in Europe until we have paid all we owe them. That is the only way to get out of the present scrape. If remittances continue in this way, with the aid of one or two cotton crops, and the realization of the present glorious prospects for the harvest, we shall not only get right, but the character of our merchants will stand higher than ever among the nations of the earth; for they will have evinced a determination to be honest in despite of the exertions of a corrupt government to make them otherwise.

The dial of the clock in the cupola of the City Hall was illuminated last night, and made a splendid appearance through the foliage of the trees in the park. It was attempted six or seven years ago, but soon discontinued, for some cause or other. A Whig corporation has been more successful, in this instance at least, in enlightening their constituents.

AUGUST 9. — I was one of a party of twenty-four who dined on turtle to-day at the Union Club House. The dinner was execrable, for a French *artiste de cuisine* knows nothing about turtle; but we had good punch and wine, some excellent songs, many good jokes, laughing in season and out of season, and noise not a little, for we had John and Charles King, Bibby, John Stevens, Otis, etc., to say nothing of myself. Chancellor Jones presided, who is as punctual in filling the seat at the head of the club table as that on the bench of the Supreme Court.

AUGUST 31. — The ocean has, by the accuracy of nautical skill, been almost converted into a railway or turnpike road. The following circumstance is worthy of note: the packet-ships "South America," Captain Barstow, and "Garrick," Captain Robinson, sailed from New York on the 1st of July, and entered the Mersey together after a fine run of eighteen days. The two ships were in sight of each other for 2,000 out of the 3,000 miles between New York and Liverpool.

SEPTEMBER 4. — Wallack opened the National Theatre (late the Italian Opera House) this evening, with the comedy of "The Rivals." He has brought with him from England a very strong company, several of whom appeared this evening. I never saw a play go off with more spirit. Wallack, in the dashing part of Captain Absolute, with a handsome scarlet uniform coat, and his one beautiful leg (the other being a little crooked ever since he broke it by being upset in the stage at Brunswick), made a most captivating *entrée*, was received with great applause, and made, at the falling of the curtain, one of the best, most graceful, and eloquent speeches I ever heard on such an occasion. But I fear he will not succeed. The National is the prettiest theatre in the United States; but it is not in Broadway, and the New Yorkers are the strangest people in the world in their predilection for fashionable locations. In Paris the theatres are scattered over the whole city, and the fashionable milliners, jewellers, tailors, and all those who depend for their support upon the gay, the rich, and the fashionable, are to be found in by-streets, or in the mazes of narrow, dark alleys; but our people must have their amusements thrust under their noses, and a shopkeeper, if he hopes to succeed in business, must pay a rent of $4,000 or $5,000 in Broadway, when he might be equally well accommodated for $600 or $800 ten doors from it. But there is a greater obstacle to the success of the new establishment in the great number of theatres at present open in the city, each one of whom has some "bright particular star" shining to attract and dazzle the eyes of the multitude.

It is almost incredible that in these times of distress, when the study of economy is so great an object, there should be nine of these money drains in operation: The Park; the old Drury, of New York, which has done well during the whole of the hard times; the Bowery, with Jim Crow, who is made to repeat nightly, almost *ad infinitum*, his balderdash song, which has now acquired the stamp of London approbation to increase its *éclat;* the Franklin, in Chatham square; Miss Monier's Theatre, in Broadway, opposite St. Paul's, — little and weakly, and likely to die; the Euterpean Hall, Broadway, below Canal street, — short-lived, also, I suspect; the Broadway Theatre, next to Tattersall's, which has been handsomely fitted up, and is to be opened next week; Mrs. Hamblin's Theatre, formerly Richmond Hill, where the Italian opera first placed its unstable foot in New York; the Circus, in Vauxhall Garden, nearly in the rear of my house; and Niblo's Vaudevilles, — the best concern of the whole at present, with a strong company playing little pieces *à la française*. Concerts, and rope-dancing, and other performances of the Ravel family, consisting of eight or ten of the most astonishing performers in their line who have ever appeared in this city. If Wallack can stand all this, he is immortal.

SEPTEMBER 6. — The President's message was sent to Congress on Tuesday. It is a long document, written with ability, but the most mischievous in its tendency that has ever been presented to the American people. It is loco-

President's Message.

foco to the very core. It echoes the opinions on the subject of finance of General Jackson, Colonel Benton, and Blair, of the "Globe;" recommends a separation of the fiscal concerns of the government from all the banks, and the substitution of the Treasury Department, and the issuing of treasury notes as a national currency, by which means all power will be concentrated in the hands of the executive and his myrmidons. It abuses the merchants, coaxes the agriculturists, and tries, as usual, to humbug the people. If the doctrines of this message are approved and supported by the representatives of the people, adieu to the present prosperity and future hopes of America ! If not, Mr. Van Buren's career is closed forever.

There are many gross misrepresentations in this message. The President puts forth his veto in advance on a Bank of the United States, and thereby deprives us of the chance of the only remedy (in my opinion) for the distresses and embarrassments of our merchants. The following paragraph occurs on this subject : " Again, to create a national bank as a fiscal agent would be to disregard the popular will, twice solemnly and unequivocally expressed. On no question of domestic policy is there stronger evidence that the sentiments of a large majority are deliberately fixed, and I cannot concur with those who think they see, in recent events, a proof that these sentiments are, or a reason that they should be, changed." Now this is not true, and the falsehood is advanced with so much boldness only to blind the eyes of the people who do not, one in ten of them, understand the subject. If the opinions of the people are to be taken from those of their representatives, they demand the re-incorporation of the late Bank of the United States ; but if General Jackson, in the plenitude of his withering power, was not only the government (as he styled himself), but the people also, then is Mr. Van Buren's assertion correct, for he defeated the intentions of Congress by vetoing the act ; and that *he* was hostile to the institution, there is, unhappily, the most abundant evidence.

SEPTEMBER 7.— There never was a nation on the face of the earth which equalled this in rapid locomotion. The President's message was brought on to this city, by railroad, steamboats, and horsemen, and carried from hence to Boston, which place it reached in the inconceivably short period of twenty-four hours from Washington, a distance of five hundred miles.

Wonderful Despatch.

Poor Lynch died in Paris, on the 31st of July. He is said in the papers which announce his death to have been fifty years of age; but I think it must be a mistake. I always supposed him to be about my age. How deeply impressive should be the decease of such a man! How many happy hours I have passed in his society! No man has ever contributed so much to the refined enjoyment of the circle in which he moved. He sang and played beautifully, was the ornament of female society, and infused spirit and joviality into the dinner-parties of his male friends, where he was a constant and favoured guest. He was for many years a wine-merchant, and we are indebted to him for some of the finest we have ever had. He introduced the Chateau Margaux, for which famous vintage he contracted for several years, and furnished it finer than we ever had it before or shall have it again. We are indebted to him for the introduction of the Italian opera, and the inimitable Signorina Garcia, and her father and family came to New York under his auspices. He also was the master-spirit who established and conducted the musical *soirées*, a few years since,— the most refined entertainment we have ever had. And now poor Lynch is gone; his friends will utter an exclamation of grief when they hear of it, and his family will put on mourning, but not a glass of wine less will be drunk, nor will one person, except his immediate relations, deprive himself of a single amusement. Like a stone thrown into a lake which agitates the water for an instant, makes a few retiring circles, and leaves no trace upon its peaceful surface; so his death will leave no chasm in the bosom of the society of which he was so great an ornament,

Death of Dominick Lynch.

and will very soon be forgotten in the hurried progress of this world's events. And so it will be with me, and with all of us; and it is better it should be so. This life is too short to be spent in unavailing regrets. Happy would it be for the survivors to reflect upon the insufficiencies of the enjoyments of this life and to prepare "for another and a better world."

I finished my job of removing the Madeira wine to the garret room in the new house, where it is nicely arranged, in an excellent place. The quantity of Madeira and sherry removed is 2,023 quart bottles and 237 gallons.

SEPTEMBER 13. — Another of my friends, one of the most delightful of my associates, died last night at Windust's Hotel, corner of Broadway and Leonard street. William Gaston, of Savannah, is no more. Mr. Gaston was a merchant of Savannah, of the most exalted and honourable stamp, upright in his dealings, agreeable in manner, amiable in disposition, benevolent in feeling, and hospitable in his mode of living. His house was the stranger's home, and Savannah acknowledged him her first citizen. I have passed many happy hours in his company, but none with so much real enjoyment as when I visited him at a cottage which he formerly owned on Long Island, at the Narrows, near Fort Hamilton. Here he was a host indeed, gay, entertaining, and eloquent; his little dinners witnessed "the feast of reason and the flow of soul." In large parties his powers were not always excited in the same degree; and it was necessary to know him intimately in order to know what was in him, and what might be gotten out of him. Like all persons of sanguine temperament and enthusiastic disposition, his spirits were unequal, and this may also have been attributed in him to another cause, peculiarly applicable to him. In early life he was engaged to marry a young lady in New Jersey (Morristown, I believe); he left New York, full of love and anticipations of happiness, to fulfil his engagement, when he found the object of his affection dangerously ill, and soon followed her to the grave instead of the altar. This, to a mind of exquisite refinement and the most acute sensibility, was a shock never to be recovered from, and a loss never to be repaired. He lived and died a bachelor.

SEPTEMBER 19.— Forrest made his first appearance since his return, at the Park Theatre last evening, in the part of Othello. I was there a short time. The house was crammed in every part, and his reception warm and enthusiastic. I think him improving; his acting is more quiet, and in person, deportment, and voice the Senate in its most palmy state never had so magnificent a commander, black or white, nor had ever Desdemona so good an excuse for her misplaced affection.

SEPTEMBER 21.— Congress are making very little progress in the important business for which they were called together; the object seems to be to develop the views of the men who aspire to lead the several parties which hope to rise to political power in the turmoil which attends the disordered state of things. Mr. Rives comes out as a conservative against the administration, hoping to receive the aid of the Whigs (a pretty strong party, thank God!) to hoist him to power; but the Whigs are not to be had for him. Mr. Calhoun, theoretical and visionary as he always is, has hitched upon Van Buren, but will not acknowledge it. He goes South against North, and would support the devil to lessen the political influence of New York. He has sagacity enough to discover that the doctrines and the measures of "New York's favourite son" are most inimical to New York, and is willing to support his suicidal measures to accomplish his object. Webster and Clay, true as steel to the best interests of the country, pursue a straightforward course. The people must come to them, or the country is ruined, and it really looks now as if they were coming to them. Congress will do nothing effectual in the present extra session, but hope is not broken.

Libels. SEPTEMBER 23.— Everybody complains of the success which attends the publication of libels on private character; everybody condemns the depravity of the times in which, and the community by which, they are encouraged; everybody wonders how people can buy and read those receptacles of scandal, the penny papers, and yet everybody does encourage them; and every man who blames his neighbour for setting so bad an example occasionally puts one in his pocket to carry home to his family for their and his own edification. It is only for amusement, it will not corrupt his morals. It is bad enough, to be sure, but the sale of one copy, more or less, will not make any difference in the circulation.

The foregoing remarks are aptly illustrated in the following remarks in an English newspaper, written no doubt by one of the numerous tribe of "preachers, not doers of the word:" "Charles Kemble cudgelled Westmacott, editor of a scurrilous paper, called the 'Age,' for libelling his daughter Fanny in the character of Juliet, shortly previous to their expedition to the United States; the editor, however, consoled himself for these dry blows by the pecuniary profit he derived from the sale of his scandalous chronicle, which was reprobated by everybody, but was to be found stowed under the sofa-cushion in every drawing-room." I wonder who cudgelled Fanny when she libelled the Yankees?

<small>Historical Society.</small> SEPTEMBER 28. — I attended this evening a meeting of the Historical Society, the first held in their new rooms, in the splendid edifice erected by the Stuyvesant Institute, in Broadway, opposite Bond street. Three rooms have been given gratuitously to the society for a term of ten years. The library (which is the most valuable in this country in books and manuscripts relating to the history of the United States, particularly the State of New York) has been well and tastefully arranged, and as it is now to be kept open during several hours of each day, it will no longer be, as heretofore, a sealed book to the members.

<small>Mr. Vandenhoff.</small> OCTOBER 2. — I went this evening to Vandenhoff's benefit, at the National Theatre. The house was crammed, for this gentleman has gotten into the good graces of the New York audience, and my friend Wallack, the proprietor, has found him a good card to play against Forrest at the Park. Mr. Vandenhoff played Hamlet, and young Wilding in

the "Liar." I did not like him in Hamlet. I consider this character the most beautiful creation of the human imagination, and have some notions about the manner of playing it which few actors can ever come up to. Cooper did in his best days; so did Kean, and, if I recollect aright, Conway did not fall much short of it. Vandenhoff's Hamlet wanted sensibility and pathos, that part of it at least which I saw, for I came away in the middle of the second act; but Isaac Hone, whom I left behind, says there was a great improvement as the play proceeded, and that it closed finely. Young Wilding was capital. Mr. Vandenhoff's reading is excellent, and he has, by long practice, acquired a perfect knowledge of the stage.

OCTOBER 5.—I dined with Mr. Wallack, at the Astor House. The dinner was given to Vandenhoff at the close of his engagement at the National Theatre. It was one of the most pleasant affairs of the kind I have ever been engaged in. The dinner was capital. I never saw a table better set out, better provided, or a dinner better cooked. The party was principally theatrical : Wallack, Vandenhoff, Rice, Hackett, Russell, of the New Orleans Theatre, Captain Marryat, Mr. Cramer, Colonel Webb, Dr. Holland, etc. We had an abundance of singing, reciting, story-telling, and imitations. Rice's negro songs and melodies were exceedingly fine. I never heard them before under similar advantages, and was perfectly astonished at Jim Crow's powers in that department. He is one of the most entertaining men I ever met in company. Wallack gave us a beautiful recitation. It was a description of a shipwreck, with many affecting incidents, as related by two different persons, a clergyman and a sailor; they were as different as the pursuits and professions of the two narrators; no two expressions were alike, and yet the same thrilling incidents were described, with the same touching effect.

There was a fine scene between Wallack and Vandenhoff. The former addressed the company as Lord Meadowbanks presiding at the theatrical fund dinner, when he gave the famous toast, "The

Author of Waverley," which brought out Sir Walter, and withdrew the veil from the great "Unknown." Vandenhoff rose as Scott, and made the acknowledgment in the very words he used on that interesting occasion. The imitation was no doubt perfect, for there was a vraisemblance about it which could not be mistaken; it was admirable. I sat until nearly twelve o'clock, and the spirits of the company were then far from being exhausted.

A letter is published in our papers which was addressed, during the panic in London about American affairs, to the governor and directors of the Bank of England, by Lieutenant R. F. Stockton, of the American Navy. This gentleman went out to negotiate a loan for the railroad and canal in New Jersey, in which he is a large proprietor. What authorized him to volunteer as the representative of the American merchants I know not; but he is not one of the timid sort, and does not often find his modesty crossing the path of his undertakings. At any rate, there is a great deal of most excellent sense in his letter, and it is said to have had a salutary effect upon the decisions of the bank, and done more to enlighten the public mind in London than anything which has been " said or sung " on the subject of American affairs. The following paragraph appears to me to contain in few words the essence of all that can be said about the connection between the banks and the people, and places the whole of the specie " humbug " in a proper point of view: " Men of wealth who hoard up gold and silver do not usually borrow. The banks loan to the industrious and working classes, and cannot of course receive gold and silver in return. They loan on personal credit, or on the security of lands and houses. The money so obtained from the banks is paid to the labouring classes, and the moment you destroy credit, and declare that nothing is valuable in a country but gold and silver, the notes come back to the bank for specie which they did not represent, whilst the property which they took in exchange for them, and which they honestly and fairly represented, is made worthless by evil combinations, and will not be received in payment."

Professor McVickar, in his most elaborate lecture on his favourite science of political economy, never elucidated more clearly this knotty subject which is now bothering the brains of all the thinking people in this country, than this lieutenant of the navy in the short passage above quoted, and Albert Gallatin and Isaac Bronson might gather some useful hints on banking and currency from one whose trade has formerly been to go "down to the sea in ships." The "big wigs" of the Bank of England must have been astonished at being schooled in such a quarter; but the writer's maxim, like that of his country and his profession, is "nothing venture, nothing gain."

OCTOBER 16. Contrary to my forebodings, and the *Congressional Proceedings.* fears of many honest men, the famous sub-treasury bill, the device which was intended to place the foot of the government upon the necks of the people, was *laid on the table*, on Friday evening, after a long and animated debate, not to be taken up again during this memorable extra session. Some of the conservatives, the balance-of-power men, held out against the force of party discipline. Congress will adjourn to-day, having done nothing but pass a bill to extend the payment of bonds for duties, for which the merchants who are short of cash will thank them.

In the course of Friday evening's debate Cambreling said something saucy to Hoffman about his changing sides, and alluded to his having served in the navy, where he learned to "tack and veer." This attack brought a reply from Hoffman, in which the "Commercial Representative" was absolutely annihilated. It is said to have been one of the most scorching pieces of eloquence ever heard on that floor. Mr. Adams rose after Hoffman finished, and declared that he had intended to reply to Cambreling, but, tearing up his notes, said there was no use in attacking a dead man. Hoffman has immortalized himself during the present short session, and given earnest of a brilliant "hereafter."

OCTOBER 26. Broadway in the neighbourhood of
Red Brethren. the City Hotel has been crowded for the last two days
by curious spectators, watching to obtain an occasional
glimpse of a large party of Indians, who, after having made a
treaty at Washington, by which their "broad lands" are diminished
in quantity by the trifling amount of a million and a quarter of acres,
are now making a tour of the principal cities, receiving presents,
and being stared at for the benefit of theatres, fairs, and lectures.
There are two tribes, amounting in all to seventy individuals; the
Sauks and Foxes, who constitute the most important part of the
deputation, are at the City Hotel, and the Sioux at the National,
opposite; for these two tribes are not on a friendly footing, and
their white keepers do not think it expedient to get up a real war-
fight for the edification of the spectators.

I went to see the Sauks and Foxes this morning, and finding
Mr. Daniel Jackson there, who is a sort of agent for the tribes, was
introduced to the principal chiefs. The whole party — warriors,
squaws, and pappooses — were seated or lying on the ground, most
of them employed in opening and dividing some pieces of colored
cord, such as is used for hanging pictures, which had been presented to them at the fair of the American Institute, and with
which they appeared much pleased. Keokuk, the chief of the
confederated tribes of Sauks and Foxes, and his favourite squaw
were seated on a small carpet separate from the rest. He is a
fine-looking, elderly man, of intelligent countenance and dignified
deportment. I have heard General Scott speak of him; he thinks
him a great man. In the expedition against the tribes, a few years
since, Keokuk was friendly to the whites and opposed to Black
Hawk, who was then the principal chief. Black Hawk is with the
party at present, but appears to have lost caste. He sits with his
son in one corner of the square, enveloped in a bright scarlet
blanket, silent, surly, and picturesque. The son is a majestic man,
aged about thirty, one of the noblest figures I ever saw, — a perfect
Ajax Telamon.

I shook hands with these Herculeses and Apollos of the woods. They are generally very stout and athletic, with immense lower limbs; but their arms and hands are delicate and small. Keokuk's hand feels like the hand of a woman, while that of young Black Hawk is not so large as mine; and yet in other respects I am much inferior in size and strength to either of them. This characteristic may be accounted for from the circumstance that they perform no manual labor, and the stoutness and great size of their legs and feet are owing to their constant exercise in the chase and other field exercises.

<small>Great Whig Meeting.</small> At seven o'clock this evening a rap upon the table in the large room of Masonic Hall took the hats off the heads of three or four thousand of as fine-looking men as ever constituted the "bone and muscle" of any community. They were the Whigs of New York; and another rap, with a glorious responsive "Aye" from this assemblage, honoured me by placing me in the chair as the presiding officer. The report of the nominating committee was read by Daniel Ullman, prefaced by a very good address.

I put the meeting in a good-humour by addressing them in something like the following words: "Now, fellow-Whigs, I have given you your way in all things. I must have mine in one: I am going to put the final question,— a course which is not usually adopted, — in a form to please myself, Are you ready for the question?"—"Ready! ready! question! question!" was the cheerful reply. "Then, as many of you as are in favour of the ticket, the whole ticket, and nothing but the ticket, and are determined to exert yourselves to the utmost to elect it, will signify it by saying Aye." Such a simultaneous, thundering, whole-hearted Aye was never before heard. "Those of a contrary opinion will say No;" not a voice responded, and the meeting adjourned in good-humour, in high hopes of success, pleased with their cause, their chairman, and themselves.

NOVEMBER 6. — The election commenced this morning. It is the most interesting one we have ever had. Former contests at the polls have been struggles for party supremacy, and, sometimes, for the indulgence of personal predilections; but on this depends the continuance or the ultimate overthrow of a course of measures which have nearly ruined our noble city, and prostrated the energies of its enterprising citizens. It may not be of great importance in its immediate results, for we can hardly hope for such a change as would give the Whigs a majority in the Legislature. The mountain of misrule in the State is too mighty to be overthrown by a single political convulsion; but the ultimate effect of a victory now would be certain, and its influence in other parts of our country, conclusive. The whole United States look to this election as the star to guide them on to victory, and Mr. Van Buren, and his cabinet, and his policy must rise or fall by its result. The Whigs enter the field with high hopes and a steady, fixed determination to do their duty; of the respectable part of the Democratic party, some have come openly over to the Whigs, others stretch their necks over the fence and drop a few votes on our side, and none give their party a full and decided support. The loco-focos, the destructives of the city, have regained possession of Tammany Hall, and the battle is to be between them and the men of character, intelligence, industry, and sobriety. Even Preserved Fish has joined us openly, and Jacob B. Taylor, Daniel Jackson, George Sharpe, and many others of the same stamp attend the Whig meetings. The "Sun of Austerlitz" rose bright and glorious this morning, and I confidently hope will set, on the evening of the third day, upon a bloodless field of battle, won triumphantly by the friends of good order and the supporters of the Constitution.

NOVEMBER 8. — The battle has been fought and won. The election closed this evening at sundown, and the Whigs have succeeded in their whole ticket. New York has broken her chains and stands erect, regenerated. The moral and political effect of this victory will be prodigious. The eyes of the whole United States were turned to us. The measures of the administration stand condemned before the nation, and Mr. Van Buren must alter his course or sink to rise no more. This contest has been conducted on the side of the Whigs from its commencement in a determined spirit, and with high hopes. Our men worked hard, but quietly, moderately; there was no bullying, no boasting, and it is greatly to the credit of the city that, notwithstanding the unusual excitement in both parties, and the enormous number of votes polled, — 36,500, — there was no commotion, no riots, and no call for the interference of the police.

NOVEMBER 16. — I received a warm letter of congratulation from Mr. Webster, in reply to one I wrote him the morning after our election, and a paper containing the result of the Massachusetts elections, which commenced on Monday. The victory there is overwhelming. Every one of the thirteen senatorial districts will return Whigs. Governor Everett's majority will be ten times greater than last year.

NOVEMBER 17. — The terrible abolition question is fated, I fear, to destroy the union of the States, and to endanger the peace and happiness of our western world. Both parties are getting more and more confirmed in their obstinacy, and more intolerant in their prejudices. A recent disgraceful affair has occurred in the town of Alton, State of Illinois, which is calculated to excite the most painful feelings in all those who respect the laws and desire the continuance of national peace and union. Alton is situated on the left bank of the Mississippi, and opposite the slave-holding State of Missouri. An abolition paper was established there, called the "Alton Observer," which, becoming obnoxious to the slave-holders, was assailed and the establishment destroyed, some time since, by an ungovernable mob; an attempt was recently made to reëstablish the paper, which caused another most disgraceful outrage, in which two persons were killed and several wounded.

NOVEMBER 22. — Such a day of continued excitement I have never experienced; for nearly twelve hours every faculty of body and mind has been on the utmost stretch.

Great Whig Jubilee.

The out-door celebration (except the firing of the cannon) was prevented by a villanous fog, which hung like a dark mantle over us at sunrise. Until noon there were occasional symptoms of better weather, but before sunset it turned into rain, and the fireworks were "no go." But the in-door operations were all carried out to the letter, and so brilliant and exciting a scene was never witnessed. At eleven o'clock I went to Masonic Hall to unite in the reception of the delegates from other States and cities, who presented themselves to the number of seven hundred and received their tickets for the dinner. At one o'clock the Mayor took the chair and addressed the delegates in an excellent speech; they were then called upon by States, and a member selected from each State addressed the meeting. It was perfectly astonishing that in this number of speakers, thus called together, and most of them entirely unprepared, there were no failures. All spoke well, — some of them with surpassing eloquence. I have never witnessed such a display of warm, glowing, impassioned oratory as some exhibited, nor so much pure, refined, convincing eloquence as fell from others. Colonel Winthrop's speech was one of the finest I ever heard,— it would have done credit to Webster or Clay; but all were excellent, and Granger's closing speech fixed the attention of an assemblage, who had remained during five hours in their several places, and most of them standing, wedged together the whole time. At five o'clock we all adjourned to Niblo's to partake of the dinner.

Seven hundred plates were set, and the floor and avenues of the saloon were crowded with persons who could not get seats. There were many speeches and volunteer toasts, but I left my seat soon after the regular toasts were done. Ten or a dozen of us, including some of the Baltimoreans, had a little supper at Niblo's; but I left them soon, and came home nearly exhausted by the labours of the day, and intoxicated, not by strong drink, but by a strong and unintermitted excitement.

This celebration will have an extensive and most salutary influence. Never before has there been such an assemblage of Whigs. A bond of union and good-fellowship has been formed which will extend far and wide, and the delegates will go home delighted with their reception, filled with confident hopes of a return of a national prosperity, and with a determination to restore the government of the Constitution and the laws.

Henry Clay. The indications of public feeling during the day, which I have watched carefully, have been in my opinion decidedly in favour of Mr. Clay as the Whig candidate for President. Whenever allusions were made to Mr. Webster and him they were received with cheers and applause; but those for Clay were more animated than the others. The delegates seemed to say that either of those patriots was good enough for them, but that "Harry of the West" would be the most available candidate. The question should not be agitated now; our duty is to get Van Buren out, and then — .

NOVEMBER 23. — I dined with Mr. Gardiner G. Howland, where I met Messrs. Meredith, Kennedy, Morris, and Dr. Alexander of Baltimore, Mr. Granger, and other gentlemen. I have frolicked too much this week, and require quiet and temperance, which I fear I shall not get.

NOVEMBER 25. — I had a pleasant dinner-party. It was intended for some of my Baltimore friends who attended the jubilee of Wednesday; but Mr. Swift, the Mayor of Philadelphia, forestalled me and took them *in transitu;* all but Meredith and Kennedy, who, like good fellows, stayed to dine with me. Our party consisted of Jonathan Meredith, John P. Kennedy, the Mayor, President Duer, Francis Granger, Mr. Graves, M.C., from Kentucky, James Watson Webb, Charles King, Abraham Ogden, and I. S. Hone.

NOVEMBER 28.—A convention of delegates from Boston, Philadelphia, Baltimore, and New York convened yesterday at the Mayor's office, City Hall. The object of this convention is to deliberate on a resumption of specie payment, at some time to be agreed upon. There is great difference of opinion on this momentous question. I think they can't do it.

Bank Convention.

NOVEMBER 29. — The great dinner is over, and I have a prospect of a day or two's peace and quietness. The dinner was given at the Astor House; about two hundred and twenty, including the guests, sat down at half-past seven o'clock, and stayed all night! We had speeches upon speeches, some very good, but most of them too long. The principal speakers were John Bell of Tennessee, Graves of Kentucky, Mr. Southard and Governor Pennington of New Jersey, Kennedy of Baltimore, Sturges of Boston, Granger, etc. Ogden Hoffman presided, with eight vice-presidents, of which I was the first. The toasts, which were intended to call out the distinguished guests, were severally given by the president and the vice-presidents. Mr. Bell spoke an hour and a half; Mr. Southard made an excellent speech, a little too much about himself; but the great gun of the evening, that which constituted the chief attraction, and kept the company together to an hour unprecedented in the annals of New York jollifications, was *Daniel Webster.* He rose at two o'clock in the morning, intending, in consequence of its being, as he said, *to-morrow,* to be very brief; but his auditors insisted upon his going on; they would not allow him to stop, and he, apparently "nothing loath," kept on in a strain of unwearied and unwearying eloquence until *four o'clock.* One hundred and fifty persons, most of them men of sober, steady habits, fathers of families, remained immovable in their seats, with no indications of fatigue or inattention until he finished at an hour when " night was almost at odds with morning." There is scarcely another individual in the United States who could thus have fixed their attention at such an unreasonable hour. I looked around frequently, and I verily believe not a person left the room while he

The Bell Dinner.

was speaking. What a wonderful gift is this public speaking, and what gourmands we Americans are when we get hold of a dish of popular oratory!

Mr. Webster was clear and distinct in his manly and patriotic surrender of personal claims upon the people, and a determination to abide in all things by the decision of a majority of the Whig party. This part of his speech did him great credit, and was received with much enthusiastic applause. When he closed, at four o'clock, I left the company reseating themselves, ready for more toasts and more speeches, and I doubt if they broke up before breakfast-time. I was glad to get away, fatigued and worn out, but too much excited to sleep.

NOVEMBER 30. — Day of general thanksgiving and prayer, recommended by the State and city authorities. There are many causes of thanksgiving, some of which our present rulers would not be willing to acknowledge as such.

DECEMBER 5. — A Mr. Price, sub-editor (as I am informed) of a scurrilous paper published in this city, called the "Herald," has addressed me a letter as chairman of the committee of arrangements for the Bell dinner, to know whether Charles King was authorized to forbid him to take notes of the speeches at the dinner, on which subject a correspondence has taken place between him and Mr. King. The gentleman is *bien enragé*. He says he bought his ticket like other people, and had a right like other people to take notes or anything else he pleased. King, who, I presume, thought he had no right to take anything but his dinner, would not allow him to proceed, and, being of the Hotspur breed, very probably showed him the door, and the man lost his ten dollars and his dinner in the bargain. For this he called King to account, and, his explanation not being altogether satisfactory, I was appealed to by the aggrieved party. In my reply I state that "the practice of reporting in the public prints the doings and the sayings of our convivial meetings without the consent, and frequently to the annoyance, of the parties who are thus unwillingly brought before the public, a practice so entirely repugnant to the feelings of our citizens, is happily confined as yet to so inconsiderable a portion of the press that it did not, I presume, occur to the committee to take any measures in advance to prevent it; but that I was of the opinion that Mr. King was authorized, by the expressed sentiments of the gentlemen forming the committee, to oppose the introduction of reporters for that object." This brought a rejoinder, and then the matter ended between Mr. Price and me; but the "Herald" will make two or three columns of the affair to dish up to his customers who like high-seasoned dishes.

DECEMBER 6. — Congress met on Monday; the President's message was sent on Tuesday. This document does little credit to Mr. Van Buren, and I trust that it seals his political condemnation. All the abominable doctrines of his September message are reiterated. He recommends the sub-treasury system, with its hosts of government locusts to eat up the people's substance, or if that will not go, then something else; but the merchants must be deprived of the use of any part of the money which their enterprise and intelligence have been the means of furnishing to the support of the government. No matter what becomes of it, so that they do not get it. Was ever a commercial people cursed with such rulers? Better would it be for poor New York if a volcano were to break out in the midst of her than that this suicidal policy should be adopted!

President's Message.

In relation to the late elections the President has his usual cant about the will of the people. He pretends that the late changes are no expression of their will. It was owing to bank influence, and the people will go round to him again, and then they will be right. Faugh! With his usual sycophancy and want of independence, he refers to "his predecessor" eight times in the course of this message.

DECEMBER 20. — We had a pleasant dinner-party, consisting of Samuel S. Howland, George Dorr, James W. Otis, J. G. Pearson, Robert Ray, John C. Delprat, P. G. Stuyvesant, Charles A. Heckscher, Peter Schermerhorn, Samuel Welles of Paris, and William H. Aspinwall.

1838.

JANUARY 1. — I verily believe there never was so pleasant a New Year's Day. The sun rose this morning through a delicious haze, which looked like impalpable gold-dust, and from which it emerged gloriously. During the day the air was soft and balmy, and the temperature warm as June. Visiting commenced earlier than usual, and was kept up with great spirit until near night. Broadway was thronged with male pedestrians, and at the open door of every fashionable house a grinning domestic was seen ushering in the visitors to the well-furnished saloon in which fair inmates were ready to receive with smiles their homage and good wishes. I began my cruise at noon, in the neighbourhood of the Bowling Green, working my way up, and intending to visit my uptown friends last. But when I arrived at St. Thomas's Church, it was five o'clock, and I was compelled to make my visit to Dr. Hawks (the most excellent pastor of that church) my last for the day; but I made some visits in the evening, and came home fatigued with my pleasant exercise.

Last evening we were all assembled in the dining-room, — myself, my wife, my six children, and son-in-law, — a goodly family party, gay, cheerful, and happy, until eighteen hundred and thirty-seven, with hobbling gait, took his ugly face away, and, turning his ill-omened back upon us, made way for his smiling, youthful successor. God grant he may not "follow in the footsteps of his illustrious predecessor," except as regards the weather, in which particular we certainly have no reason to complain of the defunct! for never, surely, was a year of such fine weather known among men. We have not had equal to a month of unpleasant weather during the year, — a lovely spring, a cool summer, and the autumn and winter, thus far, delicious as the climate of the plains of Normandy. But in other matters it has been a disastrous year. The acts of government have thrown the affairs of the country into utter confusion. The enterprise of the citizens, which, it must be confessed, led them sometimes too far, was suddenly checked and paralyzed by a sudden breaking up of all the elements which gave life to the social compact, and excited the honest industry and enlightened enterprise of our people. During this year we have lived upon each other; no wholesome business has been carried on; the sources to which we have looked for the payment of honest debts have generally failed; real estate, which in good times is the best and surest foundation of credit, has lost its value, and those who have money will neither invest in it nor lend on it. Confidence is shaken to its very centre, and the springs of national and commercial prosperity are dried up. Amidst all this scene of national and individual calamity, one redeeming ray of sunshine has burst forth, — the people have risen in their might and reproved the ruinous schemes of their rulers; the popular elections have gone generally against the administration, and nowhere has the voice of reproof been more loudly uttered than in our own State. If we hold on in the good cause the same voice will call abler and better men to the councils of the nation, and better days may dawn, and the Republic yet be safe.

During the past year I have removed to my new house, corner of Broadway and Great Jones street, which proves a most delightful and comfortable residence. I would not, if I could, have it altered in a single particular. God grant that in my prayers for better times I may be sufficiently thankful for the blessings which I yet enjoy!

JANUARY 5. — The ship "Pennsylvania" sailed from Sandy Hook at noon, on the 8th of November, and arrived in the Mersey on the evening of the 23d. I think this is the shortest passage as yet; but it is impossible to say what may happen in this "go-ahead" age. A letter which I received by the "George Washington," dated in London 15th of November, from William H.

Stephenson (he who was here on a visit last summer, and to whom we all took a liking), states that the new steamer intended for this port was to sail in about a fortnight. If she succeeds, this fifteen-day passage of the "Pennsylvania" may hereafter be considered quite a dilatory proceeding.

JANUARY 6. — The weather continues beautiful beyond all former experience, — warm as June. If we do not have a change soon, we shall want ice to cool our champagne next summer. The North river is open to Hudson. If the weather continues, the navigation will be unobstructed to Albany, — an event which I think has never occurred in the month of January during my lifetime.

JANUARY 22. — I received to-day from Mr. Webster a copy of the bill of abominations, now before the Senate, and have read it attentively. It is worse, even, than I supposed, from having given it a cursory perusal as it was published. It should be called General Jackson's rod bequeathed to his successor, wherewith to scourge the refractory merchants, and Mr. Van Buren's vial of wrath, to be poured upon his devoted city of New York more especially, as punishment for political backslidings. Its leading feature seems to be the total preclusion of the merchants, whose enterprise supports the government, from any participation in the use of money collected through their means on any security whatever. It directs it to be locked up in gold and silver in the Custom-House and post-offices in all parts of the country, and creates a host of political locusts worse than those who of old overran the land of Egypt, devoted soul, body, and conscience to their masters, to have the custody of the people's money, and to beg, borrow, or steal it, no matter how, so as the benefit to accrue from it shall be confined to the faithful. I do venture to assert that there never has been an instance, in the history of civilized man, of so much power being vested in the hands of an executive magistrate, call him as you may, — king, emperor, dictator, autocrat, or Tartarian khan, — by a legislative enactment, as this bill gives to the Republican President of a people who do

Sub-Treasury Bill.

actually dream sometimes that they are free. The amiable gentlemen above enumerated have occasionally indulged in strange freaks at the expense of their loyal subjects; they squeeze them tolerably hard, and if they prove refractory cut off their heads; but they have not the assurance to pretend that they have law for what they do. The suffering people have the consolation to know that they had no hand in forging their chains, but here representatives of the people (as they falsely style themselves) are about to twist the lash, to sharpen the sword, and hand them to their rulers, praying them to use them for the good of their constituents; and use them they will, if this ill-omened bill passes the Senate. A majority of that body are the merest tools of party, and will vote for it; but there is some reason to hope that honest men enough will be found in the House of Representatives to stay the cause.

This gold and silver currency is the prettiest sceptre with which to rule a people who do not give themselves the trouble to think much about public affairs, that a tyrant could desire. Mr. Van Buren is not exactly a tyrant yet; but wait, my masters, until this bill passes. The late Dey of Algiers thought so, and he was *the government*. The French found something in his cellars besides potatoes and cabbages; the cellars provided in this bill are more numerous than those which belonged to his turbaned highness, but the treasures they contain will be equally under the control of the *government*, and, although not intended to be applied to the purchase of chibouques and slippers for the personal use of our *revered chief*, or laid out in gewgaws for the ladies of the harem, they will be the means of corrupting the minds of the people, blinding their eyes to the faults of their rulers, and transforming a nation of freemen into a herd of time-serving and man-worshipping sycophants unworthy the name of Americans.

Kent Club. JANUARY 27.—I was favoured by an invitation to meet the Kent Club this evening at the house of Mr. William Kent. There were about twenty gentlemen, among whom were Judges Jones, Edwards, and Tallmadge, Chancellor Kent, President Duer, several eminent lawyers, and a few laymen, consisting of Charles King, Webb, and myself. There was also Mr. Mackintosh, son of the celebrated Sir James Mackintosh, and the author of his well-written biography, a gentleman who came to this country on a visit during the last autumn. We had a handsome supper, with oceans of champagne. I was right in calling it "high jinks," for a more jovial, noisy, roystering set I never met with. They seemed to contemn all law but that of passing the bottle, and the counsel on both sides summed up together without regarding the admonitions of the court.

FEBRUARY 14. — When Mr. Webster was in New York he dined on the 14th of December at the Astor House with a party of good Whigs. On this occasion he invited the party to dine with him in Washington on Washington's birthday, since which, on renewing the invitation to each of us, he has altered the day to the 21st inst., in consequence of a ball which is to be given on the 22d in honour of the anniversary, and here I am this evening in Philadelphia, on my way to fulfil the engagement.

I left New York at half-past six this morning. It was very cold, but the admirable railroad, go-ahead mode of travelling brought us to Philadelphia by one o'clock, and I got into good quarters at Head's. Mrs. Davis came on to surprise her husband, who has been here two or three days. I called upon Mr. Biddle at the bank, and had a nice little talk about matters and things.

The Biddle Plate.

I was shown this afternoon, at the shop of Messrs. Fletcher & Co., in Chestnut street, the most superb service of plate I ever saw, to be presented by the directors of the old Bank of the United States to Mr. Nicholas Biddle. It is to cost $15,000. The inscription recites all his valuable services to the institution and to the country at large, and among other things his having "created the best currency *in the world.*" He deserves all they can do for him, but the world is a big place. Fletcher & Co. are the artists who made the Clinton vases. Nobody in this "world" of ours hereabouts can compete with them in this kind of work.

The Banking House. The portico of this glorious edifice, a sight of which always repays me for coming to Philadelphia, appeared more beautiful to me this evening than usual, from the effect of the gas-light; each of the massive fluted columns had a jet of light from the inner side so placed as not to be seen from the street, but casting a strong light upon the front of the building, the softness of which, with its flickering from the wind, produced an effect strikingly beautiful. How strange it is that in all the inventions of modern times architecture alone seems to admit of no improvement! — every departure from the classical models of antiquity in this science is a departure from grace and beauty.

BALTIMORE, FEB. 15. — I was within half a minute of losing my chance this morning in the railroad cars. The omnibuses leave Market street at eight, and had started just as I got there; but I saved my distance. They go to Grey's Ferry on the Schuylkill, from where the cars start on the new Philadelphia and Baltimore Railroad, which has been in operation about a week, and go by Wilmington and Elkton, — nearly the old mail-stage route. We got here at three o'clock, an hour later than usual, in consequence of the ice and snow on the tracks. But what a contrast is this to the old winter travelling between the two cities, over a detestable road and a dangerous ferry, and two days and a night consumed on the journey. The Susquehanna at Havre-de-Grace is crossed in a steamboat superior to anything yet produced in America. The passengers descend by a stairway into this floating palace, where everything comfortable is provided. The cars are then brought on a platform overhead level with the road. The immense machine then starts, breaking the ice, whatever may be its thickness; the passengers then ascend on this side by another substantial staircase, resume their seats in the cars, and find themselves again in rapid motion on *terra firma*, having, as it were by enchantment, crossed this ferry, which was formerly one of the greatest bugbears to travelling in the United States in the winter season. It snowed when we started this morning, and has been the most unpleasant day I have experienced during the present winter. But the cars, which held about seventy persons each, are provided with stoves, which made them (as Polly Stymets said) a *little too comfortable*. The fare on this capital road is only four dollars.

WASHINGTON, FEB. 19. — Called this morning, by appointment, upon Mr. Webster, who accompanied me to the Senate at eleven o'clock, and obtained for me a place on the floor, — an exceedingly difficult thing under the present orders. The galleries were all filled two hours before the time of the Senate's meeting. I was indebted for my good place to some hocus-pocus between Mr. Webster and the sergeant-at-arms.

Mr. Clay's Speech.
Mr. Clay rose to the order of the day (Mr. Wright's bill, commonly called the sub-treasury bill) at one o'clock, and spoke until half-past five. It was a great speech, as all his speeches are; but I thought it too long. It would have borne a curtailment of an hour advantageously. Mr. Clay's physical force was not so great as usual, and I thought he laboured under the effects of indisposition; but the close of his argument was the best part. He belaboured the last and present administrations, quoting from Mr. Van Buren's reply to the nomination of the Baltimore Convention, in which he speaks of himself as "the honoured *instrument* to carry out the measures of his illustrious predecessor." Mr. Clay said that the meaning of the word *instrument* given by Webster's Dictionary is "*tool*," and continued to speak accordingly of the *honoured tool* of General Jackson.

In the course of the speech Mr. Clay bore somewhat hard upon Mr. Calhoun for his recent apostasy, and replied to his arguments in favour of the bill, to which the latter replied in a few exceedingly harsh and ill-natured remarks. He charged Mr. Clay with having " misrepresented all his arguments," and threatened " in his own good time to settle accounts with him," to which Mr. Clay rejoined that he was " ready to settle with the gentleman from

South Carolina in any way, and at any time," he chose. Mr. Calhoun, like all men whose position is doubtful in their own minds, is, no doubt, very sensitive. I thought there was a degree of acrimony and ill-nature in his reply much greater than the occasion justified. When I shook hands with this gentleman this morning I felt grieved that so brilliant a mind and so gallant a spirit had been cast away by the influence of prejudice and paltry interested motives.

FEBRUARY 20. — I called upon the President this morning, who received me with his usual urbanity. He inquired about my family and other persons of his acquaintance, talked about the weather, his habits and mode of living, but asked no questions about the state of things in New York, and, of course, did not touch upon politics.

FEBRUARY 21. — The long-expected day arrived at last. Mr. Webster's great dinner to the New Yorkers took place to-day at five o'clock. We went in a body to his house, and were met by an equal number of the most distinguished Whigs in the United States, and some of the greatest and best men which our country can boast of. The dinner consisted, as near as I can recollect, of the following party, — I shall endeavour to put them all down here, for this was an affair long to be remembered: The New York party, fourteen in number; Mr. Webster, Governor Davis, Governor Lincoln, of Massachusetts; Mr. Robbins, Mr. Tillinghast, of Rhode Island; Messrs. Tallmadge, Sibley, Hoffman, Curtis, of New York; Meredith, Wise, of Virginia; Bell and Graves, of Tennessee; Crittenden, of Kentucky; Bayard, of Delaware; Colt and Dr. Alexander, of Baltimore.

The Webster Dinner.

Toasts were given and speeches made by almost everybody. Mr. Wise was eloquent and entertaining; Mr. Webster very fine. Old Mr. Robbins delivered a beautiful eulogium upon Washington, in a soft and tremulous voice, and in language classical and pure. It was a glorious affair. When I arose at the table (at which I had the seat of distinction) I was awe-stricken, and for a moment embarrassed, but recovered instantly. I felt as if in an assembly of the gods. These were men who *can* and *will* save the country. I told them so, and they responded, Amen !

The next thing in order was the dinner which the New York party gave to the Whig delegation from our State. One senator (Mr. Tallmadge, a conservative, with us now heart and soul) and ten of the lower House, besides whom we had Messrs. Clay, Webster, Crittenden, Wise, Graves, Waddy Thompson, etc.,— in number about forty. I presided, and they all say it was the greatest thing I ever did. But how could it be otherwise? I had Clay on my right and Webster on my left. I felt inspired myself, and infused inspiration into all around me. Alluding to my relative position, I made them all pledge themselves to make one of us three President of the United States. How we apples swim ! At ten o'clock we broke up, and most of the party went to the ball in honour of Washington's birthday, which was a brilliant affair. The President was there, and the Vice-President, heads of departments, foreign ministers, etc.

Mr. Pontois, the French Minister, has been exceedingly civil to me. He wants to give me a dinner, and appears greatly disappointed that I cannot accept it. Colonel and Mrs. Howard have pressed me very hard, as have everybody here ; but we go to Baltimore on Saturday, where further honours await us. I am almost tempted to return with Charles King and some others of the conspirators, but cannot ; and perhaps it is better to break off in the midst of my enjoyment. I received this evening a letter from the Baltimore committee, informing me that an extra train of cars has been provided, to start from here on Saturday at noon. This is a comfortable and kind arrangement, as we should otherwise have been compelled to start at six in the morning, and very convenient for men who sit every night " carousing until the second cock."

BALTIMORE, FEBRUARY 24.— A dreadful affair had happened at Washington to-day, which only came to my knowledge a few minutes before I left Washington this morning. Mr. Webb, the editor of the "Courier and Enquirer," was attacked with great violence in the House of Representatives by Mr. Cilley, of Maine, who took part in the debate on the subject of the charge made by Mrs. Davis (author of the "Spy in Washington") against Mr. Ruggles, of the Senate, of corrupt and dishonest conduct in relation to a patent. Mr. Cilley, in debate, asserted that Davis was employed by Webb, a scoundrel editor, who had been bribed by the president of the Bank of the United States, etc. Webb was of our party to Washington, and soon after his arrival took measures, it appears, to obtain satisfaction. He applied to Mr. Curtis and Mr. Draper to bear his challenge, both of whom very properly refused. He then called upon Mr. Graves, of Kentucky, a very fine fellow, who has been with us almost constantly, and he unfortunately consented. He called upon Mr. Cilley, who refused to accept the challenge, on the ground that Webb was not a gentleman, and, moreover, that he was not bound to account for words spoken in debate; upon which Mr. Graves, according to the ridiculous code of honour which governs those gentlemen, insisted upon his fighting him, and after some negotiation it was agreed that they should fight this day. The first suspicion I had of what was going on arose from my meeting Webb in the passage at Gadsby's, about eleven o'clock, when I told him I was going to take leave of Mr. Clay, who lives in the same house with Mr. Graves; on which he said that Mr. Clay, not knowing of the extra train of cars at noon, had gone to Baltimore early in the morning. I went, however, to their lodgings, inquired for Mr. Graves, and was told by a servant that he had gone to Baltimore; but on inquiry found that Mr. Clay was at home, and went to his room, where I saw and took leave of him. This circumstance, together with the mysterious appearance of things at our lodgings, caused me to make inquiry, and I found that Graves and Cilley had gone out to fight with rifles at eighty yards' distance, the former with Mr. Wise and the latter with General Jones, of Wisconsin, as seconds; both adepts in this damnable practice, who would carry things to the utmost extremity, and who are said to have gone armed for the purpose of shooting any person who might come upon the ground to prevent this most unnatural combat.

The friends of Graves, who is a gallant and amiable gentleman, who has his wife here and his children at home, are doing everything to prevent the meeting and bring about a reconciliation; and Webb is much distressed at being the cause of his engaging in this quarrel, which he had nothing to do with, and much reason, I think, he has. This unhappy affair has caused a gloom among our friends, and prevented the members of Congress from coming on to the public dinner prepared for us in Baltimore. We came, however (all but Webb), in the extra car, soon after twelve o'clock, and arrived here at three. The party consisted of King, Blatchford, Giraud, Ward, Blunt, Hoxie, Patterson, Draper, Ketcham, and myself. The car on our arrival was surrounded by the populace, who expected to see Webster and Clay, and were greatly disappointed when they found none but us unimportant New Yorkers, although we were the honoured guests and they, with the other members, the adjuncts of the party. On our arrival we were waited upon by the committee, who escorted us to the Eutaw House to the great dinner.

It was gotten up in a most splendid style, and we were received by two hundred of the most respectable citizens of Baltimore, with honour and distinction never to be forgotten. Dr. Alexander presided, with a large number of vice-presidents. I, as chairman of the New York party, was seated on the right of the president, and Colonel Swift, Mayor of Philadelphia, on his left. It was, of course, my duty to reply to the third toast, which was a compliment to New York. I was alarmed beforehand for fear I should not do well, for I had no time for preparation, and my mind was engrossed with the duel at Washington; but the occasion seemed to inspire me. I spoke three-quarters of an hour, and all my friends agree that it was an excellent speech. I feel myself that it was the best effort I ever made. Speeches were made in the course of the evening by King, Gerard, and Patterson, of our party; by Colonel Swift, Colonel Finlay, Reverdy Johnson, John P. Kennedy, Judge Hanson, Mr. Poe, Mr. Barney, Mr. Ewing, member of Congress from Indiana. We had a most beautiful speech by a young lawyer named Wallace, who, if he redeem the promise given on this occasion, will be a distinguished man. We broke up at twelve o'clock precisely, the arrival of the Sabbath preventing us from sitting longer; and thus ended the most agreeable public dinner I ever witnessed, and the highest compliment I ever received.

FEBRUARY 25. — I heard early this morning of the fatal termination of this savage *rencontre*. Mr. Cilley was killed on the third fire. It was reported that Webb and Mr. Duncan, of Ohio, were to fight to-day; but it is contradicted by a letter which I received this evening from Charles King, of which the following is an extract: "The fatal issue of the duel of yesterday has caused a deep sensation. There will not be, however, in my opinion, any more fighting. Webb is truly and deeply distressed. He will remain here till Tuesday, rather so as not to appear to avoid any consequences, than because there are any consequences to be apprehended. Graves is, of course, sobered and saddened, though with the consciousness that he had done all that he could have done to avoid fighting. They fought about five o'clock, on the Annapolis road, and fired three times; the third shot from Graves passed into the cavity of Mr. Cilley's stomach. He placed his hand on the wound, made a convulsive movement to his second, fell, and died without uttering a word. It is singular that Cilley, who, in practising the day before, had shot eleven balls in succession into a space not bigger than your hand, did not hit Graves at all. So confident were Mr. Cilley's political friends that Graves would be killed, that in the House, during the day, there was, it is said, manifest exultation at the idea. Some washerwoman or servant told Mrs. Crittenden, in the hearing of Mrs. Graves, that Mr. Graves had gone out to fight, and she had to pass five mortal hours in all the agony of suspense. Mr. Clay, whom I saw in his bed this morning, told me he had had an interview with her, so fearful that it had absolutely kept him awake all night, and made him so sick and nervous this morning, from the mere recollection of it, that he cannot get up. The event of Mr. Cilley's death will be announced to-morrow. The funeral will then take place, and of course both Houses will adjourn. It is not impossible that after the death is announced some discussion may arise upon the manner of the death, and some attempt be made to censure the practice generally, and perhaps in this particular case even."

<small>Duel in Washington.</small> MARCH 6. — A committee of the House of Representatives has been appointed to investigate the circumstances attending the late duel between Messrs. Graves and Cilley, with power to send for persons and papers. In the Senate, Mr. Prentiss, of Vermont, has introduced a bill to prevent duelling in the District of Columbia, making it death for the survivor, and imposing ten years' imprisonment upon all persons concerned in sending a challenge.

MARCH 10. — The papers are filled with this painful subject. Some of the vile supporters of the administration attempt to give it a political bearing. These men, who have always supported Jackson and made him the standard of their religion, morals, and politics, are now loud in their condemnation of the practice of duelling, although the wooden god of their idolatry was known as one of the most notorious duellists in the United States, and even had a *rencontre* of the most savage and sanguinary character with another of their oracles, Mr. Benton, of the Senate. The Supreme Court of the United States, consistently with the dignity of its high station, put the seal of condemnation upon the practice of duelling, by refusing to attend officially the funeral of Mr. Cilley, and declaring the determination of the court not to unite hereafter in the funeral obsequies of any person who shall have fallen in a duel.

MARCH 15. — The speeches on this all-engrossing
Sub-Treasury Bill. subject in the Senate still go on. Mr. Calhoun has
replied to Mr. Clay, and Mr. Clay has come in with
a rejoinder. Mr. Bayard has spoken with his usual grace and
urbanity against the bill, and Benton, with his "*front de bœuf,*" has
roared in its favour; and that admirable old man, Asher Robbins, of
Rhode Island, who charmed us at Mr. Webster's dinner with his
eulogy on Washington, has added his testimony against the bill to
that of his illustrious coadjutors, in a short speech, pure, eloquent,
and classical as usual. The giant of Massachusetts, the defender
of the Constitution, came to the rescue on Monday last, on which
day he spoke five hours, and finished on Tuesday in a continuation
of four hours. It is said on all hands to have been the greatest
speech he ever made, greater even than his reply to General
Hayne, on Foote's resolutions.

The Hon. Paine Wingate, of Stratham, New Hamp-
Last of the Cocked Hats. shire, died last week, at the age of ninety-nine years.

He wasa graduate of Harvard College, and for several
years (since the death of Dr. Holyoke) the oldest graduate of that
institution, a judge of the Supreme Court of New Hampshire from
1798 until 1809. He was emphatically a gentleman of the old
school; the confidant and adviser of Washington while President.
His gait was erect and his deportment graceful. He wore a cocked
hat, breeches and top-boots, and cambric ruffles at his breast and
wrists. His lady survives him at the age of ninety-five. She is
the sister of the late Thomas Pickering.

MARCH 16. — Died last evening, John Treat Irving,
Death of Judge Irving. in the sixtieth year of his age, — one of my oldest
acquaintances; we were playmates forty-five years ago;
afterward associated in the literary institutions, to which I now look
back as the sources from which in my youthful days I derived great
enjoyment, and prospective advantages during my future life. We
have ever since been good friends, and the most cordial feelings
have subsisted between us. Of different professions, and disagree-

ing in politics at our start in life, the intimacy which commenced so happily did not continue so close as in our early years, but our personal friendship and mutual regard was never impaired; and I now mourn for his loss, as almost the last of the associates of my early years.

MARCH 24. — The Committee of Ways and Means of the House of Assembly have made a report on the finances and internal improvements of the State, said to be the production of their chairman, Mr. Samuel B. Ruggles, member from this city, — one of the ablest financial and statistical State papers which has ever been produced in this country. It presents the most glowing picture of the present resources and future prospects of the State, the result, not of sanguine and exaggerating fancy, but of plain facts and accurate calculations. It shows the most perfect ability to carry into effect all the splendid plans of internal improvement which have been projected or advised by the liberal-minded politicians of the State, and refutes most conclusively the arguments of Silas Wright, when he was comptroller, and his political hangers-on, that the works then in progress could not be completed without recourse to direct taxation. On the contrary, all the facts and arguments of the masterly report tend to support the opinion expressed in the concluding resolution: " That it is not necessary or expedient to levy a direct tax." This report appears to be the result of deep study and elaborate investigation. It is extremely well written, remarkable for close reasoning, and a style, clear, simple, and occasionally eloquent. It has no hard words, no popular clap-traps, no metaphysical humbug, but is better to read and easier to understand, by all sorts of people who can read or understand anything, than any paper on the same or a similar subject, extending to the length of eight close columns of a newspaper, that I have ever read.

When Mr. Wright, then comptroller, in order to convince the people of the State that they were going too far in the works of internal improvement, and would have to resort to taxation, told them that the revenue of the canals at that time, 1817, which amounted to $150,000, was the true basis of a prospective calculation for the ensuing ten years, and when Mr. Ruggles now shows them that this revenue amounted during those ten years to more than ten millions, they will begin to doubt, one would think, the infallibility of their wooden oracle. And when they remember how obstinately the wise plans and enlightened predictions of DeWitt Clinton, Gouverneur Morris, and Jonas Platt were opposed, ridiculed, and thwarted by this same Mr. Wright and the men who now swear by him, until they could no longer hope to deceive the people, but were compelled to come into those great plans which contributed so largely to the glory and prosperity of the State, and then ungratefully sought to deprive those men of the merit of originating the plans, — when all these things, I say, are seen and reflected upon, it would seem impossible that the people should not turn from their false prophets, no longer rely upon those who have so often deceived them, nor fail to discover that Samuel B. Ruggles is more worthy of credit than Silas Wright.

MARCH 26. — This hard-fought and long-debated *Sub-Treasury Bill.* bill passed the Senate late on Saturday night. Every senator was present; but before the finishing stroke was put upon it, it was divested of its most exceptionable features. It was no longer the monster which Silas Wright introduced, insomuch that Mr. Calhoun, who has so deeply compromised his fair fame in its support, was constrained to vote against it on the final vote. It was not bad enough for him. Its effects would not be so sudden nor so certain as he wished, to break down the North and East. It can be considered in no other light than a triumph for the talents and patriotism of the glorious band of Whig senators. The first cut of the pruning-knife slew the 23d section, which made the dues of all kinds to the government payable exclusively in specie. Mr. Webster moved to fill up the vacancy by inserting a section providing "that no distinction shall hereafter be made between the different branches of the revenue, as to the funds or the medium of payment in which the debts or dues accruing to the government shall be paid or discharged." This amendment, which was carried, 37 to 14, repeals the famous specie circular, the favourite measure of Benton and the other Loco-focos, and is a solid triumph of the Webster policy.

MARCH 27. — The administration men, who are endeavouring to make a political use of the late unfortunate duel at Washington, are reminded by the Portland "Advertiser" of the opinions of their Grand Lama, General Jackson, on this subject, by the publication of the following horrid anecdote relating to the bloody murder of Dickenson by Jackson, in 1806. The account given by Dr. May, the surgeon of Jackson, in letters dated Nashville, Sept. 16 and 17, 1817, states: "They were to fire as soon as the word was given. When the word was given Dickenson fired instantly; but Jackson, after Dickenson had fired, deliberately buttoned up his coat, took deliberate aim, and fired. Dickenson fell on his face, uttered a groan, and expired. In a letter to a friend soon after, Jackson said: 'I left the damned rascal weltering in his blood.'" This is one of the good deeds for which Andrew Jackson has been rewarded by the people with the highest honours in their gift.

Duelling.

ALBANY, APRIL 5. — The weather being fine, and a nice little day-boat called the "Vanderbilt" starting to-day, I came here to indulge my desire to see our Whig House of Assembly, and my friend, the admirable Speaker. If the Whigs are not proud of both the one and the other, they have not so much pride in their work as they had discrimination in the selection of the materials. When I arrived in Albany the House was in session; there never was so hard-working a set of men in any public body; they meet at nine o'clock in the morning, and continue in session until late in the evening, with an interval of an hour to bolt their dinners *à l'Américaine*. Never did men earn harder their stinted pay of three dollars a day, — about two shillings an hour for workingtime; a price at which I used to find it difficult to hire labourers to hoist goods for me at the old corner.

The House was in Committee of the Whole when I went in, and I had the pleasure of shaking hands with the Speaker, and my numerous other political friends, who collectively make this House a credit to the State. I certainly have never seen so good-looking a legislative body; it comprises a large proportion of talents and character, and is marked for decorum, propriety, patriotism, and zeal in the public service.

APRIL 6. — The House of Assembly has passed a general banking law, which, it is thought, will afford relief to the city of New York. It is expected to pass the Senate. Other measures also will be adopted for the relief of the banks. The time for the resumption of specie payments is near at hand, and great alarm exists in New York from the fact, now ascertained, that the same measure will not be adopted in the other cities.

Luther Bradish is the very model of a Speaker; never was a chair so filled. With a perfect knowledge of the detail of legislative business, there is a dignity of deportment, a suavity of manner, promptitude of action, and correctness of decision which has secured for him the affection of his political friends, and the respect of his opponents, in a greater degree than any of his predecessors have ever possessed. It is, indeed, "well worth while," as Ruggles said in a letter which I lately received from him, "to take a trip to Albany only to see *our own Jove* seated on his high Olympus."

Mr. Ruggles has gained great renown by his admirable report on "the finances and internal improvement of the State." It has worked wonders in the minds of the members, and all parties are now striving to be foremost in carrying out the principles of that report. The city of New York has reason to be well satisfied with its delegation, — the best we have had for many years, — and they possess an influence in the Legislature, the want of which has been hitherto severely felt. Silliman, from Kings, and John A. King, from Queens, are worthy coadjutors of their brother Whigs from New York. These gentlemen have taken a high stand and are much respected.

APRIL 21. — Gold has flowed into our city, during the present week, in streams more copious than has ever before been known. The influx of the tide is greater than was its reflux. The fall in the exchange with England, and the astonishing accumulation of specie in England, have caused shipments to the enormous amount of two millions of pounds sterling. The Bank of England sends out a million of sovereigns, the Rothschilds 250,000, and the rest by other banking-houses, while at the same time large amounts are arriving daily from South America and the West Indies. A great proportion of the shipments from England come to Prime, Ward, & King. It was to effect this negotiation that James G. King went to England, and it is presumed that he has pledged American stocks for the amount he has brought away. This change in the money affairs of the country will facilitate the resumption of specie payments by the banks of our State, which must take place in the middle of May, or their charters will be forfeited, the Legislature having adjourned without extending the time of suspension beyond that period. It is also hoped that this golden stream will force open the doors of the banks in Philadelphia, Baltimore, and other places, which have refused to come into the measure, and will produce the desirable effect of a simultaneous resumption at the time our banks have fixed. Without this the domestic exchanges will continue to be ruinous for the New York merchants; but, with a unity of action on this highly interesting subject, there is a reasonable prospect of better times. All we want is, that honest men should be enabled to realize the means of paying their debts, at least as far as those means are adequate to the purpose.

Great Britain hastened the awful crisis in this country by withdrawing suddenly the support of the bank from the American houses, and now that she finds herself suffering for the want of our custom, our merchants being determined to buy no more goods until they have paid their debts, she pours back upon us of the superfluity of her metallic treasures, by which she hopes (and with good reason) to set again in motion the wheels of commerce, and, like a kind, relenting mother, to coax back to her arms her sturdy offspring. Both parties seem to have come to the conclusion that they cannot do without each other.

I went this evening to a meeting of the Kent Club, at Mr. J. Prescott Hall's. We had a large party of judges and lawyers, with Granger and Seward, and other distinguished strangers; Charles King and myself the only resident laymen. The last hour of these very pleasant reunions bears a pretty strong resemblance to the *high jinks* which Sir Walter Scott describes so well (and no doubt from personal knowledge) in "Guy Mannering."

Arrival of the "Sirius." APRIL 23. — The British steamer "Sirius," Lieut. Richard Roberts, of the Royal Navy, commander, arrived here last evening, having sailed from Cork on the 4th. She has performed the voyage without any accident, except the slight one of grounding at Sandy Hook, from which she will have been extricated by this time. She has on board forty-six passengers.

The "Sirius" comes out as pioneer to the great steam-packet which is preparing to come to this country. She was to have sailed on the 2d inst. from Cork, and has been looked for with some anxiety the last three or four days; but the wind has been westerly during her whole voyage, and her passage has been longer than it will be hereafter. The arrival of the "Sirius" is an event of so great an interest that the corporation of the city appointed a joint committee to receive and visit her on her arrival. This committee, of which Alderman Hoxie is chairman, have made arrangements with Mr. Buchanan for that purpose, and they will probably make a jollification on the occasion. It is stated in the morning papers that the "Sirius," since her departure from Cork, has used only fresh water in her boilers, having on board Mr. Hall's condensing apparatus.

The "Great Western." It was an agreeable coincidence that the great steamboat of which the "Sirius" was, as I said, the pioneer, should have arrived this morning just in time to have the event celebrated and the officers entertained at the anniversary dinner of St. George's Society, the red-cross banner floating from the windows of the " banquet hall," the Carlton House.

The " Great Western " (for such is the rather awkward name of this noble steamer) came up from Sandy Hook about two o'clock, passed around the "Sirius," then lying at anchor off the Battery, and, proceeding up the East river, hauled into Pike slip. She is much larger than her *avant-courrier*, being the largest vessel propelled by steam which has yet made her appearance in the waters of Europe. Her registered measurement is 1,604 tons, length 234 feet, breadth from out to out of the paddle-boxes 58 feet, with her engines and machinery of 450 horse power. She is commanded by Lieutenant Hoskin, of the Royal Navy, and owned by the "Great Western Steam Navigation Company." She sailed from Bristol on the 8th inst., four days later than the departure of the "Sirius" from Cork, performing thus her voyage, under the disadvantages of new machinery and a prevalence of head-winds, in fifteen days.

The city was in a ferment during the day, from the arrival of these two interesting strangers. The Battery and adjacent streets were crowded with curious spectators, and the water covered with boats conveying obtrusive visitors on board. The committee of arrangements of the Corporation have fixed upon to-morrow, at one o'clock,. for the two Houses, with their guests, to visit the " Sirius," where a collation will be prepared for them, on which occasion her commander, Lieutenant Roberts, is to receive the freedom of the city.

The passengers on board the two vessels speak in the highest terms of the convenience, steadiness, and apparent safety of the new mode of conveyance across the ocean. Everybody is so enamoured of it, that for a while it will supersede the New York packets, — the noblest vessels that ever floated in the merchant service. Our countrymen, "studious of change, and pleased with novelty," will rush forward to visit the shores of Europe instead of resorting to Virginia or Saratoga Springs; and steamers will continue to be the fashion until some more dashing adventurer of the go-ahead tribe shall demonstrate the practicability of balloon navigation, and gratify their impatience by a voyage *over*, and not *upon*, the blue waters in two days, instead of as many weeks, thereby escaping the rocks and shoals and headlands which continue yet to fright the minds of timid passengers and cautious navigators. Then they may soar above the dangers of icebergs, and look down with contempt upon the Goodwin sands or Hempstead beach. As for me, I am still skeptical on this subject. It would be presumptuous in this age of mechanical and scientific miracles to doubt the success of any startling experiment, or even to hint the possible difficulty of a contrivance by which a man might bite off his own nose; but, after the experience I have had of such ships as the "England" or the "Sylvie de Grasse," I should hesitate to trust to the powers of the air or the fire-god for my transportation and safe-conduct over this rivulet of blue water of three thousand miles in width, which separates us from the land of our fathers.

APRIL 24. — The following gentlemen dined with us: Messrs. Francis Granger, William H. Seward, John A. King, Charles King, John Duer, R. M. Blatchford, Samuel Welles, Charles H. Russell, and M. H. Grinnell.

APRIL 25. — The arrival of the two British steamers, *First Atlantic Steamship.* the "Sirius" and the "Great Western," is the engrossing topic of our novelty-loving population; but whilst all honour is awarded to the projectors of these voyages, and every sort of compliment extended to the gallant commanders, Yankee pride is a little aroused, and the merit of originality in the daring enterprise of crossing the ocean by steam is successfully wrested from our brethren on the other side. The first voyage was made in 1819, from Savannah, in the steamship "Savannah," built in New York by Francis Fickett, owned by Daniel Dodd, and commanded by Capt. Moses Rogers. She went to Liverpool, and thence to Stockholm and St. Petersburgh, where she was visited by, and the commander received presents from, Bernadotte, Crown Prince of Sweden, and from the Emperor of Russia. The same vessel went afterward to Constantinople, where the Sultan conferred on Captain Rogers similar compliments. This experiment, it would appear, however, did not succeed entirely; it is certain that she did not make short voyages, which circumstance may account for so long a time having elapsed before the attempt was renewed.

The fact of the Americans being the first inventors of sea navigation by steam is consolatory to our national pride, but should not derogate from the credit of the British, who have now proved so triumphantly its feasibility, any more than the immortal discovery and construction of the steam-engine by British subjects should lessen the merit of our own Fulton, who first applied its power to the most important of its uses, the propelling of vessels.

APRIL 27. — Having received an invitation to accompany the Mayor and Corporation in their visit to the British steamer "Great Western," I went to the Mayor's office at one o'clock, where was assembled, besides the members of the Corporation, a large company, among whom were the judges, members of the Legislature, Mr. Webster, Governor Mason of Michigan, Mr. Bradish, the Speaker, the editors of papers, etc. From the hall we proceeded to the foot of Beekman street, where the company was taken on board the barges to the number of about twenty, each commanded by an officer in full uniform, with a fine set of bargemen and bearing the American flag in her stern. When the company was embarked, the barges formed in procession, a band of music in the first, the whole commanded by Captain Stringham, of the United States Navy, and proceeded to the steamer, which was moored a few yards from the dock, off Pike street. We were received in good style by Captain Hoskin and his officers, and, after examining the stupendous machinery of the great vessel, the company were escorted to the saloon, and seated (all who could get seats) at a plentiful collation, arranged in excellent taste, with oceans of champagne. Messrs.

Bradish, Webster, Maxwell, the Mayor, and other gentlemen, made speeches and gave toasts, and the British captains, Hoskin of the "Great Western," and Roberts of the "Sirius," appeared to be as happy as they said they were. The lovely Queen of Britain was toasted with enthusiasm equal to any which warms the hearts of her own subjects in their own country, and John Bull and Brother Jonathan were as loving as a young couple in the honeymoon. Long may these feelings continue! The whole affair went off brilliantly. The day was uncommonly fine, and the scene on the water, with the crowds of spectators on the wharves, was not the least exciting part of the pageant.

The vessel exceeds my expectation. Her steam-engine of four hundred horse power and the other machinery are upon a magnificent scale, and the accommodations for passengers in the best possible taste; the principal saloon is surrounded by forty-two state-rooms, sufficiently capacious. The ornaments are of the quaint, old-fashioned style, and the panels are decorated by exquisite paintings, in the costumes of the reign of Louis XV., which give to the whole of this beautiful apartment the appearance of a cabinet of old Dresden china. One of the greatest advantages which this saloon has over the cabins of the packets consists in the height of the ceiling, which affords light and air equal to a well-proportioned dining-room or parlour on shore. All that is now wanting to confine to the steam-vessels the patronage of all the passengers going to Europe is the assurance of safety, and that will be obtained by one or two more passages across the Atlantic.

MAY 1.—The "Sirius" sailed at one o'clock, passed the packets in fine style, and, the weather being pleasant and the sea calm, was soon out of sight ahead. The Battery was filled with spectators, who gave repeated cheers to the interesting stranger, and she was saluted from the forts on her progress down the bay. May she perform her return voyage with as much safety and expedition as the voyage out, and thereby establish full confidence in this admirable mode of communication between Great Britain and the United States!

Steamboat Disaster. The most shocking disaster on board a steamboat which has yet been recorded occurred on the 25th of April, at Cincinnati. The steamboat "Moselle" started from the wharf on her voyage down the river. She went up about a mile to take in a family; and during the time of her stopping, the steam was held up, for the purpose of showing off her speed in passing the city, when, at the instant her wheels made the first revolution, the boilers burst with a noise equal to the most violent crash of thunder. The vessel was blown into a thousand pieces, and of two hundred and eighty passengers on board only ninety were saved. Most of the persons on board belonged to Cincinnati, and in the number were many of the most respectable citizens, who were thus destroyed in an instant by the culpable conduct of the captain and other officers, in sight of their families and friends, who were assembled on shore to witness their departure. The captain paid the penalty of his crime, he being of the number killed. The papers are filled with the details of this shocking catastrophe, which cannot be read without shuddering.

MAY 4. — The subject of the late unfortunate duel **Report on the Duel Case.** between Messrs. Graves and Cilley, which resulted in the death of the latter, was referred in the House of Representatives to a special committee, of which Mr. Toucey is chairman. To the disgrace of the administration party, instead of making this lamentable case the occasion of correcting the popular code of morals in relation to these personal encounters, and thereby removing as far as practicable this stain of blood-guiltiness from our land, they seized it with avidity, and endeavoured to turn it into part of their detestable party capital. The Speaker appointed on the committee of seven, a chairman and three other thorough whole-hog men, political enemies of Mr. Graves and his second in the duel, Mr. Wise, — fellows who would sell their souls for their party, and have no more notion of political honesty than they have of the refined feelings of gentlemen. This committee has now brought in a report, recommending that Mr. Graves be expelled and Mr. Wise reprimanded by the House, — the most outrageous proceeding I have ever known in a legislative body, — a grand jury trying the accused, convicting them, and awarding their punishment; a greater violation (as Mr. Adams told them) of the privileges of the House than the offence itself, which the committee were appointed to investigate.

This report has been before the House several days, and occasioned a warm debate. Some high-minded gentlemen of the administration party cannot be made to swallow it. Mr. Adams made a great speech, in which he placed the unworthy conduct of the majority in such a point of view as would have made them blush, if their instructions had permitted. On Monday last, Mr. Graves and Mr. Wise both addressed the House, protesting against this unparliamentary course of proceeding, which would constitute four political adversaries their judges, and condemn them unheard.

Mr. Graves closed his speech with the following touching remarks, which, while they depict his sensibility and distress of mind for the part which he had to sustain in that unhappy affair, portray in glowing colours the absurdity of the tyranny which is exercised by public opinion over the minds and consciences of the people of this country in all things relating to affairs of honour, as we most unwisely call them. Who that read them would venture to decide that the lot of the survivor in this duel is better than that of the victim? And who that knows as I do, this amiable and high-minded gentleman, would not desire to pour the balm of consolation into his afflicted bosom, rather than seek to make the event which he, in common with all good men, so deeply deplores, a subject for the display of personal hostility and a weapon of political warfare? "Sir," said Mr. Graves, "I was involved in the commencement of this unfortunate affair innocently. I never conceived it possible that such consequences would have devolved upon me when I consented to become the bearer of that ill-fated note. Otherwise I should never have taken upon myself the task. I am not, and never have been, the advocate of the anti-social and unchristian practice of duelling. I have never up to this day fired a duelling pistol; and, until the day when I went to the field, I never took any weapon in my hand in view of a duel. Public opinion is practically the paramount law of the land; every other law, both human and divine, ceases to be observed, yea, withers and perishes, in contact with it. It was this paramount law of this nation and of this House that forced me, under the penalty of dishonour, to submit myself to the code which impelled me unwillingly into this tragical affair. Upon the heads of this nation and at the doors of this House rests the blood with which my unfortunate hands have been stained."

MAY 5. — Captain Marryat, having given lately at Toronto a very injudicious toast, complimentary to Captain Drew and his associates, who destroyed the American steamboat "Caroline," the wise people of Lewistown held a solemn town-meeting, at which they resolved to burn all Captain Marryat's books which could be found in the village. This most ridiculous resolve was duly carried into effect. A bonfire was kindled on the shore directly opposite Queenstown, and all the "Peter Simples," "Jacob Faithfuls," "Japhets," etc., which could be found were cast in the flames; the officiating high-priest at the altar of popular absurdity pronouncing aloud the title of each as it was immolated.

Captain Marryat, I dare say, made a fool of himself (not a very difficult task, I should judge, from what I have seen of him); but the Lewistownians have beaten him "all to smash," as the Kentuckians say. How mortified he must have been to hear that his books had been burned after they were paid for; and how sorry the booksellers, that their praiseworthy labours to enlighten the American people should be so ungratefully requited, and so many copies of their publications come to an untimely end! What a grand "flare up" of American resentment! What a glorious ending in smoke of patriotic indignation! They ought to have passed a resolution at the meeting to burn all articles of British production or manufacture, *especially coals*. The village newspaper, in its virtuous wrath, announces that "'Midshipman Easy' would not burn, its stupidity rendering it fire-proof." "Werry sewere," as Sam Weller says.

Departure of the "Great Western."

MAY 7.—This has been a gala-day in New York. The British steamer "Great Western," Captain Hoskin, sailed at two o'clock from Pier No. 1, North river. All the city went to behold the sight. The Battery was a mass of living witnesses to this event. Castle Garden was filled, and all the adjacent wharves and houses were thronged with spectators. When the steamer started she was accompanied by a dozen large steamboats with crowded decks and ornamented by flags, among which the loving embraces of St. George's Cross and the Stars and Stripes were conspicuous in every instance. I went with a party on board of the "Providence." The day was very fine, and the gallant fleet presented a scene in the bay not unlike that at the great Canal celebration, when Dr. Mitchell mingled the waters of Lake Erie with those of the ocean, and I was the fugleman to nine cheers so loud and astounding that it is doubtful if the highlands of Neversink have to this day recovered from the trembling which they occasioned.

Having reached the bay below Staten Island, the "Great Western" stopped, and the "Providence" went alongside and took off a large party of gentlemen who went down in her, among whom were Governor Marcy, Mr. Seward, and many other distinguished persons. We then left her with shouts and good wishes for her safe and speedy return to the public-spirited company who undertook this enterprise, and sent her out a successful pioneer. She pursued her course in fine style, and we returned to the city and got home to a late dinner. There was a great crowd on board the "Providence," in which were many ladies, and the excursion was quite a pleasant one. An interesting incident occurred whilst we lay alongside of the "Great Western," in the bay. The ship "Colon," from Havana, came in with a number of passengers, with all sails set. Sailing beautifully on the wind, she passed through the fleet of gay steamboats, cheered the "Great Western," went close under our bows, almost touching the bowsprit, and passed triumphantly rejoicing on her way to the renowned city of Gotham; it was a fine offset of sails and rigging against steam and paddles.

<small>A Type of Longevity.</small> MAY 8. — Died yesterday, in Philadelphia, Thomas Bradford, successor to Dr. Franklin, and the oldest printer and editor in the United States. He was in the ninety-fourth year of his age.

<small>History of Ferdinand and Isabella.</small> MAY 12. — The history of the reign of Ferdinand and Isabella, the Catholic, by William H. Prescott, an American, I am proud to say, has been published in three volumes. I have just been reading it, and I think it is entitled to a place alongside of Hume, Robertson, and Gibbon. Great care has been bestowed upon it, and no modern work displays more accurate knowledge or laborious investigation. Irving has treated some of the leading subjects of this history in the "Life of Columbus" and his "Conquest of Granada," over which he has thrown the charm of his poetical style; but here is a book, rich in all the lore of the Spanish archives, diving deep into authorities with which the reading world has been heretofore unacquainted, and making clear the dark passages of that interesting period of European history, the close of the fifteenth and the commencement of the sixteenth centuries.

MAY 14. — The Pennsylvania Bank of the United States has sent on $20,000 to Charleston for the relief of the sufferers by the fire. This is a *monstrous* act of munificence, and proves the danger of such an institution in a free country. Biddle must have

some horrid design in this, — nothing short of an overthrow of the Government and destruction of the liberties of the people.

MAY 18. — Our neighbouring city of Philadelphia was disgraced yesterday by a riot, which ended in the destruction of Pennsylvania Hall, a place of meeting for the discussion of abolition questions. A meeting was held in the forenoon, and speeches were made which exasperated the mob. Another meeting was to have taken place in the evening, but it was prevented by the interference of the Mayor. The mob, still farther instigated, it is said, by the wanton outrage of public opinion in the exhibition in the public streets of white men and women walking arm in arm with blacks, assembled in greater numbers in the evening, broke into the hall, destroyed everything they could find, and set fire to the building, which was entirely destroyed by ten o'clock. The excitement was so great that the Mayor and other civil officers were unable to prevent the outrage, and some of the number (particularly Mr. Watmouth, the sheriff) were dangerously wounded. A large proportion of the abolitionists assembled in the hall were females, of whom several harangued the meeting, and were foremost in arousing the excited populace. This dreadful subject gains importance every day, and reflecting men see in it the seeds of the destruction of our institutions.

Riot in Philadelphia.

MAY 19. — The following gentlemen dined with us: Governor Mason of Michigan, Mr. Bullock of Kentucky, Mr. Charles A. Davis, Mr. James W. Otis, Mr. Delprat, Mr. Abraham Schermerhorn, Mr. Irving Van Wart, Dr. McLean, General Fleming, and Charles A. Heckscher.

MAY 31. — The fine weather this afternoon tempted my wife, my daughter, and myself to go to Hoboken. We crossed from Canal street, walked to the Pavilion in "Les Champs Elysées" (a place better entitled to the name than the more celebrated one near Paris), and returned home at eight o'clock. It is many years since I visited this beautiful *suburb of New York*, which has been greatly improved. New walks have been laid out, the grounds beautifully arranged, the woods cleared, and a fair chance given to Nature to show off her charms to the greatest advantage.

JUNE 1. — A resolution offered by Mr. Webster to repeal the specie circular passed the Senate on the 28th by a strong vote of thirty-four to ten. On the question of engrossing this resolution for a third reading the ten votes in the minority were given by the following Senators. It is amusing to see in what company Mr. Calhoun, the great southern nullifier, has placed himself. What bedfellows political inconsistency may bring a man acquainted with! Nays: Messrs. Allen, Benton, Brown, Calhoun, Hubbard, Linn, Morris, Niles, Smith of Connecticut, Strange. Of these, five may be called Yankee loco-foco loafers; viz., two from Connecticut, one from New Hampshire, and two from Ohio, the latter being virtually a New England State, although far from its fatherland. Now, these five men do no more speak the language of their constituents than they do that of truth, honour, and patriotism, and here is Mr. Calhoun amongst them; the proud, tenacious, high-minded Carolinian, Mr. Calhoun! Well, as he likes best, so be it! As he sows so he shall reap.

Specie Circular Repealed.

This resolution was taken up in the House of Representatives on Wednesday, and carried through, without debate, in less than no time. The vote on the question "Shall the joint resolution from the Senate, repealing the treasury circular, pass?" was carried by the astonishing, unexpected vote of one hundred and fifty-four to twenty-nine, and the resolution sent back to the Senate in half an hour after the House was called to order. In the virtuous minority, our two hopeful city representatives, Cambreling and Moore, are to be found, of course; but as far as I can judge from running my eye over the Ayes and Nays in the newspaper, very few other members from our State were willing to be seen in such bad and unfashionable company. This great event, together with Mr. Biddle's letter to Mr. Adams, written in consequence of it, have infused a joyful spirit of confidence amongst our New York folk. Verily, Wall street rejoiceth! Stocks have risen and domestic exchanges fallen, and it would seem that the touch of Webster (as he said on a certain occasion of that of Alexander Hamilton) has caused the corpse of public credit to rise on its feet and stand erect.

JUNE 8. — Immediately after the passage of Mr. Webster's resolution rescinding the specie circular, business revived. Confidence was restored to financial operations, and hopes were entertained of better times; but a blight has come upon our bright prospects. The evil influence of the administration, which seems determined to oppose the wishes of the people, has again been at work. Mr. Woodbury has issued a circular, misconstruing the intentions of Congress, and prohibiting the receiving of the notes of all banks who have since some day in 1836 issued small bills, thereby " visiting the sins of the fathers upon the children." This ungracious measure of the administration, together with the tardiness of the banks of Philadelphia in declaring their intentions to resume specie payments, has thrown all things back again. Stocks in New York have fallen more than five per cent., and foreign and domestic exchanges have risen. The administration and the party which supports them seem determined to " die with harness on their backs." If they go out of office they will leave a ruined and bankrupt country to their successors.

JUNE 14. — It has been often said that a man must have great luck to get himself hanged in this country.

Acquittals by Juries.

It is certainly a melancholy proof of the depravity of our morals, that the most flagrant offences against the laws, and the most atrocious violations of the peace and good order of society, go daily "unwhipped of Justice," by the misjudging lenity, if not the base corruption, of men elected to preserve, as jurors, the purity of our legal institutions. Two cases have lately occurred, not by any means calculated to make us proud of the name of Americans.

Some time last winter a personal dispute occurred, during the session of the House of Representatives of the State of Arkansas, between a Mr. Wilson, the Speaker then presiding, and Major Anthony, a member, in the course of which the former came down from his chair, drew a large knife (a weapon which it appears these modern barbarians carry about their persons), attacked his adversary and killed him on the spot. Anthony endeavoured to defend himself (he had also his knife); but the movement of the honourable Speaker was so sudden as to render his efforts ineffectual, and I suppose it was "out of order" for other members to interfere in the parliamentary discipline of their presiding officer.

Wilson has been tried for this flagrant outrage. There is a full account of the trial in the newspapers, taken from the Arkansas "Gazette." From the testimony it does not appear that any violent provocation was offered by the deceased, and the facts above-stated were substantially proved, notwithstanding which the verdict of the jury was as follows: "Guilty of excusable homicide, and not guilty in any manner or form as charged in the indictment;" and the prisoner was discharged from custody. Further accounts state that immediately after this mockery of justice, the jurors, with the sheriffs and witnesses, had a grand drinking frolic at the expense of the defendant.

The other case has just occurred in our own Court of Sessions. During the last election for Mayor and Corporation, an affidavit was distributed at all the polls, made by a rascally Irishman, named Edmund Burke, in which our respectable Mayor, Mr. Aaron Clark, was charged with having offered a bribe of a quarter's rent to Burke, who was his tenant, if he would vote for him and the rest of the Whig ticket. This fellow was instigated to commit the perjury by James Thea and other worthy supporters of the Van Buren party, who carried him to the magistrate to take his deposition, paid the expenses, had the hand-bills printed, and let the poison work its way into the public mind, well knowing that the antidote would come too late, and knowing also that there was not the shadow of truth in the charge. Mr. Clark had never seen the man in his life, owned no such house, and the whole story turned out (as might well be supposed) an infamous falsehood. Burke was tried for the perjury. His worthy friends and coadjutors advised him to plead insanity and drunkenness, which plea found favour in the eyes of the jury, and he was *acquitted*, to be used again, when occasion shall require him, to blacken the character of some other virtuous citizen, and promote the success of the party which Mr. Van Buren calls his own.

<small>Stuyvesant's Pear-tree.</small> JUNE 15. — A great curiosity is to be seen on the Third avenue, at the corner of 13th street. A fine, healthy, patriarchal pear-tree, which annually bears leaves and blossoms, and would produce fruit if boys would let it. This tree, which, by the regulation of the avenue and streets, is now at the corner close to the curb-stone, and has been recently protected by a substantial wooden railing, was formerly one of the trees in the orchard of Governor Stuyvesant, a great distance from New York, but now in the midst of a large city population. Tradition has been ransacked for its history, which forms a part of our city statistics. Grave essays have been written upon its longevity, and poetry has sung its praises. This tree was the subject of conversation at Mr. Stuyvesant's table to-day. There is no doubt of the fact, I believe, which I now record, that it was brought out from Holland by Governor Stuyvesant, and planted with his own hands on the spot where it now stands. Governor Stuyvesant came to New York in the month of May, 1647; the pear-tree is, therefore, one hundred and ninety-one years old.

<small>Steamboat Disasters.</small> JUNE 21. — The heart sickens, and the pen falters, in recording the dreadful disasters which occur almost daily in the steamboat navigation of the United States. I fear it will soon become doubtful whether Fulton's great invention will not prove a curse, rather than a blessing, to mankind. It certainly will, or the use of steam in navigation be discontinued, unless measures are adopted to punish negligence and temerity, and to insure safety by using necessary precautions.

JUNE 22. — The unworthy representative of New York in Congress, Mr. Cambreling, brought forward the sub-treasury bill on Tuesday last, in the House of Representatives, where it has been debated ever since, many conjectures having been formed about its fate, and calculations made of the state of the vote on the passage of this obnoxious bill. It will be exceedingly close; not more than two or three majority either way. I confess I have great fears of the result. The Government is reckless of consequences; determined to support themselves by the power which this measure will give them, they put all the screws upon their political partisans, and hold out every sort of corrupt inducement to those who may have had occasional qualms of honesty or patriotism. My fears are excited in proportion to the extent of the evil which I apprehended from the passage of the bill, and my want of faith in the ability of some half-way Whigs or Conservatives to resist the bribes which a corrupt administration will not hesitate to offer. If these things continue, and the people do not arise in their might to rebuke them, the republic is at an end.

<small>Sub-Treasury Bill.</small>

JUNE 27. — This odious measure of a corrupt administration was rejected on Monday last by a majority of *fourteen*. Every new attempt to increase the President's power, and to counteract the will of the people, is frustrated by their representatives with increased majorities. The administration is on its back. May it never rise again!

JULY 12. — The members of Congress from East and North have arrived in town, glad to be released from the servitude of public duty in this scorching weather. They have been in session ten months, with the exception only of the few weeks intervening between the close of the extra session and the opening of the regular one. I called upon Mr. Webster this morning. He appears much fagged with hard work, and pants for relaxation and sea-air at one of his favorite resorts on the shore of his own State; and well is he entitled to that or any other comfort, for well has he wrought in the cause of the people, as one of the leaders of that noble band, who, although wanting in the power to do much good, have succeeded in preventing much evil. I saw, also, our worthy representative, Edward Curtis, who shows the marks of a long and distressing illness, with which he was afflicted at Washington, during which he, also, suffering as he was with the pains of inflammatory rheumatism, was compelled to keep his seat in the House when the vote of every honest man was indispensable to counteract the mischievous designs of the administration party. Honour and praise to the noble Whigs and Conservatives! They have saved the country.

ROCKAWAY, AUG. 10. — We had a very pleasant ball this evening. I had an interesting conversation with Mrs. Butler, late Miss Fanny Kemble, who is here with her husband and two little daughters. This lady, whom I greatly admired when she arrived in this country with her distinguished father, Charles Kemble, has seldom visited New York since the publication of her journal, in which she took some foolish liberties with me and my family and others of whose hospitality she had partaken. I was never seriously offended at what she said in this book, but viewed it "more in sorrow than in anger;" for I thought it a pity that a woman so brilliant, who was capable of better things, should have compromised her literary reputation by giving to the world her inconsiderate, girlish remarks upon the daily events which amused her lively and excitable imagination, when I knew her talents were worthy of better employment. This, then, was the first time we had met, and she felt doubtful of what I might consider our relative positions. As soon as she entered the room I seated myself at her side, told her I was happy to renew an acquaintance, the recollection of which had always given me great pleasure, and danced with her. In the course of our conversation she said to me, with great earnestness and solemnity, and much agitated, "Mr. Hone, I cannot express to you how happy you have made me by the notice you have taken of me on this occasion. Believe me, I am extremely grateful." I, of course, turned it off as well as I could, observing that she had no reason to be grateful; my motive was selfish, as I sought my own gratification in renewing an acquaintance so congenial to my feelings, etc. During this conversation the tear which stood in her flashing, expressive eye convinced me that this highly gifted woman, with all the waywardness of thought and independence of action which the circumstances of her early introduction into life had ingrafted upon her natural disposition, possesses that warmth of heart which I thought I had formerly the sagacity to discover, and for which I have never failed to give her credit.

SEPTEMBER 4.—Granger is in town. I called to see him this morning, at the Astor House. I told him that I thought the selection made at the Broadway House, on Friday evening, of delegates to the Convention unfavourable to his chance of being nominated Governor, for I consider them Seward men. He seems to think, notwithstanding, that he has more strength at the West than Seward. This question must not be suffered to create a schism in the Whig party. We have higher principles of action than any personal preferences between the friends of Mr. Granger and Mr. Seward.

SEPTEMBER 10.—The two curses of our country, or rather two of the curses,— for General Jackson's administration of the Government entailed enough of them upon us,— are the fanaticism of the abolitionists of the North, and the violence of the nullifiers of the South. A late transaction which has taken place in this city inculpates some of the former gentry most fearfully, and I should not wonder if they are sent to carry out their doctrines of emancipation within the walls of the Penitentiary.

The facts are these: A negro boy, the slave of a Mr. Darg, a Southern gentleman, who was here on a visit, robbed his master of $7,000 and absconded; was harboured by a fellow called Ruggles and others, his philanthropic associates, into whose hands the money got by some means; and a Mr. Barney Corse, a man of some standing, one of the Society of Friends, was employed as plenipotentiary to negotiate a peace with the master, the conditions of which were, that on the payment of $1,000, which he had offered as reward, and the manumission of the slave, with a pledge not to prosecute him for the robbery, the remainder of the money should be restored. This he agreed to, and received the principal part of the money. But the police, having received information of the transaction, interfered with the high contracting parties, and annulled the treaty. Mr. Corse and Ruggles were arrested, and I cannot very well see how they are to avoid the penalty of a pretty serious crime into which their officious interference has involved them. It is not pretended that Mr. Corse, at any rate, was concerned as instigator or party to the robbery; but their subsequent conduct will bring them in as accessories after the fact, and the excitement of the public mind on the subject of abolition and everything that relates to the blacks is so great, that these men will have little chance to escape the penalty of the law.

SEPTEMBER 14. — The Whig Convention assembled at Utica, on Wednesday, in the court-house. William H. Seward was nominated Governor, and Luther Bradish Lieutenant-Governor. These are excellent nominations, and will be supported with unanimity by the Whig party. Mr. Seward is a man of superior talents, unwavering principles, and popular manners. Consulting my personal predilections I might, perhaps, have preferred my old friend, Mr. Granger, who, having stood the brunt when there was little hope of success, seems to have had the strongest claim upon the party now, when the chance of success is so much better. But the canvass shows the undiminished confidence of his friends. He wanted but three votes on the third ballot of being the nominee, and on that ballot there were five scattering votes. As for Luther Bradish, no man in the State of New York is better qualified for any office to which the people may call him.

SEPTEMBER 21. — Died this day, Mr. Jacob Lorillard, in the sixty-fifth year of his age, — a benevolent man and a good citizen; intelligent and active in all the social relations of life, and scrupulously just in all his concerns. He retired from his business (that of tanner and currier) a few years since, having amassed a very large fortune, of which he made a good use. Mr. Lorillard and I were associated together in the German Society, in the Presidency of which he was my immediate successor, and no person in the city possessed more influence with the German population. I deeply lament the death of this excellent man.

SEPTEMBER 29. — The ex-king Joseph Bonaparte,
Joseph Bonaparte. arrived here with a numerous suite on Saturday, in the packet-ship "Philadelphia," from London. He left the United States four or five years since, as was supposed, to take advantage of some political movements which seemed to indicate the chance of a restoration of the House of Bonaparte; but he has returned, and, I trust, to spend the remainder of his days quietly in this best of all Yankee republics. He is a gentlemanly, orderly man, and has contrived to save out of the two crowns which he has worn jewels enough to make himself comfortable and to benefit his neighbors. As for his chance to reign in France, it is "no go." If the French get rid of their excellent monarch, and overthrow the present order of things, they will have something better or worse than the "House of Bonaparte" to rule them. The whole sap of the family tree ran into one branch; the rest has not fire enough to kindle a new conflagration, or strength enough to put it out if it should be kindled by others.

OCTOBER 3. — The elections in the several States
Elections. which are to settle the important question between the present administration and the people are now commencing. The interest taken in these elections is unprecedented, as well for their own importance as for the influence which their results will have upon the great crowning contest, which we are to have in November.

OCTOBER 13. — The Whigs, ever sanguine, bad politicians

certainly, discouraged by unfavourable reports, and elated by the news of success, made up hastily from unreliable estimates, have experienced several severe disappointments of late. Pennsylvania has gone against us. Porter, the loco-foco candidate for Governor, has beaten Rittner by five thousand majority at least; Ohio, which we thought our own, is, I fear, all wrong; but the strangest thing of all is our next-door neighbour, New Jersey. The election was held on Tuesday and Wednesday last. We had it all: six members of Congress by general ticket, and the Legislature by great majorities; but yesterday the tables began to change, our majorities were reduced and those of the Van Burenites increased. Our air-built castles began to totter; every fresh account was less favourable. The Whig majorities, like Paddy's candle placed before the fire to dry, became smaller and smaller; the Tories began to bet, and now our hopes are reduced so low that the most we claim is fifty to one hundred on the canvass of the whole State, and it seems probable that we may not get more than one or two Congressmen out of the whole ticket. Nothing is left for the good cause but a great victory in the State of New York, and already the despondency which succeeds disappointment has taken hold of our friends; we must fight.

Here the issue is to be tried. I cannot think that the great work which was so auspiciously commenced last fall is now to be overthrown. The cause of the constitution and the laws, the preservation of our precious institutions, are in the hands of the Whigs of New York, and there appears to be zeal and spirit in our ranks worthy of such a cause, and of a motive of action so exciting.

OCTOBER 15.— The Van Buren men have agreed upon a ticket for Congress. Loco-foco to the hub: Cambreling, Eli Moore, John McKeon, and Edwin Forrest. The latter is the celebrated tragedian, with no claim, that I have ever heard of, to the honour of representing the people

Loco-foco Congressmen.

of New York in Congress, but that of exciting, by dint of loud words and furious stamps, the pit of the Bowery Theatre to raise their shirt-sleeves high in the air and shout Hurrah for Forrest! He may be a leader of the *Pitt* party, but no statesman. True it is that these men may "steal a horse when we cannot look over the hedge." I remember well how I was berated by some of my political friends, when, as Mayor, I assisted in the ceremony of laying the corner-stone of the Bowery Theatre, and made a speech on the occasion. No act of my public life lost me so many friends, and here we have a regular-built actor presented to the people for their suffrages; and he will probably (if he should consent to serve) receive the greatest number of votes on their ticket. The *Pittites* will, of course, shout most obstreperously for him, but the better sort of men, the gentlemen (the few that belong to the party), the moral men, as well as the Five-point politicians and disciples of Fanny Wright, will vote for Forrest and Eli Moore, without the slightest compunction; and why? Because they are spell-bound, and conscience-shackled by those powerful cabalistic words, *regular nominee*.

Whig Meeting. OCTOBER 18.—I attended this evening a meeting of leading, influential gentlemen of the Whig party, at the Astor House. There were sixty or eighty present. I was appointed chairman, and R. M. Blatchford, secretary. The object of this meeting was to confer with several of our friends from different parts of the State on the prospects for the important approaching election. Thurlow Weed and Mr. Benedict, of Albany, were with us, and our candidate for Governor, Mr. Seward. The accounts were cheering, and a noble spirit pervaded the meeting, undismayed by recent disasters in other States. It was represented that a sum of about $5,000 was required, to be distributed in five or six of the counties. Subscriptions were taken on the spot, and $3,400 subscribed down, and about the same sum in addition, conditioned upon the success of the Whigs in the city elections; in addition to which a committee of seven, including the chairman and secretary, were appointed to raise further contributions. This is an irksome duty for me to perform, but, situated as I was, I could not shrink from it. The committee consists of David B. Ogden, J. P. Phœnix, Simeon Draper, Jr., Thomas Tileston, Jonathan Amory, Blatchford, and myself.

OCTOBER 19. — The Committee on Collections met this morning, and divided into separate committees of two. David B. Ogden and I sallied out in a pelting rain, in which we paddled about for upwards of three hours. We called upon several of our rich citizens, some of whom gave liberally, and others, having no regard for their own characters, or sympathy for our ducked condition, refused to give; but we have done our duty, disagreeable as it was. We shall get $5,000, but there is more required for the expenses of the city election.

OCTOBER 20. — The following gentlemen (a pleasant, jovial set) dined with us: Colonel Hunter, Mr. John Henry, and Mr. Molyneux of Savannah, Mr. Power, Mr. Nicholson, Governor Mason of Michigan, Mr. Charles Heckscher, Mr. Edward Heckscher, Mr. Thomas Moore, and J. D. P. Ogden.

OCTOBER 22. — Ten gentlemen met and dined to-day *Institution of the Hone Club.* at Mr. John Ward's, Bond street, being the first meeting of a club which was there organized to dine at each other's houses every Monday, at five o'clock punctually. The present members are, Simeon Draper, John Ward, Moses H. Grinnell, William G. Ward, John Crumby, Roswell L. Colt, Edward R. Biddle, Jonathan Prescott Hall, R. M. Blatchford, and Philip Hone.

It was agreed to extend the number to twelve by the admission of Charles H. Russell and James W. Otis, to which number the club is limited. A sumptuary law was enacted, confining the dinner to soup, fish, oysters, and four dishes of meat, with a dessert of fruit, ice-cream, and jelly. The host is allowed to invite four gentlemen, not members of the club. The members did me the honour to name the club "The Hone Club," and I was appointed the President.

OCTOBER 26. — This new enemy to the peace of
Abolition. mankind, which I fear is destined to overthrow the institutions of our country, has of late raised its head proudly in this State. The candidates nominated for office at the approaching election, from Governor downward, have been addressed in circular letters by committees of the abolitionists, proposing in rather a peremptory style certain questions regarding slavery and the political disqualifications of the free blacks. Such of these missives as were addressed to the candidates for Governor and Lieutenant-Governor are signed by William Jay and Garrett Smith. Messrs. Seward and Bradish have replied at length. Their letters are published. That of the former is exceedingly well written, somewhat evasive, and not by any means satisfactory to his inquisitors. Mr. Bradish is much more conclusive. He comes out boldly and answers all the questions in the affirmative. This does not by any means prove him to be an abolitionist, but will be so construed by that party, and will do him great injury with the Whigs in this part of the State. I regret it exceedingly, because I think this gratuitous committal was unnecessary; nor do I allow the right of a set of men, standing upon their own ground, and having views and motives abstracted from the great leading principles of political faith, to propound questions of this nature to the persons set up for the suffrages of the people, and make their favourable response the condition of their support. Such a course of inquisitorial scrutiny into men's consciences, if persevered in, will have the effect to destroy that lofty independence and integrity of mind which should characterize the representatives of the people, palsy the executive arm, and sully the purity of the judiciary. Already have I heard the most opprobrious epithets applied to my excellent friend Bradish. I know not whether the votes he loses here may not be overbalanced in the West, where the great strength of the abolitionists lies; but I regret that a man so upright and intelligent should expose himself to the reproaches of any portion of his political friends, by a supererogatory declaration of opinions which I

maintain no set of men had a right to call for. The same system is in operation here. On the announcement of my name as a candidate for the Assembly the following letter was sent to me. I copy it at length, because I consider it to be the root of a noxious plant, which in its growth will overshadow the land, corrupt the soil of republican America, and produce the fruits of anarchy and disunion : —

NEW YORK, Oct. 26, 1838.

PHILIP HONE, ESQ. : —

SIR, — We notice that you are nominated to represent this county in the Assembly of this State. As citizens and legal voters of this city, the undersigned, in behalf of themselves and others, beg leave to propound the following questions : —

Are you in favour of the immediate repeal of such laws of this State as permit slaveholders to introduce slaves, and hold them here as such? Are you in favour of enacting a law which shall secure a trial by jury to every person claimed in this State as a slave? Are you in favour of so amending the constitution of this State that civil rights shall not be granted or withheld according to complexion? Are you in favour of the passage (by the Legislature) of resolutions declaring the power and duty of Congress immediately to abolish slavery and the slave-trade in the District of Columbia, and to prohibit immediately the inter-state slavetrade; and, also, resolutions protesting against the annexation of Texas, or the admission to the Union of any State whose constitution tolerates slavery? An early answer to the foregoing questions is respectfully requested, and should you neglect to reply it will be considered equivalent to a negative answer.

Respectfully, your obedient servants,

A. LIBOLT, *Chairman.*	L. W. GILBERT,
ANTHONY LANE,	S. W. BENEDICT,
E. A. LAMBERT,	J. H. COLTON,
THOMAS RITTER,	LEWIS TAPPAN,
A. O. WILLCOX,	THOMAS F. FIELD,
W. S. DORR,	HIRAM TUPPER,
M. R. BERRY,	JOHN JAY,
THOMAS O. BUCKMASTER,	P. B. SMITH,
C. S. DELAVAN,	ADDISON A. JAYNE,
ADRATUS DOOLITTLE,	JOHN W. HILL.
ASA PARKER,	

To this letter I returned the following brief reply. I wish with all my heart that the answers of Seward and Bradish had been equally brief. "The least said," particularly in *black and white*, "the soonest mended."

OCTOBER 26, 1838.

GENTLEMEN:—I have received your letter of this day, propounding several questions to me as a candidate to represent this city in the Assembly of the State. I am relieved from the obligation of answering these questions (if such obligation exists on the part of a candidate toward a portion of his fellow-citizens), by the circumstance of my not having accepted the nomination with which I was honoured by my political friends. I am, etc., P. H.

Messrs. A. Libolt, etc., etc.

Whig Meeting.

OCTOBER 29.— The meeting was held this evening at Masonic Hall to receive the report of the nominating committee. The house was full as usual, up-stairs and down-stairs and round about. That excellent old-fashioned federal Whig, David B. Ogden, presided, with twenty vice-presidents and four secretaries. It is refreshing once in a while to see a relic of honest political principles, like David B. Ogden, allowed to take a prominent place in public affairs. It is almost the only thing of the kind I have seen in relation to the coming election. I cannot recognize the name on either ticket of a leading Federalist or National Republican,— they are permitted to work and pay money; they must bake the loaves and catch the fishes, but they get precious few of them for themselves. Every man on the Congress ticket was in full communion at Tammany Hall five years ago. They are generally good men. A better fellow is not to be found, nor a more efficient Whig, than Moses H. Grinnell; yet some of us who have borne "the heat and burden of the day" are entitled at least, one would think, to as good "a penny" as the eleventh-hour man. The tickets for Congress and Assembly went down admirably; the meeting swallowed Monroe and all without a wry face. This is all right; this unanimity "gives token of a goodly day to-morrow." We must gain the victory now, and afterward try to get some of these little matters, which are out of joint at present, adjusted to the satisfaction of all good men and true.

OCTOBER 31.—"Who reads an American book?" was the impertinent question of an English coxcomb.

American Literature.

Somebody must have read Prescott's excellent "History of Ferdinand and Isabella," with delight equal to my own, and also Stone's "Life of Brant," which I intend to read with equal pleasure one of these days. For of both these popular works three editions have been published, and the last edition of the latter was sold at an advance from that of the first of a dollar and a half, the original price of three dollars and a half having been found insufficient to leave a profit to the publisher. This is honourable to the taste of our reading public. They are not mere works of amusement, but standard histories, recording the events of days and of countries widely separated.

NOVEMBER 1.—My journal partakes unavoidably in a large degree of the subject which occupies and absorbs the minds of nine-tenths of all the folks one meets about these times. Election, Monroe; abolition, Bradish; nullification, Calhoun,—all other topics run into and are swallowed up by this troubled reservoir of party spirit and infuriated patriotism. What a happy country to be so well looked after by its citizens! A man is almost considered tainted with treason toward the sovereign people who pretends to attend to his own business.

Jersey Elections.

NOVEMBER 2.—A great meeting of Whig merchants was held this day in Wall street, opposite the new Exchange. Benjamin Strong presided, with a number of vice-presidents. Spirited resolutions were adopted, condemning the measures of the Government, and inciting the merchants to union and exertion in the approaching election. But it was not required; the spirit of the Whigs is raised to the highest pitch. The merchants have given freely, the workingmen are prepared for action, and the whole party well organized. Our hopes are high, and every man in the Whig ranks says to his neighbour, in the words of one of Oliver Cromwell's officers, "Trust in the Lord, but keep your powder dry."

I was appointed by the committee to open the meeting and read the resolutions. I spoke for about twenty minutes, and then read the resolutions with all the voice I could command. But my position in the open air, with the large openings and broken masses behind me, made the task somewhat painful; but I believe nobody could have been better heard, for my voice is strong, and I think I read very distinctly.

The scene, from the elevation on which I was placed, was exceedingly picturesque. The immense mass of heads on the level street, the groups on blocks of granite and the irregular eminences of the unfinished edifice, the heads projecting from the windows, and the crowds on the stoops of the opposite side of Wall street, with the brightness of the weather, and the animated expression of every honest Whig face that beamed upon me while speaking, presented a *coup d'œil* such as no other occasion could have produced. After I finished, Mr. Perit addressed the meeting, when the question was put on adjournment, and the feelings of the people were so strongly and so agreeably excited that it was fairly voted down. They called for Hoffman: he was not there; for Chandler Starr: he was out of town; for me again: I had spoken; for "Anybody, then!" shouted half-a-dozen voices. At length a popular orator, Mr. Reynolds, came forward, made a long speech, which nineteen out of twenty did not hear, and the meeting then adjourned.

NOVEMBER 6. — The Whig cause continues bright as ever. The greatest procession of Whigs that ever assembled paraded the streets last evening, after the returns from the wards had been received at head-quarters. They honoured me with a visit, and their fine band played several martial airs before the house. I regretted much that I was not at home to address them.

NOVEMBER 7. — The election closed this day at sunset, after the severest contest we have ever known.

Whig Success.

The whole Whig ticket is elected. The official returns are, of course, not complete; but enough was known by eleven o'clock to make it certain that the Whig majority for the Congress ticket is about fifteen hundred, and the Assembly will not vary materially from that result.

The greatest excitement prevailed during the evening. Masonic Hall was crammed full, and the street from Pearl to Duane street a solid mass of Whigs, anxious at first and exulting afterward, but orderly during the whole time. This election probably determines the question in this State, and Mr. Van Buren's chance of reëlection may now be considered desperate. The good news of the election comes in from the North and West; the river counties have turned out better than we calculated. Dutchess and Ulster have given the Whigs thundering majorities. We have, without doubt, secured a majority of members of Congress, and Seward and Bradish are elected by large majorities over Marcy and Tracy. There is one alloy to this triumph, however. Benjamin Silliman, in Kings county, and John A. King, in Queens, two of the best members in the last House of Assembly, have lost their elections, the former by one or two votes, and the latter by thirty-two. The notes of victory were again sounded this evening before my house by the Whigs. I opened the window of the library, congratulated and thanked them, and they "went on their way rejoicing."

NOVEMBER 13. — The dark clouds which covered the political and mercantile horizon at the commencement of the last volume of my journal, and overshadowed the future prospect of individuals, though not entirely dispelled, have been broken, insomuch that some bright rays of sunshine do occasionally burst forth, and men are encouraged to hope for clearer skies and better days to come.

Business has revived. Debts from afar begin to come in without the sacrifice occasioned by ruinous exchanges. The English and French creditors have succeeded in collecting their American debts much better than they expected. Mechanics find good employment; the suspended improvements of our city in private and public buildings have been in many cases resumed, and to all this may be added the glorious victory of the Whigs in the election which has just terminated in this State. The returns of the election are all in but one or two small counties, which will not materially vary the result. We have lost two or three members of Congress and Assembly by very trifling majorities, so that we do not stand quite so well as was at first reported; but we have Congress 21 to 19 and Assembly 80 to 48. Seward and Bradish are elected by ten thousand to eleven thousand majority.

The only improvement in my private affairs is the increased facility I have found in borrowing money at a fair rate of interest on mortgage of my real estate, by which I have been enabled to pay a large proportion of the debts I assumed for my sons. But the collections come in very slowly, and I have no reasonable hope that the ultimate amount of my losses will be less than I calculated at first; still I have great reason to be thankful. My health and spirits are good; my family are all under my roof, in the enjoyment of health and happiness. My daughters are with us. Mary's health is improving daily. I stand as high, I hope, in the estimation of my fellow-citizens as I ever did, and with a firm trust in God all will yet be well.

Great Defalcation. The city has been agitated to-day by reports of a defalcation in the accounts of the late collector of the port, Samuel Swartwout, to the amount of a million and a quarter of dollars. He has taken the public money and engaged with it in wild speculations of Texas lands, gold mines, and other humbugs, which have caused ruin for several years past to men of more means and greater judgment than Mr. Swartwout. A large proportion of this abstraction of the public funds took place during the first two years of his collectorship, and the amount has been increasing ever since. How it was possible that so enormous a deficiency should never have been discovered until now is perfectly inconceivable ! It is a dreadful commentary upon the manner of conducting business at Washington, and it would appear impossible that there should not have been connivance on the part of some of the coördinate branches of the department, either there or here. This is a pretty illustration of Mr. Van Buren's hopeful sub-treasury scheme, by which the collectors are made the depositaries of the public money Banks are not to be trusted. The money must not be lent, upon the best securities in the world, to the merchants whose enterprise has earned, and whose integrity has paid it to the Government ; but such men as Mr. Swartwout may take it to speculate in land in the moon, or elsewhere not much nearer home, or in imaginary treasures which the teeming earth is supposed to hold within its womb, and as yet has refused to render up even to such skilful midwives as our late collector.

President Jackson, on his accession to office, made a great fuss about public defaulters, prosecuted several petty offenders, whom he got imprisoned, and swore in his usual amiable manner that they should never be released, and at the same time appointed his personal friends, who were notoriously irresponsible, to offices of the highest trust, whose claims consisted only in their unscrupulous devotion to him and his party ; and when a committee of Congress was raised to investigate the affairs of the treasury department, which investigation would have naturally led to the discovery of this and other similar frauds, he interposed between his servants and the representatives of the people, would not allow them to answer questions, and took upon himself the responsibility.

The Hone Club dined yesterday with Moses H. Grinnell. We had Hoffman, Curtis, Wetmore, and other Whigs. There were more guests and more dinner than the law allows ; but I suppose it must be overlooked, in consideration of this being the first dinner which our friend has given since his election to Congress.

I went this evening with the Schermerhorns to the farewell benefit of Mr. Charles Matthews, at the Park Theatre. It was a full house; but he and his wife have not received the encouragement which foreign stars usually receive in this country, nor do I think as much as they deserved. They came out upon a long engagement, which their want of success has suddenly terminated, and they return disappointed, and ready (as in the case of Matthews's father) to abuse us for the want of a proper appreciation of their talents.

Visit to Boston. NOVEMBER 15. — Mr. Webster, having invited Messrs. Draper, Duer, Blatchford, and myself to dine with him in Boston, we prepared to go this day; but the weather proving unfavorable I gave up all thought of going until I received a note from Draper ordering me on board the steamboat at half-past four o'clock; so I took an early dinner, and met Draper on board the "Narragansett" at that hour. Messrs. Duer and Blatchford being prevented from going, the party was reduced to Draper and myself.

NOVEMBER 16. — Mr. Draper and I left New York in a northeast storm, arrived at Stonington at two in the morning, and came to Boston, by the railroad, at nine o'clock this morning. This is a most expeditious mode of travelling; leaving New York at the close of one day and being in Boston, two hundred and forty miles away, at the commencement of the next.

Mr. Webster called at the Tremont House as soon as we arrived and invited us to dine. He and I walked out. In the course of our walk we called upon Mr. H. G Otis and Colonel Perkins; both these worthy old sons are laid up with the gout. We did not see the Colonel, and I afterward received a kind note from him, urging me to repeat my visit. Mr. Otis wants me to dine with him to-morrow, and in the evening he repeated his invitation in a note. Several other friends called and invited me; but the weather promises to be fine to-morrow, Mr. Draper must be at home on Sunday, so I shall not extend the flying visit to Boston beyond its original limits.

We met a pleasant party at dinner at Mr. Webster's · Governor

Everett; Mr. Winthrop, the Speaker; Governor Lincoln; Mr. Ticknor, who has lately returned from Europe; Mr. Fletcher Webster, of Illinois, and his pretty wife, who are on a visit to their father; Messrs. Davis, Sturges, etc. We sat until eleven o'clock.

NOVEMBER 17. — I received the usual kind calls this morning, and pressing invitations to dinner, and availed myself of a fine cold day to walk out and see the Boston lions and make some visits; among the rest to Colonel Perkins, who lives *en prince*, and has a fine collection of pictures, to which he made many valuable additions during his last visit to Europe.

Arrival of the "Great Western." NEW YORK, Nov. 19. — On Thursday last arrived the successful steam-packet "Great Western." She sailed from Bristol on the 28th of October; has had very hard weather and heavy winds. She has many passengers; in the number are Mr. and Mrs. William H. Aspinwall, Mr. William Heyward and his family, Rev. Dr. Schroeder and his family, and my old acquaintance, Vincent Nolte.

Captain Marryat. NOVEMBER 21. — In the ship "President," which sailed yesterday for London, went passenger Captain Marryat, not any better pleased with the Americans than they with him. It would have been better for both parties if the sailor author had been known on this side of the Atlantic only by his writings. When he arrived in New York he brought me a letter of introduction. I called upon him, and he dined with us; but neither I nor my family, nor the friends whom I invited to meet him, could discover in his conversation any of the talents which his works had taught us to expect, or in his deportment the ease and knowledge of the world which is frequently to be met in its pages.

He is a good seaman without doubt, and has, somehow or other, the materials for writing good stories, and a style well calculated to give them popularity; but he has evidently never enjoyed the benefits of refined society, or intercourse with people of literary talents. He is a sort of Basil Hall, without his impudence.

Wall-street Property.   The house at the corner of Wall and Hanover streets has been sold to the North American Trust and Banking Company, by Thomas E. Davis, for the enormous sum of $223,000; higher than anything which has yet been heard of. This building is somewhat notorious from its having been erected upon the site of one built by J. L. and S. Joseph, which, about the time it was completed, fell to the ground one night with a crash which shook all Wall street; and its fall was the precursor of a much more tremendous crash in that celebrated street, commencing with the failure of the firm that erected it, and ending with the suspension of specie payments, and the bankruptcy of one-half of the merchants and traders of New York.

NOVEMBER 22. — This gentleman has just been publishing two new works, "Homeward Bound" and "Home as Found," which are reviewed, and the author most unmercifully scourged, in an able leading article of the "Courier and Enquirer" of this morning; a more severe, and, I add, a better written, castigation was never inflicted upon an arrogant, acrimonious writer than this. Mr. Cooper, spoiled at first by the kindness of his countrymen, and inflated by the praise of Europeans, who read his books without coming into personal contact with the writer, has returned to his own country full of malicious spleen against his countrymen, because, as I verily believe, he could not bully them into approving his dogmatical opinions, and liking his swaggering airs as well as the patriotic principles and unpretending deportment of his distinguished rival, Washington Irving.

Fenimore Cooper.

The works now published, of which copious extracts are made in the "Courier and Enquirer," represent everything in this country in the most disparaging light; the misrepresentations are as gross, and the uncharitable temper as disgusting, as anything to be found in Basil Hall's, or Captain Hamilton's, or Mrs. Trollope's lying histories, and (what is more wonderful coming from such a quarter) the style of the works is puerile and the incidents ridiculous; more worthy of the talents of a silly girl than of the matured genius of the author of "The Spy" and "The Pioneers."

NOVEMBER 23. — In the packet-ship "Siddons," which arrived yesterday, came passengers, Mr. William Brown and his lady, of Liverpool. Mr. Brown is the senior partner in the great house of William and James Brown & Co., of that place. They have, I presume, come out to attend the wedding of their only son, who is to marry his cousin, the daughter of Mr. James Brown, of this city.

DECEMBER 5. — Congress met on Monday. The House is so nearly divided that it is not probable that the sub-treasury scheme, or any other of the Government abominations, can be carried through. The President's message was sent to Congress on Tuesday, at twelve o'clock, and, by an arrangement made by the post-office with the railroad, reached the city of Jersey, two hundred and forty-five miles, at half-past ten o'clock last evening, and was delivered at our post-office. If this is not quick work, the deuce is in it, — twenty-three miles an hour, the whole distance, one-half of it after dark.

Meeting of Congress.

The message is long enough, six newspaper columns closely printed. There is the usual quantity of humbug about the power of the sovereign people, although all the world knows that the writer and "his illustrious predecessor" have done more to crib this power from the dear people than any who went before them; a plentiful use of such pretty, set phrases as "The anti-republican tendencies of associated wealth," "Vortex of reckless speculation," "Banks perverting the operations of the Government to their own purposes," and such unmeaning twaddle, whilst he knows in his heart and soul that he and his party in his own State have created all the banks here to subserve their political objects ever since they have had the ascendency, and now rail against them when their subserviency begins to fail. He does not say a word this time about the elections, nor does he seek to propitiate the "sober, second thoughts of the people," having found that to be "no go."

DECEMBER 6. — The anniversary dinner of the St.
Nicholas Society was held to-day, at the American
Hotel. Mr. Cozzens gave as good a dinner as I ever
sat down to; all excellent, hot and well served, and the wines
capital. There was the usual quantity of toasting and speaking.
The President (Mr. Verplanck) made a long address, in the form
of an annual report of the state of the society, in his quaint, amusing style. Dr. Francis, as physician-general, was very happy. I
made a short address when called upon, and concluded with the
following toast: New Yorkers, "at home" to all the world; let
them not forget that they are masters of the house.

St. Nicholas Dinner.

William M. Price, the United States Attorney for
this district, another of General Jackson's pets, and
one of Mr. Van Buren's depositaries of the public
money, "in spite" (as Mr. Cambreling said) "of the lamentations of the people," took himself off this morning "without
beat of drum." His flight was not known until an hour or two
after the departure of the British steamer "Liverpool," when Wall
street was in an uproar on the receipt of the intelligence that this
faithful steward of the Government was a passenger.

Another Defaulter.

These are the men who, for political services formerly rendered
(and in the case of Price continued unblushingly to the last), were
appointed to the two most responsible offices in the gift of the
general Government, at a time when neither of them could have got
the credit upon his personal responsibility for a hundred dollars.
Here are some of the fruits of the corrupt, demoralizing system
which originated with his country's curse, Andrew Jackson, and has
been unscrupulously carried out by the puppet who thought it
"honour enough to follow in the footsteps of his illustrious predecessor." Price was formerly a violent, brawling Federalist, and
when he found he could get nothing by that he became a Democrat and Tammany man, more violent and brawling louder even
than he did on the other side, but with better success. He became
the Marat, the Danton of the party, the Anacharsis Clootz, the

orator, *not* of the human race, but of the profligate race whose vigils were held at Tammany Hall and the several subordinate pandemoniums of the respective wards; supporting through thick and thin the pernicious measures of his master, and denouncing all honest men who dared to doubt their infallibility. A demagogue of the first rank, he was precisely the man they wanted. They knew their *Price*, and he knew his, and the unsuccessful Jacobin of the Federal party became the pampered minion of the Loco-focos.

The city is in an uproar; every hour brings fresh reports. This glorious election! Well are we rewarded for time and money spent and services rendered in the good cause. The light of truth is now penetrating into the dark recesses of corruption. The spoilers will be condemned to disgorge the spoils which they have themselves "told us belong to the victors," and, if it be not too late, honest men may come to their rights and the Republic be saved.

DECEMBER 7. — The breaking up of the Loco-foco forces in different parts of the country produces every day some new development of party atrocity; a state of things exists in Pennsylvania extremely alarming; little short, indeed, of civil war. The return of the judges of the election for the county of Philadelphia being in favor of the Whig candidates, they, as well as those on the other side, appeared at Harrisburg on Tuesday last, at the organization of the Legislature, and claimed their seats as members of the House of Representatives. The Whigs, having the returns of a majority of the judges, were entitled to their seats until the house was organized to receive the protest of their opponents; but this legal course of proceeding was opposed by the Van Buren men, and a scene occurred more outrageous than ever before witnessed in a country professing to be governed by written law and established rules. Both parties elected their own Speaker, and both proceeded to business in the same hall. Confusion and disorder reigned for a time, until brutal violence was resorted to and the hall was left in possession of the Loco-focos, supported by a mob of ruffians in

Party Violence.

the galleries. The whole was a scene hitherto paralleled only by the sittings of the National Assembly of France, or the Jacobin Club of Paris in the horrid days of anarchy and bloodshed which ushered in the Revolution and led to the destruction of everything "good and lovely and of good report" in that devoted country. God grant that the same causes here may not produce the same results! Virtuous men here begin to fear the worst. Now is the critical moment of our country's fate. If the Whigs continue to grow in numbers and remain firm in the good cause they may succeed in subjecting the rabble of Loco-foco Jacobins to the power of the laws; but if not, the time is close, very close, at hand, when this noble country of ours will be subject to all the horrors of civil war; our republican institutions, theoretically so beautiful, but relying unfortunately too much upon the virtue and intelligence of the people, will be broken into pieces, and a suffering and abused nation will be compelled to submit to the degrading alternative of Jacobin misrule or the tyranny of a Cæsar, a Cromwell, or a Bonaparte. To return to Harrisburg: the mob having possession of the Representatives' hall next attacked the Senate, where the Whig majority is so large that no dispute could possibly arise. That House attempted to meet in the afternoon, but the same scene was re-enacted there; riot and confusion prevailed throughout. The president's chair was usurped by a demagogue named John McCahen, who addressed the ruffians around him, instigating them to violence. The senators were assailed, beaten, dragged out, and driven from their seats. The accounts do not as yet inform us that any lives were lost. The Governor has issued his proclamation, calling out the troops, and general orders are published in the Pennsylvania papers for troops to assemble and march from other parts of the State to Harrisburg, the seat of war.

The times are out of joint. The United States are surrounded by difficulties and dangers requiring a strong arm and a better head and purer political morality than are ever to be found in a mere party manager and popular demagogue. The dishonest servants of a corrupt administration running away with the people's money; the halls of Legislature invaded in a neighbouring state by a ruthless faction, and the laws of the Commonwealth openly set at defiance; abolitionism fomented by fanaticism on one side, and restricted by pride on the other; our misguided citizens meddling with other people's concerns on the northern frontier, and running their foolish heads into Canadian halters, and sympathizing on the southern with a band of reckless buccaneers whose brotherhood would lead to endless strife and ultimate disunion; the treasure and blood of the republic expended and spilt in an Indian warfare in tenfold quantities, to remedy the bad management of our rulers; character, talents, and moral worth rendered of no account in competition with the claims of political services, — from the effect of all these evils " Good Lord, deliver us!"

Election of Benton. DECEMBER 8. — The Legislature of the State of Missouri did themselves the *distinguished honour*, on the 21st of last month, to elect that prince of humbugs and enlightener of the Loco-focos, Mr. T. H. Benton, senator of the United States for six mortal years more.

Anti-abolition Violence. The Baptist meeting-house at Reading, Conn., was blown up by gunpowder on the night of the 28th of last month. A man named Colver, an abolition lecturer, had been holding forth in the church, and was to lecture again, when a fanatic on the other side of the question placed a keg of powder under the pulpit, and blew the whole "sky high."

An Unexpected Visitor. We had to dine with us to-day Mr. Christopher Hughes, American *chargé* at Stockholm, Col. Webb, Mr. William B. Astor, and Dr. Francis. Whilst we were at dinner there was a ring at the street door-bell. The boy Daniel went out, and found nobody there; but there was a basket on the sill of the door, which he brought into the dining-room, and it was found to contain a lovely infant, apparently about a week old, stowed away nicely in soft cotton. It had on a clean worked muslin frock, lace cap, its under-clothes new and perfectly clean, a locket on the neck which opened with a spring and contained a lock of dark hair; the whole covered nicely with a piece of new flannel, and a label was pinned on the breast on which was written, in a female hand, Alfred G. Douglas. It was one of the sweetest babies I ever saw; apparently healthy. It did not cry during the time we had it, but laid in a placid, dozing state, and occasionally, on the approach of the light, opened its little, sparkling eyes, and seemed satisfied with the company into which it had been so strangely introduced. Poor little innocent, — abandoned by its natural protector, and thrown at its entrance into life upon the sympathy of a selfish world, to be exposed, if it should live, to the sneers and taunts of uncharitable legitimacy! How often in his future life may the bitter wish swell in his heart and rise to his lips, that those eyes which now opened so mildly upon me whilst I was gazing upon his innocent face had been forever closed. My feelings were strongly interested, and I felt inclined at first to take in and cherish the little stranger; but this was strongly opposed by the company, who urged, very properly, that in that case I would have twenty more such outlets to my benevolence. I reflected, moreover, that if the little urchin should turn out bad, he would prove a troublesome inmate; and if intelligent and good, by the time he became an object of my affection the rightful owners might come and take him away. So John Stotes was summoned, and sent off with the little wanderer to the almshouse.

The group in the kitchen which surrounded the basket, before John took it away, would have furnished a capital subject for a painter. There was the elegant diplomat, the inquisitive doctor, the bluff editor, and the calculating millionnaire; my wife and daughters, standing like the daughters of Pharoah over the infant Moses in the bulrushes, — all interested, but differently affected, the maids shoving forward to get a last peep; little

Emily, the black cook, ever and anon showing her white teeth; James and Dannie in the background, wondering that so great a fuss should be made about so small a matter; and John, wrapped up in his characteristically neat overcoat, waiting, with all the dignified composure which marks his demeanor, to receive his interesting charge and convey it to its destination.

DECEMBER 12. — The troops from Philadelphia, *Pennsylvania Rebellion.* under the command of General Patterson, having arrived at Harrisburg, something like order has been restored, and the two houses of the Legislature have met daily, not in their usual place of meeting, nor for the despatch of business, but for the purpose of adjourning legally. Commodore Elliott has also arrived, with other officers, under the authority of the general Government, to command the United States forces at Carlisle. These measures may keep the insurrection under whilst the troops are present; but the flame appears to be only smothered, to break out whenever they are withdrawn. Charles J. Ingersoll, the author of all the mischief, and other leaders must be hanged to restore order.

DECEMBER 14. — Hospital in the morning, Savings-bank in the afternoon, and, afterward, dinner at Mr. Abraham Schermerhorn's. I did not, of course, arrive at my last post of duty until an hour after the time I was invited for dinner, but quite in time for all beneficial purposes. I noticed a fact at the dinner table to-day, which proves the increased intercourse between the people of the United States and Europe. Of a party of twenty seated at the table every person has been to Europe, although of the number only two, Mr. Schmidt and Mr. Maitland, were foreigners. When I first dined out frequently, that distinguished class of *learned pundits* who had been "abroad," as the term then was, was so small, that if we had one native who had enjoyed that high privilege in a dinner-party he was looked up to with profound respect and deference; "a rare bird, and somewhat like a black swan." Now the streams of accumulated knowledge may be obtained at innumerable fountains: the families of Abraham Schermerhorn, of James J. Jones, of T. L. Gibbes, of Nathaniel Prime do pour forth streams of intellectuality (I wish I had the wheelbarrow which Dr. Francis alluded to at the St. Nicholas Dinner, to carry this long word) sufficient to assuage the thirst of the most ardent and untravelled seeker of knowledge.

DECEMBER 15.—A Loco-foco member of Congress, *Congressional Proceedings.* from Maine, named Atherton, brought into the House of Representatives, on Tuesday last, certain resolutions on the subject of slavery, declaring that the subject was not to be touched, that no petitions should be received, and that Congress had no right to meddle with slavery in the District of Columbia. This political tool was instigated to this measure by his brother Locos of the South, who were, no doubt, pledged to uphold him in his subsequent course. The resolutions may or may not have been proper; that is not the question; but the outrageous impudence of the fellow, and the profligate support which it received from his unprincipled party, were evinced in his speaking for nearly an hour in support of his resolutions, and concluding by moving the previous question, thereby precluding all reply, and forcing the dose down the reluctant throats of men of all political parties. And to the disgrace of the House, and the mortification of all honourable men, the motion was carried and the resolutions adopted without a word of comment (even to the phraseology, which John P. Kennedy said was so ungrammatical that his stomach, which had been to school, could not swallow it), except those which the mover had used in their favor, which it is presumed he thought unanswerable, and therefore determined should remain unanswered.

I do not recollect that this precise case has ever occurred before. Its unblushing impudence is absolutely amusing. But I would ask the *southern* gentleman from Maine, whether some of his sagacious constituents *down east* may not consider it a sort of acknowledgment of weakness, and dread of consequences a little similar to that of the school-boy, who, coming behind his companion, hits him a punk on the back, and then takes to his heels for fear of the counter-punk.

Mrs. Brevoort's Party. DECEMBER 17. — Mrs. Brevoort opened her splendid house on Saturday evening to a large party. I went with my daughter. It was a grand affair; there is not a house in the city so well calculated to entertain such an assemblage; five large rooms open on one floor, and a spacious hall besides, with a noble staircase. This is the first time all this has been shown to the *bon-ton*, and the capriciousness of the master and mistress is so great that it may remain a sealed book for half a dozen years, unless the present freak should continue.

The "Utica" brings the intelligence of the death of Mrs. Eliza Rumpff, wife of Vincent Rumpff, minister resident at Paris from the Hanse towns, and daughter of Mr. John Jacob Astor. She died at her residence in Switzerland, near Geneva. This lady leaves no children. There are, therefore, but three children to inherit the largest fortune in the State, — William B. Astor, Mrs. Langdon, and a son who is not likely to interfere with the claims of the others. If William lives to old age he will probably be richer than his father now is.

DECEMBER 25. — The club dined yesterday at Mr. Crumby's, Bond street. Of the members, Messrs. Grinnell and Duer were absent; a good dinner, good singing, and plenty of wine. The following ode, which I wrote for the club, having been set to music by Mr. C. E. Horn, was sung, for the first time, by Major Tucker: —

ODE FOR THE HONE CLUB.

I.

Our club, like a jury impanelled, we view,
Composed of twelve freemen, all good men and true;
We have hearts for our country, religion, and laws,
And we find a true verdict in her holy cause.
   Answer, then, Mr. Foreman, are you all agreed?
    President: Agreed.
    Chorus: Agreed, agreed; we are all of one mind.
      For our country and freedom, our verdict we find.

2.

Will you stand by her commerce, unfettered and free?
Shall the Star Spangled Banner still float on each sea?
Shall mercantile faith a just recompense claim,
Protection at home, and abroad a good name?
  How answer you then? Are you all agreed?
    President : Agreed.
    Chorus : Agreed, agreed; we are all of one mind,
        To stand by the merchants, our verdict we find.

3.

In the cause now before you, the plaintiffs appear,
Good order, and Reason, and Union are here;
'Gainst corruption and power they plead their own cause,
Relying on Truth, Constitution, and Laws;
  Shall the good cause prevail? Are you all agreed?
    President : Agreed.
    Chorus : Agreed, agreed; we are all of one mind,
        In support of the good cause, our verdict we find.

4.

Shall Truth, Love, and Friendship our club still unite,
And the cares of the day ne'er extend to the night?
Shall innocent mirth and good-humour abound,
And our bosom beat high as each Monday comes 'round?
  Gentlemen of the jury, are you all agreed?
    President : Agreed.
    Chorus . Agreed, agreed; we are all of one mind,
        For Truth, Love, and Friendship, our verdict we find.

5.

Shall our bumpers be quaffed as the wine sparkles bright,
And the talesmen join who are with us to-night?
Our hearts warmed by friendship, the toast shall it pass,
" May temperance fill, and joy empty, the glass " ?
  In this honest toast you are surely agreed?
    President : Agreed.
    Chorus : Agreed, agreed; we are all of one mind,
        For temperate enjoyment, our verdict we find.

1839.

JANUARY 1. — The year 1839 commences under more favourable auspices. The commerce of the country is much improved; such of the merchants as have been only sadly bent are considerably straightened; the broken ones remain broken; for myself, although not a merchant, I have been a severe sufferer as surety for others. There is an awful change in my circumstances, which can never be repaired. I have lost two-thirds of my fortune, and I have only to call to my aid philosophy and resignation, and to be thankful for the blessings I still enjoy. It is a consolation that as yet I have met all my obligations honourably, and have no reason to fear my ability to continue to do so. My children shall inherit a good name from their father; they must make the most of it, for I greatly fear it will be their only inheritance.

In a political view matters have improved during the last year. The elections, in the aggregate, have been favourable to the Whig cause. Parties in the present House of Representatives are equally balanced. The next will have a majority of Whigs, without any reasonable doubt. In the State of New York we have a Whig Governor, and a majority of about forty in the House of Assembly; but, unfortunately, we are in a minority in the Senate: that, too, we shall correct in the fall election. The city for the first time in many years will be represented in the next Congress by four Whigs, and the Mayor and a majority in both branches of the Common Council are on the same side. On the whole, we may sing

" A requiem for thirty-eight,
And a health to thirty-nine."

JANUARY 7. — The club dined at Mr. Russell's, Messrs. Duer and Colt absent. We had, among the supernumeraries, Mr. Webster, who is here on his way to Washington. He was in exuberant spirits, and more agreeable than I have seen him on any former occasion. We sat until eleven o'clock, and broke up after a grand chorus of "Auld Lang Syne."

JANUARY 28.—I heard a capital sermon yesterday morning in Trinity Church, from Professor McVickar, of Columbia College. He does not often treat us; but when he does, it is a treat indeed. He comes with a sermon well prepared, logical, learned, of the purest English, and a style surpassingly beautiful. His voice is bad, and it causes a little pain to listen so closely as is necessary for one who, like myself, has not the sharpest ears in the world, in order that no part should be lost of that which is so well worth hearing.

Professor McVickar.

Take this gentleman for "all in all," he is the loveliest man I ever knew, and I consider the intimacy which exists between us one of the greatest privileges and highest honours I enjoy. He has "dropt in" frequently of late to see us; last evening he sat about an hour, cheerful, playful, and instructive; such a mixture of learning and simplicity; a head so sound and a heart so light; a conscience free from reproach, and an imagination poetical as that of a youthful lover! And this man is seventy-five years of age. So much for good habits, early assumed and never departed from; industry, sobriety, a course of life void of offence before God and man; an enthusiastic love of literature and an habitual aversion to debt, that fell disturber of the happiness of professional men. Such is James Kent. May he live as long as this world and those "which it inherit" shall continue pleasant to him! As for myself, "I wish that Heaven had made *me* such a man."

Chancellor Kent.

This excellent man, the contemporary and friend of James Kent, I now mention on this page, not to record his living virtues, but to mourn his decease. He died on Saturday last, at his home in Albany, suddenly, whilst seated at the dinner-table. General Van Rensselaer has been better known

Stephen Van Rensselaer.

by the familiar and affectionate title of "The Patroon," — a Dutch word to express "The lord of the manor," from his extensive patrimonial estates. He has held many important civil and military offices. He was a Federalist of "the old school," and the candidate of that party on more than one occasion for the office of governor. Few men were more extensively known and beloved. Of gentlemanly manners, one of "the Lord's noblemen," of an amiable disposition, great benevolence, and active public spirit. His ability to do good, which from his great wealth was greater than that of most of his fellow-citizens, was never sparingly exerted for the benefit of his fellow-men, nor for the promotion of the public works of the State. He was closely identified with the great Canal System, and an early and active coadjutor of DeWitt Clinton in the great work which immortalized him.

JANUARY 29. — My wife and I dined with Mr. and Mrs. T. W. Ludlow; the party consisted of Mr. and Mrs. Abraham Ogden, Mr. and Mrs. Abraham Schermerhorn, Mr. and Mrs. Archibald Gracie, General and Miss Tallmadge, Mr. Gabriel Shaw, Mr. William H. Harrison, and ourselves.

MARCH 18. — We had an uncommonly pleasant
Hone Club.   dinner of the club at Blatchford's, — gay, jovial, and somewhat noisy. This was caused by the presence of several distinguished and agreeable guests: Mr. Webster, Mr. Southard, Mr. Meredith, Mr. Hoffman, Mr. Curtis, Mr. John A. King, and Mr. Young. We sat until to-morrow was near at hand.

MARCH 22. — The rumors of war on the north-
Hard Times.   eastern boundary, — burn the pine logs which have set it a-going, — together with the bank difficulties in the Southern and Western States, occasioned by a premature resumption of specie payments, have caused another panic in New York. The blossoms of hope which had sprung up in the brief sunshine of confidence are again blighted by the frost of suspicion. The pockets of rich men which had opened a little are now closely buttoned up, and "No trust" is once more the chilling maxim of

commercial dealings. Stocks have fallen suddenly; trade is at a standstill. New York cannot collect her debts, and the banks are looking to their own safety. In the mean time the markets are higher than ever. Beef and mutton sell at eighteen to twenty-five cents a pound, and how the poor man manages to get a dinner for his family passes my comprehension. Suppose we succeed in turning out Van Buren and his scurvy pack, shall we be any better off? Doubtful, very doubtful!

MARCH 29. — I went, as usual, to church this morn-
Good Friday. ing, and afterward into Wall street, where the din of business drowns the sound of the bell's invitation to worship, and the gravity of devotion is put out of countenance by the restless, anxious looks of speculative men of "this world." Good Friday was formerly kept with a considerable degree of solemnity. The banks and most of the shops were kept closed, and Episcopalians, especially, made it a point to abstain from business as strictly on that day as on the Sabbath; but it is now scarcely observed at all. A few " church people " attend worship in the morning of the day, and usually hear an excellent sermon; for if there be anything *in* the preacher, the sanctity of the occasion, and the touching service of the church for the day cannot fail to bring it *out;* but as for the suspension of business, the high rents in Broadway and the dearness of the markets will not allow the shopkeepers to lose a day.

MARCH 30. — The monster no longer keeps guard
Mr. Biddle's at the mouth of his den. The spectre which for so
Resignation. long a time frighted old Jackson "from his propriety," and subsequently disturbed the slumbers of his successor, is "laid in the Red Sea;" or, to speak more to the point, the undaunted opponent of arbitrary power, and the skilful regulator of currency and credit, has retired from the field of his triumph and his labours. The resignation of Mr. Biddle as a director and the president of the Bank of the United States is announced in the papers of this day. This event, unexpected here, and known only to a few friends in

Philadelphia, took place yesterday, in an address to the directors. He puts his resignation upon the ground of a desire for retirement, the necessity for which is indicated by a delicate state of health, which may be attributed to most laborious exertions for twenty years past in the service of the bank. This is, no doubt, the true reason, although rumor has given out others, among which is the preposterous one of his being called by Mr. Van Buren to the head of the Treasury Department. A better appointment, certainly, could not be made; but the President is not in the habit of doing magnanimous deeds, and, besides, it would not work well for his political objects. His own party would find it somewhat difficult to justify the appointment of a man whom they have been taught by their masters for the last eight years to decry and vilify at Tammany Hall, and all the outposts of the Loco-foco army of stipendiaries. Nor would he get credit with his political adversaries for honest intentions, or a desire to promote the public good. The public good! Fudge! What does it mean? The term is often used for purposes of humbug, but its meaning is obsolete.

The truth is, that Mr. Biddle is a good writer, and rather prone to trifle in the flowery paths of poetry; and now that he has had glory enough as a financier, it is not unnatural that he should seek for literary distinction. Besides, he possesses a beautiful seat on the banks of the Delaware, where there is a miniature fac-simile of the monster's marble den in Chestnut street; and he raises fine grapes, and gets a good price for them in the Philadelphia market, and has as good a right to enjoy *otium cum dignitate* as anybody I know.

APRIL 5. — Died on Tuesday last, at Wilmington, Delaware, Hezekiah Niles, the conductor of "Niles' Register" (the best statistical publication and record of national events in this country), and the father of the "American System." His name stood high on the *tariff* of private worth and public service.

APRIL 8. — Attended the monthly meeting of the vestry of Trinity Church. An application from a committee of the Historical Society for the use of St. Paul's Church, in which to celebrate the other, "Commodore Trunnion" and "Tom Pipes," from "Roderick Random," both admirable; indeed, I prefer the latter to a new picture of Mount's, "The Rabbit Trappers," which he has painted for Mr. Charles A. Davis.

I am puzzled to know how Mr. Edmonds finds time, in the midst of his laborious occupation as cashier of the Leather Manufacturers' Bank, to devote himself to an art so foreign to his ordinary pursuits, and how, under so great a disadvantage, he should have arrived at such proficiency.

Death of General Smith, of Baltimore. APRIL 24. — Mr. Christopher Hughes has just heard of the death of his father-in-law, General Samuel Smith, of Baltimore, who died on Monday last, in the eighty-seventh year of his age. His death was remarkable, and such as every old man should desire. He had returned from riding, lay upon the sofa to refresh himself, and was found dead by a servant who entered the room.

General Smith was another of the old revolutionary officers, to whom the country owes so much, and pays so little. Happily, in his case no pecuniary aid was requisite; he was a rich man. He signalized himself on several occasions during the war of the Revolution, and has been almost constantly since in public life; for many years a representative of the State of Maryland in the Senate of the United States, frequently in the Legislature of that State, and at the time of his death Mayor of Baltimore, to which latter office he was elected (although an administration man, unopposed by the Whigs) for his gallant conduct on a recent occasion when the peace of the city was disturbed by one of those mobs to which Baltimore has unhappily been rather frequently exposed.

APRIL 25. — In the packet-ship "Siddons," which sailed to-day for Liverpool, went passengers, Mr. William Brown and wife, of Liverpool; their son, Mr. Alexander Brown, and his wife, the daughter of James Brown, of this city. These are all partners or adjuncts of the great mercantile houses of William and James Brown & Co., of Liverpool, and Brown Brothers & Co., of New York.

The visit of William Brown and his wife has been very pleasant. They have married their only son to his cousin, and thereby keep the cash from going out of the family. They have travelled a great deal in the United States, visiting last winter the Falls of Niagara, passed considerable time with their friends here and in Baltimore, and now return in a fine ship, at the most favourable season of the year; and in twenty days probably the senior will again be engaged in making money, the junior in devising plans to spend it, and the ladies in telling their friends and neighbours "all about it."

APRIL 26. — General Scott has returned from his last excursion to the northern frontier, where he was sent to set matters to rights between the *loafer* royalists of Canada and the *loafer* patriots of the United States. I do not know how he has succeeded, for I was not at home when he did us the honour to call this morning. The girls saw him, and say he looks very well, considering the labour he has performed within the last two or three months, during which time he has been constantly employed in the public service, adding to his military renown the blessings which await the "peacemaker." In the course of this severe tour of duty he has travelled (by land principally) forty-seven hundred miles. He is now "the observed of all observers;" and who knows what he may be hereafter?

Celebration of the Historical Society.
APRIL 30. — The semi-centennial celebration of the Inauguration of Washington, which took place in this city on the 30th of April, 1789, was held this day, and went off triumphantly. I was one of the committee of arrangements, and, as the day approached, became extremely anxious and nervous, from an apprehension that sufficient interest had not been excited, and that the distinguished guests of the society from other States might witness a failure. But my fears were groundless. It could not have been better.

The members of the society and invited guests assembled at the City Hotel, and walked in procession to the New Dutch Church, in the fiftieth anniversary of the Inauguration of Washington, was refused (improperly, I think). Preparations are making by the society to have a grand affair on this occasion, on the 30th. Mr. John Quincy Adams has consented to deliver the oration.

<small>Arrival of the "Great Western."</small> APRIL 15. — The arrival of this packet has been looked for with great anxiety. She sailed on March 23, and arrived at twelve o'clock last night, having encountered on her voyage an unchanging series of head-winds and severe gales. This is the longest voyage the "Great Western" has ever made; but it proves, more than any other, the advantage of steam navigation. Captain Hoskin says that a sailing-vessel would not (with the wind and weather he has had) have been now more than three days on her way out.

The Hone Club dined at Mr. Amory's. All the members were present except Mr. Duer, — gone to Europe. In the number of guests was Mr. Webster, jovial and agreeable as usual. I think it not by any means improbable that if a special minister should be appointed by the President, under the act of Congress, to go to England about the boundary question, Mr. Webster may be the man. He told me that the Governor of Maine, the members of Congress, and the Legislature of that State had united without regard to party in an application to that effect, and I am tolerably sure that he expects it.

APRIL 20. — Died last evening, at Jersey City, Colonel Aaron Ogden, aged eighty-three years. He was one of the noble band of revolutionary soldiers, which is now nearly extinct. A fine old American gentleman; but, like many of his class, his latter years were sparingly cheered by the smiles of fortune, and he was compelled to rely upon the scanty emoluments of the office of collector of the port, without commerce, of the City of Jersey.

<small>"Old Ironsides."</small> APRIL 23. — The frigate "Constitution," the fine old bull-dog whose bark was heard first in the late war, is now in our harbour, waiting to sail on a cruise, under command of Captain Claxton. She lies at anchor in the North

river, off the Battery, in the tranquillity of strength. The "Massachusetts" steamer, on her return yesterday from the excursion to Sandy Hook, passed up the river close to her, and gave us an opportunity to see this noble arm of the naval power of the United States.

Artists' Supper.

I went this evening to the Artists' Supper of the National Academy, to which I was invited as an honorary member. This entertainment was given preparatory to the opening to-morrow of the spring exhibition. The number at table was about fifty, with the estimable president, Mr. Morse, at the head, who returned from Europe in the "Great Western," and myself in the post of honour, at his right hand. Our table was placed in the middle of the great exhibition-room, brilliantly lighted, and we were surrounded by the beautiful collection of pictures, fresh from the easels of the accomplished artists, who were partaking of the double enjoyment of the banquet before them and the well-earned reputation derived from the successful result of their interesting labours. How insignificant, in comparison to these, would have been the most gorgeous array of costly mirrors, luxurious hangings, rich carpets, and golden ornaments ! These are, indeed, the precious products of an art the tendency of which is to refine the mind, enrich the imagination, and soften the heart of man.

This will be one of the best exhibitions of the Academy. It is delightful to witness the improvement from year to year of the young artists, the result of study and practice under the instruction and from the fine classical models of the Academy ; and the older members grow richer and more mellow as their talents ripen into maturity.

The school of Mount, the American Wilkie, appears to have attracted many aspirants after the honours of that class of subjects in which he excels, and they have produced several capital things. Foremost in the number stands two pictures by Mr. Edmonds, an amateur painter, — one representing the reading of a penny paper ;

the other, "Commodore Trunnion" and "Tom Pipes," from "Roderick Random," both admirable; indeed, I prefer the latter to a new picture of Mount's, "The Rabbit Trappers," which he has painted for Mr. Charles A. Davis.

I am puzzled to know how Mr. Edmonds finds time, in the midst of his laborious occupation as cashier of the Leather Manufacturers' Bank, to devote himself to an art so foreign to his ordinary pursuits, and how, under so great a disadvantage, he should have arrived at such proficiency.

Death of General Smith, of Baltimore. APRIL 24. — Mr. Christopher Hughes has just heard of the death of his father-in-law, General Samuel Smith, of Baltimore, who died on Monday last, in the eighty-seventh year of his age. His death was remarkable, and such as every old man should desire. He had returned from riding, lay upon the sofa to refresh himself, and was found dead by a servant who entered the room.

General Smith was another of the old revolutionary officers, to whom the country owes so much, and pays so little. Happily, in his case no pecuniary aid was requisite; he was a rich man. He signalized himself on several occasions during the war of the Revolution, and has been almost constantly since in public life; for many years a representative of the State of Maryland in the Senate of the United States, frequently in the Legislature of that State, and at the time of his death Mayor of Baltimore, to which latter office he was elected (although an administration man, unopposed by the Whigs) for his gallant conduct on a recent occasion when the peace of the city was disturbed by one of those mobs to which Baltimore has unhappily been rather frequently exposed.

APRIL 25. — In the packet-ship "Siddons," which sailed to-day for Liverpool, went passengers, Mr. William Brown and wife, of Liverpool; their son, Mr. Alexander Brown, and his wife, the daughter of James Brown, of this city. These are all partners or adjuncts of the great mercantile houses of William and James Brown & Co., of Liverpool, and Brown Brothers & Co., of New York.

The visit of William Brown and his wife has been very pleasant. They have married their only son to his cousin, and thereby keep the cash from going out of the family. They have travelled a great deal in the United States, visiting last winter the Falls of Niagara, passed considerable time with their friends here and in Baltimore, and now return in a fine ship, at the most favourable season of the year; and in twenty days probably the senior will again be engaged in making money, the junior in devising plans to spend it, and the ladies in telling their friends and neighbours "all about it."

APRIL 26. — General Scott has returned from his last excursion to the northern frontier, where he was sent to set matters to rights between the *loafer* royalists of Canada and the *loafer* patriots of the United States. I do not know how he has succeeded, for I was not at home when he did us the honour to call this morning. The girls saw him, and say he looks very well, considering the labour he has performed within the last two or three months, during which time he has been constantly employed in the public service, adding to his military renown the blessings which await the "peacemaker." In the course of this severe tour of duty he has travelled (by land principally) forty-seven hundred miles. He is now "the observed of all observers;" and who knows what he may be hereafter?

Celebration of the Historical Society.   APRIL 30. — The semi-centennial celebration of the Inauguration of Washington, which took place in this city on the 30th of April, 1789, was held this day, and went off triumphantly. I was one of the committee of arrangements, and, as the day approached, became extremely anxious and nervous, from an apprehension that sufficient interest had not been excited, and that the distinguished guests of the society from other States might witness a failure. But my fears were groundless. It could not have been better.

The members of the society and invited guests assembled at the City Hotel, and walked in procession to the New Dutch Church, in

Nassau street. The church was filled on our arrival, and hundreds
could not obtain admission, seats having been reserved for the persons forming the procession. On the stage erected in front of the
pulpit were seats for the orator; for Mr. Stuyvesant, the president;
for myself, vice-president of the society; and for Judge Davis, of
Massachusetts; Judges Thompson and Betts; Rev. Drs. DeWitt,
Knox, and Wainwright; Governor Pennington, of New Jersey; Mr.
Southard and General Scott. The ceremony commenced with a
prayer from Dr. Knox, one of the pastors of the church. Long,
dull, and inappropriate, to which succeeded an ode, written for
the occasion by Mr. Bryant, and sung by the choir of the church
to the sublime tune of Old Hundred Psalm. The ode, in my
judgment, is very so-so, considering it is the production of the
crack poet of New York.

Then came the oration, by the venerable ex-President of the
United States, John Quincy Adams. It was in truth "well to be
there." It does not often fall to the lot of any man to hear or
read so masterly a production, eloquent in language, powerful in
argument, refined in taste, glowing with patriotism, and fraught
with instruction. The history of the formation of the government,
of the desolate state of public affairs in the dreary interval between
the termination of the war and the Declaration of Independence;
the violent and pertinacious opposition of the Anti-Federalists
to the new Constitution; and, finally, the glorious consummation
of the principles of the Revolution and the establishment of
liberty and peace by the adoption of the Constitution, the seal to
which was affixed by the event we were celebrating. All this,
together with some touching and interesting details of events
attending the triumphal journey of Washington, his reception in
this city, and the administering of the oath in front of the City
Hall, — this day fifty years ago, — were given in a voice and manner eloquent and animated, but tremulous and feeble. The orator
occupied a little more than two hours in reading it, and skipped
over many leaves. I am much mistaken if, when it comes to be

read, it does not prove to be one of the most able political papers known in this country. Broad, old-fashioned, federal doctrine, strongly laid down and stoutly supported, and proven to have been that on which alone the Government could be successfully formed and happily maintained.

The ceremonies in the church were concluded by a truly apostolic benediction from the Rev. Dr. Wainwright, delivered with all that fervour and devotional solemnity which characterizes my reverend and estimable friend.

The Dinner. Then came the tug-of-war. At five o'clock the subscribers to the dinner and the invited guests began to assemble at the City Hotel, and a few minutes before six the company were seated at the table. I had been dragged into this affair somewhat unwillingly, for I doubted if there was patriotic feeling enough in this busy, money-seeking, interested community to get up and carry through a thing of this sort, upon abstract principles of patriotism, without political excitement or present popular impulse. There was no danger about the ceremonies of the church. Admission cost nothing, and there would be naturally more or less curiosity to hear a gentleman whose talents all acknowledged, and whose public career has been marked, of late, with considerable eccentricity. There was no ground for apprehension on that subject. But the dinner — the dinner — there was the rub; and after inviting some twenty distinguished guests, to have failed there and presented a beggarly account of empty seats would have been mortifying indeed. Impressed with these feelings I worked tolerably hard, toward the last, to avert the consequence I apprehended; but my mind was never at ease until the hour of assembling, when I found that all was right. There was an assemblage of first-rate men, large as the saloon of the City Hotel could conveniently accommodate. There were three tables down the length of the room, each containing sixty-two places, all filled, besides the cross-table at the top, at which were seated the guests to the number of about eighteen. Mr. Stuyvesant, the president, presided. I was the first vice-president, and Judge Betts and Charles King the others.

The guests consisted of Mr. Adams; Mr. Southard, United States senator from New Jersey; Governor Pennington, of Massachusetts; Rev. Mr. Day, of Connecticut; the delegate of the Historical Society of Maine; Judge Thompson, Supreme Court; General Scott; Commodore Claxton, commanding the frigate "Constitution," now in port; Gen. Morgan Lewis; Col. John Trumbull; Rev. Dr. Wainwright, of the Episcopal Church; Rev. Dr. DeWitt and Dr. Knox, of the Dutch Reformed Church; Mr. Grenville Mellen; Count Roenne, Prussian *chargé d'affaires;* President Duer, of Columbia College; besides which there were present, as subscribers, all the city judges, many eminent lawyers, and distinguished literary men. A strong choir, consisting of Mr. Charles E. Horn, his son, Mr. Sinclair, and Mr. Kyle, sang fine old glees, and occasionally a solo; and performed *Non nobis, Domine*, with great solemnity, immediately after Dr. Wainwright's eloquent benediction. An ode was also recited by Mr. Mellen, which was written by him for the occasion. The hall was decorated by Stuart's fine portraits of the first five presidents, the property of Col. George Gibbs, and in front of the orchestra was suspended Pyne's original portrait of Washington, belonging to Mr. Brevoort. A transparent painting was placed behind the president's chair, representing the old Federal Hall, formerly at the head of Broad street, with the ceremony of the inauguration as it was then performed. This was covered with a curtain, and was exposed to view when, in the course of the proceedings, the first allusion was made to it.

Mr. Adams replied to the third toast in a touching and eloquent speech. Commodore Claxton acknowledged the compliment to the Navy. Governor Pennington, Mr. Southard, Judge Davis, and several other gentlemen addressed the company. The address of Mr. Southard was particularly fine; its subject, the "Judiciary," to which important branch of the government the orator paid a deserved tribute of homage.

After the regular toasts the president called upon me for a volunteer. I made a speech in allusion to the great events which occurred on the day we were celebrating within the gallery of the old Federal Hall, the view of which was directly in front of me, and read some extracts from an account of the proceedings, and from the speech which was then pronounced by Washington, all of which I had previously obtained from the " New York Gazette " of May 1, 1789. I also took occasion to pass a compliment upon the veteran Governor Lewis, now present, who then, as Colonel Lewis, commanded the troops who escorted the President from his lodgings to the hall. I concluded my speech by the following toast, which was well received : " The old Federal Hall : it witnessed the greatest contract ever made in Wall street. It is our precious inheritance ; let us ever remember that we, also, have a covenant to perform." Thus ended brilliantly the day which I had anticipated with painful misgivings.

MAY 1. — May day is fine, pleasant weather, much to the comfort of jaded wives and fretting husbands. There is a great deal of moving in the streets out of Broadway, in the upper part of the city, but less, I think, than usual amongst the tenants of good houses. But the pulling down of houses and stores in the lower parts is awful. Brickbats, rafters and slates are showering down in every direction. There is no safety on the sidewalks, and the head must be saved at the expense of soiling the boots. In Wall street, besides the great Exchange, which occupies with huge blocks of granite a few acres of the highway of merchants, there is the beautiful new Bank of the United States opposite, still obstructing the walk. Besides which, four banks — the City, Manhattan, Merchants', and Union — are in progress of destruction ; it looks like the ruins occasioned by an earthquake. The house on the corner of Broadway is undergoing alteration, which usurps the sidewalk. My poor, dear house, 235 Broadway, is coming down forthwith, and in a few weeks the home of my happy days will be incontinently swept from the earth. Farther up, at the corner of

Chambers street, a row of low buildings has been removed to make way for one of those mighty edifices called hotels, — eating, drinking, and lodging above and gay shops below; and so all the way up; the spirit of pulling down and building up is abroad. The whole of New York is rebuilt about once in ten years.

MAY 3. — Dined with Mr. William H. Aspinwall, when I met the army and the navy, embodied in General Scott and Commander Claxton, myself observing a sort of amphibious neutrality between the two.

MAY 6. — I went on Saturday evening to a meeting of the Kent Club, at David B. Ogden's.

<small>Kent Club.</small>

These have been pleasant reunions throughout the winter. The club consists of judges and lawyers, who meet and sup at each others' houses on Saturday evenings in succession; distinguished strangers are invited, and a few laymen, in which last number it has been my good fortune to be frequently included. I have not always been able to attend when invited, but when I have, the conversation of these learned "luminaries of the law" has greatly instructed and delighted me. The evening is usually divided equally between wisdom and joviality. Until ten o'clock they talk law and science and philosophy, and then the scene changes to the supper-table, where Blackstone gives place to Heidsick, reports of champagne bottles are preferred to law reports, and the merits of oyster *pâtés* and *charlotte-russe* are alone summed up.

<small>New Church of the Messiah.</small>

A splendid church edifice has been erected in Broadway, opposite Waverly place, for the congregation under the care of the Rev. Mr. Dewey, — Unitarians, who worshipped formerly in the church corner of Prince and Mercer streets, which was burnt down. The new church was dedicated on Thursday last, and there was service in it yesterday morning and evening. The congregation is very large, which, with a large number of persons of other denominations, attracted by the popularity of the preacher and the beauty of the edifice, occasioned a crowd sufficient to fill the church and all the approaches to it. The building is of stone, with a noble square tower, which is conspicuous the whole length of Broadway. The interior is very fine, and the arrangement of the pews, the pulpit, and the choir novel and commodious. The walls are painted in fresco, giving a solemn religious aspect to this splendid temple, equalled by no other in the city. But, in fact, the architecture of the upper part of the city, both in private and public buildings, is so greatly improved, that the two extremes present an appearance as dissimilar as that of the old and the new towns of Edinburgh.

Governor Seward. MAY 14. — During my absence Governor Seward has been in town for two days, Thursday and Friday. He came to attend the anniversary meeting of the American Bible Society, where he made a speech. He did me the honour to call upon me. Blatchford says that, in speaking of me, he said I was one of the few men in New York to whom he was desirous to make the first visit. I was invited to meet him at dinner on Thursday, at Mr. Amory's. Neither the sport on Long Island nor the pleasure of my recent excursion was sufficient to compensate me for the loss I sustained in not meeting my good friend, the excellent Whig governor.

New Common Council. MAY 15. — Loco-focoism triumphed yesterday in the result of their late unrighteous success. The new mayor, Isaac L. Varian, was sworn into office by his "illustrious predecessor," Aaron Clark, who appears to have performed the ceremony with an exceeding good grace. Whether the new functionary will "follow in his footsteps" is exceedingly doubtful. This, however, is not so bad, except so far as it indicates the downfall of good principles in the city government generally, for I think Mr. Varian the best man of his party. He is an illiterate man, but honest and of a strong mind, and will discharge his duties well, if his party will let him. But he will be ashamed sometimes of the shoulders upon which he has ridden into office, and the disorderly proceedings of the mob in the common-council chamber, on the occasion of his inauguration, must have given him an unpleasant foretaste of the characters of his supporters. It was a shameful exhibition of riot and blackguardism. They rushed into the area of the chamber, usurped the places of the members, interrupted the proceedings, knocked down the officers, and even in the sacred presence of "old Hays" himself didn't "care a damn for Uncle Barnacle."

The work of destruction and the distribution of the spoils is not ready, but the knife will be sharpened, and the rewards of faithful electioneering services prepared against the next meeting.

MAY 20. — The Church of the Messiah is all the fashion. The crowds which attend it on Sunday morning make our neighbourhood exceedingly gay. The ladies, in particular, pass by in great numbers, attracted by a handsome new church, and doctrines somewhat out of the regular track of Orthodoxy. Dr. Channing, the great apostle of Unitarianism, preached in the morning. I promised my friend Grinnell, last evening at Hall's, to go and hear him; but the church was filled at an early hour, to the exclusion of thousands. I went, however, to the evening service, and heard the regular pastor of the congregation, Dr. Dewey, who preaches very pretty moral sermons.

The Church of the Messiah.

MAY 30. — One hundred and sixty-one lots, being part of Henry Eckford's property on Seventh and Eighth avenues, and 22d, 23d, and 24th streets, were sold to-day at auction, at very high prices. The sale amounted to $224,045, being an average of more than $1,500 a lot, and a large part of the property remains unsold.

Sale of Lots.

Among the maritime exploits with which these adventurous times abound, the arrival, on Wednesday last, of a little steam schooner, called the "Robert L. Stockton," from England, is one of the most remarkable. She sailed from Gravesend on the 13th of April. She is only ten feet wide and seventy feet long, and her burthen is thirty tons.

Iron Steamer.

She is built entirely of wrought sheet-iron, and intended as a towing vessel on the New Jersey canal. The commander is Captain Crane. She performed her voyage in forty-six days, with no serious disaster except the loss of one seaman, who was washed off this little cockle-shell by one of the seas which were constantly sweeping her decks. Never, I presume, was the western ocean crossed in so small a craft. There was not room enough to lie straight nor to stand erect. This little vessel lies near the Battery, and is visited by hundreds of curious persons, anxious to realize the possible truth of the nursery story about the "three men of Gotham" who "went to sea in a bowl."

<small>Arrival of the "Great Western."</small> JUNE 1. — This most fortunate of all steamers arrived here last night. She sailed from Bristol on her regular day, the 18th of May, making her passage in thirteen days, — the shortest western passage ever yet accomplished. Captain Hoskin, whom I saw in Wall street this morning, says their voyage was delightful. One of our North-river steamboats could have made it in the same time, and as pleasantly.

This seems to be incredible. I turn back a few leaves of this journal, and find there, that on the 22d day of April, just thirty-nine days ago, we accompanied the "Great Western" to sea. Four days previously Mr. Pontois dined with us, and this morning I shake hands with the captain, and have the account of the minister's arrival. On my way to market this morning I met Wallack. It is exactly six weeks since I saw him act at his farewell benefit, since which he has been to England, engaged performers, made all his arrangements for a theatrical campaign at the National Theatre, spent several days with his family, and here he is again, kissing the ends of his fingers to me in Broadway before nine o'clock. I knew he was a passenger on board the "Great Western," recognized him through the disguise of a new pair of moustaches, but in the realization of the whole thing I was inclined to doubt the evidence of my senses. The steamer is full of passengers, — about one hundred and ten, — and in the number are several of our friends and acquaintances : Mr. and Mrs. E. H. Pendleton, Mr. and Mrs. Douglas Cruger, Mr. Thorn and his son Herman, John Van Buren, and George Parish.

JUNE 6. — The following gentlemen dined with us : Mr. Robert Gilmor, Jonathan Meredith, Herman Thorn, Robert Ray, Henry Brevoort, and William H. Aspinwall.

JUNE 18. — I went out yesterday with my wife and daughter to dine with my old friends, the Lydigs, at West Farms, and had truly a delightful day. The beautiful grounds on the Bronx river are in fine order ; such a profusion of roses and other flowers I have scarcely ever seen. We had an excellent dinner : Lydig's fine old wine and abundance of delicious strawberries, with a welcome hearty as the one, and unstinted as the other. Mr. and Mrs. Suydam, with some of their family, were of the party. Lydig and Suydam are both in indifferent health, and the latter dreadfully hipped, and prone to water-drinking. But our gossipings about old times, the good cheer and lovely scenery, set the old gentlemen on their legs for the time being, and both, I am persuaded, went to bed better than they have been for a twelvemonth. So much for the innocent enjoyments which this world, bad as we think it, affords.

JUNE 24. — The state of the markets in Europe for the two great products of the South and West, as reported by the arrival of the "Great Western," has produced a state of things in our commercial world of Wall street and elsewhere, disastrous and gloomy almost as that of the great crisis three years ago. Flour has fallen three dollars a barrel, and cotton has become a drug in the hands of the holders. The quantity on hand of both these great articles is unusually large, owing to the rapacity of the producers and the speculators, who, not satisfied with regular business and moderate profits, must try to get rich in a single year. Now many of the millers and cotton-planters are ruined, and their factors here have suffered severely. The natural consequence of all this is a recurrence of dreadfully hard times. The jobber cannot collect his debts nor sell his goods ; the capitalist gripes his money with the hand of death; confidence is again at an end. Stocks are low, and ordinary beef is selling from eighteen to twenty-one cents per pound.

JUNE 30. — Feeling a little in want of exercise, I crossed the Christopher-street ferry to Hoboken, this afternoon, walked on the beautiful bank to the *Elysian Fields*, and found a shady spot to smoke a cigar and read "Childe Harold."

JULY 3. — Mr. Van Buren, agreeably to previous arrangement, arrived in New York on Tuesday. The party have made the most they could of this event. There was a great military parade. His arrival was anticipated by committees who met him on the way. The Loco-foco corporation, united to the faithful of Tammany Hall, received him at Castle Garden. Mr. Edmonds, formerly of the Senate, an office-holder under the government, addressed him; and his reply, confirming all the principles of the abominable sub-treasury project, was received with shouts by his partisans. The military parade was very imposing; but, besides that, it does not appear that there was much to gratify his feelings, if he estimates at their true value the unbought attentions of gentlemen and honest men.

<small>Arrival of the President.</small>

JULY 9. — I called yesterday morning and paid my respects to the President, at his quarters in Washington Hall. He left this morning to visit Mr. Hunter at Westchester, Washington Irving and Governor Kemble on the North river, and after these and other visits to his friends, and an affectionate recognition of Kinderhook, the town that claims the honour of being his birthplace, he intends to pass a few weeks at Saratoga, where *the faithful* will, no doubt, be summoned to meet and render homage to him. During the President's stay in New York he has visited most of the public places in the constant custody of a set of men who are not (unless he has greatly changed) the sort of folks he would have chosen for his associates; but party politics, like poverty, bring men "acquainted with strange bedfellows." Moxie told me that he saw him the other evening at the Bowery Theatre, with Mr. and Mrs. Ming, a

fellow called Riall, and a young lawyer who had been discharged from the office of Davis for dishonesty. The old Republicans either choose to stand aloof, or are not allowed by the Loco-foco rabble, who have gotten possession of his person, to approach too near, lest they might do something to lessen their own influence. As President of the United States he was entitled to, and would have received, the attentions of men of all parties; but as he has avowed that his visit was intended for his own political friends, and has consigned himself to the care of the worst part of that clique, it is well to let them retain possession of him. "As he has baked, so let him brew."

JULY 10. — My wife, my daughter, and I passed a delightful day at Gardiner G. Howland's, at Flushing. Howland's noble farm is in superb order. The teeming earth groans under the weight of the golden harvest, and the whole face of Nature smiles with the prospect of abundance which she is about dispensing to mankind. Oh, if the farmer would be satisfied with his crops, the merchant with regular gains, the fruit of moderate enterprise, and the professional man with the exercise of his legitimate talents, and all of them keep clear of extravagant speculation, how much more happy and independent we should be!

Saratoga Springs. JULY 16. — We are here located (as we Yankees have it) at the United States Hotel, and no watering-place in this or any other country can boast of a pleasanter establishment, or one better conducted. We have a suite of two parlours and four bedrooms, in the delightful south wing. Several additional buildings have been erected since the last season, and the ground laid out in a well-mowed and well-rolled lawn, and clean gravel walks. A large club-house and two cottages, in an exceedingly pretty style of architecture, add to the beauty of the grounds and the comfort of the visitors. On the whole, there has never been accommodation so good at Saratoga.

The house is nearly full, but as yet not many of my intimate acquaintances have made their appearance. My excellent friend,

Mr. Bradish, the lieutenant-governor, left Saratoga this morning much to my regret. Governor Seward will, however, be here in a few days, and Mr. Clay is expected on his return from Quebec. With such auxiliaries the Whigs will hold up their heads "sky high, sky high, Mr. Speaker." The President was expected at the United States; but it is said that he will go, on his arrival, to the Pavilion. We are not Loco-foco enough for him, or perhaps not genteel enough; for it has been proved lately that he mingles with none but choice spirits, and holds communion only with Riall gentlemen. Apropos of puns: approaching a little knot in the drawing-room this evening, I overheard Mr. Mead saying, "If a man had five hundred wives, so and so." "What do you think," said St. Clair Clarke, "of a man with five hundred wives, Mr. Hone?" "Why, I think," I replied, "he must be a *harem-scarem* fellow."

JULY 17. — The papers give a gloomy account of commercial affairs in New York, which is confirmed by the reports of our New York visitors. Business is dull, stocks low, and money scarce. All are looking with anxiety for the arrival of the great new steamer, the "British Queen," while none expect favourable news by her. As a set-off against all these evil influences, the accounts of the crops in every part of the country are extremely cheering; people from all parts of the Union are here, and all agree that the prospects of great crops have in no former season been exceeded. The State of Michigan, which, two or three years ago, bought all the flour she used, will have this year a surplus for sale of a million and a half bushels of wheat. I do not know what political economists may say to this, but it does appear to me that good must come of it.

JULY 19. — A ball this evening, but I do not think it was as pleasant as the hop on Wednesday evening. I officiated as manager, with Colonel McAllister, Messrs. Wilson, Stockton, Tevis, etc. The balls are understood to require more dressing, and a greater degree of etiquette prevails, so that the young ladies do not engage in them with so great avidity as in the hops; but, on the other hand, there are champagne, and ice-cream, and blancmange, whose agreeable presence is confined to the most dignified of these amusements.

Buffaloes.   An extract from a St. Louis newspaper states that the hunters had come in with twenty-four thousand buffalo-robes and a quantity of beaver, worth altogether $100,000. Twenty-four thousand buffaloes! what a sublime idea for any man who has ever seen a buffalo or a drawing of one, or heard him described; only imagine a drove of twenty-four thousand oxen — but the imagination cannot keep pace with the magnificent scale on which the works of nature are represented in the regions of the great West. I suppose that immense number of huge living animals would look on the prairies like a flock of sheep on Hempstead Plains.

JULY 23. — The "Great Western" arrived at New York yesterday, having sailed from Bristol on the 6th. The movements of this fine vessel have gotten to be as regular as the rising and setting of the sun, or the flux and reflux of the tide. She brings intelligence quite as bad for the commercial world as was anticipated. Cotton has fallen, American stocks a drug, and the rate of bank interest five and a half per cent., and about to be raised to six. The United States of America, by the grace of God, free and independent as they vaunt themselves, have, by a course of extravagant speculations, aided by bad management of the government, and the indulgence of personal spite of "the Greatest and Best," brought themselves into a state of thraldom to their old masters nearly as great as that which existed previous to the Declaration of Independence. All we undertake to do is predicated on the chance of borrowing money from John Bull. We try to borrow so much, that the credit even of the State stocks is impaired. Cotton, the only thing we have to pay with, is placed at the mercy of the creditors, and the Bank of England becomes the arbiter of the fate of the American merchant. All this comes from the rage for speculation here; the desire to grow rich in a short time, which incites the growers of cotton and flour, instead of selling at a fair price the bounties of God's providence, to hoard them up. By and by comes "a frost, a killing frost," and then the planter loses the product of many years of regular cultivation, his factor is ruined by liberal advances, and every department of business suffers from the shock.

Saratoga. JULY 24. — Every house is well filled. It is computed that there are two thousand visitors at the place at the present time. At Congress Hall and this house there are many distinguished men and fine women; antiquated belles of a by-gone generation, enjoying with gayety and cheerfulness the scenes of their former triumphs; fine married women and lovely girls, the ornaments of the present and the hopes of the future; and men uniting as in one brilliant focus the talent, intelligence, and civic virtues of the various parts of the country.

The "British Queen." JULY 29. — The long-expected steam-packet, the "British Queen," arrived in New York, on her first voyage from Portsmouth, yesterday morning. One of her passengers came here this morning in the first train of cars. This is certainly doing business in great style. This gentleman left England only three days before we left home for this place, and what have I done in that time? Events now pass like the shadows of a magic lantern. The "British Queen" sailed on the 12th. She is commanded by Captain Roberts, formerly of the "Sirius," the Columbus of steam, who first of British steam-men reached our shores. She is the largest steamer ever built, being of the following dimensions: Length from figure-head to taffrail, 275 feet; length of upper deck, 245 feet; breadth within the paddle-boxes, 40 feet 7 inches; breadth including the boxes, 64 feet; her engine is of 500-horse power; burthen, 2,016 tons. The "British Queen" arrived in New York on the 28th. Her log is published. She had head-winds all the way. Her greatest distance in one day was two hundred and forty miles; the least, one hundred and thirty miles.

JULY 30. — Webb, of the "Courier and Enquirer," came passenger in the "British Queen." He went out in the "Great Western" on the 13th of June, and has been absent only forty-five days. Colonel Webb says that Mr. Webster is the greatest lion they have had in England, with the exception of Marshal Soult, since the visit of the allied sovereigns. He has not breakfasted or dined at his lodgings since his arrival in London. A great public dinner is preparing for him in Liverpool, as the friend of commerce throughout the world. At this banquet, which is to be attended by great numbers of the nobility and gentry, it was expected that "the defender of the Constitution" would come out with his heaviest guns.

Mr. Webster.

JULY 31. — My daughter and I visited *Her Majesty* this afternoon, where she is lying in state at the foot of Clinton street; but God forbid that either she or her royal godmother should be defunct; far from it, for such a scene of life, bustle, and animation in and about her is not often witnessed. This is only the third working day since her arrival, and she is preparing and will sail to-morrow in company with the "Great Western," which lies quietly alongside of her. It will be a trial of speed, and prodigious interest is excited in the result. The friends of both are sanguine of success, and the death-like dulness of Wall street is somewhat relieved by the betting on the race.

The "British Queen."

We were admitted on board, although the wharf was filled with persons who were excluded, and we saw every part of this leviathan of steam. Her cabin is superbly fitted up, and the staterooms adjoining it are convenient and pleasant as possible; but the sleeping apartments below are dark and confined, and I doubt whether the whole amount of good sleeping accommodations is equal to that of the "Great Western." The scene on deck was a "perfect show:" discharging in one place and receiving and stowing cargo in another; boxes and barrels of stores; cart-loads of fresh meat; great lumps of ice, and George Haws, with his pleasant, red face, reeking with perspiration, employed in stowing it away; mountains of coal sinking into the crater of the lower hold; live cows and poultry wondering what part of the pandemonium is intended for them; sentinels employed in the unthankful office of keeping back disappointed visitors; and officers more agreeably engaged in doing the genteel thing by our more favoured selves.

<small>Governor Seward.</small> When the committee of glorification were making arrangements to receive the President as the chief of their party, a note was addressed to Governor Seward at Albany, to come to New York and join the procession. This he declined in a letter, which the Loco-focos stigmatized as insulting and disrespectful, but which they refused to publish, although urged by the Whigs to do so. Their taunts all proving unavailing, the Young Men's General Committee applied formally to the Governor for a copy of the correspondence, which he furnished, and which is now published. The letter is long, and my time is insufficient to copy it, as I would wish; but it is admirable. The Whigs have reason to be proud of their man. I never read anything more "germane to the matter." Soft as silk, but cutting as a razor; manly in sentiment, but courteous in manner, — it is no wonder they refused to let it see the light. I am proud of the noble little Whig governor, and feel honoured in being allowed to call him friend.

<small>Sailing of the Steamships.</small> AUGUST 1. — The "Great Western" and the "British Queen" went to sea this morning, as well as the packets for London, Liverpool, and Havre, all filled with passengers. The crowds which lined the wharves and the Battery were greater than on any former similar occasion. I went to Castle Garden to see the two noble steamships; but as I could not see through my countrymen, and more particularly countrywomen, I had an imperfect view. The "Great Western" preceded the "British Queen" about an hour. The weather was very fine, and the water as well as the shores presented a lively and animated scene. Giving the "Queen" sixteen days' passage, she will have made her voyage out and home to Portsmouth in thirty-

six days, bringing out nearly two hundred passengers and returning with one hundred, discharging one cargo and taking on board another. Go ahead! is the impulse which now governs the world.

AUGUST 2. — The times are worse than ever. Wall street is in a state of consternation; money uncome-at-able and confidence at an end. A national bank is the only remedy (if, indeed, things have not gone too far). That, with a change of the administration, are the only straws we have to catch at. Let us try them, unless the people are determined to complete the ruin which hangs over them. If they are, so be it!

SARATOGA. — In the number of arrivals during my absence is the President of the United States, and Mr. Secretary Forsyth, with Mr. Edward P. Livingston and a few others of the faithful. The President was met some distance from the village by a cavalcade, and followed to his quarters in the United States Hotel by a motley group. The Whigs say it was a slim concern, and the Locos say otherwise. But here he is, conducting himself with his usual politeness, and making the best of everything, as he is wont to do. I called upon him yesterday, immediately after my arrival, and was most graciously received. He hoped I would pass an occasional spare half-hour in his apartment. He has been civil to my wife, and sends his bottle to her and me to drink with him at dinner. I have studied to treat him with all the respect due to his high station, and the regard I feel for an old friend, and I acknowledge the kindness with which my advances have been received. This conduct has been pursued by most of the gentlemen, political opponents as well as political adherents; but there has been one exception, on the part of a lady, which, in my judgment, was equally at variance with good taste and proper feeling.

AUGUST 6. — The President takes the head of one of the tables, and the *modest* Mr. Bennett, of the "Herald," the other. The President cannot help this, to be sure, and the juxtaposition is somewhat awkward. Bennett will make a great thing of this with those who are not aware that any person may take this seat who has impudence enough, and that it would require a pretty smart rifle to carry a ball from one end of the table to another. I wish the President would leave his seat, and give the " Herald " man all the honours of the table.

Mr. Clay.
AUGUST 7. — The village is alive with preparations for Mr. Clay's reception. I received a letter from him, dated Montreal, 4th inst., and another by a messenger who was sent hence to confer with him, dated on his voyage to Burlington, 6th inst. He is to lodge at Lake George to-morrow night, and will come to Saratoga on Friday afternoon, where apartments are provided for him at the United States Hotel. A programme of his reception is published, signed by a committee of more than one hundred Whigs. We wished to repress this public demonstration, but it could not be. The movement is spontaneous, and the people seem to be determined to out-glorify the other party.

The Whig visitors at Congress Hall have been in a ferment about the impropriety of bringing Mr. Clay in contact with his great rival at the United States Hotel. Conferences have been had and disputes held on the subject; but the difficulty is removed by the President's determination to leave Saratoga on Friday. He is to dine with the young Loco-focos at Ballston, and go to Troy, to be received there by his friends on the same evening, and will not return until the first of next week. This may be *accidental;* but it is a happy coincidence for us, and I am mistaken if we do not model something handsome out of this *Clay.*

Mr. Clay's Arrival.
AUGUST 9. — The day was ushered in by clouds and rain, thunder and lightning; but all passed away, and the glorious sun shone out by eight o'clock and dispersed the vapours from the natural, as we trust the man who comes among us will those from the political, horizon.

Secretary Forsyth took away his discontented countenance last evening, and Secretary Poinsett went this morning to Cattaraugus on business relating to the Indian Treaty. The President also went back to Ballston, and thence to Troy.

Arrangements having been made for a number of the visitors to meet Mr. Clay on his approach to Saratoga, a large number, on horseback and in carriages, left the village at eleven o'clock, and went to Emerson's Tavern, nine miles on the Glenn's Falls road. In less than half an hour he arrived, accompanied by committees from Caldwell and Glenn's Falls; and after our salutations we sat down to a collation, prepared under direction of Colonel Westcott, and served up in rather homely, but hearty style. Provisions had been sent out in the morning from Saratoga, and champagne was taken by the gentlemen. The company, which consisted of seventy or eighty, comprised many bright spirits and distinguished men. I had the honour of presiding at the feast, and it is certain that we made the most of the time allowed us.

At three o'clock we left Emerson's, and came to a place two miles in advance of the Springs, where the carriages, wagons, horsemen, and pedestrians who were to form the procession were collected to receive us. Mr. Clay was placed in a new barouche, drawn by Gerald Coster's four gray horses; the other seats occupied by Judge Walton and two other gentlemen of the Saratoga committee on arrangements. The line of march was then taken up, preceded by Frank Johnson's band of music; and such a cavalcade was never seen before in the county of Saratoga. It formed a compact line a mile and a half long. I rode in a barouche with Dr. Duncan, of Mississippi, Mr. Green, of Louisiana, and Reverdy Johnson, of Baltimore. Our approach was announced by the discharge of artillery from the hills, and the line of march preserved until we came to the United States Hotel, where quarters were prepared for "the man whom the people delight to honour." Here the avenues to the hotel were blocked up with the expecting crowds, who made the village ring with shouts of welcome. The large piazza in front of the hotel was filled with ladies, for whose exclusive use it had been reserved. It had been arranged that the address should be made, and the reply received, from the steps of the hotel; but this was rendered impracticable by the crowd, and the horses were taken out and the barouche dragged around in front. Here Mr. Clay was addressed by Mr. John W. Taylor, formerly Speaker of the House of Representatives, and replied in a speech to the assembled multitude of more than an hour; too long, I thought, for the occasion, and entering too much into political detail; but I suppose it was unavoidable. The towns-people had the regulation of this part of the ceremony, and they were not disposed to let the opportunity be lost to the people of hearing an account of the misdeeds of their rulers from the lips of the oracle of the day. After the address Mr. Clay was conducted, amidst the shouts of the men and the waving of the women's handkerchiefs, to his apartments, fatigued with travel and exhausted with excitement.

But the affair did not end here; the great dining-room of the United States Hotel had been fitted up during the day with bouquets of flowers and festoons of evergreens, and in the evening the most splendid ball was given that was ever witnessed here; eight hundred persons were present, comprising a greater number of distinguished men and fine women than have probably ever been collected in this country.

I was the senior manager, and by previous arrangement, after the first set of cotillons, Mr. Clay and his son were led into the room by me and Mr. Meredith, the band playing "Hail Columbia," and the company opening to the right and left to afford us a passage to the upper end of the room. It has been a day of prodigious excitement, and everything went off well.

August 10. — The New York papers contain every day an account of increased commercial distress, affording a striking contrast to the gayety and extravagance of this place. More money has been spent here than in any former season, some of which, I have no doubt, belongs more justly to the pockets of creditors at home than of the hotel-keepers here.

AUGUST 12. — This is the meridian of the Saratoga season. All the world is here: politicians and dandies; cabinet ministers and ministers of the gospel; office-holders and office-seekers; humbuggers and humbugged; fortune-hunters and hunters of woodcock; anxious mothers and lovely daughters; the ruddy cheek mantling with saucy health, and the flickering lamp almost extinguished beneath the rude breath of dissipation. In a few days this brilliant company will be scattered over the face of the land, and who can tell for how many of them this will be the last season?

A little circle was formed this evening in the grand saloon, which occasioned much curious speculation. It consisted of the three prominent candidates for the next presidency: Mr. Van Buren, who returned this morning; Mr. Clay; and the gallant General Scott, whose star is rising fast. Each had fair ladies receiving their attentions, and many good-natured jokes were passed between them.

NEW YORK, AUG. 21. — Our dinner to-day was interrupted by the great procession for the reception of Mr. Clay, which passed the house a little before five o'clock. Mr. Clay came down from Newburgh in the steamboat "James Madison," and by previous arrangement of the Whig committee was landed at the foot of Hammond street, whence he was escorted to Union place, and thence down Broadway to the Astor House, by the greatest cavalcade I ever witnessed on such an occasion. All Broadway was filled with spectators; from the windows handkerchiefs were waved, and shouts ascended from the crowds collected at the corners. We all left the dinner-table and went to the balcony in front of the house, whence we had a fine view. We received the salutations of Mr. Clay in passing, and I was further honoured by a salute from the band. In the barouche with Mr. Clay sat General Lynch, Dudley Selden, and General Van Courtlandt. On the arrival of the procession at the Park, and before Mr. Clay was taken to his lodgings, he was carried to the front of the City Hall, where he was addressed by Mr. Selden, and replied in a good speech of less than half an hour. In the evening he went to the Bowery Theatre, where he was received with new honour from other thousands. I went down after dinner with Gilmore and Meredith to the Astor House, which was filled like a market-place with people waiting for the return of the honoured guest from the theatre.

Viewing this affair as a spontaneous expression of public opinion, accomplished with no expense and very little preparation, and unaccompanied by military parade, it exceeded anything of the kind we have ever witnessed, excepting the reception of Lafayette. It would seem to indicate that the patriotic senator must be the favourite candidate for the presidency of the Whigs hereabouts; and I have no doubt that he is, and would stand a good chance of success, and the country be thereby saved from the further progress of ruin, were we not the most untractable, unreliable party which ever stood up against corruption and bad government.

Mr. Clay's Departure. AUGUST 24. — Mr. Clay received visitors on Thursday, in the Governor's room, City Hall. After an ineffectual attempt to see him there (for the room was so crowded that not one in twenty who went could get admission) I called upon him at the Astor House, where I saw and conversed with him for a few minutes. The civilities of the New Yorkers have nearly annihilated him. He is hoarse and fatigued; but he went, nevertheless, to the Park Theatre in the evening, where he was received, as usual, with great applause.

Trinity Church. AUGUST 26. — We are vagrants now on Sundays. Poor old Trinity being nearly razed to the ground, and a new church to be erected on the same spot, which will require two or three years to complete, we shall be compelled during that time to hire a pew in one of the up-town churches, or quarter upon our friends.

When the committee of the vestry of Trinity Church began with the edifice, it was intended to repair and remodel the interior only, leaving the venerable exterior and the noble, dark-looking spire in their original integrity; but in the progress of the work the building was found to be in such a state of decay as to be rendered irreparable, and the time-honoured temple of the Lord, the parish church of New York, the nucleus of Episcopacy, was doomed to destruction. I found, on my return to the city, a shapeless heap of ruins on the spot where my imperfect devotions have been performed for the last thirty-seven years. It occasions melancholy reflections to see the dark mass of ruins still overlooking the magnificent temples of mammon in Wall street, and to think of the changes which have occurred there during the time the venerable spire which is now removed has thrown its shadow over the place "where merchants most do congregate."

May I not also see in this dilapidation a type of my own decay and speedily approaching removal? When I first went to Trinity Church I was young, ardent and full of hopes, capable and industrious, and I should now be ungrateful not to acknowledge that in most cases my hopes were realized and my industry rewarded; but the storms within the last three years have beaten upon me, the timbers are decayed, the spire no longer " like a tall bully lifts its head," and the vestry has no funds to rebuild me.

Capture of a Slaver. AUGUST 31. — There has been great interest excited for several days past about a mysterious "low, black-looking schooner," which was seen and spoken several times off Long Island, filled with pirates, as was said. This "flying Dutchman" was captured on Monday last, between Gardner's Island and Montauk Point, by Captain Gedney, in the United States surveying brig "Washington." She proves to be very much as reported. The schooner "Amistead," a Spanish vessel. She sailed from Havana bound to Guanaja, another port in Cuba, with fifty-four slaves belonging to Jose Ruiz, a passenger on board, who had bought them at Havana from a slaver just arrived from the coast of Africa, and was conveying them to his plantation.

Pedro Montes, another passenger, had also four slaves. Four days after leaving Havana, the blacks rose upon the crew, murdered and threw overboard the captain and a mulatto cook, and compelled Montes (who had formerly commanded a vessel) to take the helm and steer easterly for their own country, under threats of being also murdered. This he did during the day, but at night altered his course, and kept upon the American coast, until on Monday last, whilst at anchor near Montauk, the blacks having gone ashore for water and provisions, the schooner was descried by the "Washington," boarded and taken possession of, the whites released from their dreadful state of bondage, and the slaves captured. The vessel was taken into New London, and an examination held on board by Judge Judson, of the United States District Court. The schooner, with the remains of her cargo, which consisted of dry goods and other articles calculated for the use of a plantation, were taken possession of, and the slaves ordered for a trial at Hartford, on the 17th of September.

The ringleader in this revolt is a Congo negro, named Joseph Cinques, about twenty-six years of age, a fine, intelligent fellow, who would be exalted into a hero instead of a pirate and murderer if his colour was right, and he had been taken under other circumstances.

I am afraid this affair will be attended with unpleasant consequences at this time, when the minds of men in this country are influenced by the question of abolition. These poor wretches were stolen from their homes, carried to a strange country, and sold to servitude, from which they sought to escape on the first occasion which offered. They committed murder, it is true; but their situation may have rendered it inevitable. They spared their owner, which would seem to prove that human blood was not their object. If these men are tried in Connecticut, and some condemned to death, Joseph particularly will be justified by one party, and his case will excite great sympathy. If, on the other hand, the revolt should be considered only as a measure of self-preservation, and the culprits escape punishment, it will be considered by the slave-holding fanatics as a new proof of the enmity of the abolitionist fanatics; so that either way it makes trouble. I wish they could all be sent back to Havana, and perhaps it may take that course.

locomotive — the only good *motive* for riding a man on a *rail*." The weather during the day and evening was delicious.

October 9. — Wall street, the commercial and political barometer, was grievously disturbed to-day. A great crash has taken place, which, now that it has happened, appears to have not been unexpected. The Bank of the United States in Philadelphia has suspended specie payments, and the other banks of that city will have to follow its example. Those in Baltimore must pursue the same course, and the thousand rotten banks of the South will be but too happy to follow suit. Our banks carry a bold front and will not suspend, they say. In order to place themselves in a situation to hold this lofty language, they have been compelled for a long time past to squeeze the poor merchants to death. They are placed under the "nether millstone," where struggling is in vain. I hope, for the honour of New York, that all their sacrifices will not be in vain; but it is hard to stand alone against the shock of universal bankruptcy.

<small>Alarm in Wall street.</small>

How that old —— Jackson will rejoice in his unsanctified retreat at Nashville, at this catastrophe! It would have been worth a play ticket to witness his triumph on the receipt of the news. "I told you so!" he must have said, as he dashed his pipe to the ground with savage joy. "Where is Nick Biddle now? — down! down! where I have tried to get him for so long a time. Shout, my liege subjects, for your master's victory! Throw up your caps, my faithful Loco-foco supporters, and renew the yell so grateful to my ears: Hurrah for Jackson, and down with the merchants!" True, indeed, he did tell them so; and we Whigs also told them so. This and all the other miseries we are suffering are to be attributed to the measures of hostility inflicted by this vindictive man upon the Bank of the United States.

October 10. — The Senatorial Convention of the Whigs of this district was held this day at the Broadway House, at noon. The members proceeded to canvass informally and inconclusively for a nominee to the Senate.

<small>Senatorial Convention.</small>

Observing my name to be high on the list, I stated to my colleagues the difficulty of my position in being present during the discussion which would naturally arise. I certainly did not desire the nomination, and would support most heartily any other candidate who might be selected; nor would I decline it. I was precluded from the latter course by implied pledges made to my political friends last year as the condition of their consent to the withdrawal of my name from the Assembly ticket, that I would agree to serve them this year if they should continue of the same mind. In order to be relieved from the awkwardness of my situation I requested and obtained leave to retire during the discussion. After an hour's absence I was sent for and the balloting commenced. On the first ballot I had eight votes, Daniel Lord, Jr., seven, and Mr. Jay one (my vote). Finding my name still before the convention, I declined voting again, and on the third or fourth ballot I received eleven votes and Mr. Lord four. On this the question was taken by ayes and nays, and I had *every vote*. So I am in nomination as the Whig candidate for the Senate of the State at the ensuing election. I hope it will come to good for the cause, and that I may be elected now that I am up; but, in truth, it would be very inconvenient for me to pass my winters in Albany. My opponent in the convention, Mr. Lord, was supported by the lawyers, who deem it important to have gentlemen of their profession in the Court of Errors; but everything that occurred was highly complimentary to me, and it is no small gratification to have had as my principal competitor such a man as Daniel Lord, Jr., who, besides standing at the very top of the New York bar, is, in every respect, one of the most estimable men in the city.

The fearful apprehensions of yesterday were realized. The banks of Philadelphia have suspended specie payments. New York stands yet — but how long?

OCTOBER 14. — My nomination for the Senate excites great interest with all parties. It is somewhat amusing to read the comments upon my character in the newspapers. The Whigs, of course, express their approbation, some of them (the "Commercial Advertiser" and "The Daily Whig") in terms of exaggerated encomium, whilst the other party are not sparing abuse. The "Herald" (Bennett's paper) says I am the most unpopular candidate that could have been put up. This must all go for as much as it is worth. I shall preserve these precious documents, and some of these days copy them here, to show hereafter the discrepancies of party opinions on plain matters.

It annoys me a little to be told that some of the Loco-focos of my own party (for we have such amongst us) are opposed to the nomination. "I am a gentleman," they say, — very much obliged to them ! — "and no gentleman can succeed." These are the men that ruin a good cause. If they are right in what they say, the party is not worth sustaining; better would it be that everything should go back to the dunghill of Democracy, and let us see if something better may not spring from it. As a set-off against the annoyance which their reports have given me, I have been gratified by the visits of several influential Whigs in the upper wards, who assure me that I shall run a better chance than any other person could have done. I have strong doubts of the success of our ticket; but I should hate confoundedly to find that I had been an injury to it.

OCTOBER 17. — Three of my young female friends have embraced the willing chains of matrimony, besides Miss Julia Coster, whose wedding I noticed yesterday. Miss Sarah Ogden made Robert Goelet happy, and to-day Miss Mary Tallmadge, loveliest among the lovely, weds Philip L. Van Rensselaer, son of the late excellent Stephen Van Rensselaer. This last marriage is celebrated at General Tallmadge's country-seat in Dutchess County, and is, I presume, a very satisfactory union to all parties concerned; pride of birth (all that we Republicans are allowed to have of it) will be gratified. Great wealth comes in to make things comfortable, and good character gives a reasonable chance for future happiness.

OCTOBER 22. — There is great excitement in relation to the arrest of the two Spaniards, José Ruiz and Pedro Montez, the owners of the revolted slaves who were taken on board the "Amistead," and are now in prison in Connecticut. This outrageous proceeding is the work of the abolitionists, who, in their officious zeal, have obtained affidavits from the wretched Africans, who, ignorant of our language, probably knew not what they were swearing about. These affidavits, charging their owners with assault and battery, were made the grounds of this arrest, and the Spaniards are in prison. Writs of *habeas corpus* have been issued, and the subject is now submitted to the judges, who, it is hoped, will see reason to discharge the men who escaped so narrowly from the conspiracy in which the lives of other white men were sacrificed. The fanatics are working day and night to make this bad matter worse; under the specious cloak of an abstract opposition to slavery, they are blowing up a flame which may destroy the Union, and light up a civil war between men who have no interest so strong as to belong to a brotherhood of patriots.

OCTOBER 23. — My old friend, Benjamin L. Swan, marries his daughter Mary, this evening, to Mr. Charles N. Fearing. My son Robert is one of the groomsmen, and Miss Eliza Russell a bridesmaid.

OCTOBER 26. — I am fairly in for it; every evening I am *toted* somewhere to show myself to the voters, to make a speech and solicit their "sweet voices," not for myself, — oh no, by all means! — but for the cause of which I am the deputed representative and organ. This is a distinction which requires some address to make, but the people seem satisfied with it. A committee called upon me yesterday to invite me to a great Whig meeting, at the Military Hall, Bowery. I went, was received with the most enthusiastic greetings, made a tolerably good speech, which was received with shouts and hurrahs, and on the whole made an excellent hit.

OCTOBER 31. — I went, by invitation of Mr. Grinnell, this morning, and partook of a collation on board the splendid new ship "Patrick Henry," intended for Grinnell and Minturn's line of packets. She is the *ne plus ultra*, or will be until another ship of her class shall be built.

NOVEMBER 4. — My vanity has been tickled again by a call signed by a large number of merchants' clerks, for a meeting to be held on Saturday evening, at the Shakespeare Hotel, of "the young men of the city of New York friendly to the election of *Philip Hone* to the Senate." This meeting, so flattering to me, was held on Saturday, at the appointed place, and was (I am told) a great and enthusiastic assemblage.

<small>Great *Hone* Meeting.</small>

NOVEMBER 6. — The Sun of Austerlitz succeeded this morning the violent storm of last night. The Whigs hailed it as a harbinger of victory, but the canvass this evening of the senatorial votes shows that we have suffered a Waterloo defeat. I am beaten by a majority of eighteen hundred, and the Assembly ticket has no doubt fared equally badly. This result is unexpected to me, and somewhat mortifying. I feel a selfish joy in having escaped the excessive labour and the numerous discomforts and deprivations which would have been the consequences of my election to the Senate; but I deplore deeply the failure of so good a cause as ours, and this triumph of principles so broadly and openly avowed by the successful party, which, in the sincerity of my heart, I conceive are calculated to destroy the only hopes of a recovery from the deplorable state in which the country is placed. Our hopes of the State have been sanguine, and it may yet save the cause; but they were equally so of the city. I fear the worst. God's will be done. Party-spirit and personal ambition and desire of power rule the country, and must rule; and their instruments are the worthless part of the population, which, unhappily, is the most numerous.

<small>Election Decided.</small>

NOVEMBER 9. — I had a dinner-party of Whigs, principally members of the "Hone Club," invited "for congratulation or for con-

dolence as the case might be," which turned out to be the latter, — no mistake about it, — so far as the host was concerned in this rascally city. But congratulation came in for a good share of the business of the day. By the time my guests assembled it was pretty clearly ascertained that the Whigs had triumphed again in the State, and secured a majority in both Houses of the Legislature. My appetite was not injured, nor was my wine less bright, from my knowledge that I was to be left at home to enjoy them and other greater comforts, instead of devoting time and labour, perhaps without thanks, to the service of the State for four years to come. It is a reprieve for which I ought to be thankful. We had a pleasant dinner. The party consisted of Moses H. Grinnell, Ogden Hoffman, Edward Curtis, James Monroe, R. M. Blatchford, John Ward, Simeon Draper, Jonathan Amory, W. T. Brigham, S. B. Ruggles, and Dr. Francis.

Gov. Seward and Office-seekers. NOVEMBER 21. — The Governor came in town to attend a public dinner given to him by the line officers of the militia, and returned home yesterday. He feels now the weight of his office. The result of the late election, by securing a majority of his political friends in the Senate, and thereby giving validity to his nominations for office, has opened the flood-gates of application, — enough to sweep him away in the current; but he seems to stand it very well. His spirits are good, his tact admirable, and he has a good word for each of the crowd of importunate solicitors for executive favour who beset him without intermission or relaxation. I have my troubles, too, in a subordinate capacity. Having been a candidate for office, and supposed to be somewhat in His Excellency's good graces, I am beset all day long by office-seekers to sign their petitions, to speak to the Governor, or to write him letters in their behalf. We Whigs are certainly the most disinterested patriots in the world. We have no interested motives, — not we! The country, and the cause, and the good of the people were our only motives in working at the elections; and now that the loaves and fishes are to be distributed, there are not more than about fifty baskets held out for each, each applicant having convinced himself that he is the only one qualified for the office, and ready to curse the Governor and desert the party if he should not be successful. I have had them every hour in the day for the last two or three weeks. I do not know of late the pleasure of eating an uninterrupted meal. I dread the sight of a square folded paper taken from a whited-brown envelope. Men are affronted if I refuse to certify that they are in all things qualified, when in truth I know nothing about them, and go off in an unappeasable huff if I hesitate to ascribe to them qualities which *I do* know they do not póssess. Persons apply to be made water commissioners, who do not know a culvert from a bridge ; measurers and inspectors of grain and flour, who can scarcely tell the difference between wheat and rye ; and inspectors of pot and pearl ashes, who would have to consult an encyclopædia (if, perchance, they can read) to ascertain if the article on which they are to pass judgment be a mineral or a vegetable production. The poor Governor has not now a refractory Senate opposed to him, as he had last session, on whom he could lay the blame of the failure of the Whigs' application. He must stand the brunt of the affair, and get over as well as he can the consequences of making one cool friend and forty-nine enemies amongst his political partisans in the case of every appointment.

NOVEMBER 22. — Poor Wallack cannot succeed with his company at Niblo's (his place of refuge after the burning of his theatre). His stock company was good, and his milky way was not deficient in stars. He has had Vandenhoff and his charming daughter, Charles Kean, Forrest, and the best opera corps in the country ; but all would not do. The theatre wàs closed the first of the present week. The stock actors are standing *stock* still, and the planets move no longer in their accustomed orbits. The Park lingers on, but it is doing a bad business. There are but few strangers in town, and the pockets of our citizens, for the most part, are too low to stand the united demands

[sidenote: National Theatre.]

of Fulton market and the theatres. Economy begins to follow reluctantly in the dirty footsteps of necessity.

NOVEMBER 27. — Mr. Samuel Ward, senior partner of the great banking-house of Prime, Ward, King, & Co., died this day at noon. There are few citizens in New York whose death would have caused so great a void in the circles of active business and social intercourse as Mr. Ward's, the moving spirit of a great financial concern, whose ramifications extended not only over all parts of this country, but were known and felt throughout Europe. Liberal and munificent in a degree greater perhaps than that of any other person, he employed a large portion of his wealth in works of benevolence and public spirit. Possessed of a good heart and a sound head, he was, nevertheless, too much the slave of systems, which he applied indiscriminately to all dispositions and characters, and measured all men by the same rules; even his own habits were subjected to a system of government too rigid for his constitution. He became all of a sudden a total-abstinence man, at a time of life when the experiment was dangerous, and drank nothing but water, when, in my judgment, a moderate use of the good wine which he had in his cellar would have been more congenial to his health. Mr. Ward was about fifty-five years old. He went to live with Mr. Nathaniel Prime at the age of fourteen, became in the course of time his partner, and continued an active member of the house, and the senior since Mr. Prime's retirement. Mr. Ward lived in a noble house, which he built a few years ago, on the corner of Broadway and Bond street, — the corner below my house, — where he had a picture-gallery and one of the finest libraries in the city. He was a rich man, and made a good use of his money; and such men are not easily spared at this time.

NOVEMBER 28. — This was the day of general Thanksgiving, appointed by the Governor of the State and the city authorities, and was very generally observed. Never had a people more reason to be thankful for the blessings of Divine Providence. The year has been especially marked by genial weather, abundant harvests, and exemption from war, pestilence, and famine, and all the minor evils with which it is the pleasure of the Almighty to visit at times his unthankful children. There are troubles enough, certainly; but they are "the work of man's hands," and show how wayward and weak he is when left to his own "inventions." Our constant prayer should be that he may not be thus left.

Coal.
I was forcibly struck this morning in examining a table of the quantity of coals produced from the mines of Pennsylvania during the last nineteen years. In the year 1820 the whole quantity sent to market was three hundred and sixty-five tons from Lehigh; in the present year more than a million of tons will have been sent. Nine years ago the Delaware and Hudson Canal Company made their first shipments, amounting to seven thousand tons; this year they have shipped to Rondout on the North river one hundred and twenty-two thousand tons, — the greatest quantity sent in any one year.

What an argument is this in favour of internal improvements, and what a reproof to the miserable tools of party faction, who, to secure their election to the State Legislature, have bound themselves by unholy pledges to break down these noble enterprises, and to check an experiment so eminently successful! Here is an increase of an article indispensable for the use of all classes of our citizens, whether for manufactures, steam navigation, or domestic fuel, to the amount of six or seven millions of dollars, and making a reduction in price to the consumers of as much more; an article which, although known to exist in an inexhaustible extent in the mountains of a neighbouring State, was as worthless as the soil which covered it, until the means were adopted by the construction of roads and canals to bring it to market; and all these glorious benefits, the fruits of public spirit and private enterprise, were to have been abandoned to secure the influence of a set of miserable politicians, who would sacrifice all the great interests of the country to promote the designs and perpetuate the power of their leaders. But, thank God! the pestilential breath of party-spirit engendered in this rotten political atmosphere has not infected the State at large, and for one year at least its councils will not be polluted by its deleterious influence.

DECEMBER 4. — I went this morning, by invitation of Monsieur François Gouraud, to see a collection of the views made by the wonderful process lately discovered in France by Monsieur Daguerre, which is called by his name. Mr. Gouraud is the pupil and friend of the inventor, and comes to this country to make known the process. The pictures he has are extremely beautiful, — they consist of views in Paris, and exquisite collections of the objects of still life. The manner of producing them constitutes one of the wonders of modern times, and, like other miracles, one may almost be excused for disbelieving it without seeing the very process by which it is created. It appears to me a confusion of the very elements of nature. It is nothing less than the palpable effect of light occasioning a reproduction of sensible objects. The reflection of surrounding images created by a camera, obscured upon a plate of copper, plated with silver, and prepared with some chemical substances, is not only distinctly delineated, but left upon the plate so prepared, and there remains forever. Every object, however minute, is a perfect transcript of the thing itself; the hair of the human head, the gravel on the roadside, the texture of a silk curtain, or the shadow of the smaller leaf reflected upon the wall, are all imprinted as carefully as nature or art has created them in the objects transferred; and those things which are invisible to the naked eye are rendered apparent by the help of a magnifying glass. It appears to me not less wonderful that light should be made an active operating power in this manner, and that some such effect should be produced by sound; and who knows whether, in this age of invention and discoveries, we may not be called upon to marvel at the exhibition of a tree, a horse, or a ship produced by the human voice muttering over a metal plate, prepared in the same or some other manner, the words "tree," "horse," and "ship." How greatly ashamed of their ignorance the by-gone generations of mankind ought to be!

DECEMBER 5. — My old friend, Henry J. Wyckoff, died last evening, in the seventy-second year of his age.

<small>Death of Mr. Wyckoff.</small>

Mr. Wyckoff was a good man, actively and efficiently engaged in public institutions of benevolence and charity. He was formerly a merchant of highly respectable standing, of the firm of Suydam & Wyckoff, and, I presume, died rich. We were formerly intimate companions, members of the same club, and meeting at dinner-parties two or three times a week. Thus another tie is broken, and another warning given.

A most outrageous revolt has broken out among the tenants of the late patroon, General Van Rensselaer,

<small>The Patroon's Tenants.</small>

in the neighbourhood of Albany, of a piece with the vile disorganizing spirit which overspreads the land like a cloud, and daily increases in darkness. The tenants of the manor of Rensselaer, which is in extent from twenty to forty miles, having waited for the decease of their respected proprietor, the late patroon, have now risen *en masse*, and refuse to pay their rent to his son Stephen, to whom that portion of the estate of his father has been bequeathed, except upon their own terms, and at their own good pleasure. They have enjoyed their leases for so many years, upon terms so easy, and have been treated with so much lenity, that they have brought themselves to believe that the lands belonged to them. Since the death of General Van Rensselaer they have had meetings, and resolved that in a land of liberty there is no liberty for landlords; that no man has a right to own more land than his neighbour, and that they have paid so little rent heretofore that it is not worth while to pay any hereafter; and that master Stephen, with as good a title by inheritance as any known to the laws of the State, shall neither have his land nor the income of it. This outrageous proceeding of the Rensselaerwickers has occasioned great consternation in Albany. The sheriff resorted to the ancient process of summoning the *posse comitatus ;* the citizens were ordered out to march against the rioters; several hundred went, and met the enemy in the disputed territory. The sheriff, with seventy followers, went forward in advance; but finding them armed and mounted to the number of several thousands, determined to resist, and swearing by Dunder and Plixsen that they would pay no more, nor surrender their farms to the rightful owner, he returned to the main body of his forces, faced to the right about, and marched back to Albany.

This is alarming, certainly, but nothing more than a carrying-out of the Loco-foco principles of the people of the State, — those principles which prevailed in this city at the late election, — to the support of which the members-elect of the Legislature are pledged, and from which the councils of the State have been lately saved by the greater virtue of the country, but which must, in a short time (perhaps the very next year), sweep away all the wise restraints of law and justice, and cause the destruction of individual rights. Let it come, if come it must; the evil will be remedied some time or other; but this fair dream of Republicanism will be dissipated by its cure.

DECEMBER 9. — The Harrisburg Convention on Saturday completed their business, and adjourned.

Whig Nomination.

The nomination is made, and nothing remains but to support it with unanimity and zeal. William Henry Harrison, of Ohio, for President, and John Tyler, of Virginia, for Vice-President, are the true, regular candidates of the Whig party of the United States. My preference was for Mr. Clay. His services have been greater than those of any other person; and his devotion to genuine Whig principles merited, and, in my opinion, should have received, from the party the highest proof of its approbation and gratitude; but this tribute which a great majority of the Whigs have ever been ready to pay him has been now withheld, from an apprehension that the opposition of the abolitionists in the Western

States, and in a large portion of the State of New York, would destroy his chance of success, and that General Harrison, being the favourite of the Whigs of the "free States," would run better. This is not the last mischief to be apprehended from this quarter. The accursed question is destined to mix up with all national questions, and in the end to alter the essential features of our government, if not to cause a separation of the States and a dissolution of the Union. The opposition to Mr. Clay from this quarter is so strong, that even if nominated he could not (in the opinion of a majority of the convention) have been elected, and it was perhaps good policy to take Harrison, who may succeed if the friends of Mr. Clay exercise that magnanimity which it appears they could not calculate upon from a portion, at least, of the friends of his rivals. But the matter is now settled, and I, for my part, am determined to forget that any other candidate than General Harrison has ever been thought of, or named to the people. The informal vote on Friday is understood to have been, for Winfield Scott, 16; Henry Clay, 90; William H. Harrison, 148.

DECEMBER 10. — In removing the foundation of the

Curious Relic. tower of Trinity Church a vaulted grave was opened, which contained the coffin and bones of Lady Cornbury, wife of the governor of the colony, who died in this city in the year 1706, and was buried under the original church, which was burned in the time of the Revolutionary war. A large plate and fragments of the coffin were found, which are now seen in the office of the architect; the former is perfectly legible, and nearly uninjured by its inhumation of one hundred and thirty-three years. The arms of this noble lady, who was sister of the Earl of Richmond, and a viscountess in her own right, are engraven on the plate, with her pedigree, age, and time of her death, etc., distinctly, but very rudely, written below. She died at the age of thirty-four. This relic is interesting and valuable, as it marks the period of Lord Cornbury's government, one of the early English governors, whose name is affixed to the charter of Trinity Church. How many generations of men have passed away, and what changes have occurred, since this plate of silver, emblazoned by the hands of an unskilful artist with the pompous display of heraldic pride and the unerring record of death's doings, was placed in its dark, cold repository, to be brought forth again to the light of day to undergo the scrutiny of a generation of men who were not thought of in those days, and who care no more about the remains of this branch of the Richmond family than those of the poor Indian chief who was driven from the spot before her husband came to it as the representative of the Majesty of England !

The place where these remains were interred was, at the time, the *northern* boundary of the city of New York. The charter of Trinity Church (a copy of which I have in my possession) provides for the erection of a church in that spot, *near* to the city of New York. It has now become in fact the *southern* boundary. The solitary tomb of this young and noble lady has echoed for more than a century the footsteps of busy men, ardently engaged in the cares of business and the pursuit of wealth; for it was close to Broadway, opposite Wall street. I proposed last evening, in the vestry, that these relics should be presented to the Historical Society ; but it was not granted. They determined to have a new tomb provided, in which they are to be re-interred.

The De Ruyters, the Von Tromps, and the Stuyvesants, of the manor of Rensselaer, remain still in an attitude of open rebellion to the laws of the land. Equally opposed to good order as to *good manors*, they won't pay their rent to him whom they style the *pretended* proprietor, oppose every attempt of the constituted authorities to enforce the demands of justice, and treat with indignity everything in the shape of legal process. This outrageous proceeding has become so serious that the Governor has ordered a body of fifteen hundred of the infantry of this city to hold themselves in readiness to repair to Albany at a moment's warning, and has provided two steamboats to transport them to the seat of war. Division and brigade orders fill a column

<small>A New Dutch War.</small>

in the morning papers, and names of major-generals, A.D.C.'s, and brigade-majors are blazoned in staring capitals. Young men with muskets, unconscious yet of murderous lead, parade the streets, "panting for the fray," and anxious to flesh their maiden swords in Dutchmen's blood; and many a one whose nose looks red and bright on frosty mornings may find it turn blue when he comes to poke into the hostile camp of the belligerent Rensselaerwickers. But in truth and soberness this is a serious business. Conduct so disorganizing must be resisted, and the laws be maintained at all events. The affair is in good hands. Our excellent little Governor understands what he is about, and if the last attempts of the sheriff in Albany county should be unsuccessful, the arm of executive power will not be raised in vain.

A correspondence between the malcontents and Mr. Van Rensselaer is published, in which it appears to me they are all wrong, and he all right. The letter of Mr. V. R. contains the description of the boundaries and extent of the Van Rensselaer patent. It is enormous, and such a territory in the hands of an individual certainly does not conduce to the public advantage. At the time of the grant it consisted of little better than wild land, inhabited by Indians, and unproductive as the prairies of Arkansas or the Rocky mountains; whereas it is now the heart of the State, near the capital, and capable of indefinite improvements if the occupants held it in fee. But these men do not go the right way to work; they have no more right to refuse the payment of the trifling rent than the tenants of houses in New York have to say they will pay but one-half of their stipulated rent, or none at all.

DECEMBER 12. — The disturbances in the Rensse-
Dutch War.   laer manor are in a fair way of settlement without calling in the aid of the troops from New York. This effect has been mainly produced by the firm and discreet course of Governor Seward, who issued a very judicious proclamation to the revolted tribes of the Helderberg, giving them little to hope from the hostile attitude in which they had placed themselves, and

much from a suitable obedience to the laws and reliance upon the justice of the Legislature.

An attempt was made during the course of this affair, by the profligate politicians who are in the ascendant in this devoted city, to get up a meeting at Tammany Hall to express their horror at the thought of troops being employed to shed the blood of their fellow-citizens, and to raise party capital by condemning the measures adopted by the Governor; but this cankered sore of Jacobinical corruption did not come to a head; their hearts were black enough, and their heads sufficiently willing to carry out such a design, but it was thought rather too radical. The time has not quite come, — it is not far distant.

DECEMBER 13. — Great anxiety has prevailed for some time past about the French packet "Ville de Lyons," Captain Stoddart, which has been out about seventy days from Havre, with two hundred passengers. Mrs. Cutting, the elder Miss Cutting, and the wife and children of Francis B. Cutting, with a number of others in whose fate great interest was felt, were known to be on board, and this day apprehensions were relieved by accounts being received that the ship had just put into Bermuda, dismasted and otherwise greatly disabled by severe weather. The perils and dangers of the voyage will be likely to induce passengers to prefer the steam-packets in making a western passage during the winter months.

DECEMBER 14. — Mr. Robert Lenox, who has been ill for several weeks, died yesterday, in the eightieth year of his age. He was formerly a merchant and magistrate of this city, and died one of its richest citizens.

DECEMBER 19. — Anthony I. Bleecker has been appointed marshal of this district, in the place of W. C. H. Waddell. In this appointment the President, it is said, has given mortal offence to the butt-enders and indomitables who form the *elite* of his party in New York. These gentry had made up their minds to the appointment of a Major Hopkins to this office, and sent a deputation of their *respectable* order to Washington to that effect, demanding that their rescript should be obeyed, and their favourite receive his share of the spoils of the victory which their prowess had gained. This demand, it would appear, was urged with a degree of insolence which the President could not brook. He smiled, however, upon his tools, rough as was their deportment, gave them soft words in return for rude enforcements, bowed the unshaven dignitaries of the Loco-foco body-guards out of his palace, and forthwith appointed this Mr. Bleecker to the office, who is a gentleman, — sufficient, one would think, at this time to disqualify him. This contumelious treatment has given mortal offence to the sovereigns, and some of their ultra papers have gone the length of abusing the President in good set terms. One or two more such acts of rebellion against the expressed will of the party will get Mr. Van Buren out of their good books. He has occasionally evinced a disposition to act like a gentleman, which will be his ruin if he does not take care.

Mr. Clay. DECEMBER 20. — The nomination of General Harrison works like a charm among the Whigs. They said that the choice of the Harrisburg Convention should be the signal of union, and that all personal predilections should be offered up on the altar of patriotism, and nobly have they redeemed their pledge. All have forgotten their first choice, and every man's banner is inscribed with the name of Harrison. In this honourable course the friends of Henry Clay have been the foremost; and the man of their choice, he who has done his country better service than any man alive, and better deserves its highest recompense, was the first to set the glorious example. Mr. Clay will never be President; but why should he wish it? He has reached a higher eminence. He has sacrificed personal interest to the public good. Is he ambitious? What is there in the title, or troublesome duty, or empty distinction of being President of the United States for four years (for that is to be the ultimatum hereafter) to fill the measure of a reasonable ambition equal to that of his present position? He has drawn off his troops at a moment when they were ready to fight for him to the death. He has submitted even to the force of prejudices, and acknowledged that popularity with the people did not follow from his best public acts. He has sacrificed the reward of a long life of public and private devotion to his country to the noble sentiment of the patriotic Virginian, " Union for the sake of the Union," and relinquished the doubtful chance of the enjoyment for four years of the glitter of office, with the vapid, dull, and useless remainder after the expiration of his term, for the proud certainty of being enthroned in the hearts of the honest, high-minded portion of his countrymen as the disinterested patriot who has always served them well, and stands ready to serve them well hereafter.

After the adjournment of the Harrisburg Convention many of the members went to Washington, where it was found that there were one or more delegates from eighteen out of the twenty-two States which had been represented in that patriotic and enlightened body. They called in a body upon Mr. Clay, to do homage to the high moral principle which had influenced his conduct. The friends of Harrison and Scott, with those who originally enlisted for Webster, were as ready to acknowledge the high claims of Clay to the proud distinction of their nomination as he and his friends had been to surrender those claims in favour of a candidate who was thought to be more available. The particulars of this touching ceremony, together with those of the great Whig dinner given on the same day, are detailed admirably in the " National Intelligencer."

DECEMBER 26. — The message was not delivered until Tuesday. It is well written, delusive, and calculated to strengthen the President with his party, — thoroughly *Loco-foco*. Two-thirds of the enormous mass of words are used to minister to the bad feelings of the anti-bankites. The President recommends, in the boldest and most undisguised terms, the sub-treasury system, — an exclusive circulation for government purposes. State banks are condemned without mercy, and the plan of a national bank is declared not only unconstitutional, but

President's Message.

altogether inexpedient. The government is to be banker, broker, and money-dealer for the whole country. These doctrines will probably be carried out in their fullest extent, and in a few months the whole policy of the country will be changed, and the general government (or rather the President and his myrmidons) become the masters of the people, and the regulators of their private as well as public affairs. Good-by, then, to all the sound influence of wholesome credit and national faith.

DECEMBER 30. — I called yesterday to see Mr. Webster. He is in good health and spirits, and greatly pleased (as he could not fail to be) with his visit. His splendid talents and high standing in his own country have been suitably appreciated where he has been, and he has met with a flattering reception and kind treatment. I had half an hour's agreeable conversation with him. He does not appear anxious to go to Washington immediately, for he sees no chance of doing any good there. His mind is full of gloomy forebodings of the unhappy result of measures which it is too certain will now be carried. The accession of Mr. Calhoun and his little squad of anti-federal nullifiers to the grasping, reckless policy of the administration, which sanctions any coalition, however corrupt, and consents to any violation of the Constitution, however flagrant, which may serve to secure the permanency of their power, gives the death-blow to the patriotic efforts of the Whigs of the North and the East. One hundred and ten good men and true in the House of Representatives are to be ruled by eight or ten who are neither good nor true, and if anything is to be gained by an occasional assistance from that quarter it must be by a sacrifice greater than the object is worth. Mr. Calhoun's party are the worst politicians in the country, — enemies of the Constitution, more dangerous than Benton and Wright, Frank Thomas, or Aaron Vanderpoel.

END OF VOLUME I.

Lightning Source UK Ltd.
Milton Keynes UK
UKOW050023040912

198435UK00001B/38/P